MAR 2 5 2021

10/01-3

W9-BJV-775

3 1299 01008 1995

East Meadow Public Library
1886 Front Street, East Meadow, NY 11554
(516) 794-2570
www.eastmeadow.info

NÖTHIN' BUT A GOOD TIME

NÖTHIN' BUT A GOOD TIME

The UNCENSORED History of the '80s Hard Rock Explosion

TOM BEAUJOUR AND RICHARD BIENSTOCK

ST. MARTIN'S PRESS
NEW YORK

First published in the United States by St. Martin's Press,
an imprint of St. Martin's Publishing Group

NOTHIN' BUT A GOOD TIME. Copyright © 2021 by Thomas Beaujour and Richard Bienstock.
All rights reserved. Printed in the United States of America. For information, address St.
Martin's Publishing Group, 120 Broadway, New York, NY 10271.

www.stmartins.com

Designed by Steven Seighman

Selections from interviews have been edited for continuity and clarity.

The Library of Congress Cataloging-in-Publication Data is available upon request.

ISBN 978-1-250-19575-3 (hardcover)
ISBN 978-1-250-19576-0 (ebook)

Our books may be purchased in bulk for promotional, educational, or business use.
Please contact your local bookseller or the Macmillan Corporate and Premium Sales
Department at 1-800-221-7945, extension 5442, or by email at
MacmillanSpecialMarkets@macmillan.com.

First Edition: 2021

10 9 8 7 6 5 4 3 2 1

To my mom, Elizabeth Beaujour (I've owed you a return dedication since 1989); my wife, Maria McKenna, who can't remember our wedding vows including anything about "listening to Hair Nation every time we get in the fucking car"; Elvis the puggle; Dino the chug (look it up . . . it's a thing); and lest we forget, Nigel Tufnel, the cat.

—TOM BEAUJOUR

To my wife, Carla Fredericks, for her unconditional and very-much-appreciated love, support, and advice—as well as her infinite patience, which was no doubt pushed to the limit over several years and across numerous continents while researching and writing this book.

To my son Levi, who reminds me every day of the pure, indefinable joy that results from a kick-ass riff hitting a young heart.

And to my parents, Gary and Leslie, and my brother, Hal, for always supporting (tolerating?) my musical obsessions . . . even when they came paired with an unfortunate mullet.

—RICHARD BIENSTOCK

CONTENTS

PART II: FEEL THE NOIZE

PART III: KNOCK 'EM DEAD, KID

PART IV: YOUTH GONE WILD

PART V: THE LAST MILE

PART VI: SHUT UP, BEAVIS

PART VII: EPILOGUE

FOREWORD

by Corey Taylor of Slipknot and Stone Sour

I remember it like it was yesterday.

I was hanging out in the living room, doing whatever ten-year-olds did in the '80s. MTV was on in the background; it was my go-to when the after-school cartoons were over. I was accustomed to the usual Michael Jackson and Dire Straits videos, so I wasn't really paying much attention. And then suddenly, something incredibly different and dangerous came on the screen that made me stop everything I was doing—playing, goofing off, and ultimately being ten years old. A bolt of lightning struck my life that afternoon and I was never the same again.

That bolt of lightning was "Looks That Kill" by Mötley fuckin' Crüe.

From there, I never looked back. Sure, I was a fan of hardcore and punk and thrash and ska and hip-hop and everything else, but I've *always* been a massive fan of '80s rock. Whether people have tried to call it glam metal or hair metal or butt rock or a host of other denigrating names, one thing remains constant: The songs were *so fucking good*. From the edginess of the Crüe and Guns N' Roses to the pop sensibilities of Poison and Faster Pussycat, from the bluesy vibes of Cinderella, Kix, and Tesla to the gutter melodies of L.A. Guns and W.A.S.P., from the punch of Skid Row and Van Halen to obscure underground gems like Vain and Life Sex & Death, there was something for *everyone,* all wrapped in leather, spandex, and silk scarves.

There were the forebears like Aerosmith and Rose Tattoo; the first wave with Quiet Riot and Ratt; the Top 40 takeover with Def Leppard and Whitesnake; the international influence like White Lion, Europe, Loudness, and Sleeze Beez . . . It was a world of huge choruses and sexual tension, and it gave you the feeling that life after childhood did *not* have to suck as hard as it appeared to suck for our parents. It was music that gave you a vision of excitement and a need for release. Every dude wanted to be cool; every girl wanted to be hot. It was the Under-Age of Utter Abandon—we were alive, and the streets were the place to be wild.

Sure, in today's mindset it was sexist, offensive, tasteless, Neanderthal, misogynistic, exploitive, aggressive, and based entirely in fantasy . . . but that was the *point*. It was *supposed* to be beyond the realms of this gray, concrete life. It was *supposed* to be a place that you dreamed about and that was ultimately unattainable. It was *supposed* to piss off the Vanilla Brigade, because who the fuck wants to be normal, passé, regular? Who the fuck wanted to be dead in the land of the living? This music had a pulse, a purpose, and a raging hard-on to *get down and get with it*. Lighten the fuck up and dress like a superhero. Find a girl or a guy and make out with the radio on. Why the fuck not? What are you waiting for?

Every mega-chorus was junk food. Every guitar riff made you mental. Every ending made you wish the song was longer. In a way, every song was a metaphor for every good time we had, clinging to the feeling and wishing it would stretch on forever. That's why we'd rewind those tunes and sing 'em again—to hold on to that feeling as long as we possibly could.

I watch those videos and listen to those albums now and I'm transported to a time when you could be a force of nature, a freak in a denim jacket, and it was okay. It was my time. It was *our* time. It was a time where music made you feel alive, where it was more than a number on a streaming list . . .

It was the rush in your pulse.

CAST OF CHARACTERS

DON ADKINS photographer

STEVEN ADLER drummer, Road Crew, Hollywood Rose, Guns N' Roses

ROB AFFUSO drummer, Skid Row

JOHN AGNELLO assistant engineer, Twisted Sister, *Stay Hungry*; producer

JOEY ALLEN guitarist, Warrant

PHIL ALLOCCO guitarist, Law and Order

MICHAEL ANTHONY bassist, Van Halen

CARMINE APPICE drummer, Ozzy Osbourne

CHRISTINA APPLEGATE actress

MAX ASHER drummer, Quest, Warrant

SEBASTIAN BACH singer, Madam X, Skid Row

BRIAN BAKER guitarist, Minor Threat, Junkyard

FRANKIE BANALI (1951–2020) drummer, DuBrow, Quiet Riot

AL BANE leather designer

GINA BARSAMIAN booking agent, the Troubadour

REB BEACH guitarist, Winger

HOWARD BENSON producer, Bang Tango, Pretty Boy Floyd, Tuff

MARSHALL BERLE manager, Van Halen, Ratt

NUNO BETTENCOURT guitarist, Extreme

RODNEY BINGENHEIMER club owner, promoter, DJ

BOBBY BLOTZER drummer, Airborn, Dokken, Ratt

RACHEL BOLAN bassist, Godsend, Skid Row

MIKE BONE executive, Elektra Records

LIZZY BORDEN singer, Lizzy Borden

VITO BRATTA guitarist, Storm, Dreamer, White Lion

BRYN BRIDENTHAL publicist, Elektra Records, Capitol Records, Geffen Records

ERIC BRITTINGHAM bassist, Saints in Hell, Cinderella

JOSEPH BROOKS DJ, the Cathouse, Scream

RIC BROWDE producer, Poison, Faster Pussycat

"WILD" MICK BROWN drummer, the Boyz, Xciter, Dokken

RAY BROWN costume designer

STEVE BROWN guitarist, Trixter

CLIFF BURNSTEIN manager, Def Leppard, Dokken, Tesla, Metallica

MISSI CALLAZZO DJ, WSOU; executive, Megaforce Records

MARC CANTER owner, Canter's Deli; Slash's childhood friend

JERRY CANTRELL guitarist, Alice in Chains

JOEY CATHCART guitarist, Strange Agent, the Nelsons, Nelson

CARLOS CAVAZO guitarist, Snow, Quiet Riot

BILLY CHILDS bassist, Britny Fox

PHIL COLLEN guitarist, Girl, Def Leppard

AL COLLINS bassist, Plain Jane

ALICE COOPER solo artist

FRED COURY drummer, Chastain, London, Cinderella

DAVID COVERDALE singer, Whitesnake

MICK CRIPPS guitarist, L.A. Guns

JUAN CROUCIER bassist, Dokken, Ratt

BOBBY DALL bassist, Paris, Poison

GREG D'ANGELO drummer, White Lion

STEVE DARROW bassist, Hollywood Rose

"DIZZY" DEAN DAVIDSON singer, guitarist, Britny Fox

ROB DE LUCA bassist, Spread Eagle

WARREN DeMARTINI guitarist, Ratt

C.C. DeVILLE guitarist, Screamin' Mimi's, Poison

JERRY DIXON bassist, Risk, Warrant

DON DOKKEN singer, Airborn, Dokken

CHRIS DOLIBER bassist, Madam X

TAIME DOWNE singer, Faster Pussycat; co-owner, the Cathouse

JEFF DUNCAN guitarist, Odin

BOBBY "BLITZ" ELLSWORTH singer, Overkill

KEVIN ESTRADA photographer

GLENN FEIT engineer, Mötley Crüe, *Too Fast for Love*

MICKEY FINN singer, Jetboy

HEIDI ROBINSON FITZGERALD publicist

JASON FLOM executive, Atlantic Records

LITA FORD guitarist, the Runaways; solo artist

BRIAN "DAMAGE" FORSYTHE guitarist, Kix

KIM FOWLEY (1939–2015) impresario, producer, L.A. scenester

ACE FREHLEY guitarist, Kiss, Frehley's Comet; solo artist

JAY JAY FRENCH guitarist, Twisted Sister

LONN FRIEND editor, *RIP* magazine; journalist; author, *Life on Planet Rock*, *Sweet Demotion*

JANET GARDNER singer, guitarist, Vixen

ROB GARDNER drummer, Pyrrhus, L.A. Guns, Hollywood Rose, Guns N' Roses

KELLY GARNI bassist, Quiet Riot

CHRIS GATES guitarist, Junkyard

DAYLE GLORIA co-owner, Scream

DANNY GOLDBERG manager, Nirvana

RON GOUDIE (1952–2020) producer, Enigma Records

LIZZIE GREY (1958–2019) guitarist, Sister, London

ALEX GROSSI booking agent, Vince Neil, Slaughter, Vixen, Kix, Faster Pussycat, Nelson; guitarist, Quiet Riot

TRACII GUNS guitarist, Pyrrhus, Guns N' Roses, L.A. Guns

CHRIS HAGER guitarist, Mickey Ratt, Rough Cutt

ROSS HALFIN photographer

VICKY HAMILTON consultant, Mötley Crüe, Stryper; manager, Poison, Guns N' Roses, Faster Pussycat; author, *Appetite for Dysfunction: A Cautionary Tale*

FRANK HANNON guitarist, Tesla

BRET HARTMAN executive, CBS Records, MCA Records

BILL HEIN co-owner, Greenworld Distribution, Enigma Records

WES HEIN co-owner, Greenworld Distribution, Enigma Records

BEAU HILL producer, Ratt, Kix, Alice Cooper, Twisted Sister, Warrant, Winger

SCOTTI HILL guitarist, Godsend, Skid Row

DARYN HINTON manager, financial backer, Stryper

CHRIS HOLMES guitarist, Sister, W.A.S.P.

JIMMY HOYSON recording engineer, Warrant, Winger

HOWIE HUBBERMAN owner, Guitars R Us; manager, Poison

BRAD HUNT executive, Elektra Records

WAYNE ISHAM video director

RANDY JACKSON singer, guitarist, Zebra

RAMI JAFFEE keyboardist, Quest, the Wallflowers, Foo Fighters

JOHN JANSEN producer, Britny Fox, Cinderella

DAVE JELLISON bassist, Mickey Ratt

JOHN KALODNER executive, Geffen Records

DEEDEE KEEL booking agent, Whisky a Go Go

RON KEEL singer, Steeler, Keel

TOM KEIFER singer, guitarist, Saints in Hell, Cinderella

MARK KENDALL guitarist, Dante Fox, Great White

AVI KIPPER engineer, Hit City West

MARK KNIGHT guitarist, Bang Tango

ALLEN KOVAC manager, Vixen, L.A. Guns, Lita Ford

RICK KRIM executive, MTV

JEFF LaBAR guitarist, Cinderella

BLACKIE LAWLESS singer, guitarist, bassist, Sister, London, W.A.S.P.

JAKE E. LEE guitarist, Ratt, Rough Cutt, Ozzy Osbourne

GREG LEON guitarist, Suite 19, DuBrow, Dokken

JOE LESTÉ singer, Bang Tango

JOSH LEWIS guitarist, Warrant; solo artist

BEN LIEMER editor, *Circus* magazine

JAMES LoMENZO bassist, White Lion

GEORGE LYNCH guitarist, the Boyz, Xciter, Dokken, Lynch Mob

KRISTY "KRASH" MAJORS guitarist, Pretty Boy Floyd

YNGWIE MALMSTEEN guitarist, Steeler; solo artist

MICK MARS guitarist, White Horse, Vendetta, Mötley Crüe

LARRY MAZER manager, Cinderella, Nelson, Kiss

DOC McGHEE manager, Mötley Crüe, Bon Jovi, Skid Row, Scorpions;
    co-organizer, Moscow Music Peace Festival

DUFF McKAGAN bassist, Road Crew, Guns N' Roses

KLAUS MEINE singer, Scorpions

DAVE MENIKETTI singer, guitarist, Y&T

JIM MERLIS publicist, Geffen Records

JOHN MEZACAPPA road manager, Plain Jane, Warrant

BRET MICHAELS singer, Paris, Poison

MICHAEL MONROE singer, Hanoi Rocks

BOB NALBANDIAN journalist

STAS NAMIN co-organizer, Moscow Music Peace Festival

DAVE NAVARRO guitarist, Jane's Addiction

VINCE NEIL singer, Rockandi, Mötley Crüe

GUNNAR NELSON drummer, Strange Agent, the Nelsons; singer, guitarist, Nelson

MATTHEW NELSON singer, bassist, Strange Agent, the Nelsons, Nelson

ALAN NIVEN executive, Greenworld Distribution, Enigma Records; manager, Guns N' Roses, Great White

EDDIE "FINGERS" OJEDA guitarist, Twisted Sister

OZZY OSBOURNE Ozzy! Ozzy!

SHARON OSBOURNE manager, Ozzy Osbourne, Lita Ford

RICHARD PAGE session vocalist, Mötley Crüe, Twisted Sister; singer, bassist, Mr. Mister

STEPHEN PEARCY singer, Mickey Ratt, Ratt

JENNIFER PERRY L.A.-based booking agent

MAXINE PETRUCCI guitarist, Madam X

ROXY PETRUCCI drummer, Madam X, Vixen

PETER PHILBIN executive, Elektra Records

MICHAEL PINTER photographer

JACK PONTI producer, songwriter

SPENCER PROFFER owner, Pasha Records; producer, Quiet Riot, W.A.S.P.

STEPHEN QUADROS drummer, Snow

STEVIE RACHELLE singer, Tuff

RIKI RACHTMAN co-owner, the Cathouse; MTV VJ; *Headbangers Ball* host

BRUNO RAVEL bassist, Hot Shot, White Lion, Danger Danger

LAURA REINJOHN L.A. scenester

KELLE RHOADS musician; Randy Rhoads' brother

HEIDI MARGOT RICHMAN costume designer

KANE ROBERTS guitarist, Alice Cooper

BOBBY ROCK drummer, Vinnie Vincent Invasion, Nelson

RIKKI ROCKETT drummer, Paris, Poison

SHARE ROSS bassist, Vixen

DAVID LEE ROTH singer, Van Halen; solo artist

KEITH ROTH musician; radio personality, SiriusXM; *Electric Ballroom* host

BILLY ROWE guitarist, Jetboy

JACK RUSSELL singer, Dante Fox, Great White

DAVE "SNAKE" SABO guitarist, Steel Fortune, Skid Row

RUDY SARZO bassist, Quiet Riot, Ozzy Osbourne

FRED SAUNDERS tour security, Mötley Crüe, Bon Jovi

MADELYN SCARPULLA radio promotion, product manager, Mercury/
   PolyGram Records; manager, Kix

RUDOLF SCHENKER guitarist, Scorpions

MITCH SCHNEIDER publicist

ANDY SECHER editor, *Hit Parader* magazine

DEREK SHULMAN executive, Mercury/PolyGram Records

GENE SIMMONS bassist, Kiss

NIKKI SIXX bassist, Sister, London, Mötley Crüe

JOHNNY "DUKE" SIZEMORE L.A. scenester, Cathouse regular

BRIAN SLAGEL owner, Metal Blade Records

MIKE SLAMER session guitarist

SLASH guitarist, Tidus Sloan, Road Crew, Hollywood Rose, Black Sheep,
   Guns N' Roses

MARK SLAUGHTER singer, Vinnie Vincent Invasion, Slaughter

ROBIN SLOANE vice president, video, Elektra Records

MATT SMITH guitarist, Paris, Poison

DEE SNIDER singer, Twisted Sister

PENELOPE SPHEERIS director, *The Decline of Western Civilization Part II:
   The Metal Years*

ERIC STACY bassist, Darling Cruel, Faster Pussycat

DANNY STANTON singer, Takashi; president, Coallier Entertainment

GREG STEELE guitarist, Faster Pussycat

JAIME ST. JAMES singer, Black 'N Blue

IZZY STRADLIN bassist, Shire; guitarist, Hollywood Rose, Guns N' Roses

DANA STRUM bassist, Bad Axe, Vinnie Vincent Invasion, Slaughter

MICHAEL SWEET singer, guitarist, Roxx Regime, Stryper

ROBERT SWEET drummer, Roxx Regime, Stryper

STEVEN SWEET drummer, Plain Jane, Warrant

HUGH SYME graphic artist, Bon Jovi, Whitesnake, Warrant, Slaughter

ROB TANNENBAUM journalist; co-author, *I Want My MTV*

PAUL TAYLOR keyboardist, Alice Cooper, Winger

KIM THAYIL guitarist, Soundgarden

FLEUR THIEMEYER costume designer

MATT THORNE bassist, Ratt, Rough Cutt

BRAD TOLINSKI editor-in-chief, *Guitar World* magazine; co-author, *Play It Loud: An Epic History of the Style, Sound, and Revolution of the Electric Guitar*

TICO TORRES drummer, Bon Jovi

MIKE TRAMP singer, Mabel, Danish Lions, White Lion

EDDIE TRUNK A&R, Megaforce Records; radio personality; author, *Eddie Trunk's Essential Hard Rock and Heavy Metal*

KATHERINE TURMAN journalist; co-author, *Louder Than Hell: The Definitive Oral History of Metal*

ERIK TURNER guitarist, Warrant

STEVE VAI guitarist, David Lee Roth, Whitesnake; solo artist

ALEX VAN HALEN drummer, Van Halen

MIKE VARNEY producer; owner, Shrapnel Records

DONNIE VIE singer, Enuff Z'Nuff

MICHAEL WAGENER producer, mixer, Mötley Crüe, Dokken, Great White, Stryper, Poison, Skid Row, Extreme, White Lion, Warrant

CHRIS WEBER guitarist, Hollywood Rose

MARK WEISS photographer

TOM WERMAN producer, Mötley Crüe, Dokken, Twisted Sister, Poison, Kix, L.A. Guns, Junkyard, Stryper, Lita Ford

STEVE WEST drummer, Hot Shot, Danger Danger

TOM WHALLEY executive, Capitol Records

MICHAEL WHITE singer, the Boyz, London

STEVE WHITEMAN singer, Kix

KIP WINGER bassist, Alice Cooper; singer, bassist, Winger

ZAKK WYLDE guitarist, Zyris, Ozzy Osbourne

GINA ZAMPARELLI (1959–2018) L.A. club promoter, booking agent

NEIL ZLOZOWER photographer

INTRODUCTION

This book, which at times seemed more like an unruly beast about to turn on its masters and engulf them in flames than a mere collection of inert words on a page, is complete. Our sincerest hope is that with its publication, an enormous debt will be repaid.

Although we've both spent our careers writing about artists who inhabit any number of musical genres, it is the hard rock music of the '80s—call it "glam metal" if you must, and "hair metal" if you're itching for a fight in the tweet-o-sphere—that first captured our ears and teenage imaginations. It gave us the bug, as they say, and we still have it. This music, inspired by '70s bands like Led Zeppelin, Black Sabbath, AC/DC, Judas Priest, Kiss, Cheap Trick, and, most unambiguously, Van Halen, sounded larger than life and incorporated unforgettable sing-along choruses, chest-beating riffs, cocky swagger, Technicolor glitz, detonated drums, and, in the fleet fingers of the many guitar gods who emerged from the era, a pure athleticism that was nothing short of jaw-dropping.

There was something else fundamental to this genre, a common thread that emerged as we were reporting back to each other on a just-completed interview or on the progress of a given chapter. Almost every person we spoke to for this book exhibited a single-mindedness, work ethic, confidence, and, yes, courage, that was nothing short of indomitable. That determination, more than the outrageous dress, massive hair, pointy guitars, and not-infrequently sexist videos, is the shared DNA that connects the characters in this story. No one stumbled into this (okay, maybe Brian Baker of Junkyard did), and you won't find a single character who confesses, "I never planned to make this a career. I was in art school and sort of just joined a band for fun." The price of admission to this rarefied world was to check your backup plan at the door and dedicate yourself to endless practice, relentless self-promotion, nonstop hustling, and, often, the gobbling of enough drugs and alcohol to kill a large dog or maybe a small horse—take your pick. This was total-immersion rock 'n' roll.

The experience of being in the audience during this era was equally all-consuming; performances were not only spectacles but also celebrations. If fans didn't leave a show grinning from ear to ear and feeling like they had just attended the biggest, loudest party in the world then they simply hadn't gotten their money's worth—regardless of how many crew members and trucks were employed in the transportation and maintenance of all the towering amplifier stacks, massive drum kits, risers, ramps, walkways, flash pots, hydraulics, lights, confetti, lasers, and, of course, sound systems that were essential attractions of this spectacular rock 'n' roll circus.

For kids living far from the bright lights of the Strip or unable to sneak out to the shows, some consolation could be found in the fact that MTV served up a steady regimen of the aforementioned music videos—clips whose production aesthetic did its best to replicate the explosive spectacle of the glam-metal concert experience while also brazenly advancing the argument that no girl or woman could resist the sexual allure of the featured players. Videos like Mötley Crüe's woman-hunting "Looks That Kill" or Warrant's firehose-flaunting "Cherry Pie" may have offended some female staffers at MTV, but to most American teens of the era they were one thing and one thing only: awesome.

Speaking of sex, this seems as good a time as any to address the fact that this work chronicles a bygone era where notions of sexism and gender politics and the disease of addiction were still relatively crude. Like the culture around them, most of the artists in this book have evolved and have also become fathers, mothers, and—*yikes!*—grandparents. That said, if you're hoping for an outpouring of regret or a litany of mea culpas, you've come to the wrong place. Our primary goal was to uncover what really happened from the people who lived it, not to make them apologize for it.

If anything, glam metal's greatest sin was arguably that by the end of the '80s it had begun to suffer from a total lack of imagination and was functioning largely by rote mimesis. New bands looked and sounded alike and were marketed so similarly that it would have been virtually impossible for them not to blur together in the eyes and ears of the fans. Something had to change, and it did, seemingly overnight. It's probably not a spoiler to note that virtually every musician you will meet in this book saw his or her career disintegrate soon after September 24, 1991, when, as the story goes, a meteor known as Nirvana's *Nevermind* impacted the musical landscape and raised a massive dust cloud that forever altered the entire climate of the business. The decade of decadence, as Mötley Crüe dubbed it, had come to a close, and acts that had sold millions of albums, packed arenas, and dominated MTV's rotation didn't just slowly fade out of fashion; they slammed headfirst into an immovable wall of antipathy. Overnight, not only had glam metal become superannuated but it was deemed unmentionable and untouchable—and anyone tainted by the genre became equally undesirable. The ecosystem suffered a total collapse.

This musical apocalypse is where we initially planned to end our story. But as we assembled the chapters that chronicle the rapid demise of the genre, we realized that it was just too much of a . . . what's the literary term for it? Oh right, a *total bummer* to finish on such a sad note. The truth of the matter is that there actually *is* a happy conclusion; it just took a couple of decades to reveal itself.

Our epilogue explores how in the twenty-first century, a significant subset of fans can't seem to get enough of this music. What once was dismissed as anachronistic schlock is the new classic rock. A reunited Poison still routinely tour arenas and outdoor sheds, compelling tens of thousands of cross-generational concertgoers to raise their lighters (or cellphones) high in the air on a nightly basis. Mötley Crüe, armed with flamethrowers, flying drum kits, and enough pyro and explosions to light up a small nation-state, played to upwards of a million fans over the course of their 2014–15 "final tour" and were the subject of a recent Netflix biopic. Guns N' Roses, with perennial adversaries Axl and Slash back in cahoots, have to date grossed an estimated half-billion dollars on their current worldwide jaunt, selling out stadiums from L.A. to Lisbon to Lima.

And while they aren't out packing "enormodomes," many of the other bands chronicled in this book are back on the road, playing festivals, corporate events, casinos, and themed cruises to a growing audience. The hard rock and hair metal fan base never went away—it just got older, became gainfully employed, and spawned children that wanna rock right along with them. That's a much more uplifting way to wrap things up, right?

Now cut those houselights and cue the fucking pyro!

—*Tom Beaujour and Richard Bienstock*

PART I

EVERYBODY WANTS SOME!!

Since its inception, hard rock has maintained a core audience that sustains it through times when the mainstream is occupied elsewhere. The period at the tail end of the '70s, where our story begins, was one of these troughs in popularity for the genre. While initiates continued to fill venues when bands like Kiss and Black Sabbath rolled through town, the vast majority of the music-buying public was more interested in new wave groups like the Knack, the Go-Go's, the Cars, the Police, and Elvis Costello and the Attractions—bands who embraced synthesizers, eschewed guitar heroics, and whose angular riffs and short, spiky hair owed much more to punk and mod fashion than to the bell-bottomed likes of Led Zeppelin or Thin Lizzy. "The industry was looking at the local new wave and punk scenes," recalls Rudy Sarzo, the bassist in a struggling L.A. "dinosaur" act called Quiet Riot.

Both inspiring and confounding to players like Sarzo was the ascendancy of Van Halen, a four-piece hard rock band from Pasadena whose electrifying live performances, striking blond-maned front man, and resident guitar wunderkind were such an undeniable force that they transcended the record industry's genre bias and landed a deal with Warner Bros. Records. The group's success, however, did not trickle down to other acts occupying the same stylistic lane. "No one seemed to be interested in the other bands," recalls Dokken drummer "Wild" Mick Brown, at the time bashing the skins in a Sunset Strip outfit called the Boyz. "Which I thought was weird, because it was like, 'Don't you think the record companies would want, like, nine more Van Halens?' "

They didn't.

Refusing to be stymied by the indifference of the major labels, many young groups like Mötley Crüe and Ratt (then Mickey Ratt), adopted a do-or-die DIY approach, self-financing recordings and pouring their resources into over-the-top concert productions that were as flashy as they were foolhardy. Whether it was Mötley Crüe's Nikki Sixx slathering his leathers with pyro gel and lighting himself on fire or the young men of W.A.S.P. hurling handfuls of raw meat at their audiences and sending flames rippling across the ceiling of the tiny Troubadour club, the bands employed whatever means they could marshal to make their mark and give the fans a night they *still* haven't forgotten. "For the early guys it was all about the music and the shows," says Metal Blade Records founder Brian Slagel.

"The record companies wanted Duran Duran. They wanted new wave," recalls Alan Niven, then toiling for an L.A.-based independent music importer and distributor named Green-world Distribution. "So if you wanted to get further you had to have some imagination. You had to have a little bit of wheel-and-deal. Because that was the only way that you were going to start building your following."

"THE PUSSY-PLUCKING-POSSE POCKET OF HOLLYWOOD"

DANA STRUM (bassist, Bad Axe, Vinnie Vincent Invasion, Slaughter) In the late '70s I was playing with a band called Bad Axe. We were a Hollywood circuit band playing the same clubs as London, which was Nikki Sixx, and Suite 19, with Greg Leon and Tommy Lee. We were headlining the Starwood, headlining the Whisky, the normal thing.

STEPHEN QUADROS (drummer, Snow) The Whisky was the house that Hendrix played, Cream played, Zeppelin . . . the list goes on and on, the people that played that place. That's the club you wanted to play, just because of the history. But the Starwood was the Wild West. It had no age limit. The behind-the-scenes stories, the dressing room, the wild partying, the drugs, the alcohol, it was a completely different vibe.

GREG LEON (guitarist, Suite 19, DuBrow, Dokken) There was the Hot 100 Club upstairs, which was the VIP area, and that led to the backstage area, which had these secret rooms. So if you met girls or you wanted to party or whatever, you could go back there and get away from everybody else. The policy was basically ask for it and you got it. Cocaine was rampant. Quaaludes were everywhere. The place was basically a front for drugs, as everybody knows.

MICHAEL ANTHONY (bassist, Van Halen) The upstairs area was more of like a local hangout scene. There'd probably be people up there doing some blow or something. It was more of just where the cool people would go.

NEIL ZLOZOWER (photographer) I went to see Van Halen at the Starwood, probably in 1977. But right around those years, those were the years of the Rorer/Lemmon 714's. In other words, Quaaludes. And I used to *love* Quaaludes. I remember going to the Starwood, probably I was upstairs in the VIP section, probably took a Quaalude before the band came on, and all I remember is waking up at the end of the show going, "That wasn't so fucking good . . ." I think I passed out during their whole set.

DANA STRUM Had it not been for the Starwood I wouldn't have seen Randy.

KELLY GARNI (bassist, Quiet Riot) I met Randy Rhoads at John Muir Middle School in Burbank in seventh grade. He was an oddball kid like me and we gravitated toward each other. We started playing together, and as far as we were concerned, you had to somehow be involved in Hollywood to make it happen. That's where all the cool clubs were. That's where all the cool people were. That's where all the rock stars hung out.

KELLE RHOADS (musician; Randy Rhoads' brother) Randy and I played together in a band called Violet Fox when we were kids. But by late '72 that had already broken up. Once Kelly and Randy met, it was always Randy and Kelly. They had like six or seven different bands before it turned into Quiet Riot.

KELLY GARNI Quiet Riot was formed in 1974, largely because of our meeting with Kevin [DuBrow, vocalist]. He really wasn't what we were looking for. We were so into Alice Cooper and David Bowie and that really glam, shock rock kind of thing. Whereas Kevin was more of a Rod Stewart/ Steve Marriott kind of a guy. We didn't think his look went with us, either. But he was extremely persistent and knew how to create a band and drive it forward, and we really kind of lacked that. He recognized that Randy overshadowed everyone with his talent, and he said, "I need to be with this guy." He saw the same thing I saw, to be honest with you.

KELLE RHOADS When Kevin met Kelly and Randy, they were playing backyard parties and just doing local, jamming, garage-type stuff. Kevin was the one who brought them into Hollywood. He told them, "No, we can play in the clubs, we can make money, there can be a career strategy here." And Randy liked that. Randy listened to Kevin and took his advice.

BOB NALBANDIAN (journalist) Locally, everyone knew who Randy was. He was supposed to be the next Eddie Van Halen. That's what everyone would say.

KIM FOWLEY (impresario, producer, L.A. scenester) There wasn't any vibe around L.A. when Van Halen first started playing. They were these guys who played Gazzarri's and now and then would sell out in Pasadena. They were a big deal at the Golden West Ballroom in Norwalk—the guitarist was hot and the singer was a James Brown version of Cal Worthington [a famous car dealer who advertised on television] and that was about it. A few nymphomaniacs, these four blondes with big tits, used to talk about the group quite a bit.

ALEX VAN HALEN (drummer, Van Halen) Gazzarri's, we auditioned twice. The Starwood we auditioned a couple of times. Walter Mitty's, The Rock Corporation, Barnacle Bill's, you name it. You name any club that was around at that time and we were there.

BOBBY BLOTZER (drummer, Airborn, Dokken, Ratt) Edward was just fucking unbelievable. And David Lee Roth was, you know, front-man king.

STEPHEN PEARCY (singer, Mickey Ratt, Ratt) I met Roth in the late '70s. And I eventually told my guys, "Hey, you gotta go and see this band. You're gonna shit when you hear the guitar player. He's nothing like you've ever seen or heard." They'd go, "Yeah, sure, sure." And when they did they went, "Holy fuck!"

MICK MARS (guitarist, White Horse, Vendetta, Mötley Crüe) They kicked ass. I had a band called White Horse who played with Van Halen a few times. At Gazzarri's. Ed was always great . . . My mouth would fall open.

KELLY GARNI Randy did go and see Van Halen at Gazzarri's, and he met Eddie Van Halen and Eddie kind of blew him off a little bit. But that was okay with Randy, because Eddie wasn't anybody to him. He wasn't in competition with him. He never saw one guitar player in his life as competition.

ROSS HALFIN (photographer) Randy Rhoads was more tasteful than Edward, who was just jerking off.

KELLY GARNI Van Halen were sort of an oddity in our world. We were familiar with them, but the best way to put it is, that we sort of ran in different circles. We were pretty much the house band at the Starwood, something we had worked our way up to from the first time we played there and got paid with a case of beer. And Van Halen was down the street at Gazzarri's, which in the '80s became a very popular heavy metal club but back in the '70s was more of a college-kid hangout. It was a different type of person that came to see us at the Starwood.

RODNEY BINGENHEIMER (club owner, promoter, DJ) There wasn't really very many local bands happening at that time, 1976. My friend and I went to Gazzarri's to see Van Halen and the crowd was just incredible. A lot of girls; I always thought that bands who had a lot of girls going crazy were gonna make it big. I used to see them setting up and they had this big bomb onstage and I guess Eddie would play off that bomb. They did "You Really Got Me" and "Runnin' with the Devil." Their fans used to park right in front and that's where they'd meet their girlfriends. And I'd say, "You should come over to the Starwood," and Eddie would say, "No, we like it here. Bill [Gazzarri] treats us so well." I said they should get more happening and then they finally said, "Yeah, maybe you're right."

"WILD" MICK BROWN (drummer, the Boyz, Xciter, Dokken) You know what? Gazzarri's was the pussy-plucking-posse pocket of Hollywood. Every goddamn rich girl who had a mom or dad that hated her and was gonna be a stripper later got started at Gazzarri's, man! When I went in there I thought I was in the movies. Gazzarri's, they'd have like a *Playboy* night and it was, "Holy shit!" Girls were everywhere. And these girls were more than willing to just take you home. "My mom and dad are out of town . . ." You'd go to these gigantic Beverly Hills mansions with these pools and you'd eat everything in the house you could and try to hitchhike back to where you lived. It was amazing.

MICHAEL ANTHONY David Lee Roth was our real connection to Gazzarri's. Bill Gazzarri, the owner, would say hi to us or whatever, but Dave was the guy that would hang out, you know, a lot.

DAVID LEE ROTH (singer, Van Halen) Bill Gazzarri called me "Van" for the first two years the band worked at his club. He was a video pioneer. These huge cameras mounted on tripods, with these huge tape decks the size of a suitcase. He would stop me as everybody was filing out to pack our equipment into our cars. "Hey Van, hey Van, wanna see some of my films?" I'd say, "Sure." He'd show me these films, and they'd always be cut off from the tits down, and here's this little dick surrounded by gray pubic hair with some hot little go-go mama just gorgin' herself.

"WILD" MICK BROWN George Lynch and I were in a local Los Angeles band at the time called the Boyz, beating our heads against the wall. Actually, Van Halen and the Boyz had a real following.

DON DOKKEN (singer, Airborn, Dokken) I knew the Boyz and we played a couple shows together. I thought they were really a good band. Honestly, I thought they would be the next band to be signed after Van Halen. They were very Van Halen–esque, you know? They had the gregarious blond-haired singer, they just had the vibe. George was a shredding guitar player like Eddie.

MICHAEL WHITE (singer, the Boyz, London) To this day, I believe George was the best guitar player that I ever was in a band with. When we used to play with Van Halen, they had similar styles but different. George was way heavier. And, I mean, when you think of Eddie Van Halen you think of heavy guitar. But George had a more evil sound than Eddie, and his vibrato was more intense. Way ahead of his time.

GEORGE LYNCH (guitarist, the Boyz, Xciter, Dokken, Lynch Mob) We were very loud, we had a lot of angst, we were very bombastic. We were not refined. A little hit-and-miss on the compositions.

MICHAEL WHITE The Boyz had a run-in with Kim Fowley around that time. Kim wanted to manage us. He was getting us gigs and stuff, and the gigs he was getting us were opening for the Runaways.

"WILD" MICK BROWN Because we were the Boyz, and they were the girls. Which was good, because they had their first record out and they had a big audience.

MICHAEL WHITE He would come to our rehearsals in Hollywood. And Kim, if you knew about him, he was very eccentric and very crazy and very high, I think. But anyway, he would come in with a group of people and they would sit and watch us rehearse and he would give us suggestions of things to do. I just remember specifically him saying, "I want you guys to be space punks. From *outer space*. I want you to dress like space punks and I want you to write your lyrics about being from outer space and coming down to conquer Earth and all that. And I want you to have costumes. I'll make you stars!" And we all kind of thought about it, like, *Really?*

GEORGE LYNCH When we were first in the band with Michael, he tried to be very theatrical, and he was kind of a combination of Robert Plant and Ian Anderson in that he would play flute. But he had this thing where he insisted on . . . His gimmick was he would blow fire out of his flute. So he would experiment with that a lot and practice and try to do it at shows. And it never went well because he ended up just spitting Bacardi 151 out of the end of his flute on the audience. And then he would insist on wearing these, I don't know what you'd call them, they're kind of like nylon material but they're pants. Stretchy pants. Kind of like a leotard but you can see through it? He would wear these things to shows but he wouldn't wear underwear. You gotta understand, we've got this guy, he's like six-two, he kinda looks like Robert Plant, and he has platform shoes on and he'd have one leg up on the monitor with these stretchy see-through pants with no underwear, standing in front of the audience, playing flute, and trying to blow fire out of his flute.

MICHAEL WHITE We did a gig at the Whisky and I had on a leather jump-suit that was made at a place called Granny Takes a Trip. But the guy made it really tight. I was onstage there and I spun, I did a spin-around, and my crotch ripped and my balls hung out.

"WILD" MICK BROWN Rodney Bingenheimer, the DJ, brought the guys in Kiss down to see a show where the Boyz played with Van Halen.

RODNEY BINGENHEIMER I spoke to this guy Ray who was at the Starwood at the time and he said, "Well, I don't know. We've never heard of Van Halen and they're a Gazzarri's band." Back then, if a band was labeled as a Gazzarri's band, they never played outside of Gazzarri's. But I said, "Yeah, but these guys attract a lot of beer drinkers," and he said maybe they'd give it a shot. So we got them into the Starwood. After a few times, I brought Gene Simmons and Paul Stanley down to see them and the rest is history.

GENE SIMMONS (bassist, Kiss) I was invited in 1977 to go see a band called the Boyz play at the Starwood, by, I believe, Rodney Bingenheimer. My date that evening was Bebe Buell. They were the headlining act but I never got to them because the first act up was a group called Van Halen, which I thought was the dumbest name I ever heard; I thought it was like Van Heusen, a shirt company. I thought the name really blew, they won't go anywhere. The first thing I thought was Dave looked like Jim Dandy [from Black Oak Arkansas] and they had kind of an old-fashioned look. But within two numbers I thought, My fucking god, listen to these guys!

MICHAEL WHITE Kiss came to see us, one thousand percent. They came into our dressing room and they were talking to us about going to New York. They said they were looking to take a band back and we were really excited.

"WILD" MICK BROWN And obviously Van Halen got picked to go to New York and record demos with Gene Simmons instead of us. As soon as that door was opened, Van Halen went in and that was slammed shut. There was a word called "new wave" that came out. Everyone had thin ties, was doing that poppy Joe Jackson thing. And punk rock came in, too.

2

"DINOSAUR MUSIC"

KELLY GARNI Van Halen got signed first. They got a great deal. We got the shitty deal.

KELLE RHOADS All the record companies, especially the main ones, had passed on Quiet Riot. RCA, Capitol, they all passed, sometimes two or three times. They didn't want anything to do with them. Partly out of desperation, their managers at that time negotiated a deal with Sony Japan. But that relegated their product to import status. People couldn't find those records. Still can't.

RUDY SARZO (bassist, Quiet Riot, Ozzy Osbourne) The first time I saw Quiet Riot they had one record out. I was new in town and I went to the Whisky to see Van Halen. They were already signed and it was sort of like a homecoming gig for them. But it was so packed I couldn't get in. So I went over to the Starwood, which was more of like the local band hangout. And Quiet Riot was playing. And you know, they came off playing at the Starwood like an arena band playing in a club. And I thought that was a very unusual and very unique approach.

I joined the band about a year later, when they were mixing the second album that came out in Japan. I'm in the photo on the cover of that record, even though their old bass player, Kelly, actually played on it. But they didn't want him in the photo. It was not my call.

KELLE RHOADS By the way, Nikki Sixx was up to replace Kelly Garni in Quiet Riot. He was with a band called London at the time. Man, did the women like that band! When London played the Starwood there wasn't a dry seat in the house. So Kevin wanted to bring Nikki in but Randy said no. He said, "Let's go with this other guy. He looks like he might be good." And that's when they got Rudy.

RUDY SARZO By the late '70s, places like the Starwood were not even the popular places anymore. It was new wave and punk places like Madame Wong's and these really underground venues that became the hot spots.

BOBBY BLOTZER The Motels, Bates Motel, Devo . . . I'm trying to resurrect these bands in my brain. Nobody knew what was coming next. It was hard to understand where we all fit in, you know?

JUAN CROUCIER (bassist, Dokken, Ratt) If you went to the Starwood on a punk night and you were a hard rocker, that could turn ugly. So you really had to be selective of what night you went to what club.

RUDY SARZO I saw Devo at their first show ever in L.A., at the Starwood. And I was blown away because they were so different. So outside the box, so original. And we were being told by all the local labels that Quiet Riot, basically what we were doing was *dinosaur* music. It was never going to come back.

DANA STRUM The Rainbow Bar and Grill, which was the famous hang, went from long-haired rocker people to skinny-tie people that looked like the Knack almost overnight.

STEPHEN QUADROS A lot of the hard rock bands were starting to make concessions. They were starting to wear, you know, white shirts and skinny ties, putting a "The" in front of their name so they would be accepted by the new wave crowd. They were starting to compromise.

CARLOS CAVAZO (guitarist, Snow, Quiet Riot) I remember me and the members of Snow, we even tried to cut our hair shorter to fit in with the new

wave kind of scene and help us achieve more success. It didn't work because our music was still metal.

GEORGE LYNCH The Boyz morphed into Xciter. We weren't making any
progress and we weren't having any luck getting signed, so we started
second-guessing ourselves and decided to become like the Pretenders.
We got a girl singer.

BRIAN SLAGEL (owner, Metal Blade Records) Xciter were probably my favorite band when I was in high school. I used to go see them a zillion times.
George Lynch was amazing. But the thing about L.A. at that time, you
had the punk rock scene and the new wave thing, and bands like Oingo
Boingo and Wall of Voodoo and the Go-Go's and that sort of stuff.

BOB NALBANDIAN But Quiet Riot, even though they had long hair and were
kind of glammy-looking, they were also real poppy. They were one of
those bands you heard on *Rodney on the ROQ* [Bingenheimer's show on
L.A. radio station KROQ] next to, you know, the Adolescents or the Circle
Jerks or whatever. Rodney would play "Slick Black Cadillac," which was
kind of a local hit back then. So that's how I remember Quiet Riot. And
then when Randy Rhoads joined Ozzy it was like, "Oh, that's the dude
from Quiet Riot!"

DANA STRUM I saw Randy play at the Starwood and my mouth was just
on the floor. I thought, How is it possible nobody's really getting this?
How is nobody seeing what I'm seeing? I looked around and I just felt
personally moved and motivated by my love for music and that style. I
was like, Jesus, he's so good! He shouldn't be here! And in my mind on
the way home from the Starwood I thought, You know what? I'm gonna
do something about it. He's *not* gonna be here. That was kind of a pivotal
moment.

   Within weeks of that, Ozzy was out in L.A. looking to put a band together. This was right after Black Sabbath. He met me at the Starwood and
he told my band at the time, "Hey guys, fuck off! Dana's going with me!"
But he had no band at the time. This was just his early steps. So I said, "Look,
I know the guy you need. You don't need to look any further. Without

question this is the guy." I thought in my mind, He's gonna change everybody's lives, Randy.

KELLE RHOADS What a lot of people don't realize is who Ozzy really wanted was Gary Moore. But Gary Moore turned him down because he was making his first solo record. So he went on this big expedition to find a lead player. He looked in L.A., he looked in New York, he came back to L.A. again. And Ozzy happened to know Dana Strum. So Dana says to Ozzy, "Have you seen Randy Rhoads?" And Ozzy said no.

OZZY OSBOURNE Quiet Riot, I never heard of 'em!

KELLE RHOADS So Dana got hold of Randy, but Randy told him he really wasn't interested because he did not like Black Sabbath. But our mom made him do it. She overheard at least one side of the conversation when Randy was talking to Dana on the phone and she told him, "You know, Randy, this might be your shot. You're going to go to that audition." So he went and played for Ozzy in a hotel room. Ozzy was all fucked up and drunk, but he recognized the talent immediately. He said, "You're the greatest guitar player I've ever seen in my life. You're in."

OZZY OSBOURNE When I met Randy Rhoads I was out of my fucking face! I was staying at Le Parc Suite [Hotel] and I'm sitting there, I'm fucked up, it's about six o'clock in the evening, and Dana Strum says, "Fucking wake up! You gotta hear this!" I met Randy and I said, "Are you a woman?" In high heels, a thin little man. Dana says to me, "You'll see him later, in the studio." So next time in the studio I'm still fucked up, Randy has a little amp on his chair and he says, "What do you want me to play?" I said, "Play anything!" Because I wanted to go home. But he started to play and even in my fucked-up state I went, "Oh, good god." And I said something to Dana like, "If he's as good as I think he is . . . look out, world."

RUDY SARZO Was Kevin DuBrow upset when Randy left for Ozzy? Yeah, of course he was. But then again, that was maybe the best thing that happened to him because as long as Randy was in the band, Kevin was always more focused on promoting Randy Rhoads. Then after that, when Kevin was left on his own, he focused on himself. And he was able to develop what Quiet Riot became later.

KELLE RHOADS It took a while, but Kevin prevailed.

INTERVIEW: MICHAEL ANTHONY OF VAN HALEN

Van Halen famously cut their teeth playing now legendary backyard parties in and around Pasadena, and eventually moved into Hollywood clubs like Gazzarri's, the Starwood, and the Whisky. Soon enough, they signed to Warner Bros. Records, became arguably the biggest and most notorious rock act of the late '70s and early '80s, and served as the template for many of the hard rock and hair metal bands that would follow.

Van Halen began playing in Hollywood in the mid-'70s. What were some of your early impressions of the Strip?

I wasn't really a Hollywood guy until I joined Van Halen. That wasn't my thing. But I think the reason Van Halen was playing gigs in Hollywood had a lot to do with David Lee Roth, because he was into the whole fashion scene and that's what was really happening out there. That's when David Bowie was really big—*Ziggy Stardust and the Spiders from Mars*, all that stuff. Everybody was walking around in platform shoes and it was like a fashion thing to go out there at night and parade around in your clothes and socialize. But if there were bands playing, for the most part it'd be local bands—except for the Starwood, which would hire name acts. As opposed to Gazzarri's, where we played, which was more like, you know, Bill Gazzarri hired whoever he could get for the cheapest.

What was Gazzarri's like at that time?

Gazzarri's was . . . I mean, we used to run the dance contest every week there. So it'd be like, "Hey, contestant number one! Come on up!" And we'd play about ten bars of "Tush" by ZZ Top or something and these chicks would dance. I mean, the club didn't really even want us to play original material. They wanted us to play dance stuff and what was happening on the radio. But we'd play five 45-minute sets a night, and sometimes there'd only be a handful of people there for the first set. But as the night went on the place would start to fill up and we would start to inject some of our own original stuff into the sets. After we'd been playing there for quite a while, they didn't really bother us too much about it because we were pulling in a lot of people.

One thing that was interesting was my sister was a Gazzarri's dancer for a very brief period of time, and her picture was on the wall there. I remember flipping out when we played there, going, "You gotta be kidding me . . ."

At that time two of the hottest guitarists on the Strip were Eddie Van Halen and Randy Rhoads. Was there a rivalry between them?

No. The only time I think we ever played with Quiet Riot was at a gig at Pasadena College. Randy was with them, but there wasn't any kind of competition. But there were a lot of guitar players that started trying to copy Eddie's tapping and all the hammer-on stuff that he was doing. A lot of gigs that we would play, Dave would say, "Hey, we don't want all these guitar players stealing your stuff." And he would tell Eddie, "When you play your solos, turn your back to the crowd." Because nobody was doing what Eddie was doing. Although I think Randy Rhoads was probably the closest guy at the time.

How about with George Lynch?

At that point George wasn't really a name yet, so no. But I remember playing with his band.

Van Halen was playing with George's band, the Boyz, at the Starwood when Gene Simmons and Paul Stanley from Kiss came to see you.

It was funny because Paul Stanley actually liked that band. But then Gene said, "*No no no no no.* This is the band right here," talking about Van Halen.

So what did Gene say to you?

I remember going upstairs after the show and Gene comes walking in and he's telling us about the business, this and that, and that he would like to do a demo with us. At that point I think he was having visions of maybe managing us. And he had an idea to change the name of the band because he wasn't sure about Van Halen. I probably still have a copy of the drawing somewhere packed away, but he had an idea to call the band Daddy Long Legs. I remember there was a picture of a spider, you could see the bottom half of the spider with the legs coming out, and then on his head he had a top hat or something. And we're like, "Hmmm . . ." We weren't really going for it. But, you know, he was in the business and we weren't.

Obviously it didn't work out.

No, it didn't. But it sure got the buzz going around town. You know, you're talking about the late '70s—Kiss were *big*. So when the name Van Halen came up, it was "that band that Gene Simmons secretly flew to New York to record a demo with." All of a sudden we had no problem getting a lot of people in Hollywood to come and see us. I think it was about a year after the thing with Kiss, at the same club, the Starwood, where Mo Ostin, who was chairman of Warner Bros., and Ted Templeman, who would end up producing us, came and saw us and we got our deal.

After Van Halen hit big, did it seem like the bands that began to populate the Strip in the '80s all wanted to be you guys to some extent?

Well, after Van Halen got signed, then all of a sudden you see these bands like Mötley Crüe and Poison and, geez, what's the common thread between all these bands? All their singers had bleached-out blond hair, they all wanted to be David Lee Roth. But you know, we did not wear makeup. And I don't know where they got that part of it from. One of those bands probably started doing it and then they all started. But it wasn't us.

But you know, in Van Halen we always used to say, "We'll play naked under one lightbulb and still kick your ass." It was visual but we wanted it to be about talent, too. And we were proud of that. Where in the '80s it was sometimes like, "If you have some talent, fine. But boy, if you have the big hair and all the clothes, even better!"

4

"JUST BECAUSE SOMEONE SAYS YOU SUCK DOESN'T MEAN YOU *DON'T* SUCK"

JAY JAY FRENCH (guitarist, Twisted Sister) We started Twisted Sister in New Jersey in 1972 as a direct response to the New York Dolls and David Bowie. I thought, There's no Jersey version of the Dolls. There's room for one more. Of course, there wasn't room for one more because the Dolls were a colossal commercial failure . . . and nobody wanted another version of a colossal failure. Then there was a period where Twisted Sister was a Rod Stewart–ish kind of band with another singer named Rick Prince. When Dee Snider finally joined in 1976, he introduced harder stuff like Alice Cooper and the shock rock stuff.

DEE SNIDER (singer, Twisted Sister) When I joined Twisted Sister, they were playing a couple of Jay Jay French originals, but Jay Jay said, "We have to announce them as, like, deep cuts." Like he'd say, "This is off an early Deep Purple album." You would have the odd person come up and go, "I really liked that Deep Purple song you played." But you couldn't even say you were playing it. It was that taboo.

JAY JAY FRENCH Bar bands that play covers tend to be behind the curve because they're solely reactive to and trying to catch up with the current trend of music. Twisted Sister was with makeup, then we were without makeup, and then we were with makeup, then we were in kind of transvestite-ish *Rocky Horror*–type makeup, then we were in shock makeup, then we were in glam makeup. We were always behind the curve.

EDDIE "FINGERS" OJEDA (guitarist, Twisted Sister) We used to play every-thing within a hundred-mile radius, and every club was packed, so it'd be four or five nights a week. There were people that used to follow us everywhere, no matter how far we went.

DEE SNIDER Clubs like Hammerheads, for example, had maybe a five hundred to seven hundred capacity and closed and reopened with like a two thousand to three thousand capacity to accommodate the audience that we had. And they would literally bring our crew guys in to tell them what the club needed in order to have Twisted Sister play there—size of stage, power, dressing room positioning—because we were very specific about what we wanted. The club owners knew that if they had Twisted for a weekend and Zebra for a weekend they could make their nut in those two weekends. And then the rest of the bands, lesser bands, would fill things in.

EDDIE "FINGERS" OJEDA We played Fountain Casino, Speaks, Hammer-heads—those were the three biggest clubs. And also we played at the Chance in Poughkeepsie a lot. Eventually we started doing the Civic Center because we could do it, even without a record deal.

DEE SNIDER Some of the club owners were pretty mobbed up, and we bor-rowed money from them on occasions. They would help finance us if we were doing something, like a recording or like when we had to go to England because we had a chance to be on TV. We'd come back and do a weekend or a couple of shows and pay them back. They loved us, and we had no problem. A bunch of those guys were at my wedding!

VITO BRATTA (guitarist, Storm, Dreamer, White Lion) Around 1978 or '79, I was in a high school band called Storm with Nicky Capozzi, who would also be the original drummer in White Lion. The band only played originals, and it was insane stuff, because you had one guy who was into David Bowie, one guy who was into King Crimson, one guy that was into Rush, and one guy that was into Van Halen. And we blended that. We were doing Seattle before there was a Seattle. That band broke up, and right around that time, I went to see Twisted Sister at the Rock Palace on Staten Island. Dee Snider would stop the show if there was somebody in the front who wasn't getting into it. He would say, "Hold on, hold on, hold on! Everybody stop!" And he'd put a spotlight on the guy. I was in the front row with my arms crossed, studying everything because I'm a gearhead: "There's a Shure 57 on the drum set. Okay, he's got a Marshall hundred-watt head. He's got DiMarzio pickups in his Les Paul . . ." So Dee stops the show and the spotlight is on me. He chewed me a new one from the stage and humiliated me, but it was all in good fun. It was part of the show.

DEE SNIDER I *crucified* him. I just destroyed him from the stage.

KEITH ROTH (musician; radio personality, SiriusXM; *Electric Ballroom* host) Dee really fucked people up. I honestly believe that some of those people he singled out are on a couch right now with their therapist still talking to them about it.

VITO BRATTA Afterwards, I'm going out to the car at the end of the night and I hear, "Hey!" And it's Dee Snider. And I'm like, "Oh, shit. What's he gonna do, beat the shit out of me?" He goes, "Hey, you look like a rock guy. What do you do?" I says, "Well, my band broke up." He's asking me about it. I says, "Yeah, we do all originals. I'm not going to do this cover stuff." Meanwhile, it was like an insult to him, because they did half and half. And he's like, "Listen, if you're doing all originals, you're never going to play anyplace in front of people. You've got to mix it up. You got to get out there." So, because of that, I said, "All right, I'm going to get on the same circuit as you."

DEE SNIDER I've talked to Vito about this, and he said that was like a life-changing moment. He sort of checked himself at that point, and I'm like his hero. Honestly, I was just being a dick!

VITO BRATTA I went searching for a band, and I found Dreamer.

DANNY STANTON (singer, Takashi; president, Coallier Entertainment) Dreamer had a buzz and they were good-looking guys, so the girls would show up. When I saw them, I immediately thought that Vito was very Punky Meadows–esque and should have been in Angel. He was tall, lanky, he had the long hair.

STEVE WEST (drummer, Hot Shot, Danger Danger) The drinking age was eighteen, so with a fake ID you could go see a band if you were sixteen, you know what I'm saying?

KEITH ROTH We all had the fake IDs from Playland in Times Square. Once in a while you would sneak into a Jersey club, and being at that age, it was larger than life. Getting in to see Zebra or Twisted Sister was like a home run.

BRUNO RAVEL (bassist, Hot Shot, White Lion, Danger Danger) I actually went to see Twisted when I was probably fourteen. I took my brother's fake ID and went to Speaks out on Long Island. It changed my life. They had an energy and they just kind of bowled you over in an unashamed, non-forgiving way. They were basically like, "If you don't like us, fuck you. You're the one who's missing out." They almost kind of hypnotized you into thinking, like, Oh shit. If I don't like these guys, I'm an idiot! It was like a bullying thing, but in an endearing kind of way. But the main thing that made Twisted Sister stand out from the other bands on Long Island was their shtick. The way they spoke onstage, Dee and Jay Jay were like a comedy team. I could just sit there and listen to the raps in between songs. Forget about the playing. I didn't even care about the playing. I just wanted to hear them talk because they were so funny.

EDDIE "FINGERS" OJEDA The Fountain Casino in New Jersey was an event hall that also did a lot of big catering jobs. It was one of those really big rooms where all these panels would open up and the place would get bigger and bigger. And they used to have to open up every wall for us. I remember getting five thousand people in there on a Wednesday.

VITO BRATTA It was a great scene, and a lot of guys came out of it. We were all friends. Every Monday night at the Fountain Casino was a band, Steel Fortune, which was Dave Sabo from Skid Row.

DAVE "SNAKE" SABO (guitarist, Steel Fortune, Skid Row) We would open up for Dreamer at the Fountain Casino. Vito was really low key, but he was really, really funny. I used to have an MXR six-band EQ on the stage floor and I was really meticulous about it—you know, making the most incremental movements on the sliding faders to make this EQ perfect. Steel Fortune would come out and we'd go into the first song and it'd sound nothing like how I set it. And I'd look over and all the sliders are pushed all the way down and Vito's on the side of the stage, laughing his ass off. So he would sabotage me all the time. But I love that guy.

KEITH ROTH Steel Fortune played whatever they felt was fab, like "Neon Knights" and "Children of the Sea" by Sabbath. I was really impressed . . . but then again, I was fifteen.

MARK WEISS (photographer) The bands seemed pretty happy with packing it in these clubs . . .

DAVE "SNAKE" SABO I remember I went to one of Twisted Sister's SMF [Sick Mother Fucker] parties at the Fountain Casino. There was easily two thousand people there. And the party started on, like, a Sunday afternoon and went all the way through until the club closed. I was there with my buddy Jim, who was the original guitar player in Skid Row, and we were there the whole day. I loved Twisted Sister.

DEE SNIDER Well, we were making $1,000 a week, cash, and I did the research—in today's money, that would have been about a salary of, like, $370,000 a year, taxable. Of course you're driving Mercedes. You're driving Corvettes. You're buying houses. And all these other bands that are driving Mercedes and Corvettes and buying houses, they think they're actually rock stars. They're living it. They're doing coke. They got the groupies. They got everything. But they're not stars except in this microcosm. I mean, Twisted had bodyguards. We had unlisted phone numbers and had to lose fans on the way home, so they couldn't find your house.

TOM KEIFER (singer, guitarist, Saints in Hell, Cinderella) It was so lucrative on the East Coast and the cover bands were so popular, it was like living the fantasy without doing the work to create your own music. But I just felt that as long as you're doing that, you're imitating other people and not developing your own thing. The best you could do is maybe, in a night where you would play three or four sets, sneak in, "Hey, here's one of ours."

RANDY JACKSON (singer, guitarist, Zebra) A lot of clubs would say, "Don't do any originals, we just want covers." So we would just go ahead and play the originals, but we just wouldn't announce them. It was a good way to see how the songs were going over, and that's a good indicator of whether a song is working or not.

VITO BRATTA At eighteen years old I was making a living playing, doing covers in Dreamer. Club owners knew that when we played, we sold out the club. We did one hour of Black Sabbath and all this stuff. And at the end, when we were getting tired, I said, "Let's try some originals." It never happened.

DAVE "SNAKE" SABO I couldn't believe that Twisted weren't signed. They sold out the Palladium in New York but they still couldn't get a record deal.

JAY JAY FRENCH None of the labels would touch us, and I don't necessarily think that they were wrong. Just because someone says you suck doesn't mean you *don't* suck. We could have sucked. We generally were not ready for prime time. When we were ready for prime time, we were ready for prime time.

EDDIE "FINGERS" OJEDA I don't think we were worried about how popular new wave was in the late '70s and early '80s because at that time, you had hard rock bands like Aerosmith and Judas Priest, so there was a market for both, even though the new wave thing was big.

TOM KEIFER On the Northeast club circuit we were on, it was kind of a trend at the time to really push the envelope visually, even with cover bands. The band I was in, Saints in Hell, took a lot of inspiration from the Plasmatics in the attitude and the look. We had a pretty wild front man, and he'd breathe fire and cut himself onstage with glass.

BRIAN "DAMAGE" FORSYTHE (guitarist, Kix) We basically started out as a cover band. Especially at the end of the '70s, punk rock and new wave was big.

STEVE WHITEMAN (singer, Kix) There were clubs all over Maryland, so you could make a living just playing in Maryland. We were definitely into Led Zeppelin, the Stones. We played a little bit of everything. We played the Clash. We played Devo. We played Rod Stewart. Cheap Trick, Aerosmith, Grand Funk, Deep Purple—you name it, we played it. The first time we heard AC/DC, we loved them.

BRIAN "DAMAGE" FORSYTHE We hadn't even heard of AC/DC yet, and a friend of ours turned us on to them. When we started covering them, this is probably around '79, before *Highway to Hell* broke them in America, we played the whole of the *Let There Be Rock* record—every song on there. And it was funny because not too many people were aware of AC/DC at that point, so when we started playing those songs, people thought they were ours.

STEVE WHITEMAN We used to do a club called the Wharf in Waldorf, Maryland, that was six nights a week, five sets a night. Man, did that make us mad-ass tight.

BRIAN "DAMAGE" FORSYTHE It was right on the water and had an outside porch thing. It burnt down at some point.

STEVE WHITEMAN I remember one time playing in front of one guy on a Tuesday night. All night long. And we kept going to the owner, "Can we please just knock this off?" And he wouldn't let us.

BRIAN "DAMAGE" FORSYTHE This guy would watch the clock, you know? He was really relentless. And our set couldn't be short, it had to be right on time.

STEVE WHITEMAN By the time Friday and Saturday rolled around, we were a little fried, and our voices were a little fried, so the biggest crowds got to see the band at its worst.

BRIAN "DAMAGE" FORSYTHE For some reason there was a spot where there was a hole in the stage. And we were doing "Whole Lotta Love," and when it got to that *way down inside* thing, Steve would go and stand in the hole, and sing the rest of the song from there!

STEVE WEST We were just out of high school, and just playing the scene and learning how to do it. And eventually, that morphed into Bruno and I starting our own bands and cutting our hair short and becoming a new wave cover band called Hot Shot doing Duran Duran and Flock of Seagulls and all that for a couple of years. We were playing five nights a week and that's how we made a living. It was great. Then that morphed into more of an AOR thing. We were playing Night Ranger, 38 Special, ZZ Top, whatever was happening. That ended when they raised the drinking age to twenty-one.

BRUNO RAVEL The audiences were cut literally in half, maybe even more.

MARK WEISS With the drinking age change, I think all these bands started honing in on doing originals, trying to be rock stars, MTV, go to the West Coast, that whole thing.

EDDIE "FINGERS" OJEDA We got signed just in time because the drinking age went from eighteen to twenty-one and a lot of these places were going disco and doing DJs and that whole scene in New York dropped out. We left and went to England to record the first album. It was really tough for some of the other bands on the circuit . . . They had to break up.

5

"RHYMES WITH ROCKIN'!"

BRIAN SLAGEL Everybody who was still playing anything heavy in L.A. was all kind of in the same boat. We were all friends with each other because it was such a small scene then. And we all grew up on the same stuff—AC/DC, Kiss, Judas Priest, Zeppelin, Sabbath, all that stuff. So we had a lot in common.

DON DOKKEN There wasn't just the Hollywood scene. There was also the South Bay scene—Dante Fox, which became Great White, Bobby Blotzer, Alan Niven, Juan Croucier, Mick Mars . . . We were all down there. We were just commuting to Hollywood.

JUAN CROUCIER There were a lot of musicians in that area. Rent was cheap, okay? I remember Don Dokken and I shared a rehearsal place with a band called Vendetta, and the guitarist in that band was Mick Mars. They all lived together in an apartment, and Mick had, like, three Marshall stacks about three feet away from the front wall of the living room, and behind that was a sleeping bag and a pillow.

MICK MARS I used my Marshall stacks to kind of wall me in so I could be away from everybody; kind of like my own little room made out of Marshalls.

DON DOKKEN We were all pretty honestly starving. We would work in the daytime, practice at night, try to get gigs anywhere we could.

BOBBY BLOTZER Me and Don were in a band together in '76 and '77 called Airborn. We were doing gigs with Van Halen, doing cover material. We were South Bay, which is the Redondo Beach, Manhattan Beach, Torrance, Hermosa Beach section of Los Angeles. And Van Halen was from Pasadena, Snow was from inland L.A. You had Quiet Riot, and they were from . . . I don't know where the fuck they were from, Hollywood, I guess. But all of us bands were out doing gigs together and such. We went and played up in Hollywood, anywhere we could, honestly.

CARLOS CAVAZO I remember the Boyz, I remember Xciter, I remember doing shows with Don. I remember Great White; they were Dante Fox for a while.

MARK KENDALL (guitarist, Dante Fox, Great White) I grew up in the suburbs of Los Angeles—West Covina, Huntington Beach—but always within, like, a hundred-mile radius of L.A. In the '70s I was in a band and we'd play places like the Starwood and the Troubadour and the Whisky. And during the week we'd play covers gigs, like a five-sets-a-night kind of thing. Then one day a friend told me he saw this guy at a backyard party who was sixteen years old and just a great singer. And it ended up being Jack Russell.

JACK RUSSELL (singer, Dante Fox, Great White) I grew up in Whittier in a real nice family. I joined my school choir when I was in fifth grade. I started my first band right around then, at eleven years old. Started with drugs and alcohol, too. I had an overprotective mom and a really strict father. I guess it was my way of rebelling.

By the time I was sixteen, I was playing with a prog-rock band because they were gigging on the Strip. It was me and these twenty-two-year-old guys and I didn't really like the music, but it got me into Hollywood. Then I left them and got in another band, but they kicked me out for being all drugged out. After that I was playing backyard parties doing cover songs. That's when me and Kendall met and decided to start a band together. This was '78, '79.

MARK KENDALL Just three or four months after that, Jack got in a bunch of trouble and was sentenced to eight years in prison.

JACK RUSSELL Here's what happened. And let me just first say the reason I tell this to people is not to make me sound like a badass. I tell it so that people might learn from it and realize that, you know, with drugs, no matter how you think you've got control of your life and how impossible you think it is that something bad might happen, it's possible.

Anyway, here's how it went: Me and a friend of mine used to find out where the coke dealers lived in our area, right? Then we'd put on ski masks and go in their house with a gun and a knife and say, "Hold your hands up and take us to your coke or we're gonna blow your head off." Of course we weren't gonna do that. But we would load the gun because it was a revolver, and with a revolver you can see when it's pointed at you whether it's loaded or not. And we didn't feel like getting our butts kicked.

So we did this a couple times and it was no problem. And then one time my regular partner couldn't go so I borrowed a gun from a friend of mine—same type of gun, a .22 revolver—and another friend agreed to go with me. So we put our ski masks on, we go to this house, and we go up to the front door. And before we go in, I say, "Look, let's smoke some PCP, just to get us in that mood." And this PCP I had was so strong. I had no clue. But we did it and then we walked into the house. And the rest of what I'm gonna tell you, you have to understand, is from the [police] transcripts. Because I have no recollection of any of this. I really don't. I was in almost, like, a sleepwalking state, you know?

So we go in the house and my friend notices that I'm not acting quite right. And he splits. Now I'm in this house with this gun, and I guess I went into the backyard. And from what I've been told, there was a maid out there and she was watering the plants by the pool. And apparently I said, "Give me your coke!" She goes, "No coke. Just Pepsi. Help yourself it's in the refrigerator." She thought I was a friend of the guy who lived there and that I was playing a joke, right? So I guess this made me upset, and I went over to her and I grabbed her. She had her arms over her head and she was squirting me with water and the gun went off. And the father, who was downstairs in the house, looks out and sees this guy in a ski mask wrestling with his maid. So he goes to the side of the house, grabs a briefcase full of money, and runs into a bathroom. And by this time the maid had gotten away from me and ended up in the same bathroom as him. According to the transcript, I put huge cracks in the door from hitting it. It was a solid-oak door, but I guess I had that super-strength type of stuff that happens when you're high or whatever. And then the report also said, for some unknown reason, I shot at the door. And the bullet went through the door, hit the Saint Christopher necklace over the maid's heart, and ricocheted into her shoulder. Saving her life. Saving my life, as well.

Next thing I know, I wake up on my knees on the floor by the bathroom door, and I hear, *"Come out of the house. This is the county SWAT team."* I go outside and they say, *"Drop the gun!"* I drop the gun. I walk forward and they grab me and get me on the ground. And the one cop starts hitting me. He's going, "What did you shoot her for?" I'm like, "What are you talking about?" "You shot her! The maid!" I shot *who*? And then I heard my dad's voice: "When you're all hopped up, you're gonna shoot someone." And there I was.

MARK KENDALL I was walking by the newsstand one day and I see on the cover of the paper: WHITTIER-ITE JACK RUSSELL SHOOTS LIVE-IN MAID. I mean, the letters were like four inches high! And I'm going, "Well, it can't be the same Jack Russell. This isn't the guy that's singing with me. It can't be!"

JACK RUSSELL They gave me eight years. But then they sent me to this place called California Youth Authority, where they resentence you. After a clerical error and just a bizarre set of circumstances, I ended up getting out in eleven months.

MARK KENDALL By that time I had gone out and started over and basically made a band with a bass player named Don Costa and a drummer named Tony Richards, who both wound up playing with W.A.S.P. later. And I had a female singer named Lisa Baker, who George Lynch stole for his band, Xciter. We went on with another singer for a while and then when Jack got out he asked if he could audition.

JACK RUSSELL I did my first show with them six days after I got out of jail.

MARK KENDALL Jack's very first show with Dante Fox was at the Troubadour. He was scared to death and I don't blame him. You know, when you're confined for any length of time, just walking around and going to the store's a big deal. So imagine how he felt, you know? But he worked his way into it.

JACK RUSSELL It was a great show! They got me all dressed up and we went up to the Troubadour and just got plowed.

GREG LEON The clarity in Jack's voice, it reminded me of Robert Plant. And he never hit a bad note. Whereas Kevin DuBrow? Sharp, all the time. It would drive you crazy. I didn't care for the rest of the band, but to this day I believe Jack was probably the best lead vocalist on the scene.

MARK KENDALL With Dante Fox, at first we would just go up onstage and play. But then we started dressing up and doing this good-versus-evil thing. It was pretty goofy.

JACK RUSSELL It was like this "duality of man" thing, you know? The bass player was all in black. Mark was all in white. I was dressed in black and white. The whole thing was kind of stupid.

BOB NALBANDIAN Kendall looked like an albino. He had that platinum-blond hair and you couldn't tell if it was natural or if it was a look he was going for. But they were just a fun band, great band. And the music was very Van Halen–ish. Kendall was a great guitar player and Jack was a fantastic singer and front man. And Don Costa, the bass player, he was a maniac.

MARK KENDALL Don Costa would play his bass with a pickaxe. And he put this cheese grater on the back of it, and he would grind his knuckles on that and then bleed all over the stage. He was a real character. I remember later on when he was out of the band, George Lynch called me going, "Where's that crazy bass player?" And I'd seen the Boyz many times. I knew all those bands. When George got the girl singer out of my band, he was in a band called Xciter. He wanted to make it more than anything.

"WILD" MICK BROWN Don Dokken had his eye on Xciter. And after the Van Halen thing closed the door on other bands, everyone was making a move to try to do something new. So he approached us and said, "Listen, I'm gonna go to Germany. I know Dieter Dierks, who produced the Scorpions. I'm gonna record some songs. Can I take your song 'Paris Is Burning' and record it?" And we said, "No!" And he did it anyway.

GEORGE LYNCH That's not *exactly* true. I did say yes under the condition that we work our business out and he come over to the house and we kind of talk about it and we do an agreement and I show him the songs and all that kind of stuff. And that he keep me posted as far as what the business opportunities were for these songs and what exactly he was doing with them. Well, none of that other stuff happened. He just felt he got an okay and then he took two songs that were Xciter songs that I wrote.

DON DOKKEN I asked them if I could use the song "Paris"—the riff and the chorus. I didn't like the lyrics or the melody. I wanted to change it. And finally George said—he just doesn't remember—he goes, "Yeah, we don't play that song anymore. It's over with." Because they had moved on to kind of a new wave vibe. They had a girl singer in their band, they cut off all their hair, and they were going full-on toward the whole new wave thing. Otherwise I wouldn't've done it. But I just kept the riff and I kept the chorus and then I rewrote all the lyrics and melody and that's how it came to be.

GEORGE LYNCH I saw years later in a contract he had signed to a publishing company in Germany, World of Music, that he sold these songs for twenty-five or thirty-five thousand deutsche marks, which is quite a bit of money. And, um, you know, that's pretty underhanded, to say the least.

DON DOKKEN I went to Germany and Dieter Dierks was gonna be in Hamburg for a night and he came to see me play and he said something to the effect that Klaus Meine from the Scorpions had hurt his voice and things were going slow and he thought my vibrato sounded very similar to Klaus'. So that's how I ended up singing background vocals on the Scorpions' *Blackout* album. Then I did more demos after I sang for the Scorpions and Gaby Hoffmann, the manager of Accept, who were also recording in Dierks' studio, took my demo to Hamburg and got me a record deal on a French label, Carrere Records. But I had no band at this time, so I went back to L.A. with a deal but no band. Mick and George weren't doing anything, so that's when I asked them to join. They said no. I said, "Well, I'll give you guys, like, fifteen hundred bucks and you get a free trip to Germany. We'll throw some songs together and make an album."

"WILD" MICK BROWN Don called and he goes, "Hey, I recorded some of your songs and I have a small record deal. Would you like to be in the band?" I was living with George at the time and I looked over at him and held my hand over the phone. I said, "Listen, this *sonofabitch* took our songs and he recorded 'em and he's got a record deal. And he wants me to be in the band." And George was just steaming! He was like, "Wow, you just raped me of the last thing in my life I have!" But before he could think about it I went back to Don and I said, "I'll do it . . . if George can be in the band as well." And he went, "Well, I don't know . . ." He knew there was gonna be problems! Because he'd already lied to him. But I convinced George. I said, "Listen, we've got nothin' else going on. Let's take a chance." All I could think was, Man, we're hittin' the wall here, it's getting late in the game. I'm already twenty-two! I said, "Let's go to Germany. At least our music will get recorded with us playing on it." And goddamn, it did.

DON DOKKEN Of course after I got the record deal, George said, "You stole my song!"

ALAN NIVEN (executive, Greenworld Distribution, Enigma Records; manager, Guns N' Roses, Great White) I think there was some sort of creative friction there, too. George definitely had an extremely high opinion of himself. He claims to have developed the hammer-on tapping technique before Eddie Van Halen. And I tend to sit there and go, "Both of you fuckers are liars. I think Harvey Mandel did it before both of you." But that's musicians. And Don is very much a songsmith. I would say that it was just chalk and cheese in terms of personalities.

JACK RUSSELL There's a lot of people that talk trash about Don, but they just don't know Don. He helped Great White so much in the beginning, and he never asked for anything in return. He's got a rough exterior, but people get the wrong ideas about him. He can be a little high on Don Dokken—"Enough about you, let's talk about me"—but all of us can, you know? It comes with being a musician.

MICHAEL WAGENER (producer, mixer, Mötley Crüe, Dokken, Great White, Stryper, Poison, Skid Row, Extreme, White Lion) We recorded Dokken's first album, *Breaking the Chains,* in Germany, which was basically my first production. There was tension in the band between Don and George— their egos kind of did their little thing. To me that tension was not necessarily bad, but then again, I only saw it in the studio and I kind of tended to control that between the two.

DON DOKKEN When we did the album in Germany, George never even finished the record. He left before it was done. And I had to finish it by myself. Mick and him hopped on a plane and went home. They basically decided that "if you can get a record deal, we can *definitely* get Xciter back together and get a record deal." So I gave them their money, their fifteen hundred bucks, and they took off.

"WILD" MICK BROWN We didn't want it to be called Dokken. But Don was using that name prior to the recording. We didn't want to be that. So it was, "Yeah, we'll get a band name." And I remember George and I left and Don had to stay in Germany to mix and sing and everything. And George, he was smarter. He goes, "I know that guy's doing something. When we get back over there it's gonna be called Dokken."

GEORGE LYNCH So one day we're back in Germany and drive to this city to a warehouse to go see our first record. It's at the printing plant. And we're sitting there in front of a pallet of records and we open it up and we look at it and there's a picture of Don on the cover and it says *"Don Dokken"* and there's no picture or mention of any of us on the record. And we're like, "Don, what the fuck is this?" And he goes, "Oh, man, I don't know how this happened. Some heads are gonna roll. I'm so pissed . . ." I go, "Oh, I bet you are."

"WILD" MICK BROWN So we got him to drop the "Don"!

GEORGE LYNCH That's a compromise that he set up for himself to make it appear that he had compromised.

"WILD" MICK BROWN That pissed George off completely. And I can see why. He was being lied to. And, listen, to an artist, music is the most sacred thing. Sometimes it's the only thing you have in your life. And George, he never really let go of it.

DON DOKKEN I figured, well, Van Halen, that's an unusual name. I'll call it Dokken, you know? Rhymes with "rockin'!"

6

"BLUE-BLACK HAIR AND HIGH HEELS"

BOB NALBANDIAN The thing about a lot of these L.A. bands is that when they became famous, they weren't new bands. You hear about, you know, Mötley Crüe, and it's a "brand-new band that just came out . . ." People didn't know the history. They didn't know that Nikki Sixx had been in London and all these different bands.

DON ADKINS (photographer) I didn't know the details of Nikki's backstory. What I do remember is him telling me about living in the projects in the Seattle area and that life there was really, really hard. He said he had to come to L.A. to find a way to make it, and just to get the hell out of where he was. He thought that L.A. was the place to follow his passion because everything was happening here.

MICHAEL WHITE I was playing at the Starwood, and Nikki was working there as a janitor or something.

GREG LEON He would paint walls, do whatever side jobs needed to be done. I'd go there sometimes to book a gig and I'd see him sweeping the floor, changing a room around, or whatever.

MICHAEL WHITE He saw me play and he came up to me and we talked, and he said he wanted me to be the singer for his band. They were called

London. I went out and I saw them and I joined the band and we started doing gigs.

DON ADKINS The lead singer of London was a guy named Nigel Benjamin. Nigel was the singer of Mott the Hoople after Ian Hunter left and they were called Mott. I think there was some frustration that things weren't going the way he wanted, and London eventually wound up losing Nigel and they went in search of another lead singer. And that was Michael White, who had been with the Boyz. Then that kind of devolved and for about a month London ended up having [future W.A.S.P. front man] Blackie Lawless as their singer.

LIZZIE GREY (guitarist, Sister, London) Before Blackie ended up in London he had Sister, which was his version of Alice Cooper. This was a few years earlier. Sister was an interesting band. Blackie used a lot of the shock rock approach, eating worms onstage, lighting stages on fire with these massive flames.

MIKE VARNEY (producer; owner, Shrapnel Records) The guy ate worms! Out of a live bait box!

LIZZIE GREY Yeah, a box of night crawlers. Extra large. It was fun to watch.

GINA ZAMPARELLI (L.A. club promoter, booking agent) I just remember standing there in the Starwood being absolutely shocked. I was still, I think, in high school. And I was just like, "What is going on? Who is this guy?"

LIZZIE GREY Back in the day, I would go see Sister play, and then I joined the band. Then we ended up getting a guy named Frank Feranna. But Sister kinda fell apart because Blackie wasn't really pleased with Frank's playing. Blackie fired him. At the time Frank and I were so close it was a pretty easy thing for me to leave with him and say, "We're gonna do this London thing."

GREG LEON I knew Nikki as Frank Feranna. He auditioned for my band Suite 19 a couple of times and he did not get the gig. Because he couldn't play! But he looked great. I mean, he was a great-looking guy.

MICHAEL WHITE He was Nikki when I joined London. He wanted to be Nikki so everybody called him Nikki. But every now and then when somebody was mad at him they'd say, "Frank! *Fuck off!*"

LIZZIE GREY Van Halen would come to see London because we were dressing up like the New York Dolls and making a big noise. We started getting people coming to the Starwood shows. I mean, we had Jagger and Richards there, the huge rock stars. Because we were providing shock rock, too. But ours was more of a fancy dress, I guess I'd call it, than the death rock kind of thing.

DON ADKINS I was going to all of London's shows for at least a year, a year and a half. And the manager of the Starwood was a guy named David Forest. He took a liking to the group and basically gave them headlining spots all the time on key weekends. So London built up a good following. They were sort of like one of the original hair bands. Just incredibly tall hair, with the platform heels and boots. And they had the typical thing at the time, which was hot girlfriends, or girls that liked them that would help them make their clothes and all kinds of stuff.

GREG LEON I took Tommy Lee to the Starwood when London was playing. He was still Tom Bass, and he was playing with me in Suite 19.

DON ADKINS Tommy was from West Covina. He lived at home with his parents.

GREG LEON Tommy had been following me for the longest time, begging me to play drums, but he was only seventeen. I'm going, "Dude, you're a kid!" He goes, "You gotta hear me play. Just come over to my place." So we got together, he had a great rehearsal room. His dad, David, had built a room inside of a room in the garage. And then the bass player that we had, his mother was a booking agent, so she had us playing all over the place almost every weekend. And I was booking the Hollywood clubs, and we did a lot of parties. It was young kids having fun, girls everywhere and stuff. It was awesome.

STEPHEN QUADROS Suite 19 would open for Snow. Greg Leon was an amazing guitar player and Tommy was a great drummer. Really solid. I remember that. He was really an enthusiastic guy. I liked his energy.

GREG LEON We went to the Starwood one time to see London and Tommy just fell in love with them. He goes, "Man, there's something about that guy . . ." Talking about Nikki.

STEPHEN QUADROS Nikki was the wildest-looking guy. He would show up all decked out, with his big leather heels on with Doberman pinscher dogs with him. He was like this maven.

DON ADKINS Then London went ahead and broke up and went their separate ways. But Nikki was always thinking about the next big thing. And that's when he started formulating, I want to have this new group. I want it to be hard, heavy . . .

NIKKI SIXX (bassist, Sister, London, Mötley Crüe) London played the Starwood all the time, and we drew really well. So when I was getting ready to quit London, I sat down with David Forest, who ran the club, and I told David that I wanted to do a new version of London but I wanted it to be a lot harder.

DEEDEE KEEL (booking agent, Whisky a Go Go) One day Nikki came up to see me in the Whisky office. I had never seen London, but he said, "I have a new band. This band's going to be really great. You have to book us." I didn't really know what to think but he was very persistent and so eventually I gave him a date. And the band was Mötley Crüe.

GREG LEON They wanted me to be the guitar player in Mötley Crüe but I didn't want to do it. That just wasn't appealing to me. I wanted to be in a band like Rainbow or Frank Marino and Mahogany Rush.

DON ADKINS I forget how it all came together. Tommy was there, and then Mick Mars, who had had some previous groups in L.A. came in . . .

DON DOKKEN I knew Mick Mars from the South Bay—he was playing in a band called Vendetta. I told him I thought he was stuck playing in that club band and he should try to branch off and start his own band.

JUAN CROUCIER One thing I told Mick was "You're never going to make it in a band if you're playing the covers circuit. It's highly unlikely that a group of people are gonna walk in, see you playing 'Can't Get Enough of Your Love' and go, 'That's the guy we need for the next huge multiplatinum band!'" or whatever.

MICK MARS I asked the guys [in my band], "Please let's do some writing, let's do some real music?" No, they all wanted to do cover songs. So I go, "Okay, see ya." And I put an ad in the *Recycler* and I think everybody knows that story: "Loud, rude, aggressive guitar player." That was late 1980, just after John Lennon was shot. I remember because it was '81 when Nikki called and we started, like, playing around in January and early February.

NIKKI SIXX When I met Mick he had his shoes duct-taped together and he had duct tape on his pants to keep his pants on. The guy had no money. He had a Marshall stack and a Les Paul. He had his priorities straight!

DON ADKINS Mick was older. I thought he was in his late thirties, at least. He had more of a seasoned adult sense of humor and everything. But also there was a seriousness to him, because he was dealing with a lot of financial hardship and child support and crap like that. Basically what I saw with him was a drive, like, "I gotta get out of this. I gotta do something. I gotta make it."

MICK MARS At the time we first got together I was listening to a lot of different artists that were kind of obscure, like Rare Bird and Be-Bop Deluxe. I was into Trapeze, Glenn Hughes' first band. Lots of Jeff Beck, some Aerosmith, some Kansas. And the other guys, being younger, they were listening more to Kiss and stuff like that. But I had, like, ten or fifteen years on them. Hell, I'd been playing guitar longer than Tommy or Vince had been alive.

NIKKI SIXX We had this little guitar player kid named Robin who was in there for a second before Mick came in. He maybe rehearsed with me and Tommy for a week.

MICK MARS My first job. Nikki and Tommy were like, "You tell him!" So I said to Robin, "We don't need ya!" Basically. I can't remember the exact words. It was kind of cruel but I was put on the spot.

NIKKI SIXX And then it was the three of us.

DON ADKINS They went and found this other lead singer named O'Dean. O'Dean kind of looked like . . . the best analogy I can have with him is he looked like Paul Williams with black hair. The same height and everything. A really short guy. And if I had to pin his vocal style it was heading toward the direction of [AC/DC singer] Brian Johnson. Nothing that stood out about him. But they started going ahead and playing with O'Dean at this rehearsal studio, I think it was at SIR when I saw them. They had one reused song from London called "Public Enemy #1," and they started rehearsing.

MICK MARS One day we were rehearsing with O'Dean and I told Tommy outside, "This guy isn't right." He was . . . different. So Tommy calls Nikki out and goes, like, "Hey, Nikki, Mick doesn't dig O'Dean." And I go, "No. I want that little blond-haired guy we saw at the Starwood the other night!" I go, "I don't care if he can sing, because I was pretty high, but I know that the girls were going nuts over him."

STEPHEN QUADROS I remember Vince Neil coming backstage at a Snow concert when he was about seventeen years old. He was in a band called Rockandi. Not to lift a Montrose title or anything! He was, like, the prettiest David Lee Roth kid, you know? He looked like the total perfect rock star.

GREG LEON He had a good image and his voice was really high. And the girls loved him. When Rockandi played, there would be all these girls at the front of the stage. And they weren't in front of the guitar player or the bass player, they were right in front of Vince. Hoping he'd sweat on them or something.

MICK MARS O'Dean had a Roger Daltrey–sounding voice. Vince's was much higher pitched—and he was much better lookin'! So Vince came to an audition and that was it. Goodbye, O'Dean!

DON ADKINS Nikki just immediately fell in love with Vince's voice. So even before I got to meet him, Nikki's telling me, "Don, this guy has this, like, not-of-planet-Earth voice. I can't describe it. It's out of this world." And it was the perfect formula. The perfect mix.

NIKKI SIXX The first song we ever played together was "Live Wire."

LIZZIE GREY Did I think they'd make it? No. I just felt like . . . I felt it was lacking something. Ironically, the vocals. I wasn't really crazy about it. I didn't like where they were coming from. But everybody else liked Vince's voice just fine. So, it shows what I know.

DON ADKINS Mötley had an apartment on Clark Street, right above the Whisky a Go Go. It was just a scene up there all the time.

VICKY HAMILTON (consultant, Mötley Crüe, Stryper; manager, Poison, Guns N' Roses, Faster Pussycat; author, *Appetite for Dysfunction: A Cautionary Tale*) When I moved to L.A., after a few cocktail waitress jobs I ended up being a record buyer at the Licorice Pizza on Sunset, across from the Whisky a Go Go. And punk rock was kind of ruling on the Strip. It was Black Flag, the Circle Jerks, Oingo Boingo, those kinds of bands. We did an in-store with the Go-Go's and there was a line all the way down the block. But at the same time, the picture window at Licorice sort of faced the Whisky and Clark Street, and I kept seeing these guys in blue-black hair and high heels and a blond-headed guy walking up Clark, which ended up being Mötley Crüe.

NIKKI SIXX We stuck out like a sore thumb, and I think that we gave hope to all those guys running around and still loving rock 'n' roll. That they could do something. They were like, "What the fuck are these guys up to? These guys don't make any sense." Because we were part punk rock and part power pop and we acted like punks but we looked like the Dolls. Even though the Dolls were punks, but you know what I mean. The new wavers were like, "Wow, this is kind of cool," and the punkers were like, "This is really cool," and the metallers were like, "This is *awesome!*"

DEEDEE KEEL For me it was a natural transition to go from a band like the Dolls into a band like Mötley Crüe. It was the same thing, only more radical. It just got more crazy and more crazy.

DON ADKINS I did a shoot with them where it was something like an eleven-hour day, and I think nine hours of that was hair. It was a really elaborate procedure. Basically all the guys would bend over and hang their heads upside down and girls would go ahead and spray their hair. Then they would carefully walk back out with their heads still down. When they were ready to get photographed it was, "Okay, Don—*now!*" They'd flip their heads up and you'd photograph before their hair started falling down.

NIKKI SIXX You can't use aerosol. If you do, then you've got to dry your hair upside down and pull it out while you do it. And of course you've got to sleep upside down. You sleep on your forehead. When you wake up in the morning your hair is all messed up. And you look at yourself and you say: "I look fine."

JACK RUSSELL You know, I thought they would do well only because they looked totally weird. And I thought, That's probably a really smart move, coming up with your own thing. Because it's hard to come up with an image that hasn't been done. To be honest, in Dante Fox we were like Judas Priest look-alikes. Like, "Okay, go down to the Pleasure Chest and buy all the leather bracelets . . ." You know, it's a sex shop, you could buy anything in there. I remember chasing Mark Kendall around with a three-foot black dildo. He was screamin', "*Aaaahhhhh!*"

DON ADKINS Their big debut in L.A. was going to be at the Starwood [on April 24, 1981]. They opened for Y&T, who had just changed their name from Yesterday and Today. And they had more of a traditional hard rock, slight heavy metal crowd. More of a macho type of thing. Mötley Crüe came out and they musically killed it. But there were some people doing the old, "Hey, look at these guys . . ." Some of these macho guys that were troubled by the glam look.

CHRIS HOLMES (guitarist, Sister, W.A.S.P.) Mötley Crüe, I used to call 'em chicks with dicks.

DAVE MENIKETTI (singer, guitarist, Y&T) We knew that they were gonna open the bill for us that night and we had heard that they were this up-and-coming band. So me and Phil, our bass player, we got up into the balcony at the Starwood and we watched about three of their songs when they first came on. And we looked at each other and we said, "These guys aren't that good!" They were pretty raw. I mean, there's no question about it. But we were very critical about other people if they didn't have, like, amazing chops. But with Mötley it wasn't about that. It was about the vibe of their band, their attitude, and of course, you know, their stage show and everything. Although they didn't really have much of a stage show at that particular point . . .

NIKKI SIXX We would take the amp line, with white borders made out of painted two-by-fours with stretched black material on them. So it looked like walls of amps, right? Not! We'd have one 8 x 10 SVT cabinet and Mick had his Marshall stack. The reason that we did that was that everything looked really big.

DON ADKINS One thing that did happen at the Starwood was that one of the a-holes in the audience who was like, "Eff you, eff you!" and kinda flipping off Nikki and all this stuff while he was playing, Nikki was telling me about this later, he said to himself, "I'm gonna win this asshole over . . ." And he just starts aggressively playing his bass so much so that he cut his thumb open and he's spewing blood everywhere. And the guy just shut up.

VINCE NEIL (singer, Rockandi, Mötley Crüe) Those were crazy days. Nobody knew who we were, and we didn't exactly look normal. So people would see Mötley Crüe and be like, "What the hell is this?" People wouldn't even stand near the stage when we played. There were some good bar fights back then where it was just like, "Fuck you, buddy!"

NIKKI SIXX I just remember sitting in a fucking cowboy bar surrounded by fucking rednecks in Grass Valley [California] and I'm wearing like yellow pants with the black stiletto boots and some leather jacket and no shirt and my hair all freaked out and Vince is like the same and Tommy's the same, and just fucking sitting there, man. And the people are like, "Hey, man, what's *your* fucking trip?" "I'll tell you what our fucking trip is, man, we're a rock 'n' roll band!"

7

RATT 'N' ROLL

STEPHEN PEARCY Mötley were about a year ahead of us. We'd troll the Strip, trying to see who the biggest, baddest band was when we moved up to L.A. And people kept saying, "There's this new band, Mötley Crüe." And we were like, "Oh, yeah?" "Yeah, they light their legs on fire and they do this and that, they're crazy. They're partiers and there's chicks around." And so we're going, "Okay . . ."

CHRIS HAGER (guitarist, Mickey Ratt, Rough Cutt) Stephen and I were from San Diego. And there's a big history of people who migrated up from San Diego who actually wound up becoming notable people in the scene. I'm talking people like Jake E. Lee, Warren DeMartini, Robbin Crosby, just to name a few.

BRIAN SLAGEL Ratt saw how Mötley had done it, and they naturally kinda followed the lead of Mötley and went in that direction. Once they did that, then the whole scene kinda took off.

STEPHEN PEARCY People were going, "Who's the next band around here that's doing something?" And people would say, "Oh, it's a band called Mickey Ratt."

CHRIS HAGER Stephen wanted to call the band Mickey Rat after this magazine cartoon character. He was sort of the antithesis of Mickey Mouse, this kinda fucked-up guy who drank and smoked and fucked a lot of chicks, right? Mickey Rat was a scoundrel. And he was funny. And Stephen loved it. Then we added another *T* to the end of the name to avoid copyright infringement.

DAVE JELLISON (bassist, Mickey Ratt) Stephen knew someone who had a house in Culver City. And he could live in her garage. And he's like, "I'm going to go to L.A. and make it . . ."

STEPHEN PEARCY It was my friend's mom's house. Mrs. O'Neill. The garage's back room was converted into a big, square white room.

CHRIS HAGER So we moved all the band equipment into the garage and put our little mattresses and stuff in there. We lived in this garage, we rehearsed there, we partied there. And that was the genesis of Ratt, basically.

DAVE JELLISON Stephen's chief skill, to be honest, was his steadfast belief that he was going to be famous. I was like, "But you're not that good of a singer and you're not really that good onstage and you've got no rap . . ." But, I mean, from the day I met him, we were playing a backyard party in San Diego in 1978, he was like, "I'm going to move to L.A. and I'm going to be famous." It was like *"What?* You're playing a shitty party!"

CHRIS HAGER We played together for about a year and a half, doing all the clubs that were around at that time, like Madame Wong's and Club 88. We even did the Starwood right before it closed down [in June 1981, roughly two months after Mötley Crüe's debut performance there].

STEPHEN PEARCY We played the Troubadour once in a while but they were strict about "you can't play down the street for two months . . ." and all this stuff. So you had to play the game until you became a house band, which Mickey Ratt did.

CHRIS HAGER We became the house band at Gazzarri's.

STEPHEN PEARCY Stryper also played there, only they were called Roxx Regime at the time. They became really good friends with us.

MICHAEL SWEET (singer, guitarist, Roxx Regime, Stryper) We used to hang out in front of Gazzarri's and smoke cigarettes together and talk.

DAVE JELLISON This is before they decided that being a religious band was going to be their focus. Because they weren't religious. They were in the parking lot, you know, with chicks just like everybody else. There was no indication of any Christianity in them.

MICHAEL SWEET The way it worked was you would do three to four short sets, maybe forty-five minutes each. And the minute you would stop the next band would go on. And there would be two or three bands each weekend. And this went on starting from seven or eight o'clock at night until two a.m.

CHRIS HAGER Bill Gazzarri was a quintessential Hollywood kind of a guy. Kind of a gruff, shady, tough old bird, you know what I mean?

DAVE JELLISON Bill Gazzarri was one of the most disturbing human beings ever made. He would get onstage and say, "Nothing but the hottest bands on my *staaaage!*" He kept referring to how good-looking all the guys were. And then there were the Miss Gazzarri's contests, which were just a bunch of super-hammered nineteen-year-old chicks.

CHRIS HAGER As far as girls, Stephen and I were pulling a lot of women from day one. We had this thing where we would always . . . not always, but a lot of times, we would wind up with sisters. Even twins in some cases. This happened more than a couple times.

DAVE JELLISON You get a band that is appealing to the women and the men will follow. That's been around since time began.

CHRIS HAGER Mickey Ratt was actually doing pretty well. But it came to a point where, musically, it wasn't quite working for me. So we parted ways. And the name of the band gradually changed from Mickey Ratt to M. Ratt to, by the time I left, just Ratt.

MICHAEL SWEET And then Jake E. Lee was in Ratt. So that was really cool.

JAKE E. LEE (guitarist, Ratt, Rough Cutt, Ozzy Osbourne) When I was in San Diego I was in a band called Child. We were a big San Diego band, but I realized that we were never going to get any bigger than being a big San Diego band. I tried to talk all of them into going up to L.A., but they were all older than me. They all had jobs. Half of them were married. They didn't want to do it. So I moved up to L.A. on my own, but I knew Stephen Pearcy and the guys in Ratt. It's not like we were close or anything, but we had played shows together and partied together and stuff like that in San Diego. When I got to L.A. I'd go check out Stephen's shows and hang with the band and stuff, and that's how I got into Ratt.

MATT THORNE (bassist, Ratt, Rough Cutt) And then the bass player, I think it was Dave Jellison, quit. And Jake was my roommate at the time, so he said, "Hey, you want to audition for this?" So I learned the songs and went down there and I was in.

My first gig with Ratt was a house party in Culver City. But then we played the Troubadour, and we played Gazzarri's a lot. But nobody was packing the clubs yet except for Mötley Crüe. And Mötley Crüe wouldn't have played a house party in Culver City.

RON KEEL (singer, Steeler, Keel) The first time I ever went to L.A. I got in a rental car and went straight to Gazzarri's. Coming from Nashville, I didn't really have any gauge of anything. Back then your conduit of information was basically *Circus, Creem, Hit Parader* . . . There was no MTV, there was no internet. So I went inside Gazzarri's and to me it was rock 'n' roll heaven. And Ratt was playing. I'm pretty sure they were doing "Rock Bottom" by UFO when I walked into the room. And Jake, he was obviously the center of attention. I thought, That guitar player's pretty good. I think I can take that singer, but that guitar player's badass!

JAKE E. LEE Pearcy had been playing rhythm guitar up until when I joined the band, but I'd always pretty much been in one-guitar bands. And Pearcy knew it. And he knew that I could handle all the guitar parts by myself and make it sound full. So we became a one-guitar band for a while. And that's when Robbin moved up to L.A. from San Diego.

DAVE JELLISON Robbin Crosby came from money. His dad worked for *National Geographic,* his dad was successful, they had a nice house in La Jolla. Basically he told his dad he wanted to be a rock star. He said, "I want you to give me the money you would give me for college and I want to apply it to being a rock star." I was like, "Fuckin' A . . ."

CHRIS HAGER Robbin had the nickname "King." He was, I don't know, six-foot-four or whatever. And a great-looking guy. But a little intimidating if you didn't know him. And he was the kind of guy that was not afraid to speak his mind. So he'd give you shit, but usually good-natured shit.

JAKE E. LEE So he would come to all the shows, hang out, help us move gear. And he started hounding me, saying, "Jake, don't you want another guitar player?" "No, Robbin, I don't!" But he was a real likable, charismatic guy. We'd go out, party, get drunk, and he would harangue me about being in the band. And eventually I succumbed.

MATT THORNE Robbin had a hard time getting in a band because he was so tall. Nobody really wanted him because he was like a giant compared to everybody else.

JAKE E. LEE So finally I told Robbin, "Okay, you can be in the band, but you're just the rhythm player. And if I just want you to play one power chord throughout the song, that's what you'll do, right?" He said, "Yes, yes, absolutely." But as soon as he got in the band it was, "Okay, what leads do I get to do?" I said, "What are you talking about? You can't do any leads!" And he was like, "Come on, there's gotta be one or two . . ." So I said, "Tell you what, any lead in any song that you think you can do better than me, that's the one you can play." But he just kept talking himself into being a bigger and bigger part of the band. And that was one of the reasons I eventually left.

CHRIS HAGER Once Robbin and Stephen got together, they became the nucleus of what Ratt was.

JAKE E. LEE I think Robbin was living with Stephen for a while, in the garage where we rehearsed. Because I remember I showed up for rehearsal early one day, and I walked in and he was jacking off. The funny part was that I was embarrassed and kind of grossed out, and Robbin was totally casual about it. He's like, "Hey, Jake, you're early!" I was like, "Sorry . . . I'll get out." He goes, "Oh, no problem!" He was still talking to me as I was trying to back out the door. But Stephen and Robbin were always more flamboyant, whereas I was a little more subdued.

CHRIS HAGER Stephen also had this eye for fashion. A lot of the stuff we wore was, like, girl's jeans and stuff like that. Everybody was wearing spikes and leather, but Ratt, they had more of this pirate thing going on.

MATT THORNE He had, you know, big, padded shoulders, with pants that look like riding pants that would be puffy and then tight at your ankle. And then these little booties. It looked really feminine to me.

STEPHEN PEARCY We would call ourselves Cement Pirates. We were looking like a cross between Adam Ant and Duran Duran. That was the image that Robbin and I kinda stuck to. Because we didn't want to alienate the girls whatsoever, and we kinda catered to them by looking nice. So it was full-blown Cement Pirates for years.

JAKE E. LEE Then one day Stephen said something about the way I dressed onstage. And he told me that I really needed to up my game as far as how I looked onstage. I was like, "Really?" And he says, "Yeah. More like Robbin. Robbin's a Ratt guy. I'm a Ratt guy. You're not so much a Ratt guy." And that was the moment I quit. You know, problem solved. I'm out. See ya later! I know that Stephen likes to say that I quit because I got the Ozzy gig. But I can say definitely that was why I quit Ratt.

"DON'T JUST TACKLE THE QUARTERBACK—BREAK HIS ARMS AND LEGS, TOO!"

MICHAEL PINTER (photographer) Allan Coffman, who started managing Mötley Crüe, was from Grass Valley. He had a brother-in-law who happened to be a professional roadie in Los Angeles, working for different bands.

DON ADKINS The roadie's name was Stick, because he liked Thai sticks. So Mötley had two guys, Stick and Slug. I forget who Slug was. Another friend of theirs.

MICHAEL PINTER And this roadie would come up to Grass Valley to visit his sister and Allan, who at this time was a residential contractor, building houses and stuff. He would tell all these tales of life in the fast lane down in L.A., and I guess that sounded pretty exciting to a guy in Grass Valley doing residential construction. So Allan told his brother-in-law, "If you find an up-and-coming band that looks really promising, why don't you let me know? I might want to invest in them." And the band he came up with was Mötley Crüe.

DON ADKINS Allan was straitlaced but looking for something. Looking for a little excitement in his life. It seemed like he had a very traditional family. I met his wife. Very mom-looking.

BRIAN SLAGEL I was working at a record store in Woodland Hills and I had a metal show on a local radio station on Sunday nights. And I was friends with the Mötley guys. I'd see them all the time. I knew their manager really well. So when I first started putting together the *Metal Massacre* compilation record I said, "Hey, would you guys wanna be on it?" They said, "Sure, why not?" At that point, being on a record was somewhat of a big thing. But then they ended up making their own record instead.

NIKKI SIXX We did [*Too Fast for Love*] at a place called Hit City on the corner of La Cienega and Pico and basically cut it live.

AVI KIPPER (engineer, Hit City West) Hit City West was a small, low-overhead facility. Two rooms. A couple offices and a shop. We did a lot of R&B, we did a lot of Persian music. The Beach Boys were there at one point. We had everything from the Mystic Knights of the Oingo Boingo to Andraé Crouch. We could stay in the black at a fifty-bucks-an-hour rate and come out with a decent-sounding product. As is evidenced by that first Mötley Crüe record.

GLENN FEIT (engineer, Mötley Crüe, *Too Fast for Love* [credited on album sleeve as "Gleen Felt"]) I knew the owners there and they gave me a deal, $35 an hour.

VINCE NEIL I think it cost us, what, three grand to make and we did it in just a couple days? It was basically just a glorified demo tape.

GLENN FEIT We cut the whole album in four or five days. And unfortunately at the end of it I came down with the flu and, you know, you don't want to mix with your ears full of fluid and stuff. I finally got better about three days later and they were in the studio with Michael Wagener.

MICHAEL WAGENER I knew Mick Mars because I had recorded a demo for his band Vendetta when I was in the States for the first time from Germany in 1979. When I came back in '81 he said, "Hey, you gotta help me with my new band. It's called Mötley Crüe."

MICK MARS I'd known him a long time and he was doing a band called Accept with Udo Dirkschneider. I almost played in that band. About a week before Nikki had called, Michael Wagener asked me if I would play in Accept. So, I was almost a German guy!

MICHAEL WAGENER They were just crazy . . . a crazy bunch of people. Mick was the calmest of them all and obviously Tommy and Vince were absolutely crazy. When I walked in the first time, Tommy was laying on the ground on his back and was lighting his farts on fire. So, that's how I met Mötley Crüe.

MICHAEL PINTER I owned a photofinishing company in Grass Valley, and Allan Coffman would come in when he was back from L.A. and have me print up photos. One thing led to another and I said, "Well, why don't you let me do the cover for your album?" And he said, "Okay."

He got my plane ticket and he picked me up at the airport. We went right to a place called Sunset Sound, a rehearsal stage place on Sunset Boulevard. We wanted a gritty, black-and-white look. Because everything else . . . remember bands like Loverboy, the Canadian band? They all had these nice pretty pastel colors in their covers. And we said, "We're just gonna go maybe the opposite of all that." I found this one album by Marty Balin, his first solo album [*Balin*], and the cover was black-and-white with a red title. I thought, This is the look we need to go for. So that's kind of how *Too Fast for Love* came about. I mashed the picture into that concept. The resemblance to *Sticky Fingers* was not completely lost on me, either.

NIKKI SIXX When the lights were all white and cut and industrial-looking it gave things a sort of stark, coked-out feeling. It would sort of make people's skin crawl.

MICHAEL PINTER The lighting in the back was four times more powerful than the lighting actually lighting the figures. But one of the things that did was that the band's hair got completely blown out of existence in the photographs. Their big hair turned small. So we added the hair back into those pictures with airbrush. I told the airbrush artist to make it look big.

VICKY HAMILTON On the back cover of *Too Fast for Love* Vince's hair was a mess. He had that Roseanne Roseannadanna sort of look. And he was furious about that, you know? But I think they only printed like a thousand of those.

GLENN FEIT I had taken demos around to the labels. I talked to Epic, I talked to Columbia. I played it for people at A&M. They were not into it. It was too hard for them. They said, "It's not really what's going on right now." So the record was released independently. Leathür Records was a business entity that Allan Coffman put together because no one was interested in the band.

DEEDEE KEEL Mötley Crüe's first show at the Whisky was on a Monday. I went to Elmer [Valentine, co-founder of the Whisky a Go Go] and I said, "I really want a big favor. I really want to book this band." He was totally against it. It wasn't his cup of tea. But Monday and Tuesday were off nights—if I could fill them I could have them. They got $50, at most.

NIKKI SIXX Bro, we were fucking poor back then. We were broke. The only way we ate was when we picked up girls and raided their refrigerators or got them to buy us McDonald's. Most of the clothes we wore were T-shirts and shit we stole out of their houses.

DEEDEE KEEL I couldn't figure out how they knew every day when Elmer went home from the club. Because they'd come running upstairs to see me and they'd scour the trash cans for little bits of roaches, the ashtrays for cigarette butts, my desk for whatever lunch I might have left over. I got into the habit of not eating all my lunch so I could give some to them. They also took all my phone books. I said, "What the hell? Why are you guys taking my phone books?" And Tommy said, "We don't have any toilet paper."

STEPHEN PEARCY Their place was really easy to get into; the door was always open. People would crawl in the window to their bedroom. Robbin and I went to hang out there, we wouldn't leave for three days. It was a party that never ended.

DEEDEE KEEL I went to their apartment around the corner from the Whisky a couple of times. It was too terrifying to ever go back to. It was horrible. The first time I went there, the entire front pane of glass from the window was gone. They'd crashed through it. And the porch was completely filled from top to bottom with beer cans and whiskey bottles. The inside . . . I don't even want to tell you, it was so disgusting. And there were girls in there half-dressed. It was quite a sight.

DON ADKINS It was a total divey apartment. Paper-thin walls, shoddy construction. I got up one morning after sleeping there and I just remember the three of them, Tommy, Nikki, and Vince, eating . . . it was either Kaboom or Trix cereal. They're all wearing bathrobes, sitting on the couch eating cereal and watching *Looney Tunes*. It was the greatest sight ever.

DEEDEE KEEL And Vince, he would use the Whisky to bring girls up during the day and have sex with them in our light booth. I caught him up there many times and had to throw him out.

BRIAN SLAGEL Right around that time their manager guy—Coffman was the name—came to my mom's house, sat on my mom's couch, and said, "Hey, we have nine hundred Mötley Crüe records that we made. What do we do with 'em?" This is the version of *Too Fast for Love* that they put out on Leathür Records. I said, "Well, there's this distributor here locally that I buy stuff from called Greenworld. You should probably talk to them." So he said, "Okay, cool."

ALAN NIVEN Greenworld basically started as an import house. We brought in a lot of records from Europe and Japan, the likes of Kitaro, for example. One day Wes Hein came into my office, because in '81 I was handling the sales for the company, and he said that somebody had come in with a tape that they wanted to sell to Greenworld. Would I take it home and listen to it and evaluate it?

WES HEIN (co-owner, Greenworld Distribution, Enigma Records) We did not have a record label at this stage. But we were pressing some people's records and we were doing what were called exclusives, where we said, "Oh, you pressed X-thousand copies of whatever? We'll take them all and we'll help you with marketing and so forth."

ALAN NIVEN So I took it home and put it on my little boom box, put my Sennheiser headphones on, and it was the original *Too Fast for Love*. And there was a track on there called "Piece of Your Action" that I thought was a really good, *bona fide* rock 'n' roll song. It was something that I personally connected to—certainly more strongly than the very eclectic records that the Heins brought into the company to distribute. And more so than the prevalent new wave stuff. Wes asked me if I would take over the negotiation of the contract with Allan Coffman, which I duly did. And we signed Mötley Crüe to Greenworld. I think we scratched up $15,000 for the advance. And everybody laughed at us. They thought we were crazy.

BILL HEIN (co-owner, Greenworld Distribution, Enigma Records) The band had a nice little buzz, but there was no giant rush of people going out to sign Mötley Crüe.

ALAN NIVEN I was a little surprised that it had come all the way down to the bottom of the barrel to Greenworld and no one else had picked it up. But in those days, you have to remember, it was A Flock of Haircuts and the Thompson Durans, you know, everything was Brit new wave pop. And Mötley were viewed as a throwback dinosaur that couldn't play very well. But I rather thought that *Too Fast for Love* was kind of a glorious train wreck of a record that had a spirit to it and an attitude. There was an element of Cheap Trick to it. There was an element of Alice Cooper to it. And I thought, This could be a lot of fun . . .

BILL HEIN People viewed them as sort of punkish, which, you know, if you think there's a line from punk rock that starts with the New York Dolls, you can kind of see that.

TRACII GUNS (guitarist, Pyrrhus, Guns N' Roses, L.A. Guns) In tenth grade my best friend, Danny Tull, had a *Music Connection* magazine and there was a little ad for Mötley Crüe in there. They were playing at the Troubadour.

I saw that picture and I was like, "Whoa, are these guys punk rock? Are they metal? What are these guys?" And Danny goes, "I don't know, man, but we should go see them." So we went down to the Troubadour and it was, like, five bucks to get in and it was a completely life-changing experience. The music was loud and heavy and the guitarist had two Marshall half stacks, one on either side of the drummer, like, *yeeeaaah*! I think I dyed my hair black later that week.

SLASH (guitarist, Tidus Sloan, Road Crew, Hollywood Rose, Black Sheep, Guns N' Roses) I was in a "special" program at my school called Continuation Education, and there were these three girls—total rocker chicks with ripped shirts, makeup, tight pants, all of that—that were all about Mötley. They had just come out with the indie version of *Too Fast for Love*. I have this vivid memory of Nikki and Tommy, all decked out, with their heels and leather and teased-up hair, the whole nine yards, hanging out in front of the school, smoking cigarettes. And these girls ran out to meet them, and they were excited. Nikki and Tommy gave them all these posters and flyers to hand out. Basically, these girls were gonna do whatever they told them to do.

NIKKI SIXX Yup. They were "marketing." Street Team 101, way back in the day!

GINA ZAMPARELLI With Van Halen, I watched them promote. And they were good at it. But there was nothing like Mötley Crüe. There wasn't a phone pole, there wasn't a magazine . . . I'd drive down streets in Pasadena, then I'd be down on Hollywood, down on Ventura Boulevard, Mötley Crüe was in your face 24/7. It was just over-the-top and they wouldn't stop until every last person in every single city in Los Angeles saw a flyer or a poster that said Mötley Crüe.

VICKY HAMILTON Around the time *Too Fast for Love* came out I started doing some management consulting for Allan Coffman. I would do these big displays at Licorice Pizza, and a friend of mine got some mannequins from Sears and we painted them white and we built towers with the album cover. Then we called up the band and I said, "Bring down some personal effects." So they brought down whips and chains and handcuffs and cop hats. Nikki gave me a tarot card of the devil. And Tommy had some broken drumsticks. And Vince goes, "Close your eyes . . ." And he dropped a pair of pink panties in my hand. And they were, like, not clean. It was kind of gross.

DEEDEE KEEL Nikki became a staple in my office at the Whisky. He'd come up and Elmer let him design posters with me, he let him do advertising with me. And I would allow him to use the telephones and he would throw ideas out at me. Just kind of do a game plan for the band.

SLASH I think it was that same night that I went out to the Whisky and saw Mötley play for the first time. The thing I remember most was the band's impact. They had the audience in the palm of their hands, and they had a production going that was as professional as you could get at the Whisky. They had the flash pots, the lights, the drum riser, all the blood, the outfits, and everything. Back then, Van Halen was the band that really defined the L.A. scene, but as cool as they were, there was an element to them that was so glitzy that I couldn't stand. And that spread across L.A. when they took off. When Mötley came out, it was something that was pretty different. They were a little bit more hardcore, and that appealed to me.

STEPHEN PEARCY They were amazing. I mean, they were actually *new*. Not new in a sense like, you know, where they got part of their image and this and that, but they just, Nikki knew just what to do with it and he accomplished it.

CHRIS HOLMES All that stuff where Nikki used to light his boots on fire, Blackie figured that crap out way before, in the Sister days.

NIKKI SIXX Vince and Tommy used to light me on fire in our apartment. And, you know, the carpet was all burnt. We would practice with different things. I remember I used to hang out by a dumpster behind this pyro company in Hollywood. Finally they were like, "What d'ya want, kid?" And I was like, "Can you show me how to do this? Can you show me how to do that?" I was very inquisitive about pyrotechnics. I still am.

VINCE NEIL We would experiment with putting pyro gel on his boots.

NIKKI SIXX It was a pyro gel, which I only used once. It worked great on instruments because it would burn for a long time very hot. But you can't put it on the body because it would get so hot. And I had leather pants, leather boots. Sometimes I would have to wrap my legs underneath. Then we started using just straight rubbing alcohol, but it burned really fast. It was just, Holy shit! And then it was over. With Tommy, Mick, Vince, and myself, it was never a question of "Should we do that?" It was always "Yes!" Should Vince chainsaw the head off a mannequin filled with blood during a song called "Piece of Your Action"? Of course! Who wouldn't? Well, 99.99999 percent of all other bands wouldn't. But we would.

VICKY HAMILTON Mötley Crüe was kind of the right cocktail for the Sunset Strip.

TRACII GUNS What they were able to do was create a lifestyle in the Hollywood music scene. Even the audience started dressing more and more like Mötley Crüe. And it was really fun. You know, they really did it.

DON ADKINS They did a New Year's Eve show at the Troubadour at the end of '81 that sold out immediately. And they had David Lee Roth introduce them onstage. That was a big deal. Afterward they have a party at their apartment, and David Lee Roth shows up, everybody in L.A. is there.

ALAN NIVEN For me, I thought the exceptional thing was their three nights at the Whisky [in February 1982]. To play three nights at the Whisky was not done at that time. It was a full house every night. There was a vibe there, there was an audience there, and, oh my god, the girls were there, too. And these girls came pre-ravaged in their attire. I'm looking at this going, "There's more going on there than people realize . . ."

NIKKI SIXX I remember back then somebody in my band saying to me, "Bro, we're doing three nights at the Whisky. We made it." And I said, "Made *what*? I wanna sell out the Forum. I don't care about the fucking Whisky a Go Go." Everything Mötley did in those days was always, at least in my eyes, a stepping-stone to something bigger. We approached everything from the perspective of "Don't just tackle the quarterback—break his arms and legs, too!"

9
THE YELLOW AND BLACK ATTACK!

VICKY HAMILTON I was working as a cocktail waitress at Gazzarri's in '81 and Ratt and Roxx Regime seemed to play, like, every Friday and Saturday night. They both did versions of Judas Priest's "Breaking the Law."

MICHAEL SWEET As Roxx Regime we were playing Gazzarri's all the time. But we wouldn't make any money. And I remember Bill Gazzarri used to always pay us with a smile on his face, as if he was paying us really well. Then we would lug our gear out the back door and load it into our station wagon and drive an hour back home to La Mirada, just thinking, Man, this sucks . . . But we never thought the gig itself sucked. We were thrilled to be able to play at Gazzarri's. So we were there what felt like every weekend.

ROBERT SWEET (drummer, Roxx Regime, Stryper) Hollywood was where we really cemented the beginnings of what we have today.

MICHAEL SWEET When I was a kid I was hearing about Van Halen and seeing the name around town. I never saw them, but I saw Quiet Riot. I went to the Starwood a few times and saw Y&T when they were Yesterday and Today.

ROBERT SWEET Our mom and dad and so many people in our family were really into music. We used to have these get-togethers where seven, eight, ten people would come over and there would always be music going on. And for some reason I gravitated towards the drums.

MICHAEL SWEET Our family moved around a lot—Pasadena, La Mirada, Fullerton, Whittier. We moved to Oklahoma for, like, a year. But then we moved back.

ROBERT SWEET Probably around the time I was seventeen and Mike was maybe fourteen we started playing music together. And I knew my brother could sing. I had a lot of people coming to me, saying, "You two as brothers have something that's kind of unique, you vibe off of one another." And I'd seen it with other brothers, like the Van Halens.

MICHAEL SWEET I joined my brother's band and we started playing backyard parties and local venues. And then I found myself in Hollywood, playing the Whisky, the Troubadour, Gazzarri's. I was playing those places when I was very young, lying about my age because I looked older than I was. Our band was called Firestorm. And we were also called Aftermath. But then we wound up joining forces for a brief period with this local guitar player, and he had a band called Roxx.

ROBERT SWEET Then we found out someone had already used that name. So I just tacked "Regime" onto it.

MICHAEL SWEET We were just trying to find our sound and the right team. We were even a three-piece for a while, with me as the only guitar player.

ROBERT SWEET We had gone through probably five or six guitar players. C.C. DeVille was one of them.

MICHAEL SWEET We met C.C. out in front of Gazzarri's. This was '82, '83. He had come out from New York. He was all glammed out with big hair. He was looking for a band. And we're hanging out and we go, "Hey, dude, what's going on? What's your name?" He was still Bruce [Johannesson] at that time.

ROBERT SWEET We gave him a phone number and he called us. He came down and jammed and he was awesome.

MICHAEL SWEET He was a great guy. We liked his energy, we liked his attitude. And he was going to join the band. But I recall that when we told him about how everything's gotta be yellow and black, he wasn't into that. He said, "Ahh . . . it's not really my thing. I'm more into pink and purple."

ROBERT SWEET He wanted to do, you know, pink fingernail polish and pink lipstick and fur. And, hey, more power to him. But I didn't really want to wear lace. I didn't want to wear lingerie. I enjoyed seeing women in it, but I dunno, it just wasn't my thing.

MICHAEL SWEET I remember one time my brother was talking to C.C. about his guitars—he had some B.C. Riches, I think one of them was pink. And Robert was saying, "We're going to have to make that yellow and black . . ." And you could just see C.C.'s eyes bulge out. It was like, "No, god, no."

But Robert loved everything yellow and black. He was just fascinated by it. He painted his kit yellow and black and then it eventually spread over a two- or three-year period to everything being yellow and black. We started going out and taking road signs off of poles and putting them on the garage walls where we rehearsed. And then the walls were striped yellow and black and then we were wearing yellow and black and we became the Yellow and Black Attack.

ROBERT SWEET I'm not a guy that was super in love with wearing yellow clothes. But I thought it was cool when you put it together in the form of stripes. Only because it stood out. I wanted an idea that was an eyepopper. And you know, the last time I talked with Bill Gazzarri, he walked up to me and he said, "Robert, you guys are too big now. A lot of bands are complaining. You bring in too much gear. You're too loud. You've made it. Get the hell outta here and go become famous."

MICHAEL SWEET We did a showcase for Enigma Records [initially launched as a division of Greenworld Distribution] at this rehearsal studio/warehouse.

WES HEIN They came out and everything was striped. All their equipment. Every guitar, all the drums. I think their girlfriends and moms had made their outfits. It was probably just yellow clothes and black electric tape.

MICHAEL SWEET We would go buy pieces of, like, white shag carpeting, and we would paint them yellow and put black stripes on them and pin them around our legs from the knee down. And then we would wear black spandex underneath. From a distance it looked amazing. But then you got up close and it was like, "Oh, man . . ." They still smelled like paint.

BILL HEIN We thought it was nuts. But you have to remember—at that point nuts to us was good.

WES HEIN Honestly, the only thing I ever really asked them to do was to change the name. Because I was not crazy about Roxx Regime.

MICHAEL SWEET Thank god they didn't care for the name. I didn't either.

ROBERT SWEET They felt it was too hard to remember. We needed something more to the point.

MICHAEL SWEET We came up with Stryper, and obviously it just made perfect sense, as we were sitting there looking at striped walls and striped gear. We spelled it with a *y* because otherwise it looked like Stripper. Then we applied the scripture with the stripes—Isaiah 53:5, "by His stripes we are healed." And then we had an acronym for the name: Salvation Through Redemption Yielding Peace Encouragement and Righteousness. Everything took on a meaning and made sense.

RON GOUDIE (producer, Enigma Records) They hid the whole Jesus thing from us.

WES HEIN We had no idea. But then Ron and I were down at the Casbah [Recording Studio] with them one day, because we wanted to listen to some of the tracks they were working on. And the lyrics were a lot clearer in the studio than on the bad cassette dub they had given us. So we're listening, and one line is "Jesus is the way." We look at each other. And then we look at Robert and Michael. There's this silence and we say, "Are you guys Christians?" And they're like, "Yes."

10

"IT'S MALE DOMINATING. MACHO-ISM OR WHATEVER"

RON KEEL In those days, you'd walk into any gig and you'd see three or four bands that went on to sell multiplatinum records. And just those guitar players—George Lynch and Jake E. Lee and Mick Mars and Mark Kendall, the list goes on. I saw W.A.S.P. at the Troubadour, lighting stuff on fire, throwing meat out at the audience. I thought that was cool because we didn't have meat, man. We had peanut butter and jelly. I'm like, "Wow, these guys are badass! They're throwing steaks!"

BRIAN SLAGEL I think I got hit in the head once with some meat.

GINA ZAMPARELLI When W.A.S.P. came along . . . if Mötley Crüe was scary, W.A.S.P. took it over-the-top. They were so tall and the stage show was so menacing. There's no words for it. I went to every single show. I couldn't *not* go. They were unbelievable to watch. It was this progression of theatrical music that went from Alice Cooper to them to, later, Marilyn Manson. At that time, we'd never seen anything like it.

TRACII GUNS The first time I ever saw W.A.S.P., it was at the Troubadour on a Wednesday night. I was maybe fifteen or sixteen, and Blackie lit the W.A.S.P. sign on fire and Chris Holmes spit in the air and it landed on his arm . . . They were just, like, they were *foul*. It was awesome!

BLACKIE LAWLESS (singer, guitarist, bassist, Sister, London, W.A.S.P.) Our foundation was in theatrics. We didn't want to stand there and play. That wasn't us. Basically, it started out as entertainment for us. We quickly discovered that whenever you have the attention of eyes and ears, sight will always win over sound. People listen with their eyes, not their ears.

BRIAN SLAGEL There was a buzz around this guy Blackie Lawless. None of us had ever met him, but we all kind of knew who he was.

BOB NALBANDIAN Blackie had a reputation. I guess he was in the New York Dolls for a while, and he had had his band Sister. People seemed to know about him.

DON ADKINS Did Blackie ever tell you about his sports days? He told me his real name was Steve Duren, and when he was younger he had actually gotten drafted for the farm team of the Tigers. And he goes, "Yeah, I was a helluva baseball player. I had a ninety-mile-an-hour fastball in high school," something like that. He was telling me the story of how he got drafted but then he got the offer to go be in the New York Dolls, what became the final version of them, and he took that instead.

BLACKIE LAWLESS I only did a couple of shows with [the Dolls]. I was nineteen years old. And I was stunned because it was like five guys all trying to be like Jim Morrison and succeeding . . . Much more has been made out of my time with the Dolls than should have been. The big thing for me was it got me from the East Coast of the U.S. to the West Coast.

CHRIS HOLMES Back in the late '70s I'd worked with Blackie in Sister. I grew up in a place called La Cañada, right by the Rose Bowl. It's where the NASA Jet Propulsion Laboratory is. And the next town is Pasadena. Back in '73, '74, Van Halen would play backyard parties there. I met Eddie Van Halen and we became friends. He'd borrow my amps all the time, and I'd be able to go down to the clubs and see the soundcheck and stuff. I was in high school.

Then in '78 I got in a motorcycle accident and I was laid up in a hospital and I was gonna be there for a while. Eddie had just gotten off the first Van Halen tour and he had taken his guitar and cut a big V out of the back of it. It changed the tone of the guitar—made it a lot more trebly. So he came and visited me in the hospital and asked to borrow my Ibanez Destroyer for their record. He wound up using it on *Women and Children First,* and then went out on the road again.

Anyway, then I get out of the hospital and I want my guitar back. So I go over to his mom's house and she opens the door and I say, "Hey, I think my guitar's here . . ." She goes, "Look in his room." I go back into Eddie's room and I find it, and it doesn't even have a bridge or a pickup in it, the prick! But I kinda didn't care.

AL BANE (leather designer) Chris Holmes was a friend of mine from high school. He was the guitar hero. Whereas I didn't have an easy time— I'm Hispanic and it was a pretty white area and pretty damn racist. But Chris didn't care about any of that. He treated people the way they treated him. So we became friends. Then one day he called me up and asked me to help him make a costume for this band he was playing in. It was called Sister.

BLACKIE LAWLESS Sister was put together in 1977.

STEPHEN QUADROS I saw Sister one time at the Starwood and I think it was Blackie, he actually set himself on fire and it kind of went a little haywire. I was like, "What's he doing?" It looked like he actually burned himself a little bit. And the music was okay. It wasn't great or anything. But when he put W.A.S.P. together, W.A.S.P. was light-years better than Sister. They were better musicians, they had better songs, and they had a better show.

CHRIS HOLMES When Blackie talked to me about joining W.A.S.P., I didn't even wanna join the band. But I asked him, "How long until it gets a deal?" He said, "Guaranteed it'll be in a year." So I came in and we did our first show. We had Don Costa and Tony Richards from Dante Fox.

GINA ZAMPARELLI Don Costa did one show with W.A.S.P. And he was grating the flesh off his knuckles with a cheese grater. I have this memory of standing there going, "Oh my god. He's not doing that!" It was sickening.

CHRIS HOLMES He was playing his bass with a pickaxe, all out of tune. I came into rehearsal the next time and I went, "Don, you're probably one of the best bass players I've ever played with. But if you ever play out of tune onstage with me again I'm gonna chew your cock off and spit it in your face in front of everybody!"

The funny thing is, Don quit that day anyway because he had gotten a gig with Ozzy. Blackie was playing guitar at the time and he didn't wanna disband us so he said, "I'll play bass." And that's how Blackie became the Geezer Butler of bass that he is.

BRIAN SLAGEL The first time W.A.S.P. ever played at the Troubadour it was insane. The place was packed. They went up and they were unbelievable. They had this huge show. They had fire. They had girls tied to this gigantic cross. At that point nobody . . . Mötley was doing some theatrical stuff, but nobody had done anything like this. It was *crazy*. The music was really heavy and it was really amazing. We couldn't believe this band had come out of nowhere and had this massive production.

KATHERINE TURMAN (journalist; co-author, *Louder Than Hell: The Definitive Oral History of Metal*) I saw W.A.S.P. at the Troubadour and I was standing right up front. As a sixteen-year-old girl who was somewhat sheltered, I was just like, shocked. I mean, I thought it was awesome as well . . .

TRACII GUNS I thought Mötley Crüe were the greatest thing in the world until I saw W.A.S.P. When I saw W.A.S.P., I was like, "Ah, now *this* is how you do it!"

MIKE VARNEY Nobody ever came up in the clubs and did stuff like that. This was like a major arena show being done for, you know, four hundred people or something. That's why the lore of W.A.S.P. grew so fast.

GINA ZAMPARELLI It sounds funny to say now but you felt like you didn't know if you would live or die. It's like you were going into something treacherous. Meat would be flying everywhere, the stage would be on fire . . . You didn't know what was going to happen.

JAIME ST. JAMES (singer, Black 'N Blue) I was at one of the early shows at the Troubadour. They had the W.A.S.P. sign behind them and when they lit that thing on fire . . . I was sitting up in the balcony and I could feel the heat roll across the ceiling and right down on me.

KEVIN ESTRADA (photographer) I remember the skin on my face was just boiling. It felt like it was going to peel off because that place was so damn hot.

CHRIS HOLMES That was kind of my idea, to play by firelight, you know? We just took the regulators off a barbecue grill, made a pipe around the sign, and hooked it up to a propane tank.

AL BANE Imagine a six-foot-by-three-foot frame, like a picture frame. We drilled holes in the plywood and fashioned up a big rectangle that the gas would go through. I built it at [NASA] Jet Propulsion Laboratory, because I was working in the plumbing shop at that time. I stole the pipe from JPL, drilled it, bolted it together, and took it home. We put that thing in the Troubadour and fucking burned the ceiling, dude.

CHRIS HOLMES There's butane and propane—two kinds of fuel. And one's heavier and one's lighter, so one goes up and one goes down, right? I don't know which one does which. But all I know is you've gotta get the right mixture so it doesn't go up into the ceiling. But one time it caught some of the cables on fire that went up to the monitors.

AL BANE All of a sudden the room's at 110 degrees. Twenty linear feet of exposed flame. *Whoosh!*

CHRIS HOLMES But we always had fire extinguishers there. We're not *idiots*.

AL BANE With W.A.S.P., they had a friend named Curt who came from a wealthy family. His dad was, like, a heart surgeon. So he had this bitchin' six-car garage in La Cañada and all the tools you could ever want. Me and Chris and Blackie would go hang over there and work on stuff. We started making the fire sign and the torture rack and the raw meat box, all this stuff.

BLACKIE LAWLESS The whole germination came from *The Road Warrior.* Nobody ever picked up on that. We were astonished. We never got busted.

CHRIS HOLMES I didn't like the little glittery, glam clothes. I was not gonna wear that crap. I was gonna wear leather *Road Warrior*–type stuff.

AL BANE We literally went into Curt's garage and grabbed his mom's garden tools and made things like spiked bracelets out of little three-claw planter tools. Chris put it on his arm and there's an armband from hell. Okay, that works. Let's keep going. What's next?

CHRIS HOLMES I remember one time I found these really big shark hooks in the garage. And I thought, Man, these would be cool onstage . . . So I had this shark tooth on my arm and this chick reached up from the audience and grabbed me and it hooked her. She couldn't get her hand off of it. I remember one of the roadies came up and pulled her off and ripped a big hunk of meat out of her hand.

BLACKIE LAWLESS Not many bands, at the time, were wearing huge nails coming out of their shoulders and stuff like that. Look at the saw blade thing. It was totally unique.

JAIME ST. JAMES Blackie would wear, like, real thin women's nylons with some kind of codpiece thing with a saw blade crotch. I remember it was pretty insane because his balls were hanging out the sides of the fuckin' thing!

AL BANE Blackie's first codpiece was actually a twelve- or eighteen-inch blade from a table saw. Then we said, "Okay, we gotta mount this thing." So we welded washers onto the side of it and cut the profile to fit the cup from a jockstrap. It would go underneath his legs and come up and then we riveted it onto the cup. All this stuff, the raw meat box, the fire sign, the torture rack, we were just making it ourselves.

BLACKIE LAWLESS With all the props and everything, when we came out, we looked like a million bucks. We looked like we had *huge* money behind us. But we were broke—less than broke!

CHRIS HOLMES The idea for the torture rack came from *The Road Warrior*, too. Remember the guys tied to the front of Humungus' car with the hoods on their heads? That's exactly where that came from.

LAURA REINJOHN (L.A. scenester) One night I was out at a club with a friend, and my friend said, "Oh, there's that guy that everybody is talking about. His name is Blackie Lawless." And I turn around and this real tall, kind of weird-looking dude comes walking over. I wanted to kind of burst out in laughter. Because it was a weird scene. He said they were doing a show, and would I be interested in being a part of it? I was going to school for journalism and I was still living with my parents at the time.

Anyway, they had a girl they were working with at the time, her name was Pam. And she was doing this thing where they put her up on a cross. It was kind of like a pre-Manson show. Real shlocky, a lot of blood, a lot of gore. Inappropriate lyrics. One thing led to another and I became that girl on the cross.

CHRIS WEBER (guitarist, Hollywood Rose) Laura, they used to tie her up and throw meat at her. Raw meat.

CHRIS HOLMES We had an abundance of women that wanted to do it. They were excited to be onstage naked, you know?

LAURA REINJOHN I was topless, and I had this custom-made leather thing that covered the bottom half of me. It was very misogynistic. Blackie would pretend to slit my throat, and we had this contraption that was rigged up so that I blew through a tube that had these blood packets. I'd chew on the blood packets and the blood would run down my throat and *ahhh*!

CHRIS HOLMES Have you ever smoked pot, dope, whatever? Okay. If you take a water pipe and blow in the bowl, water comes out the mouthpiece, right? Same concept. People like that kind of shit. It's male dominating. Macho-ism or whatever. Plus, the audience sees a naked chick with tits.

BLACKIE LAWLESS To understand us in the beginning, it may sound kind of silly to you now, but I thought what we were doing was social comment. I never cared about shock rock for the sake of shock rock. I thought it was boring, to be honest.

LAURA REINJOHN It was so bizarre and so, like, *What the fuck?* And the music was really, really bad. There was no message. It was just to be as over-the-top as possible. It was not a very glamorous gig by any means.

AL BANE That whole era, the bands that were succeeding were the bands that were pushing the limit on anything they could do. And it was because you had to draw a crowd. And at that point there were lots of crowds, right? But you had to draw them in. You had to have a reason to go. And now you've got this crazy fucking band that, you know, is wearing assless chaps and the fucking guy spits blood and he's torturing a chick and there's pyro and fire and smoke . . . They're turning it into this spectacle and people had to go check it out. That's the thing that people don't do now. Nobody does *anything*. People are lazy.

BOB NALBANDIAN It was crazy, man. It was almost like the Wild West, just anything goes. It was before record companies and MTV got hold of all this stuff, and it was all underground and word of mouth. People just heard about this shit.

BRIAN SLAGEL It was a total DIY effort in the beginning, way before the labels got into it. And it was a great scene back then. Very independent-minded. I think the later versions of a lot of that stuff, the bands wanted to do it because they saw Mötley and Ratt become rock stars and they wanted to become rock stars. But for the early guys it was all about the music and the shows. Nobody there was thinking, I'm gonna do this and be rich and be a rock star. They were trying to do a show and make it something other than just guys in jeans and T-shirts. And Mötley and

W.A.S.P., they were doing production. It was above what anybody else was doing on a theatrical level.

ALAN NIVEN The record companies wanted Duran Duran. They wanted new wave. Nobody took rock 'n' roll seriously. They thought it was passé. So if you wanted to get further you had to be self-determining. You had to have some imagination. You had to have a little bit of wheel and deal. Because that was the only way that you were going to start building your following.

GINA ZAMPARELLI I remember Blackie saying to me one night, "Uh . . . I have to go because I have to go get some meat." And I was like, "This is a weird world I live in . . ."

CHRIS HOLMES My mom came down to a show once. We played with Warrior, right? They played after us. And my mom sat there and she goes, "Chris, these guys sound a hundred times better than you guys." Which they did! But I go, "Mom, there's this one thing they don't got. The energy. We got the *energy*!" You know, W.A.S.P., it was raw.

BRIAN SLAGEL They were really one of the first bands to really create a big buzz in the L.A. scene, where all of a sudden record company people were paying attention to them. We were all like, "Wow, that happened *really* fast."

KEVIN ESTRADA I remember walking out of the Troubadour just, like, amazed. I went to school the next day—I was in tenth grade at the time—and I was telling my friend, "W.A.S.P. were awesome! They were incredible! They're everything you heard about!" But then I said, "I don't think they're ever going to get out of L.A. They're just too crazy. Too extreme." But you know what? Two, three years later, they were playing arenas around the country.

MIKE VARNEY I made Blackie an offer to do the band's first record on my label, Shrapnel. And Blackie said to me, "I'm gonna wait. I believe I can get a major label deal." Then he goes, "One day I'm gonna walk up to the Capitol Records building, my feet on the cement, look in the twelfth-story window in the A&R department, and I'm gonna say, 'I'm Blackie Lawless. My time has come.'" Like he was King Kong or something. Which I thought was really funny. Because he ended up being on Capitol Records.

"WE PRAYED IN THE LIMO, SURE"

MICHAEL SWEET Around 1983, that's when we had a few of our friends in the music world who had changed their lives come into our rehearsal studio and tell us about God. And that's when the light went on for us. And Oz [Fox, Stryper guitarist] had grown up in a Christian family. Tim [Gaines, Stryper bassist], his dad was a preacher. And Robert and I came to know God through Jimmy Swaggart. My brother started watching him on television when we were kids, like I'm sure a lot of people at the time.

ROBERT SWEET I would watch the telethons. I mean, he was very famous. He'd sold over a hundred million records, which very few people know. His cousin was Jerry Lee Lewis.

MICHAEL SWEET We were kinda more drawn to his music than his preaching. My dad's a big Elvis fan and Jimmy kinda sounded like Elvis.

ROBERT SWEET Even as a little kid, something was pulling on me and I remember talking to my family about accepting Jesus. And I did when I was fifteen years old. I think it was April 20, 1975.

MICHAEL SWEET So we actually accepted Christ, the whole family, and then we started going to church. But the more Robert and I got into music and playing the clubs, the less we were going to church. And that whole cliché that goes along with rock 'n' roll, you know, sex and drugs, I was doing all that. I remember standing out in front of Gazzarri's and the Arthur Blessitt folks, they would walk down Sunset Boulevard with this big wooden cross with wheels on the end of it and they would preach to people on the Strip. And I was one of the guys that they preached to. Here I am knowing that what they're saying is true, at least according to my beliefs. But at the same time I'm standing there with a drink in my hand smoking a cigarette and talking to Stephen Pearcy. So I wasn't living the life.

ROBERT SWEET Then one day I just looked at the guys and I said, "Guys, this is how it's got to be."

MICHAEL SWEET It was an easy thing for us to say, "All right, let's do it." We said a prayer, we started rewriting lyrics, and from that day forward we changed everything and went down a different path.

VICKY HAMILTON After working with Mötley Crüe I became friendly with Wes and Bill Hein. And Wes was like, "Maybe you try and book Stryper and help us with this." I had never heard of Stryper, but when I figured out it was Bobby and Michael from Roxx Regime who I used to see at Gazzarri's, the instant rapport was there. But I had no idea they were Christian. I went to their rehearsal space in La Mirada, I saw the 777, the Isaiah quote on the wall. It still didn't dawn on me. And my parents were fundamentalist Christians! You would think that that would not slide by me. But back then I smoked a lot of pot and whatever.

Anyway, I decided that I would help Stryper and that I would start booking them. I booked them at the Country Club to open for Bon Jovi, which was Bon Jovi's first night in town.

MICHAEL SWEET They had a decent following. I would like to believe that we pulled a lot of those tickets as well because we did have a big following there. The only thing I remember about that, it's the only time I've ever really met Jon. I didn't even really meet Jon. He didn't really have anything to say. He just kinda did his own thing. The rest of the guys all said hi and were very cordial and very nice. Jon was just Jon.

ROBERT SWEET I remember the drummer for Bon Jovi walked up to me, he looked at my drum set, and he said, "What the eff is *that*?"

VICKY HAMILTON That night was the first time I saw them throw Bibles at the crowd. They had stickers in them, with the 777. I saw them hit a girl in the head with a Bible and it sort of knocked her back a little bit. I was like, "Okay . . ."

ROBERT SWEET Drummers always throw out drumsticks, right? Guitar players throw out picks . . .

WES HEIN And people were clamoring for these Bibles. It was pretty amazing. Nobody was throwing them back at the band or anything.

MICHAEL SWEET In the early days we used to throw out Bibles with no stickers, and they used to get left on the floor of the venues. Then we started putting the sticker on and they would all get taken, because I think people viewed it more as a souvenir than a Bible.

WES HEIN Sometimes the band would come to us and say, "Hey, can you advance us some money?" They were buying all the Bibles themselves. So I'd cut them a check. Because if they had, you know, twenty shows for a particular tour, think about the number of Bibles they'd need for a show, times twenty.

VICKY HAMILTON After that Bon Jovi show I took a meeting with the woman that was their investor, who was somebody they knew from the church.

MICHAEL SWEET That person's name is Daryn Hinton. She was part of a ministry called the Eagle's Nest. Her dad was an actor, she grew up in Bel Air in the movie industry. She had inherited some money and whatnot and so she invested in the band.

DARYN HINTON (manager, financial backer, Stryper) I saw them first at a Bon Jovi concert at a little place called the Country Club. I had already pre-judged in my mind that they were doing this as a gimmick and using

God's name. But after seeing the show, and seeing and feeling the spirit and seeing the reaction from the kids, I was totally turned around.

ROBERT SWEET I remember being in the dressing room, and I open the door and Daryn's standing there and her mascara's running down her face. She's crying. And she told me she was there that night to kind of rebuke us, telling us we were doing the wrong thing. But then she said, "I am so touched by what I saw tonight." And two nights prior I'd asked God, I said, "God, we need money, nothing in this world happens without money." I asked for $100,000. So now this is just a couple days later, and Daryn says, "If you're interested, I have $100,000 I'd like to invest." Same amount.

VICKY HAMILTON The next thing you know she's buying them a limousine and they're striping it out in yellow and black.

MICHAEL SWEET We didn't paint it yellow and black. It was a black limo and then we had yellow pinstriping put on it. I never really got the limo thing but, you know, Daryn liked to do things, and still does to this day, in a big way. She just thought, Okay, we're gonna have our own limo, we're gonna get our own billboard on Sunset Boulevard—which we had, she paid for that, too—and that will make everybody around town go, "Who are these guys?" It made noise. It created a buzz. And you know, if you don't have people talkin' about ya, then you don't have people talkin' about ya.

VICKY HAMILTON I remember them pulling up to a gig at Radio City and I got in the car with them and they're, like, leading a prayer circle. In the limousine! And girls are sort of beating on the window to try to say hello to them and stuff. It was a little odd for me.

ROBERT SWEET We prayed in the limo, sure. But that's all part of it all, right? Where would we be without beautiful women? None of us would exist. So thank God for it.

MICHAEL SWEET But we really went out of our way to not partake in that stuff. *Prior* to Stryper we did. But during Stryper? No. But we did have a lot of girls that followed us around from venue to venue.

ROBERT SWEET With Stryper, we were always one hundred percent rock 'n' roll. We're not these Christians who are trying to be rock 'n' roll guys. We love rock 'n' roll music. But when it comes to Christianity, we mean what we say.

WES HEIN When we were getting ready to put out the first record [the 1984 EP *The Yellow and Black Attack!*], we were getting phone calls going, "When it's out, I want to buy a box." And we're like, "What do you mean you want to buy a box?" "We're going to give them out at our church." And then the shows, I was seeing how well attended and well organized they were. The Christian community was starving for a band like this, because the music was great.

RON GOUDIE They were some of the best musicians I've ever worked with. The Sweet brothers, they're not twins, but they're *like* twins, they can finish each other's thoughts and all this shit. And they're fantastic players.

BILL HEIN A lot of Christian kids liked rock 'n' roll, and they were bored with a lot of the Christian music they were hearing. It just didn't speak to them. So Stryper comes out and they're doing rock 'n' roll. If you like Ozzy Osbourne, if you like Judas Priest, but you're a Christian? Well, here's Stryper. Put it in rotation.

MICHAEL SWEET We were different, man. We really were. That's why it's even more disturbing when people say, "Ah, it's just a gimmick." Those people weren't there. They didn't walk in our shoes. They didn't live it. They have no right to say it was a gimmick because they don't know. They don't have a clue.

"WE KNOW WHAT WE'RE DOING, FUCK YOU!"

TOM KEIFER I started playing the club circuit in Jersey and Philadelphia and the Northeast five nights a week at a pretty young age. I was still in high school, and I was on what they called the work-study plan program; they thought I was going to a job during the day, but actually, I was asleep. There was a lot of partying going on and I struggled with a lot of that stuff through high school and a few years after that, and through a lot of the club bands I was in, including Saints in Hell.

ERIC BRITTINGHAM (bassist, Saints in Hell, Cinderella) I was living in Ocean City, Maryland, and Tom's band Saints in Hell, which was basically a cover band with a few originals, was playing at this local club on Halloween. The band had gotten in a day early from Philly and were hanging at the bar the night before the show. I was in the bathroom just taking a leak and Tom and another guy from the band walked in and were bitching about their bass player. And then Tom just sort of tapped me on the shoulder lightly and was like, "Hey, do you play bass?" And I was like, "Actually, I do. But I don't really have a bass right now." And Tom said, "Well, if you want to come down to jam tomorrow morning, you can use our bass player's stuff." So I showed up the next morning, played a couple of Kiss songs or whatever, and they were like, "All right, you have the gig. Just figure out where you can get a bass and we'll see you in Philly."

TOM KEIFER We did that for a while, and I woke up one day and felt like my life was going nowhere. I actually moved back with my parents and got a job and started writing songs, tried to clean my act up a little bit, and pretty much stayed on that path from there on.

LARRY MAZER (manager, Cinderella, Nelson, Kiss) If you remember, Fotomat had kiosks in shopping-center parking lots where you could drop off film in the morning and the photographs would be ready to be picked up at the end of the day. Tom had a route of x amount of kiosks that he would drive to in the morning to pick up the film to take it to wherever and then later in the day, at five, drive back the prints. Then as soon as that was done, he would drive to the Galaxy club in Somerdale, New Jersey, where the owner let Cinderella practice upstairs. He would literally work from, like, six in the morning to five in the afternoon and then go right to New Jersey to rehearse. It was just ridiculous dedication and he already had twenty or thirty really good songs written.

TOM KEIFER It's kind of living the two lives, working during the day and then we would rehearse at night and work on songs, and every once in a while get into the studio and bang out some demos. That was the goal: to create a sound and get a record deal.

ERIC BRITTINGHAM We did that for about a year before we even played a gig.

LARRY MAZER There was a recording studio in suburban Philadelphia, called Veritable Studios, and I was very close with the engineer, a guy named Joe McSorley. It was a little studio, mainly for local bands, whatever. One time I was there working with a band, and he said, "Can I play you something?" He played me a couple of Cinderella songs and it blew me away. He said, "Well, I know they're talking to Gene Simmons, who heard some stuff and is interested in working with them, but he's asking an arm and a leg," which is typical. It's ironic that I then managed Gene Simmons three years later.

ERIC BRITTINGHAM Our guitar player at the time, Michael Kelly Smith, had actually auditioned for Kiss around the same time that they ended up picking Vinnie Vincent, so he had Gene's number. We met with Gene at his apartment in New York . . . It was pretty surreal sitting in Gene's living room with him because this was like 1982 before they took the makeup off for *Lick It Up,* so none of us had really seen his face before. But then he sent us some songs, because it turned out that he wanted to do a production deal where he would write the songs for us and produce the records and manage the band. And honestly, the songs he sent us were really bad. So here we are, like huge Kiss fans, telling Gene Simmons, "No thank you. That's not what we want."

LARRY MAZER They had a Saturday-night residency at the Galaxy, which was ten minutes from my house, so I went one Saturday night and there were about forty, forty-five people there, and they came on, and you would have thought that Tom Keifer was at Madison Square Garden. The guy just came on with an attitude like there's twenty thousand people here and it blew me away.

TOM KEIFER We had a lot of potential and I'm glad somebody saw that, but we had a long way to go. I think the beauty of being that age is not only the abundant energy that you have, but there's also a confidence; there's no self-doubt. It's like, "We know what we're doing, fuck you!"

LARRY MAZER There was enough interest that every label came, but I could not get them a deal because people didn't like Tom's voice. Whereas I thought his voice was a plus because at that point in time Aerosmith had just reformed and had come out with *Done with Mirrors,* which was not a great record because they were still in their heroin phase. AC/DC was in that period of *Fly on the Wall, Flick of the Switch, Who Made Who,* which weren't great AC/DC records. And here's Cinderella, right down the middle of Aerosmith and AC/DC. The closest we got was Jason Flom, who at that time was A&R at Atlantic Records and who said to me, "Well, I *kind* of like it, but it's either this or Savatage and I think Savatage has a much bigger future."

13

"OKAY, WHERE'S THE KNIVES?"

RIKKI ROCKETT (drummer, Paris, Poison) I met Bret through a guy that I grew up playing with. He played bass and I played drums. His name was Dave. He was a short-order cook at a place called the Amity House in Lewisburg, Pennsylvania, and Bret had just gotten a job there busing tables. He goes, "Look, I don't know what this guy sounds like, but he's got his own PA." I said, "We'll figure out how to make him sound good if he doesn't!"

BRET MICHAELS (singer, Paris, Poison) They didn't necessarily want me because I was cool, they didn't want me because I could sing; they wanted me because I owned my own PA system.

RIKKI ROCKETT He came down with his PA, it was the middle of winter, and he was trying to unload his dad's Lincoln in clogs. I'm like, "This guy's fucking dedicated. I'm in." I liked him right away because I just knew that we both had the same kind of drive and dreams. Even though we had slightly different musical likes, it didn't matter.

BOBBY DALL (bassist, Paris, Poison) The reason I would never join a band before was that I wanted total commitment. These guys are great people and great players and the package was great, but I think it was the commitment, the willingness to do whatever it takes to make it that sold me. That was something very important to us, because we don't come from rich families.

RIKKI ROCKETT If somebody said to Bobby Dall, "If you slit your wrists and come within an inch of dying, you will get a record deal," he'd be like, "Okay, where's the knives?"

MATT SMITH (guitarist, Paris, Poison) The three other guys put something in the classified ads in the newspaper and I happened to call. They were looking for a guitar player. It said something like *"Guitarist wanted for theatrical band, has to be willing to move to L.A."*

BOBBY DALL We've always worn makeup, we've always looked real flash, since we put the band together. It's not like there was a glam scene and we said, "Let's go glam!" and jumped on the bandwagon.

RIKKI ROCKETT Yeah, we would get shit. We got into a lot of fights over it and that kind of stuff.

MATT SMITH It was mostly covers at first, but the first thing we did at the first rehearsal was try to write songs.

RIKKI ROCKETT Even though we grew up on Kiss and Alice Cooper and bands like that, by the time we were at the age where we could go out and play, the punk rock/new wave template was what we had to take from, because that's what was happening. So we lied a lot of times. We'd say that we'd do Greg Kihn Band and Tommy Tutone and all this kind of stuff and then we'd come out and do Judas Priest's "Screaming for Vengeance." We'd also do hard rock versions of songs like "Get Ready" by the Temptations, because we realized that a lot of those classic songs were very pivotal to the bar owners who were of that age. They started to really like us for that and we developed a good relationship with the few bars that we did play, like the Pine Grove Inn in Pine Grove, PA.

BRET MICHAELS The motto was "Shake your hiney at the Piney." We would play five sets and have to dress in the bathroom. The "dressing room" was a stall.

MATT SMITH Aerosmith, Kiss, we'd even do some current stuff like Mötley Crüe. Let me think . . . a *lot* of Kiss.

MITCH SCHNEIDER (publicist) I was hanging out with Poison on their bus once and I asked Bobby Dall, "What band inspired you?" And he looked up and he said, "Foghat." I was horrified but didn't express it.

BRET MICHAELS Somewhere, there's a Polaroid image of me out behind a U-Haul truck with me on the ground nailing together stands for the PA to go on because the bar's roof leaked.

RIKKI ROCKETT The only time we'd get a chance to play a lot of our own stuff was with Kix. We opened for them numerous times back there in the early days—especially in Maryland, because Maryland's drinking age was eighteen at the time and Pennsylvania was twenty-one, and we were nineteen and twenty.

BRIAN "DAMAGE" FORSYTHE When they used to open for us, as Paris, they were horrible. We would be backstage and listen to them and go, "Man, these guys are terrible." But they'd be getting over because we'd be doing all-ages shows, like up around Scranton, PA, and the little girls would just be going insane! It would be like the Beatles, the way the girls were reacting to Bret Michaels. But we'd sit back there and we wouldn't be seeing them, we'd just be hearing them from behind the stage, and we'd be going, "God, these guys, they can't even play! What's going on here?"

RIKKI ROCKETT We could only play so many places because we were so young, so we started to rent out VFW halls and skating rinks and bring in our own bleachers. We promoted our own stuff. We sold our own tickets, the whole nine yards. We hired a company called Fly by Night Sound. They were soup to nuts. They'd bring lighting and they'd bring sound and just pull up in a truck and it looked like it was ours. We felt cool. Because back then I didn't dream about having a Porsche, I dreamed about having a big PA system and a big lighting system.

BRET MICHAELS It was New York or Los Angeles, and L.A.'s warm and the chicks were better looking.

BOBBY DALL We sold everything we owned and went to L.A.—sold our cars, sold our stereos, our records. I sold my record collection! . . . "They tore him from his Aerosmith albums, weeping!"

BRET MICHAELS We had a kind of naive belief in ourselves and in what we wanted the band to be: a combination of the glam look and the party sound. We thought music kind of sucked. It had no energy. We did have the energy and we just wanted to be rock stars, man.

RIKKI ROCKETT We were young guys. I was twenty-two when we moved out here to Los Angeles. Bobby, who is the youngest, was nineteen.

BRET MICHAELS The day we left was my younger sister's birthday, March 2, 1983. We had an old ambulance van, a Chevette, and a green pickup truck. Nothing but gear and a dream. We had CB radio as communication. And I'm a diabetic so I'm taking four or five injections a day.

MATT SMITH We had this river rescue van that Rikki's dad had. That's how we got the equipment out, and it broke down as soon as we crossed into California. We had to rent a tow bar and hook it to Bobby's car for the rest of the way. Then we trashed it.

BRIAN "DAMAGE" FORSYTHE When they went out west, I remember our singer, Steve, saying, "If these guys get signed, I'm gonna quit the business and start making pizza."

PART II

FEEL THE NOIZE

Although they had struggled for years to secure a deal in the U.S., when Quiet Riot released *Metal Health* on producer Spencer Proffer's CBS-distributed Pasha label in 1983, the timing coincided perfectly with the then fledgling MTV's insatiable demand for videos by acts that were compelling not only musically but visually. The album's first single, "Metal Health (Bang Your Head)," gained some traction at radio, and it was MTV president Les Garland himself who requested a video from the band. The resulting clip connected immediately with viewers and the album quickly went gold. But it wasn't until the band delivered their second music video to the network, this time for their cover of Slade's "Cum On Feel the Noize," that Quiet Riot became a genuine mainstream phenomenon. "At one point, you couldn't turn on the radio without hearing the song or switch on MTV without seeing that video," recalls Quiet Riot drummer Frankie Banali.

Metal Health would unseat the Police's *Synchronicity* from the number one spot on the *Billboard* album chart and go on to sell six million copies, demonstrating beyond a shadow of a doubt that hard rock was anything *but* the "dinosaur music" it had recently been dismissed as. In fact, it was the sound of *now*. And likely, of the foreseeable future as well.

"Quiet Riot didn't just break through. They didn't just put a hole in the wall. They knocked the fucking wall down," says Dee Snider of Twisted Sister. After struggling for the better part of a decade to gain recognition, Snider's band would storm the pop charts with "We're Not Gonna Take It." The song's accompanying concept video, which starred actor Mark Metcalf reprising his *Animal House* role as the spittle-spewing Doug Neidermeyer, was an MTV staple. "It was a really melodic, anthemic song, and it was a fun video," says then network executive Rick Krim. "We knew it wasn't just for guys who liked metal."

The question at the major labels was no longer whether hard rock had commercial potential, but which acts in the genre had the most. Elektra would align itself with Mötley Crüe and Dokken, while Atlantic Records added Ratt to its fabled roster after label head Doug Morris flew from New York to Los Angeles to witness them play to a packed house at the Beverly Theater. "Doug never really ventured an opinion of 'I really love this music,'" recalls Ratt producer Beau Hill. "He just sat there, with his mouth open, watching two thousand fans singing the words. And like a good businessman, he went, 'Okay. I'm hearing the cash register ring on this one.'"

Realizing that Los Angeles was the place to be seen and heard, bands like Paris, from Mechanicsburg, Pennsylvania, and Plain Jane, from central Florida, packed up their belongings and made the pilgrimage west. Paris changed their name to Poison soon after arriving in Los Angeles, while Plain Jane and their front man, Jani Lane, eventually merged with existing local act Warrant. At the same time, a group of young Hollywood natives named Slash, Steven Adler, and Tracii Guns were playing musical chairs with a number of newcomers to the scene, among them Seattle transplant Duff McKagan and two refugees from Indiana who would take the stage names Axl Rose and Izzy Stradlin.

Not all bands found the idea of uprooting themselves to be particularly appealing. Making a go of it on the East Coast,

Philadelphia's Cinderella caught the eye and ear of an up-and-coming New Jersey rocker named Jon Bon Jovi and secured a deal with the singer's label, Mercury/PolyGram. Cinderella's debut album, *Night Songs,* which featured the group posing under a pink and purple logo sporting sky-high hair and animal-print spandex, would move three million copies, ushering in a boom era when such dizzying sales numbers and over-the-top imagery became the new normal and hard rock bands were the roaring engine that kept the music industry whizzing down the fast lane.

14

"ANTHEM PARTICIPATORY ROCK"

DEE SNIDER Quiet Riot, they don't get enough credit. They get *dis*credited. But I've screamed it from the mountaintops. I will continue. Quiet Riot should be immortalized. What they did . . . first of all, they were on the West Coast doing it for years and years and years, carrying this glitter rock/glam rock torch, putting out these independent records, going to Japan, doing everything they could. And then, finally, against all odds, they break through.

PETER PHILBIN (executive, Elektra Records) Quiet Riot, everyone passed on them. They were a shitty band. And somehow CBS/Sony in Japan signed that band. But everyone here passed on them. Epic passed. Columbia passed. But there was a guy who had a label deal named Spencer Proffer. And this is my memory—I might be wrong 'cause I wasn't involved—but Spencer forced that record out on his label and everyone was holding their noses.

SPENCER PROFFER (owner, Pasha Records; producer, Quiet Riot, W.A.S.P.) I was driving around L.A. working on an Eddie Money single as a day job, trying to make a few bucks and I heard the 1973 Slade version of "Cum On Feel the Noize" on the radio, on a pop station. It was sandwiched in between "Roxanne" by the Police, one of the great songs in life, and Soft Cell's "Tainted Love." But it jumped out of the radio. This was anthem participatory rock. It *invited* people to participate: "*Come on feel the* *noise, girls rock your boys.*" And I said, "Holy shit. If I could find a band to sing this song . . ." Then I might be able to get CBS, who I had a deal with, to pay attention to me. Because they didn't. They thought I was nuts. I used to wear these silk robes, I would come into the offices barefoot. You think Rick Rubin is eccentric? You didn't know me in '81, '82.

But when I heard "Cum On Feel the Noize" on the radio I literally felt I needed a band. So I called everyone I knew in town and they told me there was a band playing at a place called the Country Club in Reseda called DuBrow. Fronted by a guy named Kevin DuBrow. I was told they were very animated and they would do anthem participatory stuff.

RUDY SARZO Quiet Riot was done when Randy left for Ozzy's band. At the time, I was living with Kevin in his apartment and he started DuBrow, and in order to pay my part of the rent I joined a band called Angel and I also played with Kevin. A lot of the stuff he wrote for DuBrow later ended up on *Metal Health*. But we couldn't get record deals. We were still suffering from the mentality that the record companies had that we were playing dinosaur music.

FRANKIE BANALI (drummer, DuBrow, Quiet Riot) Kevin asked me to join Du-Brow in January 1980. At the time I was playing in five other bands so I turned him down. But we had this connection, and eventually I started working with him. DuBrow was definitely a part of the L.A. scene, but you also have to understand, L.A. at that time, you know, when everybody thinks of the Strip, they think of the big hair and the crazy clothes and all of that. That really hadn't started yet. At that point in time the bands that really were working a lot were the new wave bands. That's who we had to compete with.

RUDY SARZO Then I got the opportunity to go play with Randy in Ozzy's band. And that was the opportunity of a lifetime. I did not realize how big that was going to become, but at least I was able to play with my friend Randy again, and also make a living from playing.

FRANKIE BANALI Quiet Riot and Twisted Sister, both bands had gone through different incarnations, up to the point that each band got signed and went out and did it. But essentially, you know, we weren't '80s bands. We were '70s bands that had already paid enough dues to make it possible for us to really be able to appreciate the sort of gift that we got.

DEE SNIDER Twisted Sister were dismissed as a club phenomenon, a local phenomenon, whatever. We played cover tunes as well as originals, and we had makeup, and we were dinosaurs. The "the" bands—bands like the Cars—were stripped down, CBGB's, minimalist backlines, no grandeur. We had walls of Marshall stacks and all of the costumes and makeup and all the pomp and circumstance of "yesterday's bands."

JAY JAY FRENCH Maybe we did suck, or maybe the act was not polished enough to go. Whatever it was, what happened happened, you can't change it. It makes me think, Did we get famous too late? I don't think so. I don't think we had learned all the lessons we needed to learn yet.

DEE SNIDER With Twisted Sister, it took so fucking long and we had to work so hard. It was so anticlimactic when we finally got success. We'd already been in arenas. We'd already sold out theaters without a record deal. We had an outdoor show that drew twenty-three thousand people. It was a long time before anything. We'd been in Electric Lady Studios with Eddie Kramer recording our demos. There was nothing grand about going into Cherokee Studios with Tom Werman. There was nothing grand about walking into an arena; we'd been in arenas.

FRANKIE BANALI In maybe '82 Spencer came down to the Country Club to see DuBrow and came back to the dressing room afterwards. And he showered the band with praises.

SPENCER PROFFER There was twenty people in the audience. They were singing songs like "Bang Your Head." They were singing songs like "Party All Night." Meaning, songs that would invite you to join along. So I went up to Kevin, who was the leader of the band and very, very outspoken. And I said, "Hey man, this stuff is really cool. My name's Spencer Proffer." And Kevin, who's a student of rock music, said, "Spencer Proffer—weren't you that guy who did that Tina Turner album [1975's *Acid Queen*]?

Didn't you put her in *Tommy*?" He knew my whole life story. And he said, "Didn't you build a studio?" And I had a studio called Pasha. I said, "I'll tell you what—I'll give you studio time. If you do a song that I think could be a hit, I'll do three of yours. I'll pay for it, I'll record it. I just made a label deal with CBS, I think I can put it through the system. Would you do this?" Well, little did I know they had been passed on by everybody in the business. They went up and down the Strip, they played the Troubadour, they played the Roxy. Everybody passed on them. But Kevin said okay. So I made a deal with them.

CARLOS CAVAZO My band, Snow, was on that bill, too. DuBrow had a different guitar player at the time. But soon after that Snow broke up and I was sitting around the house we were living in, wondering what I was going to do next, and I got a call from Kevin and those guys saying, "We're looking for a guitar player. Wanna come down?" I'd seen the original Quiet Riot with Randy and I'd met Randy a bunch of times, and I thought they were good guys. And I knew they had put out a few records on a Japanese label. But I didn't think they were past their prime or anything. I looked at it like, because of punk rock and new wave, it prevented them from getting a record deal here. So I joined.

SPENCER PROFFER I took Quiet Riot into the studio and we cut those first four songs on *Metal Health* in a weekend.

CARLOS CAVAZO Rudy wasn't even in Quiet Riot when we started recording the first side of *Metal Health* at Pasha. He was still with Ozzy, and that was right when Randy had his horrible accident and passed away. [On March 19, 1982, Rhoads, age twenty-five, was killed in a plane crash in Leesburg, Florida, along with pilot Andrew Aycock and makeup artist Rachel Youngblood.] And Rudy and Kevin had been talking and he kinda wanted to come back to Quiet Riot and we were like, "Yeah, we love Rudy. Of course." And so he came back.

RUDY SARZO After Randy died I lost my joy of playing onstage. But being in the same room with my old bandmates Kevin and Frankie, and also Carlos, who I knew from the local scene, that gave me a lot of joy. But there was no record deal yet for Quiet Riot. That album was done on what is called "spec time." There was no budget. I left one of the biggest bands in the world for the complete unknown.

FRANKIE BANALI Spencer wanted us to do "Cum On Feel the Noize," and I never had a problem with that. It really didn't make any difference to me. However, Kevin was livid at the idea. He saw himself as the consummate songwriter. He didn't need to do outside material.

SPENCER PROFFER It was part of the quid pro quo. Because they didn't find me—I found them. And I said to them, "You let me arrange and produce 'Cum On Feel the Noize' with you. In return, you've got a couple of songs that I think are in that spirit. I'll record those." They didn't want to do a song written by others, but they did.

RUDY SARZO I witnessed the conversation between Kevin and Frankie in the studio about how to sabotage that song. So yes, that is true that they tried to do that.

SPENCER PROFFER No. That's not true. Once we went in to record it, they didn't play it poorly. They played it terrifically! Are you kidding? They were professionals. They didn't slag off. They treated it equally as they treated "Bang Your Head" or some of the other songs.

FRANKIE BANALI Here's what happened. We needed to have this thing move forward, and we knew that without agreeing to do that song it was not likely to move forward. I also knew that Kevin was not going to agree to it. So what I did is I said to Kevin, "Listen, we've got a potential situation here where we can maybe do a record, maybe it gets released, maybe it sells a few copies. So let's just tell Spencer that we'll do the song, and then not work on the song, not rehearse it, not do anything. Then when the day comes to play the song it'll be a giant train wreck. And Spencer will just say, 'You already have these other songs, let's just keep going, forget about that.'"

So then the day comes to record "Cum On Feel the Noize," and we're in the live room at Pasha and Kevin is sitting on this tall stool in the back corner of the room giggling away, because he knows what's about to happen. I start playing that drumbeat, the intro, which I had never played before, and then all of a sudden everybody is joining in and we're playing the song.

CARLOS CAVAZO It actually came out really good. And Spencer wound up loving it.

FRANKIE BANALI Spencer goes, "Man, I wish we had recorded that!" And the engineer says, "Come on in. I did!" So Spencer bolts out of the room. And as he bolts out, Kevin comes in from the corner, grabs me by the arm so hard he almost dislocates my shoulder, and drags me out of the room. And he goes, "What the fuck was *that*?" I say, "I don't know, man. I just started playing . . ." I'm tap dancing at this point. He goes, "What am I supposed to do now?" So I told him, "Well, you can fuck it up by singing like shit." And I turned around and walked away. Because I knew in Kevin's mind he wouldn't allow himself to be the one that sucked. And he didn't. He sang it great.

CARLOS CAVAZO I remember Spencer going to New York with the masters from that session and pitching the album. I don't think a lot of labels were signing metal bands.

SPENCER PROFFER I called my friends at CBS Records and I said, "I have the next band." I flew to New York and they set up a conference room with all the promotion guys, everyone. I played them the four songs we had recorded, and by the time I was finishing "Cum On Feel the Noize" I got a note from one of the executives. And the note was: "Spencer, we hate this." So I took the songs and went shopping to other labels. And everybody I went to passed. To a man. Later, I called Walter Yetnikoff, who was the chairman of CBS. And I said, "You guys made a deal with me because you thought I had vision. Please let me finish this record that you all hated and let me put it out." And Walter, to his credit, said, "Go ahead." So I finished the album.

FRANKIE BANALI The label didn't want the band to be called DuBrow and they came up with all these ridiculous names—Periscope, Wilde Oscar . . .

I mean, I'm serious about these names! And Kevin says, "Well, if it's not going to be called DuBrow then it's going to be called Quiet Riot." They were really, really reluctant to let us do that. So that gives you an idea about how much they were behind the band.

CHRIS HAGER Quiet Riot were one of the first bands to get signed on the scene. I remember the night it happened. We were down at the Troubadour. Carlos was there, I think Frankie was there. And we were like, "Fuck yeah, man!" Congratulating them and stuff.

RON KEEL *Nobody* was cheering on Kevin DuBrow when Quiet Riot broke down the barricade for all of us! At the time it was competition, man. Somebody else gets a record deal? It was, "Screw those guys!" We're all jealous. We want that. I want that. *I want that car, I want that girl, I want those drugs, I want that sold-out stage, I want that crowd.* It was very, very aggressive and competitive.

SPENCER PROFFER Quiet Riot opened that door wide. None of those bands could get a record deal. 'Cause the nature of what was getting signed by the labels and industry was more passive. And you know, it was good stuff—the Police, Soft Cell, Duran Duran. There was cool stuff being done. But none of it was *rockin'*.

15

"THIS IS GONNA GO"

BILL HEIN One of the things that kept the major label A&R people away from Mötley Crüe was that it wasn't trendy. It wasn't new wave-y. It wasn't what was happening at the time. It was raunchy metal, you know?

ALAN NIVEN I took them to KMET. I took them to KLOS. There was no interest at radio in playing them. So basically everything was done by word of mouth and press. I had a relationship with Sylvie Simmons, who was based in L.A. and wrote for the British magazine *Sounds*.

WES HEIN Sylvie Simmons was writing about them as if they were the biggest thing on the planet. So people in L.A. were reading about this L.A. band, but in a London-based magazine. It made them seem larger than life.

SOUNDS MAGAZINE, February 20, 1982 *Four of the most striking looking guys this city has to offer the exiled headbanger, with their un-L.A.-pale skin, ratted hair, killer leathers and stiletto heels . . . the first LAHM [Los Angeles Heavy Metal] band I've seen in a long time that can really give Van Halen a run for their money.*

BILL HEIN Eventually we sold something close to thirty thousand records of *Too Fast for Love*. And that was in a very short period of time. It was just blowing up. And Tom Zutaut and Elektra Records came calling.

VICKY HAMILTON Licorice Pizza is where Tom Zutaut heard about Mötley Crüe. He saw the display we did and went into the Whisky and saw them and ultimately ended up signing them to Elektra Records.

ALAN NIVEN I was at a NAMM [National Association of Music Merchants] convention at the Century Plaza hotel. I grabbed the few Mötley Crüe posters that Allan Coffman had and put them up in our booth. And this young man came up to me and looked at the posters and said, "Do you have something to do with Mötley Crüe?" I said, "Yes, they're signed to our label." He said, "I'm very interested in them." I said, "That's wonderful. Why don't you come and have dinner on the weekend?" He did, and that was the start of a very long friendship with Tom Zutaut.

The one thing I understood from Tom back in the day was that a good friend of his had told him to look out for Mötley Crüe. And that good friend was Cliff Burnstein.

CLIFF BURNSTEIN (manager, Def Leppard, Dokken, Tesla, Metallica) Tom Zutaut was at Elektra, and Tom knew about Mötley Crüe. This is what I think happened: I think Tom maybe hipped me to Mötley Crüe and asked me what I thought. And I heard their first record and I said, "This is gonna go . . ."

ALAN NIVEN There was a highly entertaining moment when Tom Zutaut and I were having a drink with Allan Coffman at a place called Casa Cugat, which was right next door to Elektra when it was still on La Cienega. Allan went off to the bathroom and came back very red of face and perspired, and told me and Tom that he'd just had a "battle with some gooks." Obviously trying to infer some sort of Vietnam flashback, if he had ever been there. So I went to investigate, and there was a pay phone hanging off a wall by a wire or two. I went back into the bar and looked at Tom and said, "I think it's time we should go . . ."

CLIFF BURNSTEIN I had a meeting with Mötley Crüe and I thought, I could never handle these guys. Plus, they had Allan Coffman, who didn't want to give up managing them. So I decided, This is too messy. They have a manager, they're unmanageable anyway. Or at least that was my impression. I can't do it. I'm not cut out to do that kind of thing.

ALAN NIVEN The minute they were at Elektra, Allan Coffman was no longer the manager.

VICKY HAMILTON Allan just seemed to disappear at that point. And Doc McGhee and Doug Thaler came in.

BILL HEIN Elektra offered what was for us a very nice deal to buy out our contract with Mötley Crüe—give us a nice advance payment, give us a royalty, which was very welcomed.

ALAN NIVEN So one day I roll into work and the receptionist at Greenworld asks if a friend of hers can come in and talk to me. He has a record that he wants me to listen to. I said sure. And a white 1956 Bentley pulls up outside . . .

DON DOKKEN I was a mechanic, so we'd go out and try to find these really cheap beat-up cars and just try to bandage them back together and sell 'em for a couple hundred dollars' profit, just to make the rent. So I was totally poor but I've got a white Bentley. It was sitting in a movie sound lot a couple blocks from the house with flat tires, just rotting away. I asked someone who it belonged to and they said one of the directors. I hunted him down and I said, "Would you consider selling it? I'll give you five thousand bucks for it." I borrowed the money from various people, and my brother and I fixed it up and got it running. It was such an ostentatious car. The old, big giant fenders, the giant round headlights. So the joke was, I'm a starving musician but I'm driving around in a Bentley. People thought, Wow, Don got a record deal. He made it!

ALAN NIVEN And out steps this guy. He comes into my office, puts his feet up on my desk, throws the European release of *Breaking the Chains* at me, and says, "I want you to do for me what you did for Mötley Crüe!" And that was a guy called Don Dokken.

DON DOKKEN Alan knew somebody that worked at Elektra. And *Breaking the Chains* had come out on Carrere and he says, "You should take it to this guy I know, Tom Zutaut, and play it for him."

ALAN NIVEN But Tom had just made a major decision by signing Mötley Crüe and was a bit reluctant to make another one. So for Dokken I said, "Tom, look, I know you've got a relationship with Cliff Burnstein and Peter Mensch at Q Prime management. Do you mind if send this record to them?" And he connected me to Burnstein, who said, "Have Don call me." And of course with Cliff and Peter on board that enabled Tom to be more aggressive at Elektra and that's how Don got on Elektra.

DON DOKKEN I get a phone call from a guy named Cliff Burnstein and he says, "I saw your record in an import store and I liked it." So he comes to L.A. and meets me. And you know how Cliff looks, right? Like a homeless person. He has that big scruffy beard. I was expecting someone in a suit and tie.

CLIFF BURNSTEIN I felt that I was excited about Dokken and that I could do something with them. So Tom Zutaut said, "Great, let me sign them over here to Elektra." And Joe Smith was the head of Elektra at the time, as I recall. So Tom goes in there and, quote, "gets them signed." And we make some kind of deal. It's not an expensive deal. It's a cheap deal. The record is already made. Then Joe Smith leaves the company and Bob Krasnow takes over and Tom Zutaut calls me and says, "Cliff, I have some bad news. Krasnow is not interested in this, so we're backing out of the deal." And I said, "Oh, this is terrible." Because, really remember, obviously we had Def Leppard as management clients then, but they weren't *Def Leppard* with a capital *D* and a capital *L*. We didn't know if we had a future with Def Leppard. I would know it in a few months, but I didn't know it then. So this was really kind of a big blow.

DON DOKKEN It became like a joke: "So, Don, do you have a record deal or do you *not* have a record deal?" I'd say, "I don't know. It depends on what day it is. Ask me tomorrow."

ALAN NIVEN Don and I formed a friendship, we lived together. He was the guy who introduced me to Dante Fox, who became Great White.

MARK KENDALL Back then there was only a handful of bands getting deals. The crazy signing mania had not really begun yet.

JACK RUSSELL It all happened through Don Dokken. Our drummer at the time, Gary Holland, had played with Dokken in Germany, and he introduced me to Don. So Don brought Alan down to the Whisky to see us, and Alan liked what he saw.

ALAN NIVEN Fucking abysmal. Mark Kendall was in white. The bassist was in black. The drum kit was half black and white. Jack Russell was half black and white. He had a huge fucking knife gaffer-taped to his biceps. The songs were not very good. I was unimpressed.

MARK KENDALL I didn't know this till later, but Alan had seen us a couple times and kinda passed. And Don Dokken told him, "No, man, you're missing it. These guys really are good!"

ALAN NIVEN I went a second time and they were just as awful. But after the show I was driving back to Palos Verdes at something like three o'clock in the morning and I had one of those rare moments of lucid thought, where I evaluated the situation and I said, "I trust Don. He has a competence in songwriting and performing. I must be missing something."

So I went to the Troubadour and looked a *third* time. And the third time I saw them they *still* weren't very good. But when the encore came around, if I remember correctly, they did Humble Pie's version of "I Don't Need No Doctor."

MARK KENDALL That's what sold Niven, believe it or not. A cover song.

ALAN NIVEN Kendall just took the fucking roof off. And Jack had a voice. So I realized it was just the material that was an issue. At that moment, I said, "Here is something that definitely has possibility . . ."

JACK RUSSELL He wanted to sign us to Enigma. And we're all like, "Yes!" So one night we go to Alan's house up in Palos Verdes and he's like, "Guys, I've got some bad news. I quit my job today." What? He goes, "Well, the company didn't want to sign you, so basically I told them to eff off."

ALAN NIVEN I had been running the sales and marketing at Greenworld, and after the Mötley Crüe thing, I asked to be a partner and they said no. So when I threatened to leave, one of the guys there said, "Let's start another label and you can be the label." And that was Enigma. But when I wanted to sign Great White to Enigma, that wasn't going to happen. Bill Hein wouldn't do it. So I left.

JACK RUSSELL So I said to Alan, "We're out a record deal. You're out a career. Why don't you manage us?" He said, "C'mon, Jack, I know nothing about managing." I go, "You'll learn." And not only did Alan become a manager, he became one of the best managers in the business. He ended up managing Guns N' Roses.

MARK KENDALL Niven flat-out hated the name Dante Fox. I was less than thrilled with it myself.

JACK RUSSELL He said, "What do you think about changing your name?" Me and Mark looked at each other and we went, "We'll lose all our following!"

ALAN NIVEN I said to him, "All thirty-seven of them, Jack?"

JACK RUSSELL So we finally said okay. And Alan goes, "What about Great White?"

MARK KENDALL I was just like, yuck. I mean, that's a really stupid name, too.

JACK RUSSELL I used to call Mark the Great White, because I'm a shark fisherman and he's got a really light complexion. So when we'd play a show, before he would do his solo I'd announce, "Mark Kendall—the Great White!"

MARK KENDALL Jack did used to call me that onstage. But I don't think Niven had ever heard that. What he told me was one night he was standing outside a club where we were playing, and I drove by and screamed something into the crowd. And the kid next to him says, "There goes Great White!" And that's when the light went on in his head.

JACK RUSSELL I said, "You get us a record deal, you can call us whatever you want."

ALAN NIVEN We did an EP with Don Dokken and Michael Wagener. It cost us $5,000 to record it. In hindsight it makes me smile when I remember Wags would be in the studio and Jack would be doing vocals and Wags' guidance would be [in German accent], "Make a fist, Jack! You've got to make a fist!"

DON DOKKEN Great White asked me if I could help them do a record and I said, "Sure, I can help you. Michael Wagener's a great engineer and I could probably get you studio time cheap and *yada yada yada.*" And I took them in the studio and recorded them.

ALAN NIVEN At the time, neither KLOS or KMET played independent records in regular rotation. But I went and managed to get KMET to play "Out of the Night," which was a big breakthrough. So the record companies were sitting there and they're looking at someone who has a certain amount of energy and determination, and who can get a little bit done because here's KMET playing a record in regular rotation.

MARK KENDALL I'd never heard of a band with a song in rotation. Not Ratt, not Dokken, none of them. It was something that was unheard of. But Alan was able to do it. And that really got a buzz happening. Everybody was going, "What the heck's going on here? Great White's on the radio!"

JACK RUSSELL I remember the first time I heard myself on the radio. Alan came into rehearsal and he goes, "Hey, stop, guys. I want you to hear something." He turns the radio on and here comes *"Out of the nii-yiiight. Your mama tells you baby . . ."* We're like, "Are you kidding me?" We were just high-fivin', jumping all over each other. It was like a tree full of monkeys. It was one of the greatest moments I can remember.

16

"THEN I GOT THE OZZY GIG . . ."

JAKE E. LEE After I quit Ratt, they were looking for another guitarist and I recommended Warren, who was a friend from San Diego. He was nineteen and he was a great player. And I remember he was thinking about going to college. But I called him and talked him into coming up to L.A. instead. I said, "You can always go back to college if that's what you want to do. But right now, there's this thing happening up here and I think you want to be a part of it."

WARREN DeMARTINI (guitarist, Ratt) The deal was I had to move up to L.A. that day, because there were Ratt shows that weekend. And you know, canceling a show at that point in your band's career was just an impossibility. You just could not do it. You would never get another job.

JAKE E. LEE I was living in an apartment with my girlfriend, and I let . . . well, my girlfriend let Warren live with us for a month or so.

WARREN DeMARTINI I basically moved to L.A. with my equipment and the chords to "Round and Round."

JAKE E. LEE And I was writing the riff to "Bark at the Moon," which was originally for Rough Cutt, the band I joined after Ratt.

WARREN DeMARTINI Jake and I, we're both night owls, so, you know, a typical night at that time was us at twelve, one in the morning, sitting on the floor and leaning back against a couch that's got the stuffing coming out, and there's a black-and-white TV with stations going in and out but we're not really watching it, and we're both playing unamplified guitar, just working on these two songs.

JAKE E. LEE Then I got the Ozzy gig . . .

WARREN DeMARTINI One day Jake said to me, "Oh, you'll never believe this, but I got a call from Ozzy's manager and I'm going to try out." And what was weird was that, not long before that I was on the phone with George Lynch and he's like, "Yeah man, I'm pretty sure I got the Ozzy gig . . ." That was a strange thing because at that moment I think I was probably the only person that knew what was going on, you know?

DANA STRUM When I first found Randy for Ozzy, George Lynch was actually my second pick. And when Randy died in the plane crash in Florida, I was the person that held the auditions and brought Jake and George in.

GEORGE LYNCH After Randy died, Ozzy had Brad Gillis from Night Ranger playing guitar for him for a little bit. And I left Dokken for a minute and toured with Ozzy. I never played onstage during a live show, but I would go up and play at soundchecks and at rehearsals. They were grooming me, basically. Then we did rehearsals in Dallas for a week or two, and then I flew back to L.A. to do more rehearsals at SIR. And that's when they got Jake.

DANA STRUM I was put in a bad position because I was told, "Dana, we're going with this other guy." And I was like, "But this guy quit his job! He's got his bags here!" And then Jake had the gig.

JAKE E. LEE George was there for my audition and, um, yeah . . . that *sucked.* Because I knew who he was; he was part of the scene. And after my audition I'm packing up my gear and I'm by the exit door, and nobody has said anything to me. So I just figured I didn't get the gig. And that's when Sharon Osbourne walked up to me and said, "We think you're the guy." And then Ozzy walked up next to her and he said, "Do you want the fucking gig?" "Yeah, I do." And at that moment, George came over and stood next to us. And he says, "Hey guys, what's up?" And Ozzy turns to him and goes, "You lost it! It's his now!" And he walks away.

Then it's just me and George standing there looking at each other. It was just a very awkward moment.

GEORGE LYNCH I gotta say, it was pretty coldhearted and really hit me hard. Because I pretty much had nothing at the time. My wife and I had two little kids and we had an apartment. I was even working a side gig delivering liquor down in South Central. It was a dangerous job. And so when the Ozzy thing came along we thought, This is it. This is really going to change our fortunes.

SHARON OSBOURNE (manager, Ozzy Osbourne, Lita Ford) Everybody took it for granted that George Lynch would get the gig. But Ozzy wasn't like, "Oh my god, I have to have this George Lynch, this is the guy for me." It wasn't a done deal. And then came Jakey, and everybody was like, "Yeah, this is the one." Jakey came in and was just . . . he was phenomenal.

OZZY OSBOURNE George Lynch is an excellent guitar player. But Jake was a more tasty guitar player to me.

JAKE E. LEE If you ask George, he'll say I got the gig because I had better hair.

SHARON OSBOURNE Of course he had better hair! He had better everything than George.

GEORGE LYNCH I think their big thing with me was that I had cut my hair short. I didn't have that big rock look. But, hey, I could've worn a wig. Ozzy was *bald* at the time!

WARREN DeMARTINI That whole thing was a shocker. Because everyone that was hanging around in L.A. in that circle thought for sure that George was gonna be the next guitar player in Ozzy.

GEORGE LYNCH The Ozzy thing happened over the course of what was probably a couple of months, and when that ran its course and didn't work out for me I thought, Okay, well . . . So one night I went to see the Dokken guys at the Whisky, they were there hanging out or something, and I go, "Are we putting this back together?" And they were like, "Well, we don't know, George . . ." I remember even Mick saying that to me. *What? Really?* I think they actually had Warren in the band for a second.

"WILD" MICK BROWN During that period when George was running around with Ozzy we thought he was leaving. So we said, "Well, we've gotta get somebody . . ." And everybody was emulating George at the time. But then here comes Warren DeMartini! I don't think he ever did a gig with us, but we had claimed him as the guy.

DON DOKKEN George had quit the band. And in this interim I was going to do one more showcase for Elektra to try to get them to keep us on the label. Juan Croucier was on bass. And I had met Warren DeMartini. He was kind of in Ratt, but Ratt hadn't really made it.

GEORGE LYNCH Ratt and Dokken rehearsed in the same facility. And I think Warren came in and was jamming with them for a while. So I went over and started jamming with Ratt!

WARREN DeMARTINI I rehearsed with Dokken once. Maybe twice.

DON DOKKEN And in the middle of all this Warren and Juan are playing with Ratt at the same time. Everybody was kinda playing musical musicians. But Warren and Juan decided to go with Ratt and that was the end of it.

GEORGE LYNCH At some point Warren and I ran into each other in the hall and I go, "What are we doing? Why don't we just go back in our respective bands?" So that's what we did. It was kind of funny.

"WILD" MICK BROWN I remember looking at Warren one day and telling him, "Listen, dude. Don't go with Ratt. You'll never go anywhere with that band. They don't have any songs!" When I hear myself say shit like that . . . Warren and I are still friends, and we laugh about it when we're drunk. Like, Wow, how wrong can you be?

17

"WHEN YOU'VE GOT NOTHIN', YOU'VE GOT NOTHIN' TO LOSE"

BOBBY BLOTZER I went down to Hollywood to see Ratt play the Whisky and I wasn't quite into the band. I was waiting for this other gig to open up, in a band called Bruzer. They were amazing. But with Ratt, I saw that there was potential in the band, but I wasn't really fond of Pearcy as a front man, you know? But by this time months had gone by and these Bruzer guys were fucking lingering.

JUAN CROUCIER Bobby called me one day and said, "Hey, I wanna go jam with the guys from Ratt." They had a rehearsal space in this garage in the backyard of this house . . . I think the lady's name who lived there was Mrs. O'Neill. So Bob goes, "Can you take me up there?" 'Cause I had a little pickup truck. So I said, "Yeah, no problem. Maybe buy me a burger and I'll give you a ride." I don't think he ever bought me the burger.

BOBBY BLOTZER So in March of '82 I joined Ratt, just to play.

JUAN CROUCIER Then about two weeks after that he calls me and he goes, "Hey man, I need you to help me out. I can't play with this bass player. I'm gonna kill him. Can you come down and jam with us?" And, you know, I was a starving musician. So I go, "How much is the band making?" "I think we make about fifty bucks a gig." And I went, "Fifty bucks? I'm in!" That was groceries for a week. And so Ratt began basically from there.

BOBBY BLOTZER We rehearsed in that garage in Culver City for, like, a year and a half, maybe. And that's where we wrote a lot of that stuff.

WARREN DeMARTINI Ratt was starting to do better, and what happened was DeeDee, who was booking the Whisky, had seen Ratt and she had an idea that it could be something. So Saxon was playing the Whisky and I think the opening act couldn't make it or something like that. But I remember it was very quick, like that day: "You've gotta get your stuff to the Whisky." We got a chance to play, and they were doing two shows in one night. Totally packed and sold out. And we got up there and played and it was the first time we'd ever played to that many people and got the response that we got. That was a turning point.

STEPHEN PEARCY Eventually we became a house band at the Whisky. Just like Mötley.

DEEDEE KEEL I tended more toward the pretty boys. I liked a band that would go up there and put on costumes. I loved the circus. So as soon as I heard about Ratt, I got them into the Whisky as fast as I could. And I really thought they had great tunes. They didn't take off or get the attention as fast as Mötley Crüe, but if I had to score them they'd be number two, for sure. People were coming, particularly girls. And Stephen, have you ever met him? My girlfriend was with me once and she said, "Oh, my god, this guy just exudes sex." He touches. He's all over. And particularly if he wants something.

STEPHEN PEARCY We didn't really eat but I had girls taking care of us, feeding us, giving us stage clothes. Bailing us out of jail.

BOBBY BLOTZER And then it started getting big. I was starting to trip out. I was really getting a buzz off it. We were packing the Whisky. Sellouts, two nights at the Troubadour, everywhere we played around SoCal.

WARREN DeMARTINI But even though things were doing better we never really got paid, you know? There was no manager or anything like that. I remember one night at the Troubadour, this was after that Saxon gig, and it was like we'd seen with Mötley Crüe, where there's a line going around the corner. We did two shows, both totally full, and when we were done it was like, "Where's the guy with the money?" When Marshall started managing Ratt that stuff didn't happen anymore.

BOBBY BLOTZER Marshall was managing the Whisky at the time. And I knew who Marshall Berle was. He was somewhat infamous. He had been on the scene since the '60s and shit. He worked with the Beach Boys. He worked with Creedence. He was, like, legendary.

MARSHALL BERLE (manager, Van Halen, Ratt) I go back to 1960, when I started at the William Morris office in the music department. I signed the Beach Boys. I brought Van Halen to Warner Bros. I had an office at the Whisky, and one of the girls there told me about Ratt.

DEEDEE KEEL That would have been me.

MARSHALL BERLE They had some great songs and they had a huge following already. I personally liked them. But I always go by what the people see, you know? So cementing the relationship and wanting to sign them was based on the reaction of the audience toward them.

DEEDEE KEEL When Marshall got his hands on Ratt, he got involved pretty heavily. And Stephen Pearcy was the kind of guy who would walk on people's shoulders to their head to the next lily pad, if you will. So you could see that coming a mile away. But I can remember telling Stephen, "Ride that pony as far as it takes ya."

STEPHEN PEARCY If I'm correct, we were doing a Whisky show and Marshall just came up and introduced himself. He said, "Hey, I used to manage Van Halen." We go, "*Van Halen?*"

MARSHALL BERLE I didn't bring Van Halen to Warner Bros. I brought Warner Bros. to Van Halen! I had a relationship with Ted Templeman, and Ted Templeman and Mo Ostin and one other guy from Warner Bros. came to the Starwood. I told the band I was bringing some people down.

And it was pouring rain. Of course, David Lee Roth likes to tell it different. I don't want to get into all that. The bottom line is I did my job. I did what I said I was gonna do.

BOBBY BLOTZER Marshall, he's a little old-school shifty, you know? But god bless him.

STEPHEN PEARCY All we heard was "I was Van Halen's manager for two tours. I can get you in the studio."

MARSHALL BERLE Even if I hadn't worked with Van Halen, here's a bunch of guys on the street. You offer them a record deal, I'm sure they're going to take it no matter what.

STEPHEN PEARCY We talked. Because everyone was getting signed at that time, but we still had nothing goin' on.

JUAN CROUCIER Marshall had a label called Time Coast and offered Ratt sort of a production deal. And back then, it was just a different world. Oftentimes groups that really had nothing going on were offered these deals that were maybe not the most lucrative deals. But when you've got nothin', you know, you've got nothin' to lose.

BOBBY BLOTZER So we did this EP in one week in November of '82. I forget the name of the studio. It was on Melrose.

STEPHEN PEARCY I think that record only cost something like three grand.

BOBBY BLOTZER I remember walking out of that studio Thanksgiving morning, after mixing that record for a day and a half straight. And I had to go to my in-laws for Thanksgiving. I was so fucking tired. I got in my [Datsun] B210, pulled the seat back, put my feet outside the window, and went to sleep. But the record sounded killer!

STEPHEN PEARCY The artwork was Robbin and I throwing live rats on Tawny Kitaen's legs, at Neil Zlozower's studio. She was Robbin's girlfriend.

NEIL ZLOZOWER These weren't wild rats that we found in the gutter or something like that. They were rented from, as Stephen called it, a place called Rent-a-Rat. I'm like, "Dude, they got a place that rents rats?" He goes, "Yeah."

STEPHEN PEARCY It was just some weird idea—"Get some rats, throw 'em on her legs, it'll be kinda creepy." So we did. And Tawny was a little squeamish but she went with it. She was a trouper! The only thing was, we rented five white rats. But if you look closely at the cover, there's a sixth one. Black. Don't know where that came from.

JUAN CROUCIER That was one of the things we were always kind of laughing about. Like, "Hey, man, didn't we have five? How come there's six in there now?"

NEIL ZLOZOWER I've gotta be honest with you. I'm an animal lover. Probably the best pets I ever had in my life were pet rats. I loved them. So I don't know whose idea the whole thing was, but it wasn't mine.

MARSHALL BERLE I hired some promotion men to get the EP some legs in L.A. and it took off like crazy. I did what any record company would do. Which was, number one, get some airplay. We got it into heavy rotation.

BOBBY BLOTZER KLOS *and* KMET, in an unprecedented move, they were both playing "You Think You're Tough."

JUAN CROUCIER It was like, "Whoa! We're on the radio!" I'm driving down Prospect Avenue in Redondo Beach, and here comes "You Think You're Tough." And I thought, Oh, yes! And you know the fans picked up on it, we sold somewhere in the neighborhood of forty thousand copies on our own, as an independent band, and that's what helped to bring about the Atlantic deal.

MARSHALL BERLE My experience after Van Halen and before Ratt was that there was a lot of independent record activity going on. I was helping out the Go-Go's and I saw how all the bands were promoting themselves.

That's what needed to be done to get interest from the labels. But you sell forty thousand, fifty thousand units, somebody's gonna jump all over that.

BOBBY BLOTZER And that led us to the Beverly Theater, July 27, 1983. That's when we got our deal.

STEPHEN PEARCY Lita Ford was also supposed to play, but she pulled out because she didn't want to open for Ratt. We said, "We don't care. We'll just play alone." And that's what we did.

BOBBY BLOTZER She was trying to show up late and fuck with us somehow, this is the story we were told. But we just went on. We said, "Fuck it." She showed up but it was too late.

STEPHEN PEARCY And that's when the president of Atlantic came down with a couple of his guys.

BEAU HILL (producer, Ratt, Kix, Alice Cooper, Twisted Sister, Warrant, Winger) I had worked on a Sandy Stewart record for Modern Records, which was a subsidiary of Atlantic. And one day I got a call from [then Atlantic Records president] Doug Morris. He said, "Are you willing to go to California with me to look at a band? Because if you'll produce them, I'll sign them."

WARREN DeMARTINI I remember a feeling that it was this or nothing, because my memory is that every label had passed on us and Atlantic was the last big one that hadn't seen us yet.

STEPHEN PEARCY Marshall had been instigating meetings, having labels come and check us out. Major labels. And a lot of people didn't wanna deal with us.

BEAU HILL So we flew out and we saw Ratt play at the Beverly Theater and the place was packed. There were two thousand screaming kids and they're going completely nuts.

STEPHEN PEARCY And then it was done. Next thing you know we're signing contracts with Atlantic Records.

MARSHALL BERLE Doug and Beau came backstage after the show, *bing, bang, boom,* that was it.

18

"I'M NOT RUNNING ANY FUCKING CIRCUS!"

BRYN BRIDENTHAL (publicist, Elektra Records, Capitol Records, Geffen Records) When Tom Zutaut first signed Mötley Crüe, it was really funny because they came in through the underground parking garage, and people went and hid in their offices.

TOM WERMAN (producer, Mötley Crüe, Dokken, Twisted Sister, Poison, Kix, L.A. Guns, Junkyard, Stryper, Lita Ford) Elektra did not have much of a rock 'n' roll roster then.

BRYN BRIDENTHAL The band came to the label to meet everybody, and they came in to a lot of closed doors. You know how they looked—they were tall and they jingled with all the bracelets and stuff, and the hair, and people were scared of them. But I liked it. The "scared sell" has always been my favorite. To sell through sex is powerful, but to sell through fear is much more powerful.

Anyway, I took them down the street to Benihana, and we just had a fabulous time. I really connected with Nikki. He's sort of always been like my oldest son.

DOC McGHEE (manager, Mötley Crüe, Bon Jovi, Skid Row, Scorpions; co-organizer, Moscow Music Peace Festival) Joe Smith was the head of Elektra at the time, and he signed Mötley Crüe. Then when Bob Krasnow got there, Bob basically said, "If I was here when Mötley Crüe got here, they wouldn't be here."

TOM WERMAN Bob Krasnow, he was a talented guy. Didn't know shit about rock 'n' roll. When he first became the head of Elektra, he came to L.A., which was the Elektra headquarters, and announced that he was going to have a headquarters in New York as well and that his first official duty would be to drop Mötley Crüe.

BRYN BRIDENTHAL Well, Krasnow didn't want any circus acts on his label, is what he said.

DOC McGHEE "I'm not running any fucking circus!"

TOM WERMAN He called them an embarrassment.

DOC McGHEE So I said, "Well, why don't you just let them go?" But Bob said he wouldn't let us go because we had sold two hundred thousand records [of Elektra's 1982 remix of *Too Fast for Love*] and that we should go make a new record. My question was, Who was going to determine what that record would be? It certainly couldn't be Bob. And he said, "No, we've just hired Tom Werman, he's the producer." So I sat down with Tom. We had kind of the same visions, and we made *Shout at the Devil*.

TOM WERMAN Mötley Crüe were young, uncomfortable, surly . . . kind of concerned that they were being fed to the corporate machine. They were pretty combative. They were concerned about being misinterpreted and led down the wrong road. But Tommy Lee finally said, "Listen, if this guy's going to produce our record, we ought to listen to him." And so I said something along the lines of "I'm going to work with you. I'm hired by you. I'm not a dictator, I'm a collaborator, and I'll try to help you make the record you want to make."

BRYN BRIDENTHAL Nikki had the whole concept in his head right from the beginning. He's a very smart guy, and very ambitious.

NIKKI SIXX We had the goods for that record—songs like "Looks That Kill" and the title track were just killer. Plus, Tom Werman knew how to help us crystallize our vision without imposing his own.

TOM WERMAN So we made *Shout,* and it was quick . . . and difficult.

NIKKI SIXX If *Shout at the Devil* is a darker album than *Too Fast for Love,* it's because it reflects that we were into this whole heavier trip. I was dabbling in black magic, and I think that that generated a lot of bad, negative energy. It was like Sodom and Gomorrah.

DOC McGHEE I think some of it was shock value, but a lot of it was just Nikki's personality. He loved to shock people. He was kind of a spooky kid at the time.

BRYN BRIDENTHAL The lore is he slept in garbage cans and was raised mostly by his grandparents. He came to all of this . . . There was no training or preparation.

DOC McGHEE Whereas Vince and Tommy were more like Van Halen, *Fast Times at Ridgemont High* guys, you know what I mean?

BRYN BRIDENTHAL The moment I felt like I was finally accepted by them was when they started changing their clothes in front of me. That's how I knew Mick Mars was a redhead.

DOC McGHEE But Nikki was this gothic, kind of *Billion Dollar Babies-* influenced kid that had a real dark side to him.

TOM WERMAN There was one story, I was not there, but there was one story about a female and a coke bottle, and that after one session . . .

NIKKI SIXX I was doing a lot of drugs, and lots of weird shit was happening, especially sexually. There were orgies, and days and days of being in some person's house that I didn't even know. I would wake up out of a binge and there'd be naked people and drugs everywhere. I'd have blood all over my hands and my feet and not know what happened. I remember that one girl wanted me to take her up into the Hollywood Hills and sacrifice her.

DOC McGHEE Nikki separated his shoulder during the *Shout at the Devil* sessions. He crashed his Porsche—how unusual—going down Laurel Canyon or Benedict Canyon. He had to go do what he had to do, but it hurt.

TOM WERMAN He was playing the bass parts with his arm in a sling, and that was very slow. It would take us hours and hours to do a track.

NIKKI SIXX I had to finish the bass on "Red Hot" with a metal pin in my shoulder and a huge cast. I could barely move my arm, but I did it. It was so painful that I took ten Percodans that day.

TOM WERMAN There were drugs involved. I never saw them actually do heroin, but I know that they were doing heroin while we were in the studio. But we worked through it. I was pretty lenient. I mean, if they started yelling and running around, I would say, "Come on, sit down," or "Go outside, we're working here." But I didn't mind. I wasn't strict, like, "Silence!" I wanted the artist to be happy.

RICHARD PAGE (session vocalist, Mötley Crüe, Twisted Sister; singer, bassist, Mr. Mister) I remember walking into Cherokee Studios in Hollywood and there was a bottle of Jack Daniel's on the console. And I said, "Okay, here we go! This is gonna be good." That was my first memory of that session.

TOM WERMAN I would hire background singers for my records. Tom Kelly [who went on to co-write Madonna's "Like a Virgin" and Cyndi Lauper's "True Colors," among other hits] was on all of them, and he was the guy who brought in Richard Page. Richard Page was the son of a minister, and he wouldn't sing some of the Mötley Crüe lyrics.

RICHARD PAGE I don't know where the story came from that I didn't like their lyrics. It wasn't my kind of music, and I may have mentioned that to someone at some point and that got blown out of proportion. But I thought that what they were doing was cool. I remember that when we were singing the song "Bastard" I really blew my pipes out. It wasn't even like there were any notes. It was just me screaming, *Bastard! Bastard!* over and over again.

BRAD HUNT (executive, Elektra Records) *Shout at the Devil,* this was a metal band. I mean, that's what the perception was. It wasn't easy to get them on the radio. It took a lot of work. Because it didn't fit an easy model. It wasn't holdover Flock of Seagulls—it was something different. You know, you think about the transition period from the late '70s to the early '80s, and then, oh my god, here comes *Shout at the Devil,* and it's right in your face.

MIKE BONE (executive, Elektra Records) When *Shout at the Devil* came out, Zutaut came to a marketing meeting and, you know, we're telling him we're gonna take out some trade ads, we're gonna do a video, we're gonna do some consumer print, we're gonna take an ad in *Kerrang!* and *Thrasher* and *Rolling Stone* . . . And Zutaut came in and he said, "I don't give a fuck about trade ads. I don't give a fuck about consumer press. I don't give a fuck about pricing and positioning. Here's what I want." And what he wanted was a gatefold package—a single record, but in a gatefold sleeve. And everyone was just like, *"Are you fucking crazy?"* The CFO said, "That's gonna cost another twenty-five or fifty cents a unit." Tom said, "Look, if you do this gatefold package, this makes the band seem bigger than they actually are. 'Cause kids will get this record, they'll open it up, and they'll see the band." He said, "That's the marketing plan."

So per Tom Zutaut we did a gatefold. And the finance people were having heart palpitations. We also did all the other stuff, but that gatefold took up a lot of bandwidth. But Tommy, god bless him, he knew that market up, down, and sideways.

"WILD" MICK BROWN *Shout at the Devil,* here's this album cover, you open it up and here's these amazing photos. Mötley Crüe and Dokken were both on Elektra and I said, "Oh my god, we're gonna get lost in the shuffle."

TOM WERMAN The record became a hit so quickly that Bob Krasnow couldn't drop the band.

MIKE BONE Thank god Bob didn't drop them, 'cause we sold a fucking shit-ton of those records!

DOC McGHEE But I had to pay for the photo shoot, I had to pay for the videos. Bob wouldn't pay.

ROBIN SLOANE (vice president, video, Elektra Records) Bob Krasnow and Mike Bone hired me to start a music video department at Elektra, and "Looks That Kill" was the first video I made there. We did it for, like, fifty grand. It was a dominatrix kind of thing. It was ridiculous. I was terrified meeting the band. Mick Mars was the scariest guy imaginable to a twenty-six-year-old neophyte. And I'll say as a woman it was sort of horrifying to see women objectified as they were in that particular video. But the other side of it is no one held a gun to those women's heads to be in the video. So, you know, it was fine. And it got into heavy rotation.

BRYN BRIDENTHAL The first press they did was them on the cover of, I think it was *Circus*. There were girls in the shot, too. I had approval on the girls to make sure they looked right. But when we got there for the photo shoot, the magazine had switched them out and had other girls there who weren't as hot. I was not happy with that.

19

"YOU'VE GOTTA MEET MY FRIEND AXL"

STEPHEN PEARCY In '83, '84, we would walk down the Strip and it was like twenty-four-hour Sodom and Gomorrah Mardi Gras, you know? Then new bands started coming in and they got into their own thing. And the next thing that made the scene in L.A. was Guns N' Roses. That's when people went, "Oh, there's some different shit coming out. These hair metal guys aren't gonna hold up to this!" Well, yeah we could. And we did. For many, many years. It's just that it was such a strange thing that took everybody by surprise.

CHRIS WEBER Before there was Guns N' Roses, even before there was L.A. Guns, Tracii had his band and we all went to Fairfax.

ROB GARDNER (drummer, Pyrrhus, L.A. Guns, Hollywood Rose, Guns N' Roses) I met Tracii in electronics class at Fairfax High soon after I moved to L.A. I grew up in Westchester, New York, and I went to school with Matt Dillon—we lived down the street from his family. Then I was new at Fairfax, but Tracii and I got to talking and then we started playing together.

TRACII GUNS We started our band, which was called Pyrrhus.

CHRIS WEBER Slash's band was Tidus Sloan.

ROB GARDNER Tracii, Chris Weber, Slash, and I all went to the same school. We all knew each other.

TRACII GUNS Slash and I actually used to walk to Bancroft Junior High School together. And it was all about the guitar for us. Later on at Fairfax he turned me on to Randy Rhoads because he saw Ozzy play in L.A., and the next morning I was waiting outside electronics class and he couldn't wait to tell me about it. He goes, "You know that picture on the Starwood of that band Quiet Riot? Well, the blond guy, he plays guitar for Ozzy now and he's going to be your favorite guitar player." I was like, "Yeah, right. Whatever . . ."

CHRIS WEBER Slash was Saul Hudson back then. I remember him and Tracii, they played some guitar-offs at Fairfax, at one of the little showcase rooms that was connected to the school. They had this dueling banjos thing for electric guitars. It was actually pretty fucking cool. But I don't know how much they were friends at that point.

ROB GARDNER Over the years I think it was a case of "I'm getting pretty good." "Oh, *I'm* getting pretty good." Then you start playing in bands and people start watching and all the kids have different opinions. "I like this guy better." "Well, I like *this* guy better."

TRACII GUNS I never really saw it that way. I think we both really encouraged each other. If anything, it was maybe just a natural kind of healthy competition. But Slash would come over to my house and my mom, who was a pedal steel player, would always approve of his guitar playing. She would say, "You know, he's really bluesy . . ." "Yeah, Mom, I know." And she would tell me, "You should be more bluesy." "No, Mom, I'm into metal!"

MARC CANTER (owner, Canter's Deli; Slash's childhood friend) I met Slash in the fifth grade because he saw my motorbike parked outside a Kentucky Fried Chicken and he was thinking about stealing it. And then he said to himself, "Instead of trying to steal it, why don't I just say, 'Hey, can I ride it?'" And that's what happened.

Then in the summer of tenth grade we bumped into each other. He told me he was in a band, and that same day I went with him after school to his rehearsal. This was Tidus Sloan. And I watched him play Black Sabbath's "Heaven and Hell" on a B.C. Rich Mockingbird through a Sunn amp. The tone he was getting would've blown Tony Iommi away. It was so rich and so thick and so heavy. And of course, he nailed the guitar solo. So, long before Guns N' Roses, long before Hollywood Rose, I knew he was going to make his living playing the guitar.

ROB GARDNER Slash's band and our band were two of the more popular bands at Fairfax. But we always got along. We'd do backyard parties, just your typical high school kind of stuff. I don't remember how it went down but we played a party at a studio.

TRACII GUNS What it was actually was that Ron Schneider, who we all called Schneidy, he played bass in Slash's band and he said to me, "Hey, Slash wants to do this New Year's Eve party. We can all go there and jam."

MARC CANTER Slash had an idea of renting out a rehearsal studio downtown [in L.A.] called Curly Joe's, and charging three dollars to get in. And then he booked everyone he knew. He knew Tracii and Pyrrhus, and he knew Josh, who was the guitar player in Warrant at that time. None of these bands had ever played the Troubadour yet. They were all just high school bands that knew each other. And they were all bands that made it eventually, with different lineups.

JOSH LEWIS (guitarist, Warrant; solo artist) Slash was a few years older than me but we both went to Fairfax. All the Chili Peppers went there, too. Talk about rock 'n' roll high school . . . But Slash asked us to play this New Year's Eve party at Curly Joe's, this was '83 going into '84, and it was our first gig as Warrant. Pyrrhus played second, and Slash's band, which had been called Tidus Sloan but had just changed their name to Road Crew, played third.

MARC CANTER If you think about it, that night in 1983 you're seeing L.A. Guns, Warrant, and part of Guns N' Roses.

TRACII GUNS I mean, man, we were like fifteen years old. I still had braces on!

ROB GARDNER Tracii's dad had a plumbing shop over in the Valley, so we used to go over there and play after the shop closed. And then we'd also play at my house. We started writing songs, just me and him, and then we added a bass player.

TRACII GUNS The bass player was my friend Dani Tull, who also went to Fairfax, and then we got Mike Jagosz, who somehow Rob Gardner knew, to sing. We would ditch school and go to Mike Jagosz's house and play *Risk* and then rehearse and try to not get caught for ditching school.

ROB GARDNER Mike had a garage that was soundproofed. And his brother, Dave Jagosz, had a band called Shire that would play in there, and then we would play in there, too.

TRACII GUNS I went to see Shire play at the Roosevelt Hotel, and this guy Izzy was their new bass player. He had on a pink leather jacket and white cowboy boots, with dyed black hair. I could relate to that right away. I just figured he was a Mötley Crüe fan. So right after they got done playing I walked up and said, "Hey man, I'm Tracii." He said, "I'm Izzy." And it's like, "Okay, cool. We're buddies now!"

ROB GARDNER Back then he wasn't calling himself Izzy Stradlin yet. He was Jeff Bell, actually. He got rid of the "Is" [Stradlin was born Jeffrey Isbell] and just called himself Jeff Bell.

TRACII GUNS When I was about sixteen, Izzy moved into my mom's house and lived with us for, like, a year. And we always agreed that we liked Aerosmith and the Stones and the band Accept, but he turned me on to a lot of other stuff, like Hanoi Rocks and Girl with Phil Lewis . . . this kind of alternative rock scene. And I don't mean alternative music. I mean just the alternative to mainstream metal.

CHRIS WEBER I was looking for a band and Tracii introduced me to Izzy. I think I wanted to play with Tracii, but he said, "No, I'm sort of a one-guitar-player dude." But one night I was at the Rainbow, and Tracii was there with Izzy. They were outside in Tracii's dad's truck. Everybody that was under twenty-one kind of hung out in the Rainbow parking lot.

TRACII GUNS The Rainbow and the Rainbow parking lot were two different things. Inside the Rainbow was for scary people. The parking lot at one thirty a.m. was for nice rocker people!

KATHERINE TURMAN I started going to the Rainbow constantly when I was also sixteen or seventeen. We wouldn't even go to the Rainbow—we would go for the Rainbow parking lot. Then everyone hooks up or goes to an after-party.

CHRIS WEBER There'd be a couple hundred people finding someone to go home with, whatever. Everybody was just kind of easy and drunk. It wasn't a big deal, you know? HIV really wasn't around in that way yet.

But that night Tracii had probably said something about me to Izzy, like, "I wanna introduce you to this guitar player, his parents have a pad here, he's got gear . . ." Probably something that would've been pretty attractive to Izzy, who didn't have enough money to buy a drink at times. So Izzy and I meet, and he was talking about bands I hadn't even heard of, like Hanoi Rocks. I was like, "Yeah, whatever, that's great. Judas Priest and Rush and Zeppelin!" But he brought a different sensibility to it. It was like, here was somebody who seemed like they knew what they were doing. And he looked great.

IZZY STRADLIN (bassist, Shire; guitarist, Hollywood Rose, Guns N' Roses) I was seventeen when I came out to California . . . I grew up in Florida and moved with my mom to Lafayette, Indiana. I started pissing around with a drum set, met Axl, and we hung out a lot. It was nowhere. We decided to put a band together. It was a bad time, being there. The people, the girls, it was so backward. The girls didn't even know how to dress when they went to gigs! So the prospects were absolutely zilch. Axl and I were into anything that had a hard, loud beat. I think that's how we managed with all that was comin' down.

TRACII GUNS Izzy would always tell me, "You've gotta meet my friend Axl." Or, you know, Bill at the time. He would say, "You guys are gonna get along great. He can scream that way you like it and he's into Nazareth." He kept telling me he was into Nazareth. And I was like, "Yeah! I like Nazareth!"

IZZY STRADLIN The first thing I remember about Axl, this is before I knew him—is the first day of class, eighth or ninth grade, I'm sitting in the class and I hear this noise going on in front, and I see these fucking books flying past, and I hear this yelling, and there's this scuffle and then I see him, Axl, and this teacher bouncing off a door jamb. And then he was gone, down the hall, with a whole bunch of teachers running after him. That was the first thing. I'll never forget that.

BILLY ROWE (guitarist, Jetboy) Jetboy started to go to L.A. in '83, when I was still in high school. A friend of ours was super into W.A.S.P., but they hadn't played San Francisco yet. This is pre the first record. So one time we tagged along with her to see W.A.S.P. at the Troubadour. And there was this dude standing outside who had the look that we were all about, that rock 'n' roll trashy punk look. He was wearing all black, he was wearing the creepers, he had a black leather jacket that he had spray-painted pink with shoe polish. He just had that look that I connected with, that Hanoi Rocks look. And it was Izzy. And we started hanging out. We used to all hang out at Chris' parents' house.

CHRIS WEBER So I brought Izzy up to my house, I know that my mom called him Jeff, and we started to write some songs together. I don't remember exactly when this was, but I know that [Aerosmith's] *Rock in a Hard Place* was out, because I was really inspired by "Jailbait" for [the Hollywood Rose and eventual Guns N' Roses song] "Anything Goes." In the very beginning, me and Izzy were listening to that.

BILLY ROWE One album that Izzy used to listen to a lot was *Restless and Wild* by Accept. And if you listen to a lot of those songs on that record, especially "Fast as a Shark," you'll hear where Hollywood Rose and Guns

N' Roses probably got things like "Reckless Life." And Axl had that whole Udo [Dirkschneider, Accept singer] vibe. You never read this stuff, though.

CHRIS WEBER In any case, we wrote some songs, and the way I remember it is that Izzy said, "You know, my buddy's out here, he's a singer and I want him to sing for us." It kind of just became apparent that this guy Bill Bailey was going to be our singer.

TRACII GUNS For maybe six months, it was just, "This guy, Bill, you know, he's the man. And he's coming back and we're going to put the band together, we're going to be like Hanoi Rocks." I was like, "Great!"

CHRIS WEBER Axl had already been in L.A. with a band called Rapid Fire, but then I think he went home to Indiana for a little bit.

IZZY STRADLIN He came out like three times before he stayed.

TRACII GUNS So finally Axl came back out from Indiana, but he was staying with Izzy's ex-girlfriend, Jane, which was kind of a weird living situation because Izzy was living at my place. It was bizarre.

CHRIS WEBER You could tell that Izzy and Axl were on this sort of voyage together. That's what it looked like from the outside. I never really felt like I had that same relationship with them. Maybe it's because I'm from Los Angeles and they grew up in Lafayette.

LAURA REINJOHN Izzy and I picked up Axl at the bus station downtown, and we drove him back to the apartment he was staying at on Whitley. I cut his hair for the first time. He had this long red hair when he got here.

CHRIS WEBER One day Izzy brought me over to where Axl was living, on Whitley just north of Franklin. It was an old apartment with sort of a sliding elevator door gate. So we go up to the top and just sort of walk along the roof. And as I'm looking out over the rooftop I see this really white guy just laying out in the sun. It was a burning hot day and I just remember he was *very* white. And Izzy is like, "This is Bill!"

ROB GARDNER And then they did Hollywood Rose.

CHRIS WEBER The first band name was AXL. I don't know who came up with it. It wasn't me. Probably Axl. But you know, he wasn't calling him-self Axl yet. I don't think I ever called him Axl the whole time I was in a band with him. He was always Bill. So it was me, Izzy, and Bill, but then there was a small falling out and I remember Izzy telling him, "Look, let's get the band back together." But he said, "We have to change the name. I'm not gonna play under the name AXL anymore."

So then we were called Rose, but we would go to import record stores and we saw that there were other bands in other countries called Rose. So we changed it to Hollywood Rose. We would go back and forth between the names. It's very *Spinal Tap*.

20

"WE JUST MADE IT A FRIGGIN' PARTY"

BRET MICHAELS When you're coming from towns like Mechanicsburg and Butler, PA, and you pull into L.A. and there's umpteen billion people, it's a moment of going, "Holy shit, this is fucking awesome!" And a moment of "Holy shit, I'm looking at the Strip and there's gotta be 150,000 band guys walking around." You're not in competition with four other bands—you're talking about 40,000 other bands trying to make it.

RIKKI ROCKETT Kim Fowley, who managed the Runaways, was actually the person who prompted us to come out.

MATT SMITH We met with him our first night in L.A. He was even weirder in real life than he comes off in the movie about the Runaways. He wanted us to pretty much scrap the glam thing and do a *Road Warrior*-type theme. Sort of like armored suits, maybe.

BRET MICHAELS Kim and a bunch of other people took us to see Hollywood Rose in Chinatown. What would eventually become Guns N' Roses. It was a Monday or Tuesday night. To me that was awesome.

RIKKI ROCKETT We saw the genius in Kim and we listened to what he said and took a lot of what he said to heart, but then you could also see the craziness in him. That's the stuff where we'd go, "Yeah . . ." Then he tried to sign us to his little label. We're like, "Look we haven't even tried to shop for labels yet. Why would we do that?" When we said that we weren't willing to do that right away that's where he started getting really weird to us. He got kind of aggressive, actually.

BOBBY DALL When we pulled into town every band wore leather and studs, they were all trying to be the rudest, toughest, most manly band they could be. And we stuck out like sore thumbs because we were wearing what we've been wearing ever since we put the band together.

BRET MICHAELS We stayed at the Tropicana Motel, which was like the rock 'n' roll hangout. We played the Troubadour and the Music Machine, which I believe was with Siouxsie and the Banshees. At the Troubadour it was maybe a couple weeks after we got to L.A. We got thrown on as an opening act. You go on at six but the doors don't open until seven. It was one of those things. You were the first of four or five bands on the bill. There were a few people there.

JEFF DUNCAN (guitarist, Odin) I saw Poison's first-ever gig in L.A., at the Troubadour. We were there because we had a full-page ad in *BAM* and so we were taking all the *BAM* magazines and folding down the page with our ad because we had a gig coming up.

RIKKI ROCKETT It was just bizarre to me that in L.A., people would play once or twice a month maximum. Back east, we were playing every weekend, two or three nights a week, two or three sets a night. Here, people were playing one set once a month. How do you do that? Then we figured out that if we went to the outskirts, places like Covina, we could go play cover songs, make some money, and then come back to Hollywood and do what we did. Most people wouldn't make the connection. That worked for a while. We had other jobs, too—bit parts in movies or whatever, background stuff.

MATT SMITH I only worked for, like, two days, at a telemarketing place where we'd call and try to sell office supplies. And then I was riding my skateboard to work one day and I fell off the curb and I scarred my knee up really bad and I said, "I'm not coming back." Then, after a couple of months we met Vicky Hamilton, who became our manager.

VICKY HAMILTON I was just coming off managing Stryper, and after the whole Christian thing, a band named Poison seemed really appealing, you know? I've always kind of liked the girly boys.

RIKKI ROCKETT Once Vicky was in our lives, I felt like even at our worst I wasn't going to starve to death. Before her, I didn't know.

VICKY HAMILTON At that point in time they were not good musicians at all. They could barely play their instruments. I went home with them to Harrisburg for Christmas and they showed me these videotapes of when they were still called Paris and they were doing all these Mötley Crüe covers. I was like, "Uh, do not let *anyone* see these!"

GUNNAR NELSON (drummer, Strange Agent, the Nelsons; singer, guitarist, Nelson) They were all about attitude and about being the world's greatest party band. I remember being at a party and listening to Bret's demo on the porch and I thought, Oh my god, this is embarrassing. Then it turns out to be Poison. I mean . . .

VICKY HAMILTON They lived on North Orange Drive, in between Franklin and Hollywood Boulevard. Rikki and Bret had a room and Bobby and Matt and the roadies had a room. There was like a little card table and that was where all the dinners and all the business meetings went down, and Bobby was always the cook. It was just spaghetti. It was like a lucky day if they had garlic bread. Bobby and I wrote these proposals to get investors and they had put a hundred industry people's names and phone numbers on the wall, and a hundred girls' numbers. They were sure that whatever the scenario was, the answer was on that wall. Girls would call up and say, "Can I come over?" And they would say, "Ah, if you'll clean the apartment. Or bring us a bag of groceries."

BOBBY DALL Sure, we'd have girls buying our groceries, stuff like that. If they wanted to come hang out with the band and stay over at the house then, yeah, that's what it took. We were hungry. We'd get money from gigs, but we used that to keep the band going. We needed to eat . . .

RIKKI ROCKETT I think girls in that age group, they tend to mother a little bit. I honestly wish I could go back and thank every single person that did that because, shit, we wouldn't have made it without that help.

GUNNAR NELSON Mötley Crüe was trying to go after all the hot chicks, but Poison intentionally paid extra attention and were extra kind to the ugly fat chicks who actually were much more ardent fans. Those were the girls that, you just treat 'em with a little bit of respect, make them feel beautiful, and they're loyal like you wouldn't believe. Those girls were an army for Poison. It was the smartest marketing plan I've ever seen in my career, I can say that. It was genius.

VICKY HAMILTON With Poison, the first following was like the fat girls' club. There'd be a line of fat girls across the front of the stage. And then, like, the gay boys showed up. You know, there was a *Sex in the City* episode about, like, the fat girls and the gay boys? That was absolutely about Poison. Then the cool girls came, and then the guys came.

TAIME DOWNE (singer, Faster Pussycat; co-owner, the Cathouse) Poison always fucking put on a good show. They'd get the bitches at the show and that was basically, like, eighty percent of what it was about back when you were fucking twenty. The other fifteen was about the brews and the other 5 was about the music. Like, "I'm just gonna play fuckin' Ramones covers and have fuckin' fun," you know what I mean? You prioritize your shit when you're young. Put the pussy and booze first.

DON ADKINS I went to see Poison at the Roxy in '83, '84. They had the makeup and the hair and everything. And at the Roxy they were very accepted. Every hot girl in L.A. was just, like, getting wet over them.

BOBBY DALL If you were living in Los Angeles in 1983–84 like we did and you were a guy rocker, it was all about pussy. That's what it was.

VICKY HAMILTON I got them a couple of investors to put money into their clothes and their equipment and things and I made a deal with the Troubadour to have them play once a month. And the Troubadour paid their rent and their phone bill every month.

GINA BARSAMIAN (booking agent, the Troubadour) The Troubadour helped them a lot financially. But they had a good show. The music was very nice and they were very good at it. They were pretty boys in those days with their long hair and their makeup and everything.

RIKKI ROCKETT We had this whole idea that whatever songs we wrote we wanted them to be a soundtrack for our live show. If we were doing a show for Halloween, we would fully just focus on how to make a Halloween show. We'd create mic stands made out of broomsticks and everybody would come out with witch hats, and we'd have an intro tape of the theme song from *Halloween* and things like that. We were very themed out and into those things. Black streamers going out into the audience and spiders that people can rip off of them and take home. We just made it a friggin' party; our idea was to connect the stage with the fans.

BRET MICHAELS We moved into the back of a dry cleaner's all the way down on Washington and Palm Grove Avenue, which back then was a little suspect. Threw a mattress on the floor.

VICKY HAMILTON It was Keel's old rehearsal spot, and it was kind of dangerous. I mean, chicks were getting raped and all kinds of stuff. It was a horrible place. I was always afraid going down there.

RON KEEL We were out of there as soon as we got a record deal. It was a shithole. When you walked in there, there were swarms, *swarms* of cockroaches. I mean literally you were just fightin' them off, waving your hands in front of your face. They're flying cockroaches. It was not only dangerous but really filthy.

RIKKI ROCKETT We were pretty much the only white guys in about a fifteen- or twenty-block radius at that time. They were putting a club in called

TVC15 next door, and so we just started stealing wood, two-by-fours, paint. That's how we built that warehouse. The warehouse was just an empty vessel, basically. Then we built all the bedrooms and all that stuff. The only thing we ever paid for were studs to go into the concrete. We were little thieves.

VICKY HAMILTON They basically tied off sheets to divide their rooms.

BRET MICHAELS We spent one Christmas in there. We got this little tree and we sat there ripping up our flyers and making them into decorations for the tree. In many ways those were my favorite days for the band because it was that all-for-one time. We felt like it was us against the world, which sounds fuckin' corny but it's how it was.

RON KEEL I know Poison had even some rougher issues after we left in terms of guys breaking down the door and storming the place, assaults and things.

RIKKI ROCKETT Bobby Dall, me, a guy named Russ Rents who was one of our road crew guys, and I were confronted by four other guys who had weapons and had probably ten of them behind them. I thought I was going to die that night. Then the police actually came around the corner. The timing was impeccable, and they took off, but then they started throwing stuff through our windows. We got harassed to the point where it was really hard to live there.

BRET MICHAELS You have to survive. You have to eat. You have to have shelter.

DON ADKINS I think one thing I noticed . . . the really good bands that rose to the top, and I'm talking, you know, Mötley Crüe and Poison and a couple of others, they all had this one thing in common where, yeah, they were living the rock-star life, getting laid, having girls do all this stuff for them, but they were all really, really focused on making it. Absolutely driven. And that's the biggest thing I remember with Poison. They had this plan laid out. And they all wanted to take it to the next level and make it.

BRET MICHAELS We were workaholics with a dream.

"IT'S HARD TO BELIEVE, BUT AT THAT TIME JANI WAS REALLY KIND OF SHY"

MAX ASHER (drummer, Quest, Warrant) Me and Adam Shore, Warrant's original singer, were elementary school friends, and then in junior high, we had a band called Quest. In the beginning it was me, Adam on bass and singing, Scott on guitar, and then Rami Jaffee, who is in the Foo Fighters now, on keyboards.

RAMI JAFFEE (keyboardist, Quest, the Wallflowers, Foo Fighters) They were all one year older than me, so I was the underdog and super stoked to play with the dudes. I brought in cue cards from my dad's office to rehearsal with markers and tried different fonts to feel out if Quest was the right choice. I did the same when we changed it to Quadrant but was never really there when they went on to be Warrant.

MAX ASHER We played a graduation party because we were all leaving for high school, and we were planning on breaking up after the gig.

RAMI JAFFEE The set list, as were all of Quest's sets, was all covers. Mainly classic rock ranging from "Won't Get Fooled Again" and "Baba O'Riley" to newer bands like the Cars, Pretenders, and the Police.

MAX ASHER Adam saw a classified ad that was like, "*Randy Rhoads, Eddie Van Halen, whatever whatever, call me—Josh.*"

JOSH LEWIS I put an ad in the *Recycler,* which was a classified-ad magazine, and Adam Shore answered it. Then we set up a meeting, we were from the same neighborhood kind of, and he stole his mom's car to come pick me up. I think he got in trouble for it later.

MAX ASHER I came up with the name Warrant right around that time. We were huge Ratt fans, and the name Warrant comes from Warren DeMartini. I'm thinking "Warren" and "Warrant" and I pitch the name and everybody likes it.

WARREN DeMARTINI I remember that I was at the intersection of Franklin and Highland at a red light and this kid was putting up flyers on telephone poles and he's like, "Are you Warren DeMartini?" I said, "Yeah." He hands me a flyer and goes, "My name's Josh, I like your playing. I'm in this band Warrant and we named the band after you." I was totally blown away.

STEVEN SWEET (drummer, Plain Jane, Warrant) Jani Lane and I grew up in rural towns that were about forty minutes from each other in Ohio, south of Cleveland. The first time I met him was around 1982, long before we moved to Los Angeles and joined up with the guys who had started Warrant out there. He was playing drums in a band with my brother.

AL COLLINS (bassist, Plain Jane) The band was called Crack the Sky. They let Jani sing one or two songs from behind the drums. I was a fan, so I introduced myself to him at a show and found out he lived around the corner. I started going over to his house pretty regularly with my bass, and we'd do these epic bass and drum instrumentals in his garage.

STEVEN SWEET Jani was a good drummer—a natural player. He was one of those guys that did a little bit of everything. In high school, Jani was into musical theater and music, but he was also on the football team. He was, like, in the non-cool circuit and the cool circuit.

AL COLLINS We were in his house and there was an acoustic guitar in the kitchen. And he said, "Hey man, I've written some songs. You want to hear 'em?" So he played some songs for me, and I thought, Wow, these are really good . . .

JOHN MEZACAPPA (road manager, Plain Jane, Warrant) Jani's songs, even being raw, had amazing hook lines. You could imagine listening to them on the radio as you're driving down the road.

AL COLLINS I thought we should try to put a band together to do those songs, and that eventually became a band called Dorian Gray.

STEVEN SWEET I think we had like one rehearsal together with Jani singing, myself playing drums, my brother playing guitar, and Al Collins on bass.

AL COLLINS This was Jani's first attempt to come out from behind the drum kit. I don't think it lasted more than a couple weeks before he told us he wasn't ready and we needed to get a lead singer. So that's what we did. It's hard to believe, but at that time Jani was really kind of shy.

STEVEN SWEET I wound up graduating high school and I moved to Connecticut with my family. My brother stayed with Dorian Gray in Cleveland, playing the circuit there with Jani playing drums. They stayed there for a year, and then they moved to central Florida.

AL COLLINS We hired a singer that Jani really liked and started playing cover material. And then when the band told me they were moving to Florida, I left.

STEVEN SWEET I spent a year woodshedding in Connecticut, and Jani, who was in Florida, decided he was going to quit Dorian Gray to work on his own material and be a lead singer. He said he wanted me to be the drummer for that band.

AL COLLINS Jani called me up, asked if I could come to Florida and audition for his band. We decided to try to put another band together and do his songs with him coming out from behind the drum kit. He was ready.

STEVEN SWEET I had my drums already shipped out to Florida by freight, and the night before I was set to come down from Connecticut, Jani calls me and says, "Oh, we found another drummer, don't bother coming." I should have taken that as a real sign of his true colors, but I didn't. My brother, who happened to be visiting with me in Connecticut for Thanksgiving said, "Well, just keep your plane ticket, come down with me anyway. I'm sure you'll find a band in no time." I joined a band down there called Los Angeles, and after Jani saw us play, he realized that I was the drummer he actually wanted.

AL COLLINS We just worked day jobs and got this demo together, and then we decided to move to California.

STEVEN SWEET We were looking at *Hit Parader* and *Circus* magazines and all the bands that were getting signed were bands that we really liked, like Mötley Crüe, Ratt, and Great White, and we were just like, "Man, we ought to get out of Florida."

JOHN MEZACAPPA I had stayed back in Ohio, and Jani called me and said, "We're going to go to California and I'm going to put the band together, and I want you to put the crew together. Let's make it happen." That band was Plain Jane.

AL COLLINS I had an old Cutlass Supreme, like an early-'70s, mid-'70s vehicle that I had gotten from my grandmother. We pulled a trailer with that, and we broke down probably in just about every state. By the time we got to California, we didn't have any money.

STEVEN SWEET For the first week we wound up living off of baloney and bread sandwiches and sometimes just mustard; we'd get mustard packets from the drive-thru of a restaurant and just put it between bread, because it would keep in the dresser drawer of the hotel room.

JOSH LEWIS I never would have imagined that the original Warrant lineup, with all the success we were having, would soon lose two core members and have them replaced by a couple guys from Ohio.

"EVERYBODY WOULD BE THROWING UP, PASSING OUT, HALLUCINATING, OR BANGING OUTSIDE"

WARREN DeMARTINI Doug Morris told me he signed Ratt because of "Round and Round." He thought that song could go the distance.

STEPHEN PEARCY "Round and Round" was written in the living room at "Ratt Mansion West." A couple guitars, two tape decks, and me, Warren, and Robbin sitting around throwing ideas back and forth.

WARREN DeMARTINI I was refining that riff all the time. And then when we all lived together at Ratt Mansion West, I was practicing one day and playing the riff and Robbin and Stephen were like, "What's that?" And we just gathered around in a circle and in thirty minutes we had what you hear today.

STEPHEN PEARCY I had rented a one-bedroom apartment pretty close to the Strip, and me, Warren, and Robbin all lived there. So did all of our gear and a couple of our roadies. And we decided to call it Ratt Mansion West. People actually thought we lived in this huge mansion.

WARREN DeMARTINI It was this two-level apartment building in north Culver City that kind of wrapped around a crummy old swimming pool. And it was not unusual for it to be, like, two thirty in the morning and half of the Troubadour would show up. All of a sudden it's an after-party.

STEPHEN PEARCY They were just crazy parties, man. Anybody and everybody would show up—it could be W.A.S.P., it could be David Lee Roth, it could be Dio. I remember one time we had that mountain booze that's, like, 150 proof and that you could light it on fire and shit. What was it called? Everclear! We'd get some containers of that, do some fire tricks, pass that around, and by the time it got late everybody would be throwing up, passing out, hallucinating, or banging outside. If you wanted to be where shit was going down you either went to the Mötley house or Ratt Mansion West.

BOBBY BLOTZER We would party there all the time. Then they had chicks that would come over and bring them food and cook and all that.

STEPHEN PEARCY So we had "Round and Round" done in probably a day and a half at Ratt Mansion West. And then Beau got a hold of it and he went, "That's the first song you're gonna record." And it was, "Wait a minute, we've got heavier songs. We've got better songs . . ." "Nope. That's it. That's your song."

BOBBY BLOTZER We started recording *Out of the Cellar* in September of 1983 at the Village Recorder. We were in the big room, which Fleetwood Mac had spent two million dollars to completely remodel. It was insane.

BEAU HILL Everybody in the band hated me. Because Doug made it very clear that if I didn't do the record, they're not going on Atlantic.

JUAN CROUCIER We talked about different producers, but Beau Hill was Doug Morris' hot new producer.

WARREN DeMARTINI I remember it was like, "We think it would be great if you tried working with Beau . . ."

BEAU HILL On a visceral level, I felt bad for them because they were put in the position of having to trust a completely unknown quantity. And in all fairness and honesty, I was not a proven producer at all. I was still learning. I mean, I knew how to be in a band, I knew how to engineer, I knew the mechanisms of that stuff. But the subtlety and psychology of herding the cats was something that was on-the-job training for me, basically.

STEPHEN PEARCY [In the studio] I was always mojo'd down somewhere with somebody. In cupboards, in rooms closed up, under things. They had to look for me all the time, see where I was at. And then they'd find me and say, "Time for you to sing." I'd say, "Okay."

JUAN CROUCIER There were people coming and going, there were beautiful girls showing up, there was some partying, if you will. But 99.99 percent of the time we stayed really focused on making that record. I was generally easy to find.

WARREN DeMARTINI I remember that we finished the record, and then there was months of nothing, you know? It seemed like huge gaps of not much happening. Then suddenly we get a call that we have to be at this address downtown to shoot a video.

"POP SONGS WITH HEAVY GUITARS"

CARLOS CAVAZO The first single from the *Metal Health* album was "Bang Your Head."

SPENCER PROFFER I thought Quiet Riot's "Bang Your Head" could be an anthem for the time. But it was a bitch to get it played. I had to mortgage relationships in a couple of markets. I called program directors personally. And there were only four or five markets in the country that played "Bang Your Head." They put it on the air and within two to three days that record soared to be the most requested record on their stations. And that was the beginning. Then a guy I was socially friendly with named Les Garland became head of programming at MTV. Les called me up and he goes, "Hey man, you've got a really cool record happening in Texas and Oklahoma. Would you give me a video?" I said, "Sure."

CARLOS CAVAZO That was actually the first video we ever shot. It was filmed at some art college in Simi Valley. It was kind of a weird experience. I didn't know that MTV was even a big thing yet.

SPENCER PROFFER Les put it on the air at three in the morning, the phones went berserk. Four days later he moved it to midnight, the phones went berserk. Five hundred thousand units later my friends at CBS, they were my best friends, man. I couldn't do more for them!

FRANKIE BANALI After we started touring we came back to L.A. and did the video for "Cum On Feel the Noize." And that one busted the doors open.

RUDY SARZO MTV influenced *everything*. All of a sudden everything was image-driven. Even bands like the Police, they had so much talent but they were also very image-friendly. All you had to do was grab a camera and shoot those guys horsing around in the studio and you had a hit. For bands like us that were colorful and had a lot of personality, MTV was the perfect tool.

RICK KRIM (executive, MTV) It felt like it was something bigger and broader than an Iron Maiden video. Iron Maiden made some entertaining videos, but it wasn't for the masses, it certainly wasn't for girls. I've got to believe there was a good female audience who liked "Cum On Feel the Noize" and "We're Not Gonna Take It" and a lot of the stuff that was to follow. Because they were pop songs with heavy guitars.

FRANKIE BANALI Dee has been really complimentary about how he had heard "Cum On Feel the Noize" and that was in part how Twisted Sister developed "We're Not Gonna Take It."

DEE SNIDER It was totally influential. "Cum On Feel the Noize" was a big hit, and I said, "Let's steal the structure." Drum, chorus, song kicks in. Audience participation was always paramount to me. And not to take anything away from Frankie Banali, because he's a dear friend, but I wanted to next-level that shit.

TOM WERMAN Doug Morris, the president of Atlantic, called me at home. And he said, "I have this band that has had some success in Europe but I can't get arrested with them here, and I feel that you're the only guy who can make a hit with this band."

JAY JAY FRENCH We knew that Werman was there with us because Doug Morris said so, and Doug Morris was the key to the band's future.

Because you make Doug happy, you make it all happy. We all understood that.

DEE SNIDER Let it be known that when we were doing *Stay Hungry* I was in the studio fighting every day with Tom Werman to keep him from killing my band.

TOM WERMAN All I could figure out was that when I came into the picture, Dee had been working on the band for seven years, putting his heart and soul into it and getting nowhere, and so finally, I'm introduced into the picture, they have a huge hit, and I get the credit. And he's pissed. He's like Trump.

JAY JAY FRENCH Tom didn't like some of the songs that Dee wrote and wanted us to do Saxon songs. Dee always brings it up. "Motherfucker, he wanted six Saxon songs!" We had a fight.

DEE SNIDER He didn't want "We're Not Gonna Take It" or "I Wanna Rock" on the album.

TOM WERMAN I thought "We're Not Gonna Take It" was a little bit like a nursery rhyme.

DEE SNIDER I remember Tom's sitting in a folding chair in the studio, and I'm on one knee, because I'm trying to talk in his ear. I'm going, "Tom, trust me." He goes, "It's so, like, a kid song." I said, "It's going to be more aggressive when we record it." And literally, he says, "I don't care. If you want it on the record that bad, fine."

TOM WERMAN They claim that I didn't want to record it. That I wasn't going to allow them to record it. Producers don't have that kind of power. They hire *me*, for Christ's sake. The band is hiring you, they can fire you!

DEE SNIDER "We're Not Gonna Take It," the single, was released a couple of weeks before the video hit, and we had 145 radio adds the first week.

An incredible amount. But the video by Marty Callner was like adding rocket boosters, or fuel injection to a hot rod. No one had done anything like it before. And it showed the band. It was a game changer at MTV.

MITCH SCHNEIDER Marty Callner made everybody look like a fucking million dollars—better than they ever have in their life. He had done specials for HBO, and when he was shooting videos, he carried those lighting techniques into that. It looked cinematic because he was somebody who was shooting big-time shit.

DEE SNIDER Les Garland cut off the whole front end of "We're Not Gonna Take It." He said, "This isn't a rock video. This is method acting."

SPENCER PROFFER Quiet Riot went out on tour with Black Sabbath during the "Bang Your Head" period. Once the record went gold, we said, "Let's open it up, let's put out 'Cum On Feel the Noize.'" That record was a hit and we sold seven million albums. It kicked *Synchronicity* out of the top spot. It was the first metal record to hit number one. The record that nobody wanted to touch. And not only at the label—nobody in the entire industry.

FRANKIE BANALI November fifteenth was the day after my birthday and we were playing Rockford, Illinois. Before the show our manager came up to us in the dressing room and said, "We just got the *Billboard* numbers for next week and *Metal Health* is going to be number one. You'll be jumping over Michael Jackson's *Thriller* and knocking the Police's *Synchronicity* out of the top spot." We were dumbfounded. I mean, it went from absolute silence in the dressing room to us screaming and yelling and dancing like fools. And the guys in Black Sabbath came in with a case of champagne. And we drank the entire case.

CARLOS CAVAZO And then Sabbath start cracking open bottles and somebody had some cocaine and we're all fucking snortin' and drinkin'. And then we had to go on and do our show. I was like, "Oh my god, I can't even play right now!" I was stiff as a board. I had to drag my hand around that guitar neck. It was horrible. I never did that again.

ZAKK WYLDE (guitarist, Zyris, Ozzy Osbourne) I saw Quiet Riot open for Black Sabbath at the Meadowlands in New Jersey. And Quiet Riot, you would've thought it was their show. Without a doubt. *Metal Health* was *huge*. It was the height of the power of that record. When they played "Bang Your Head" the houselights went on, it was twenty thousand people with their fists in the air. When they got done playing, it was like you just witnessed the headliner. It was that crushing.

SPENCER PROFFER Then they went out on the road with Loverboy. And Loverboy was a huge pop band. So we opened up the demographic to an even wider audience. When the band got on pop radio they blew up big-time. But all of this was by design. Which is not to say I knew *how* big it would get. I just wanted to get it on the radio and make a dent. Who knew it would be the biggest debut rock record of all time until Guns N' Roses happened?

JAY JAY FRENCH Quiet Riot was responsible for all of us. The success of Quiet Riot allowed the success of everybody else.

DEE SNIDER The day *Stay Hungry* went platinum we were out in the Midwest somewhere. Y&T was our support, and I think Lita Ford was in there, too, underneath Y&T. Not literally—figuratively. But we were there at soundcheck and we were told the record was platinum. We just started doing this big sort of rumble with the band and crew, just going around chanting and screaming, "Platinum! Platinum! Platinum!" That was huge.

FRANKIE BANALI Everyone around us on the charts, it was Lionel Richie, it was the Police, it was Michael Jackson, it was everybody that had nothing to do with hard rock at all.

DEE SNIDER I remember getting a fan letter saying, "My favorite bands are Kajagoogoo, Duran Duran, and Twisted Sister." And I was like, "*Ruh-roh.*" That was a moment where we said, "This is wrong. These three names shouldn't be on the tongue of this fourteen-year-old girl." I was not ready for that.

JAY JAY FRENCH MTV did us the biggest disservice on the planet. It gave us this super-Technicolor, larger-than-life thing in America. And it was overwhelming.

RICK KRIM Twisted made enough entertaining videos. A lot of their videos had the same vibe to them, so I guess at a certain point it could be, "That's what Twisted Sister is." But that's what they wanted.

FRANKIE BANALI I mean, there just wasn't really any rock at the time, heavy metal, whatever you want to call it. There had been bands before us like Van Halen and Def Leppard, but there is no question that once the *Metal Health* record went to number one and the single was number five and we sold millions of copies—which was unheard of for most bands, and certainly at the time unheard of for a hard rock or metal band—we really opened up the door for everyone else. Because what happened is at that point, every manager, every accountant, every attorney, every booking agent wanted whatever was going to be the next Quiet Riot.

RIKKI ROCKETT Quiet Riot really, truly saved rock 'n' roll. A lot of people don't give them credit for that. Because at that time people were still stuck . . . They just wouldn't let go of the new wave stuff. But the hard rock, heavy metal, rock 'n' roll surge, Quiet Riot started that.

RUDY SARZO The '80s MTV generation hard rock and metal bands, at least the first ones, they were actually bands from the '70s. I mean, there was a version of Ratt named Mickey Ratt at the same time as Quiet Riot in the late '70s. Great White was there. The Dokken guys were around. Nikki Sixx was playing with London. So it wasn't like Quiet Riot made it big and all those bands like Mötley Crüe and Dokken decided to get together. We had all gigged together, and we had been through the same merry-go-round with the record companies, that whole "You guys are never going to make it." Right. Of course. But you know, we all just had to be ourselves.

DEE SNIDER Kevin DuBrow once said to me—we were having dinner together—"Don't you hate that these fucking bands, all these fucking bands, they're together a couple years, they get a deal, and they have an album and they're out on tour? Don't you fucking hate that?" I looked at him and I said, "Are you kidding? Kevin, I wouldn't wish what we went through on my worst enemy." He was shocked by my saying that. I go, "It took the fucking joy out of it for me."

24

"I BROKE NIKKI'S NOSE. I BROKE TOMMY'S NOSE. I PUNCHED POOR MICK JUST FOR THE HECK OF IT"

MIKE BONE *Shout at the Devil* was selling like gangbusters. I was the head of promotion at Elektra, and the guy who was my predecessor was this guy named Lou. One day Lou comes into my office and he goes, "Hey, Bone, look at this. This Mötley Crüe record just clicked past five hundred thousand. We've got a gold record here! We should go and show this to the band." I said, "Yeah, they're out on the road." They were in Binghamton, New York. Doc McGhee had them opening for Ozzy.

FRED SAUNDERS (tour security, Mötley Crüe, Bon Jovi) Because they were the opener it was absolutely crazy. They're on for forty-five minutes and that's it. The rest of the twenty-three hours and fifteen minutes of the day they wore me out just trying to keep an eye on 'em. But they did a lot of in-stores, a lot of promotional stuff. They worked a lot.

BRAD HUNT The in-stores were nuts. One of them, I think it was a Record Town, and by the time we got there the line was out of the mall. It's snowing like a mofo and these girls are standing there in torn sweatshirts in the snow because, quite frankly, one of the big things at a Mötley Crüe in-store, aside from buying the record and getting it signed, was to get your breast signed.

MIKE BONE That night we were in Binghamton, they were staying at some cheap motel, a Ramada Inn or something like that. And because we were the opening act we got back to the motel relatively early. There was a restaurant there, and Lou and I were gonna have a beer with the band and then get in our car and head back to the city. So we're having a drink, and while we're doing this buses are pulling up to the hotel, and they're dropping off all these ski people in their ski outfits who are coming from New York up to Binghamton. So now on one side of the room are the ski people with their knitted caps and everything, and on the other side is Mötley Crüe and their road crew and some groupies. And Vince has this girl at the bar, and he takes her underwear off and . . . Let's just put it this way, he used a longneck beer bottle on her. In the restaurant, in full view of everyone, including the skiers. This girl's friend was right there with her as this was going on, and she says, "I can't believe you're letting him do this to you!" And the girl looks at her friend and she goes, "I'm with Vince Neil of the *Mötley Crüe*!" I'm like, "Oh boy, let me finish my beer and get out of here . . ."

DOC McGHEE Listen, Mötley Crüe was this band that every day you apologize. It wasn't like, "Oh, geez, that's a surprise!"

FRED SAUNDERS When Doc McGhee offered me the job of security director he said, "These guys are so wild they need to be put in check." In fact, jokingly, he said, "I'll give you a bonus if you've gotta hurt 'em." I said, "You got yourself a deal."

DOC McGHEE Fred was a great security guard but *he* needed a security guard after ten o'clock at night. He turned into one of the dark angels as well.

FRED SAUNDERS Shit. Let's see here . . . Vince I beat up many times. I broke Nikki's nose. I broke Tommy's nose. I punched poor Mick just for the heck of it.

SHARON OSBOURNE Ozzy and Mötley together was just insanity.

OZZY OSBOURNE It was a band of lunatics on the road. Because they were just breaking through to a new audience. It was after the show that the mayhem started.

SHARON OSBOURNE It was a fuck fest. It was insane—Ozzy pissing on fucking cop cars and not realizing it's a cop car, you know, all of those things.

FRED SAUNDERS I can remember Ozzy climbing up over my balcony and coming into my hotel room with just a bathrobe on. And I was on the tenth floor! I remember the guys jumping into pools with their clothes on, standing there pissing in the pool . . . It was goofy stuff, you know? Just some guys trying to outdo each other.

NIKKI SIXX Ozzy is one of the sweetest men I've ever met. But when Sharon wasn't around, it was like a five-person gang. It was always like, "He topped us again."

SHARON OSBOURNE The guys in Mötley Crüe, I was like Debbie Downer because I would always try and get Ozzy away from them.

CARMINE APPICE (drummer, Ozzy Osbourne) Sharon wouldn't allow anyone backstage. So Mötley Crüe, they used to draw pictures of a limp penis and call it the "No Fun Tour." Because, you know, they're young, they're vibrant, they're ready to screw anything that walked and drink and do drugs and have a great time.

SHARON OSBOURNE I was like, "One of you guys is going to die and it ain't going to be my husband."

MICK MARS I remember Ozzy just had his daughter Aimee and I remember seeing her as a tiny, tiny little baby. Sharon had just had that kid when we were doing that tour. But Ozzy was still fuckin' up everywhere. He'd come up to our bus singin' "Iron Man" but he was singin', "I . . . am . . .

krelly man." And he'd have about half an ounce of cocaine in a baggie and he'd come on the bus and cut out a bunch of cocaine lines and stuff. We called 'em Texas power rails. And the next thing that I know is, I was going to my room, the other guys went to the pool, Nikki pissed, and Ozzy started snorting ants.

JAKE E. LEE I was there for the whole snorting-of-the-ants thing. I think my version's a little bit different than anybody else's, but I also was the only guy that wasn't drunk. I'll just tell you the way I remember it. We're at the hotel swimming pool during the day and Ozzy was there bragging about how fit he was getting. Because my martial arts instructor was out on tour with us as Ozzy's bodyguard and trainer. And I think it was Nikki who said, "Yeah? How many push-ups can you do?" And so they had a push-up contest. Ozzy did about three, I think. Then they had a sit-up contest. Ozzy lost that, too. Then Nikki said, "Well, let's change the rules." And Nikki was out there with a girl that he had met the night before. She was lounging in the sun and Nikki pulls his dick out and starts pissing. She didn't like it, she ran off. It was getting weird, because there were families out there at the pool.

OZZY OSBOURNE We would try and out-crazy each other. Why, I can't remember.

JAKE E. LEE Then Ozzy was sitting on the concrete and we were looking at him to see what he was going to do. And he had this funny look on his face, and that's when I could see that he was pissing in his trunks while he was sitting down. There's this pool of piss forming around him, and because he was quote-unquote in physical training, he must have been taking a lot of vitamins because I remember his piss was almost fluorescent. So Nikki's kind of looking at him, like, "I dunno if that beats me . . ." And then Ozzy got on his hands and knees and started licking his piss up. That's when I gathered my things and I said, "Okay, I'm out." And as I was walking away I saw him snorting something on the ground, which I assume was the line of ants.

If they did anything after that, I don't know and I kinda don't want to.

SHARON OSBOURNE A lot of it has obviously been exaggerated. But it was nothing new to me. It was like, "Been there, done that. Move on, kids." I was brought up at a time where there were real gangsters in the music industry, and people had guns and artists had guns and it was a much tougher business. I'd been around all of that and all the groupies and all the insane behavior. So it did nothing to me. It was just like, "Oh, fuck off." I was just trying to keep my husband alive.

DOC McGHEE If we went to a nice hotel, which never happened in the first five years—I mean, we never were able to stay in anything but a Howard Johnson—we had to put out cash. Otherwise they wouldn't even let us stay in the hotel, because the Mötley guys were funny guys. They didn't do stuff that was malicious, but they would trash stuff and not say anything and then we'd get the bill afterwards. I would always say, "Hey, if you smash something you have to tell us before you leave. Otherwise you have to pay double for it." So then I'd be getting calls at three o'clock in the morning from Sixx: "Put me down for a TV." "Put me down for a lamp."

BRAD HUNT I mean, the scenes in hotels were pretty wild. You learned after a point to try to not stay on their floor.

OZZY OSBOURNE Mötley Crüe were a force to be reckoned with back then. They were the heavy version of the glam rock kind of deal.

JAKE E. LEE But I don't think Ozzy was worried about it. Ozzy knew he was Ozzy. And all of the opening bands—Mötley, Ratt, shit, even Metallica opened for a while—pretty much worshipped Ozzy. I don't think he looked at them as any kind of competition.

FRED SAUNDERS As far as Mötley were concerned it was Ozzy's show. But in reality, you look at the merchandise and it was Mötley who were selling. Mötley merchandise was, like, twelve bucks a head at the time. It was amazing.

JAKE E. LEE The arenas were always full when Mötley went on. Nobody wanted to miss them. They had a great audience reaction. And definitely a lot more girls were interested in meeting Mötley Crüe after the show than they were in coming to the Ozzy bus. You could tell they were going to be huge.

CARMINE APPICE When those guys were on tour with us, they were on fire. They were out to *kill*.

BRAD HUNT They partied hard, no ifs, ands, or buts about it. But they were really hard workers.

MIKE BONE The Crüe, for all the stories—and god knows there's plenty of stories about them—it did not make a fuckin' difference. If you told them to be in the lobby at seven thirty a.m., they were there at seven twenty-five. If they had to go do a morning show at some rock radio station in order to sell tickets, they'd ride through the night and park their bus in the station parking lot and go in and rev up the morning DJs.

BRAD HUNT I remember every jock would say, "You can't swear on the radio." And of course, within the first seconds of the interview inevitably a "fuck" would come out of one of their mouths. But everybody loved 'em. I mean, what was not to love? They were fun on the air. They were a great interview. They were terrific.

OZZY OSBOURNE I was well established but Mötley Crüe were coming up fast. It was a good package. But it was one of the most dangerous tours I ever did. I said that to Doc one day, "It's getting so crazy . . ."

DOC McGHEE I don't think there was anyone in Mötley Crüe that went, "If we do this, that's going to be cool and people are going to . . ." You know what I mean? These guys weren't bad guys and they didn't do it to be rock stars. They did it because that's what they did.

BRYN BRIDENTHAL If bad is good, they were perceived as bad. Which turned out to be really good.

25

"I BELIEVE OUR BUS GOT CRABBED OUT"

MARSHALL BERLE I don't know if you know this, but when "Round and Round" was released as a single by Atlantic, we had promotion guys on it and we couldn't get arrested. We got a few spins here and there, but it was sort of dead in the water. But when that video came out, everybody jumped all over it and it just took off.

WARREN DeMARTINI We knew Milton Berle was going to be in it, and everybody was very excited to meet him. It was the juxtaposition of this total shoestring-budget video being made with this ultra, super-professional legendary TV superstar.

MARSHALL BERLE Funny story: I told Atlantic, "We gotta do a video." So somebody at Atlantic sent me to a production office in L.A. And I'm there talking to a bunch of English guys, and I say, "Why don't we get my uncle to be in the video?" "Who's your uncle?" "Milton Berle." And they go, "Who's *that*?" But we made that thing for under $25,000. We shot it in a day in a warehouse.

STEPHEN PEARCY The idea was "We're gonna build it around a dinner party, and the dinner party's gonna be invaded by rats." And we were the rats. Basically, the band would play, shit would fly, and Warren would fall out of the ceiling and land on the table. And Miltie, he was the funniest piece.

JUAN CROUCIER Milton took over. He was in drag, he was both husband and wife at the dinner, he started ad-libbing. We just let him roll with it.

STEPHEN PEARCY One of the directors was Don Letts from Big Audio Dynamite, right? The black guy with the real long dreads. Well, he thought he was just gonna tell Milton, "All right, you're gonna do this . . ." Milton stopped him and went, "I'm going to do what I want to do in this video." Don said, "All right, it's all yours." And walked away.

MARSHALL BERLE Milton was actually excited about doing it. Because he saw this as a new medium. I was telling him, "This is going to be the biggest thing. *Music videos.*" So he got excited. And he was very nice to all the guys.

STEPHEN PEARCY He'd look at me like, "What are you nuts, kid? You don't know about me? My nephew hasn't told you what I'm about?" I'd go, "Yeah, I know who you are, Mr. Berle." He'd be like, "Fuckin' rock 'n' roll faggots . . ." But it was all tongue-in-cheek.

MARSHALL BERLE I used to take the guys to Friars Club roasts, where Milton would be the MC. They got a big kick out of that.

WARREN DeMARTINI I remember meeting Tom Bosley at the Friars Club. I was a huge *Happy Days* fan.

JUAN CROUCIER We loved Milton very much. He had a heart of gold. He'd sit down with us and light up a cigar and start telling us stories about some of the people we'd heard rumors about. He'd go, "All right, lemme tell you a story . . ." And all of us would just riddle him with questions.

STEPHEN PEARCY I asked him if he banged Marilyn Monroe.

JUAN CROUCIER To be honest with you I don't remember that part. Maybe I was in the bathroom or something, I don't know.

STEPHEN PEARCY He said, "Of course!" He was proud! We actually tried to get him a hooker, or maybe a stripper. I don't think he went there, though.

JUAN CROUCIER So we released the video, it went onto MTV, and it was a whole new medium. Now you could not only hear the band—you could see 'em. So people throughout the greater United States could finally see what was happening in Hollywood. It really catapulted the band into a position of being able to actually get out there and do some great touring.

STEPHEN PEARCY You had to lock into one of these good tours. Mötley scored the Ozzy tour and then they moved up the ladder. They became an arena band. Who was next in line? Well, how about those Ratts? And sure enough, we got his U.S. tour, his European tour, and everywhere else. Then after that we opened for Billy Squier. And after that tour we were on our own. And we had a blast, man. We had a great time.

WARREN DeMARTINI We had a bus that we called the Free Bird, because it had a big bald eagle painted on it. We also called it the Rolling Hilton. And that was what we called home. We used that bus for, god, I can't imagine how many miles.

STEPHEN PEARCY Oh, shit. The Rolling Hilton was the ultimate party bus. We probably had more girls on there than guys. There was so much lingerie, panties and bras. We started hanging them up everywhere. You couldn't even walk through the place. But it started *really* stinkin', you know? Getting funky. We were all loving it but it got crusty after a while.

JUAN CROUCIER And what started out as six weeks turned into ten months before we came home. We'd do runs, I believe our longest run was twenty-three shows without a day off. So people started telling us, "Hey man, you guys are on the radio." And we'd be going, "Really? Because we're out here in Des Moines, just sitting in a hotel waiting to play."

STEPHEN PEARCY At some point we had to get a new bus, because I believe our bus got crabbed out. It had to be fumigated.

JUAN CROUCIER I mean, look, you've got a bunch of guys that are basically young, single men in their prime. A lot of testosterone, and a lot of very, very beautiful young ladies. It's a really simple equation, right?

STEPHEN PEARCY It wasn't the first bus that had been fucked up, I'm sure. But you'd be surprised who brought in those crabs. It wasn't us. It was other people who brought those things around.

BEAU HILL When I met those guys, they were all starving street urchins, and the first year, they went from zero income to declaring an income of 1.2 million each. In one year.

MARSHALL BERLE I think their look was one of the main contributors to their success. Stephen, I mean, he's a rock star. Just look at him. And all of them were into looking good. There was never a doubt in my mind, from the time before we made the EP, that they would be a big band. I knew it.

BOBBY BLOTZER Honest-to-god story, dude. At the end of the *Out of the Cellar* tour we came home . . . rich. Like, fucking filthy rich. Especially compared to what we were, which was filthy poor, you know?

BEAU HILL That's both good and bad. It's good because obviously they were enjoying some success. But some people are mature enough to be able to handle going, literally, from rags to riches, and others are not mentally prepared to deal with it.

STEPHEN PEARCY For me it was just the alcohol and the smoke. The booze. The girls. Those kind of "nature" drugs. But a little later you start meeting creepier people and then the other drugs start coming in. And everything's for free. So what do you do? Somebody gives you an ounce of blow, a big bag of pills, you don't know what it is. It turned into, like, CVS or whatever the drugstore is, you know?

BOBBY BLOTZER We had a hard time getting along. There was a lot of fun times, don't get me wrong. But there was also a definite struggle for power.

HEIDI ROBINSON FITZGERALD (publicist) There was definitely a vibe there: "It's all me. I'm the one." There were some members who had that a little bit more than other members, but I think that that gave them a really interesting dynamic.

NEIL ZLOZOWER I found with all the bands, whether it's Mötley, Ratt, Van Halen, when they're out there in the beginning they're all living in a one-bedroom apartment, they're all eating Taco Bell and McDonald's, they're all starving to death. They're all fucking the same girl and passing her around, maybe Robbin's got this chick, and two days later Juan's boning her, and Stephen will take over, whatever. Then, once the bands start getting money, that's when the egos and the jealousy and the animosity starts moving in. It's like, "Okay, I just got a Lexus," so now someone else has to go out and get a Mercedes. Or, "This guy's girlfriend has a thirty-six-inch bust, so I've gotta go out and buy my chick a forty-inch rack." Or, "He's got a three-bedroom house in Encino, well, I gotta go buy a five-bedroom house in Beverly Hills." That's when the band starts drifting apart and things start going to shit.

BOBBY BLOTZER I was the first person to buy a house. First person to buy a brand-new car. That red Trans Am in the "Back for More" video that Warren drives away in? I bought that the day before the shoot. But we had just sold four million records, we had a record deal for five records. So I bought a house, I bought my mom a brand-new car, I bought her a house, too. It was that sort of thing. It was surreal, man. Unbelievable.

26

"GEORGE AND DON HATED EACH OTHER ... *REALLY* HATED EACH OTHER"

GEORGE LYNCH For the "Breaking the Chains" video, I remember the director or somebody else on the crew saying, "Yeah, we have these ideas ..." And one of the ideas in the storyboard was to put these little chains on my guitar instead of strings, you know, because the song was called "Breaking the Chains." They were just riffing. So, yeah, it was great. People remember it!

DON DOKKEN The bummer was we had what they call a "passive hit," apparently. Everybody in the country was playing the song "Breaking the Chains," it was getting Top 20 requests on the radio. But we didn't sell any records. Because Elektra didn't believe in the record. They only printed, like, a hundred thousand copies. That hundred thousand copies sold and when they were out of the record they didn't make any more of them. So now they're like, "Wasted money." You know? "Let's drop Dokken." But we convinced them to give us one more shot. That's why I came up with the title *Tooth and Nail*.

CLIFF BURNSTEIN When it came time to make *Tooth and Nail* it would have been me who would have said, "Let's bring in an A-list producer." And Tom Werman was an A-list producer at that time. He had made some big records in the late '70s—Ted Nugent, Molly Hatchet, Cheap Trick—and he had just produced Mötley Crüe's *Shout at the Devil.*

TOM WERMAN George and Don hated each other . . . *really* hated each other. It was weird. I would let them just fight it out. Basically the guys in the band didn't like Don's songs. Don liked "Alone Again" and they wanted to rock! Don wanted to be a crooner.

DON DOKKEN They were totally against "Alone Again." Period. "Not gonna happen," they said. I said, "Who made you guys king? The band's called Dokken, and you guys just can't arbitrarily vote what we're going to put on the record." I had three songs that were going to go on the record. They wanted to kill them all. Because George wanted all his songs on the record. Typical band infighting. And I actually threatened, I said, "I'm quitting. It's over. You guys are fired, I'm leaving."

CLIFF BURNSTEIN Today, if I knew how bad the situation was between two band members like it was with Don and George, I would probably have the conversation up front and say, "Unless I can solve this to my satisfaction right now, I'm not interested." Back then, much younger and with lots less experience, I might have thought, I'll figure out a way of dealing with it. But now I know that there are some things that are so deep-seated that even if you're an expert in human psychology or behavior, there's not much you can do about it.

DON DOKKEN Tom Werman negotiated it for us: "Don has three songs on the record, you gotta at least let him have one more song on the record." And of course at this time, you gotta remember, on the radio all the bands were doing ballads. Def Leppard, Journey, they all had singles out that were ballads. But George saw us as being a metal band. Which we weren't. Because I'm not a metal singer.

"WILD" MICK BROWN Tom Werman confused us completely because, as far as I could tell, he didn't do a goddamn thing! Basically he was on the phone the whole time, talking to someone else about a trip he was going to take to Hawaii with his family or whatever. We'd end the track and we'd look up at the booth. "How was that?" And Werman, he'd get off the phone real quick and he'd go, "Um, yeah, that was good for me. Were you guys in tune?" He wasn't even listening! It was very strange for us.

CLIFF BURNSTEIN I think I started getting calls pretty quickly from one person or another saying that they didn't like Werman and that he didn't seem particularly engaged in the process. My response to that always was "Look, guys, he did all these great records, and they're all fucking hits and maybe this is his method!" I don't fucking know. I never made a record with Werman before, so how the fuck would I know? If he has success, and his method of getting success is pretending like he's not really engaged, then fine! I don't care, okay? Go with the guy . . . He's had more hits than you have, that's for goddamn sure! That would have been my response for whoever was calling me with this stuff, and it might have been Don, it might have been George, it might have been both of them, it might have been Mick. Who knows? It might have been all of them calling me separately or together, but I would have said, "Who are you to say?" Werman's the guy who has the fucking multiplatinum records on his wall.

GEORGE LYNCH One of the things that was really strange is he brought in a truckload of video game machines, and he encouraged us to play them a lot, saying it would relax us in between takes. He'd get on the mic and he'd say, "Okay, guys, take a break, go play some video games. You look tired." And he actually had one of those change things on his belt! So he'd make change for us. He'd tell us, "Make sure you have your dollars. I can change ones, fives, whatever."

TOM WERMAN That is stunning. Just unbelievable. I don't even know if they had any games there or where they would have been.

"WILD" MICK BROWN We were in good hands, though, because we had Geoff Workman, and he oversaw it all. But, goddamn, he would come in with a case of beer that he already drank six of, throw those in the fridge and a magnum of Jack Daniel's. Every day he carried a case of beer with the magnum of Jack on top. And he would snort blow from this little . . . well, not a little ball, a big ball, and then drink Jack. I guess the beer was to get it going in the morning. Then it was Jack for the rest of the night. And blow.

TOM WERMAN I only worked with Geoff Workman as my engineer for three albums—*Shout at the Devil, Tooth and Nail,* and Twisted Sister's *Stay Hungry*. He was a divisive, evil alcoholic.

JOHN AGNELLO (assistant engineer, Twisted Sister, *Stay Hungry*; producer) I was the assistant engineer on Twisted Sister's *Stay Hungry* and just loved Geoff Workman. He was this giant hunchbacked British guy with crazy teeth who was a great engineer and just so good with the bands. But he was also really nuts. He would drink like a bottle of Jack Daniel's a day, which was phenomenal. At one point we hooked up a bottle of Jack to an IV to an Atlas microphone boom stand and he just walked around the studio with it because he thought it was hilarious.

TOM WERMAN What he did with Dokken was that he secretly recorded my conversations . . . my speech in the control room, and then edited it into a different meaning. You know? He used hours and hours of it—he was very good, *a very good engineer*—and made it sound like I was gay and wanted to fuck the band.

DON DOKKEN Yes. When Geoff Workman first started the record, we were recording Tom talking and they just kind of edited this whole thing of, like, hours and hours of footage where, like, let's say they'd say, "Oh, you know that chick, Tom? Would you like to fuck her?" And he'd go, like, "Yeah, I'd love to fuck her," you know? Geoff would record that and cut it. And then Tom, maybe down the road he said, "So, anyway, about you guys . . ." Geoff would record it and go back and put in the words "you guys." So it would say, "Yeah, I'd love to fuck . . . you guys." Why'd they do all this? Well, they did all this because they were all doing coke. Geoff Workman was an infamous coke addict. He did a ton of coke, Jack Daniel's, he was fucked up from the day . . . He was *always* fucked up. So they'd sit up after a session at night and spend hours and hours and hours with this footage to make it sound like Tom was talking about how he wanted to have sex with George. But beyond that tape, George was really,

really difficult in the studio. Everything Tom asked him to do, maybe try this solo again, maybe do this, George basically shot him down. He'd just argue with him incessantly.

TOM WERMAN Geoff played the tape for George, and George flipped. And I didn't know any of this. George had already done the lead break on "Tooth and Nail" . . . and it was a piece of art. An unbelievable solo. And we were doing another song and he was just shredding but not going anywhere. And I said, "You know, George, I love the 'Tooth and Nail' solo. It went from point A to point B and it really had something to do with the song and it was musical and it lifted it and pushed it along. Could you come up with something a little more substantive like that?" And he went crazy and threw his guitar down on the floor and he had a little fit.

"WILD" MICK BROWN I guess George bought into it. Which sounds weird to me because he's a prankster as well. And so they got in an argument and George goes, *"Listen, you sonofabitch, you cocksucker"* something or other! He called Tom every ugly name. And Werman had no idea. He was like, "What the hell is he talking about?" It was hilarious. I guess it really got out of hand.

TOM WERMAN So I went out in the studio and I said, "George, you seem to be pretty angry, would you feel better if you could hit me? Do you want to hit me? I'll give you the first shot." He was tough, but this line works a lot.

GEORGE LYNCH Yeah, it wasn't a huge blowup. I think it had culminated in that . . . because what Tom kept coming up to me and doing was telling me that I should play more like David Gilmour. He was like, you know, every day, "Yeah, that fast shit, nobody wants to hear it. Just give me a *bawrn na na . . .*" Over and over again. And I'm thinking, We're paying you a lot of money. I don't need you to tell me to go *bawrn na na . . .* I know how to do that all by myself. That's not valuable input.

TOM WERMAN It came to a standoff and I said, "You know, I think you'd be better off if you finished this record with somebody else." And I walked out and called the manager and said, "I'll give you a point back." And that was that.

CLIFF BURNSTEIN I never heard this story. Oh, god . . .

"WILD" MICK BROWN Listen, we just pissed our pants. It was funny to me but I was horrified. I was very young and very naive and trying to be real serious. And between all this pranking shit going on I was like, "Wow, is anyone paying attention to our band?"

CLIFF BURNSTEIN I'm not sure how the record got finished. I let Zutaut take care of it. Zutaut brought in Roy Thomas Baker.

MICHAEL WAGENER I just got called by Elektra, or actually by Don, because they needed to mix the album and they had Roy Thomas Baker, who was at Elektra. He had a position at Elektra, vice president of production or something. It was actually a position that didn't exist, one of those. He decided that he was going to mix it, and then Don insisted that I would be there along with Roy to mix the record. Maybe I was a little bit of Don's security blanket.

"WILD" MICK BROWN So Roy Thomas Baker comes in, and it's Roy Thomas Baker, man! We're all like, "*Wow!*" He's very polite. He does this mix and he turns and he goes, "So, this is what I think you sound like. I want you to listen to it and give it some thought. Tell me what you think." So we listen and then everyone's going to each other, like, "I *hate* this fucking mix. We sound like the goddamn Cars, man." So Jeff and George told me, "You're gonna have to tell Roy Thomas Baker that we have to fire him." And I'm like, "*What?* You can't tell Roy Thomas Baker that you have to fire him!" And they go, "Well then tell him his mix sucks." So the next day I said to Roy, "Listen, we discussed it and we're not happy with the direction of the sound." And he goes, "Ah, that's what I thought you'd say. You're a guitar band and you'll probably sell eight hundred thousand as opposed to three million. But, okay." And he just backed right off of it.

MICHAEL WAGENER Roy and I mixed the first song together and then the band came in and didn't like it. It was very poppy in a way and then Roy just pulled all the faders down and goes, "Just do what you always do with those rock bands." And then he left. And then that was it and I was basically mixing the record.

"WILD" MICK BROWN So he was gone. Out of the project. So, really, we paid him a fortune just to mix one song. And we marched on.

DON DOKKEN Roy was very eccentric. He had two Rolls-Royces, a black one and a white one. So he'd show up in the daytime in his white Rolls-Royce and he'd wear a white suit. Then he'd have to leave at six to go have dinner. He'd go home, get his black Rolls-Royce, and put on a black suit.

"WILD" MICK BROWN He had a plexiglass piano that recorded itself when you played. Back then it was the highest-tech thing. And his house was really neat. He had a pool in his backyard that looked like it came out of Disneyland, with one of these slides that went around.

DON DOKKEN I met Freddie Mercury because I went over to his house one day, looked at the pool, and, lo and behold, there's Freddie Mercury laying by the pool, you know? Laying out in the sun. And I'm like, "Holy shit . . ."

"WILD" MICK BROWN And there was always these young girls hanging around. George was like, "Jesus Christ . . ." And there was a little jam room. So we'd play drums, play guitar, and there's Roy Thomas Baker, going down the slide. You had a pretty big day at the Roy Thomas Baker house!

DON DOKKEN When it came out, *Tooth and Nail* just barely, barely crept to gold. And we toured for sixteen months. We could never get that Top 5, Top 10 hit. We were definitely the band that just stayed on the road and toured and toured and toured until we just fell down.

"WILD" MICK BROWN We had a video camera on the bus that was filming girls in the back lounge. You could tape it in the front with a VHS. Then you could call back: "No, no, move her butt to the left a little bit . . ." The first time we had a black-and-white camera.

JAY JAY FRENCH Dokken opened for us after *Tooth and Nail* came out. There was blow jobs in the back lounge with cameras stuffed in speakers so you could watch the girls giving head in the front. It was total rock 'n' roll debauchery.

"WILD" MICK BROWN It got around and other bands would go, "I wanna go make a video in your back lounge!" Well, come on in! We did, like, six months with that camera on the bus. And it's always just horrifying as well. Because your girlfriend would be sitting in the front of the bus! And the girl would go, "Well, I would never do that with these guys . . ." And then she's in the back doing . . . a lot of weird things! And the girlfriend's watching it on the video monitor in the front of the bus going, "Oh my god!" It was kind of rude but these girls just wanted to have fun. It was hilarious . . . and then it got to be disgusting. So then we got a color camera and a little more high-definition. Well, that was a hit, too!

DON DOKKEN The first single that came out from *Tooth and Nail* was "Into the Fire." Then we did "Just Got Lucky." But then the same thing—the album wasn't taking off. It hadn't gone like everybody else had, with their multiplatinum record. By then, you know, Ratt's playing the Forum, they've got a huge hit. Mötley Crüe's taking off. Everybody's taking off, and we're just kind of eking our way out on tour and we're up to a couple hundred thousand records sold. *Again.* And I'm like, "Fuck." So I begged and pleaded to put out "Alone Again." I really had to fight the fight. Nobody wanted to do it because there was no money. The label didn't want to spend any more money on us. So we ended up playing the Palladium and we hired Wayne Isham. He said, "I'll bring in a couple guys cheap, with some sixteen-millimeter cameras." That's why, if you look at the video, it's live. We played "Alone Again" and they filmed the show and it became, like, a standard. And then, finally, we hit it with our next albums, *Under Lock and Key* and *Back for the Attack*. And the rest is history. We just took off. But it was a long, hard fight.

27

"GUNS AND ROSE"

ROB GARDNER Hollywood Rose's drummer used to go MIA. They wouldn't know where he was. So I used to fill in with them all the time. Because I just knew the songs. But I wasn't a permanent drummer for them, because I had my thing with Tracii.

TRACII GUNS Okay. So the next step was changing the name of the band from Pyrrhus to L.A. Guns. I loved the name Hollywood Rose, you know? And I had this girlfriend, Dina, who would call me Mr. Guns all the time. And then my friends started calling me Mr. Guns. And so I became Tracii Guns.

And then one day Izzy and I were at my mom's, and I took a black vinyl album cover and used a stencil to draw up an L.A. Guns logo. And I showed it to Izzy. I go, "Hey man, is this cool?" And he looked at it, like, "L.A. Guns?" I said, "Yeah. I wanna change the name of my band to L.A. Guns. Like Hollywood Rose." And he goes, "That's awesome!" That was, like, a two-minute conversation. And L.A. Guns was born that day in my mom's living room.

CHRIS WEBER Hollywood Rose played the regular Hollywood places. There was the Orphanage, which was our first gig [in January 1984], there was the Troubadour, there was Madame Wong's West . . .

TRACII GUNS Izzy said, "Do you guys want to play with us at Madame Wong's West?" I was like, "Sure, let's do a gig together." And so we were down there during the day, pulling our crap in for soundcheck, and there's Axl by himself at the microphone, just wailing. I'm like, "Holy shit, that guy can sing!" That's when I wanted to be close to Axl, when I saw him sing like that.

CHRIS WEBER Then Hollywood Rose played a show with Stryper at the Music Machine. The way I remember it is something happened onstage, I think I swung around and hit Axl with the top of my guitar. My memory was that he was pissed off. And I wouldn't be the first person to say that Axl's got a relatively unique ego. It could be easily damaged and easily inflated at the same time. Anyway, nobody got fired, but we kind of disbanded.

TRACII GUNS Somehow Chris Weber was out of the band and then Slash was in the band. And it was funny because nobody knew that we were friends. But they decided Slash was playing guitar for Hollywood Rose. And, you know, cool-looking man, obviously. So that happened.

STEVEN ADLER (drummer, Road Crew, Hollywood Rose, Guns N' Roses) Me and Slash, we were walking down Sunset Boulevard and we saw this one flyer and it just stood out . . . The singer and guitar player, they just looked so cool. It was Rose. Hollywood Rose. It was Axl and Izzy. And we went into Gazzarri's and we watched them.

MARC CANTER Slash and Steven had known each other for years. He was his friend from Bancroft Middle School. They lost touch for a few years after that but then Steven eventually wound up playing drums in Road Crew. And then Duff was in Road Crew for, like, a week, when he first got into town from Seattle.

DUFF McKAGAN (bassist, Road Crew, Guns N' Roses) I moved down to L.A. in September of '84. As a punk kid from Seattle, it was total culture shock. Of course I knew about, like, Eddie Van Halen and that kind of guitar playing. And I knew that first Mötley record they had put out themselves. But moving here and seeing all the flyers on the telephone poles and shit . . . it was a lot of bands, a lot of long hair, a lot of *outfits*, you know what I mean?

MARC CANTER Somehow he answered Slash's ad in the *Recycler* and they started jamming.

DUFF McKAGAN He had this ad that said, "Influences: Fear, Aerosmith, early Alice Cooper." And his name was Slash. So I thought he was a punk rock guy like me. I called him up, we talked on the phone, totally cool guy. Then I went to meet him and Steven at Canter's Deli. He said, "We'll be in the left booth at the end." So I look in the left booth and there's, you know, basically all this fucking hair! But also, I was wearing like this long red-and-black, like, super-fly pimp jacket with an anarchy A on the back of it, and I had short blue hair. So I'm sure they're looking at me and going, "Huh?" Slash's girlfriend at the time, she was a very out-front kind of girl, and she goes, "Are you gay?" I'm like, "No, I'm not gay." She goes, "Okay, well, maybe we can find you a girlfriend."

We ended up that night going back to Slash's mom's house. We're hanging out in his room in the basement and drinking vodka and he starts playing guitar. And I'd never been in a room with a guy my age who played guitar like that. But the Road Crew thing, there was no singer, and they're like, "Maybe you can sing . . ." But I had already moved away from home, I was ready for the next step. I wasn't going to play with some guys who just got out of high school the year before and had a bunch of riffs. Even if they had a fucking guitar player like Slash.

MARC CANTER Slash could never find a singer that was good enough to start playing real gigs at the Troubadour and stuff like that. So he realized he was going to have to pluck one out of a band that was already established. And Rose was already playing gigs, or Hollywood Rose—I guess it kind of went back and forth between the names. So I went with Slash and Steven to Gazzarri's. I think it was a battle of the bands, it was like a dollar to get in and Rose only played three songs. All I remember is Axl was good and Izzy was good.

STEVEN ADLER I said, "If we get that singer and that guitar player and a great bass player, we will have the greatest fucking band ever."

MARC CANTER Right after that Rose gig at Gazzarri's Slash joined up with Axl. And then they got Steven Adler in the band, and this guy Steve Darrow to play bass.

STEVE DARROW (bassist, Hollywood Rose) I had been playing with a band called Kery Doll, and I remember hearing Hollywood Rose had another gig booked for later in the month, probably at the Troubadour. So I saw Izzy one day and I said, "How's it goin'? I heard you got another gig booked." He goes, "What are you talking about? You're playing it! You wanna play bass for us?" So I basically faded out of Kery Doll and faded into Hollywood Rose.

We started playing, and Slash at that point was kind of a shredder. He had the B.C. Rich with the tremolo bar and he was doing a lot of dive bombs. But then he could also play the Joe Perry stuff and that kind of bluesy rock. And Steven had his double bass kit. He was really flashy and showy and had a lot of cymbals, a lot of drums. But at the same time Axl would be like, "We worked out a version of 'Honky Tonk Women' . . ." trying to get more of that sort of rock 'n' roll into the metal stuff.

SLASH There was Izzy and Axl, and then there was Steven and I. And then there was us in different combinations. We weren't ready, though, and it didn't last long.

MARC CANTER And then Izzy kind of walked away from it. Maybe he made it to one rehearsal and then he was gone. He left and joined the band London.

STEVE DARROW It was one of those weird things where Izzy was there and the next time he wasn't. And then Axl was a little bit more involved in the way things were going than the way things were before. And then it also was the beginning of Izzy's drug time. He started hanging out with different people and his priorities were more in that unfortunately. So anybody who wasn't really directly involved in either making him a rock star or buying drugs was sort of low priority in his life.

MARC CANTER Izzy . . . I was less than thrilled with Izzy. For that reason only.

CHRIS WEBER I don't think I even remember Axl or Izzy getting drunk when I was in the band. I don't think they could afford it, to be honest with you.

TRACII GUNS I mean, I guess Izzy was always really curious about heroin. He had a girlfriend at one point that was doing junk. But it was very mysterious to him. One time my mom found some books at the house that Izzy had gotten from the library about heroin. She brought it up to me and I went, "Ah, he's a smart guy, he's just checking something out . . ."

MARC CANTER After Izzy left it was almost like a new band. I think they actually changed the name from Hollywood Rose to the New Hollywood Rose. Because it was just Axl from the band, and then Slash and Steven came in together and they found a new bass player. But that version of Hollywood Rose only lasted for about three months. They had like four or five gigs, a couple of rehearsal parties, and then it kind of fell apart. And then Axl went ahead and joined Tracii in L.A. Guns.

TRACII GUNS My manager, this guy Raz, fired Mike Jagosz because he was being a dummy or something. And then I just hit up Axl. "Hey, you wanna be in L.A. Guns for a while?" And he said, "Yeah." We did that for a solid nine, ten months before we finally did the gig with London.

MARC CANTER I went to see L.A. Guns when they were opening up for London at the Troubadour. And Axl was upset that London somehow screwed them over.

TRACII GUNS Axl swore he saw Nadir [London singer Nadir D'Priest] detune my guitars before we went on and all this shit. Which makes sense because when I went onstage all my Les Pauls were completely out of tune. Like, four notes down on every string. So he made a big stink about that.

LIZZIE GREY Axl hated Nadir.

MARC CANTER He vented about it during the gig. And then he tore up a London poster onstage. But that's Axl. Axl will say what's on his mind.

DUFF McKAGAN I saw that show at the Troubadour. Slash took me. And the thing about Axl, I'd seen so many shows by this time. My old band, 10 Minute Warning, we opened for Black Flag when it was Henry Rollins' first show with them in Seattle. And Henry was the most intense dude I'd seen. I saw him before the show, like, stretching out in his little short dolphin shorts, not talking to anybody, super intense. Ready to fight. And when Axl came out onstage at the L.A. Guns thing I saw that same intensity, but kind of more fucking unhinged. It was *real*. And the guy was hitting these notes . . . I'd never seen anything like Axl.

TRACII GUNS Izzy quit London after the Troubadour show. Because he didn't want to be associated with that.

MARC CANTER Then Izzy booked a New Year's Eve show at a club called Dancing Waters in San Pedro. They were going to put Hollywood Rose back together.

STEVE DARROW That was one of Izzy's "book a gig, get a band together later," kind of moves. He asked me to do it and I said, "Sure." And he had asked Axl and he actually said no at one point, because he was still in L.A. Guns. But then he convinced him later on and he said yes. And then they asked Slash.

CHRIS WEBER If I remember right, Slash was working at Tower Video or something like that and couldn't get off for the show. So they called me to fill in.

STEVE DARROW Slash had a job at Tower Video, and Axl had worked there, too, around the same time, behind the counter. And Slash couldn't get the night off. Even though it was New Year's Eve he had to work until midnight. He was a responsible employee, I guess. So Izzy reverted back to Chris Weber. And then I don't know how Rob Gardner came into it, probably because he was playing with Axl in L.A. Guns at that point.

MARC CANTER So Hollywood Rose did that gig, which was a one-off. And I guess they wanted to continue with it but they just couldn't figure it out exactly. And maybe they didn't want Chris Weber. I'm not sure what happened. But the next thing I knew Axl had put together a band with Tracii.

TRACII GUNS Axl had actually been fired from L.A. Guns by our manager, Raz. He was just like, "I'm not going to deal with you anymore." And so then we got Mike Jagosz back for a second, which is probably when that Hollywood Rose reunion happened.

But at that time, Axl and I were attached at the hip. So we decided we were going to continue playing together, we just had to figure out in what configuration. And then I was like, "Well, Izzy's not doing anything, why don't we just add him to the band?"

The initial idea with Axl was "Hey, let's just write and record and we'll go out and play new songs." And somehow we came up with the name Guns and Rose, which was just his last name and my last name. And then within five minutes Axl's like, "Nah, man, Guns and *Roses*." And I'm like, "Yeah, that's a *great* band name."

28

"FOR ONE THING, WE NEVER WORE ANY FUCKING LIPSTICK!"

TOM KEIFER We were playing at a place in Philadelphia called the Empire, and Jon Bon Jovi was in town working on *7800° Fahrenheit* at the time and walked into the club and saw us play. I think some people look back and they look at Jon and say, "Oh, multiplatinum artist went in and waved the magic wand and got Cinderella a record deal." He wasn't a multiplatinum artist at the time. But he did tell Derek Shulman at PolyGram that we were worth checking out, and I'll be forever grateful for whatever words he uttered, which eventually—and I say eventually—led to a record deal. Because Derek came down and saw the band.

DEREK SHULMAN (executive, Mercury/PolyGram Records) I went down to see the guys and Thomas was superb, as was Eric. But they had a couple of other guys who weren't superb. And I told Larry Mazer that the songs were great and Thomas was a fantastic guitarist and a great singer, but the band was not quite up to snuff . . . and that if he could get a new guitar player and drummer, I'd be very interested in doing something.

LARRY MAZER Derek basically sat with Tom and he said, "Look, I want to be honest with you. You're a star. Eric's great. I don't buy Tony Destra and Michael Kelly Smith. Here's what I'm willing to do. I will sign you. I will give you $25,000 for three months, but you need to get rid of those two guys and replace them and show me that it's more of the band that I want to be involved with." This was a mega moment, because Tom had known these guys for almost his entire life.

TOM KEIFER The only way I can put it is that if I had disagreed with the criticisms, I wouldn't have let them go. But let's just say there were musical differences before Derek ever came into the picture. And it was still a very hard decision. And to their credit they went and started Britny Fox and they did well for themselves, too.

BILLY CHILDS (bassist, Britny Fox) Britny Fox were modeled on Cinderella. We did step right into their spot. We had a buzz because we had two of their original members. We had Michael Kelly Smith and we had Tony Destra. I mean, it gets thrown at us a lot, it gets denied a lot, but there's really no denying that we were pretty much just by luck and by design modeled after Cinderella. I couldn't really help the fact that I had long blond hair kinda like Brittingham, you know what I mean? It was what it was. And Dean I think consciously and subconsciously did model himself after Keifer.

"DIZZY" DEAN DAVIDSON (singer, guitarist, Britny Fox) Tony Destra and I, we were painting a house. We walked into the kitchen to get coffee and here's a magazine and Cinderella is on the front cover. He lost his shit! He was a Sicilian and if they had been anywhere within ten feet of him they would've had broken arms and legs. He was like, "That was a shitty move that they did!"

BILLY CHILDS Tony died in a car crash on February 8, 1987, in Somerdale, New Jersey. It was about two hundred yards from where Pelle Lindbergh, the goalie for the Philadelphia Flyers, had died two years before. We'd played a gig and we're hanging out, typical Saturday night. And me and this girl and ironically this guy Adam, who became our next drummer, were outside sitting in a car smoking a joint. And Tony and our light man came out and said, "Yeah, we're going to this party, blah blah." And they split.

Well, it couldn't have been more than a few minutes and here comes the light man back. And we're still smoking this joint. That's how fast this all happened. And we said, "What the fuck's going on?" And he said, "Tony just had an accident down the street." So we start driving down and we're like laughing. I remember going like, "We better get there quick because Tony's gonna fucking kill somebody if they fucked up his car." And all of a sudden we see a fucking transmission laying in the road. I mean this accident was spread out like a fucking plane crash. We got up around the next turn and we saw his car. And we saw the engine of his car about fifty yards away sitting on a front lawn near this house. It was like smoking because it's so fucking cold out. And we got out of the car, there was nobody there, man. No cops, no ambulances, nothing. And I went over and Tony was laying behind the car. And I remember looking at him and thinking, Well, there's not a fucking mark on him. And I looked around a little bit and then I realized the whole back of his head was gone.

DAVE "SNAKE" SABO I auditioned for Cinderella. Jon Bon Jovi turned me on to the band. They were playing at the Galaxy in South Jersey, and Jon called me up and said, "Why don't you come down and hang out?" And Jon's A&R guy, Derek Shulman, was there, there was this big buzz going on. And it was either Jon or Derek who told me that they were probably gonna get rid of their guitar player. And I was like, "That's all I need to hear." And I went up and introduced myself to Tom after one of their shows, when he was outside. I said, "My name's Snake, I'm friends with Jon, blah, blah, blah." And I said, "I know you're gonna get a deal and I know you're gonna get rid of your guitar player and I'm your next guitarist." I guess he was taken aback by my unabashed forwardness and confidence but he invited me down after they made that move. And I jammed with them three times. As did Jeff LaBar. And Jeff got the gig and I was heartbroken. I was crushed. But it was great because I told myself, I'll never audition for anybody ever again. I'm gonna do my own thing. That was the kick in the ass that I needed to start putting Skid Row together.

ERIC BRITTINGHAM It was down to Dave and Jeff LaBar. We were like, Well they both play great and look cool, but Dave has an edge because he's Jon's friend and Jon helped us get the deal, so we should probably go with him. But Dave used to call me and Tom twenty times a day like, "Do I have the gig? Do I have the gig?" And we were like, This guy is gonna drive us fucking nuts if we hire him! So we went with Jeff.

DAVE "SNAKE" SABO I was relentless 'cause I wanted it so bad. I knew how good of a band they were and I knew that they were going to do well. And I wanted to be a part of that. I called Eric and Tommy like crazy!

JEFF LaBAR (guitarist, Cinderella) The way it was quoted to me, Derek's words were "You need a flashier guitar player, a Jake E. Lee type." And that's what they got basically, they got somebody that's half Asian as well! I met Jake in '85, maybe '86, and we look like brothers.

TOM KEIFER Jeff was in a band that opened for Cinderella at the Galaxy from time to time. We had seen him onstage, and he just had kind of a vibe about him. Then when he came in to actually play with us, he locked right in. There's always an intangible that's hard to put your finger on, something that just feels right.

JEFF LaBAR There was a band down on the Jersey Shore called the Dead End Kids, and that's who we got the move from where we flip the guitar around our backs. They had two guitar players and the bass player that would all do it at the same time. I would go out in the yard and try to do it: I hit myself, I cracked my elbow, I hit myself in the back of the head. But when I got into Cinderella, Eric showed me that you use a seatbelt and you get extra-long screws and washers and bolt the seatbelt right into your guitar. All it really takes is someone to show you, someone in front of you to show you where to place the guitar and exactly how to do it. And then after that, all it takes is the balls to do it.

FRED COURY (drummer, Chastain, London, Cinderella) I was in L.A. playing in the band London and I knew Eric Singer, who is in Kiss now but was in Lita Ford's band at the time. I called him out of the blue and was like, "Hey, anything happening? Do you know of any bands?" He said there was this band called Cinderella looking for a drummer and I said, "I don't want to play in a band with girls unless it's Heart." He said, "There are no girls in the band." I said, "Then why the dumb name?" He said, "Before you make fun of the name, listen to the band. It's like Kiss or Queen. When you hear it, it's not what you expect." I got the demos, and the first thing I heard was "Night Songs," and I was floored. Everything was so raw and I was like, Oh, my goodness, this is AC/DC and Aerosmith in one band! I have to get this gig! Eric gave me an address of someone to send my tape to at PolyGram.

ROSS HALFIN Fred Coury was Persian, as you'd call him now. As a kid his mother was so wealthy, he'd been all over the world. He was a spoiled bastard. I would shoot the band and everyone else would look at the pictures and say, "These are great." And he'd go, "Well, I don't like my cheekbones." Tom used to make fun of him all the time.

JEFF LaBAR PolyGram's first choice was Eric Singer and Eric turned us down. But I actually knew of Fred because I was a big collector of all the underground Shrapnel, Megaforce, guitar hero records and Fred had played on *Mystery of Illusion* by Chastain. So when I saw his name, I was like wait, Fred Coury, you mean the drummer for Chastain?

FRED COURY When Eric and Jeff came to pick me up at the airport, I had a big bag of candy. You've got to hedge the bet, as they say. You've got to stack the deck, and I don't think anybody else showed up and was like, "Hey, you guys want some mints?" Eric met me in the terminal and I was like, This guy looks like a rock star. This is awesome. Then we get to Eric's Datsun B210, and Jeff pops out of the back seat and goes, "Hey, is this you?" And hands me the Chastain record that I played on when I was sixteen. Then he goes, "Would you sign it?" The first autograph I ever gave was to Jeff LaBar on a Chastain record that I had recorded a year prior, which he bought, not knowing anything about me. I was like, This is really good. I've got candy and this guy wants my autograph. I'd better get this gig!

LARRY MAZER I got a copy of a record by a band called Stone Fury, which was Lenny Wolf's band that later on became Kingdom Come. Andy Johns, who of course worked with Zeppelin and the Stones, had produced it. It was very Zeppelinesque, and the production was just in your face. I called Tom and I said, "You've gotta come to my house right now, I've gotta play you this," and he came over, I played it for him, his head exploded, and we called Derek Shulman on Monday morning and said, "You should reach out to Andy Johns to produce *Night Songs.*"

DEREK SHULMAN Andy absolutely had the right feel for what this band needed but he was completely crazy.

LARRY MAZER He was the best rock engineer that ever lived, but then you had to deal with all the other bullshit. He was a mess. He trashed his hotel room in Chinatown here in Philadelphia.

FRED COURY I think he scared everyone in the band once or twice, like seriously scared like . . . "I don't want to get killed."

TOM KEIFER I could sit here and list all his flaws, but everyone has flaws. The thing that was just amazing about Andy was that he had an endless passion and energy to get it right. He was the one who taught us everything about making records and music. And he reminded us constantly of my heroes and how great they were, almost to the point of belittling us sometimes. He was very intimidating and hypercritical, and that was good for us; we needed it. I remember one night, we were working really late, and I was trying to be my best, but he was just wearing me out on this one overdub. And he finally just stopped the tape—he loved to imitate John Houseman, particularly when he was a bit buzzed—and said, "Thomas, what we're trying to achieve here is when the listener gets to the end of the record, they pick the needle up, and put it back at the beginning again." And then all of a sudden, a lightbulb went off. It was like, What's going in these grooves is for all time. There's no do-overs.

JEFF LaBAR When we were working on basic tracks up at Bearsville Studios in upstate New York, Andy told me that I was one of the best rhythm guitarists that he had ever worked with. And then when we went to do guitar solos he said the exact opposite. He said, "Jeff, you're terrible." I was like, Oh my god, are you serious? But I'll tell you man, that was better for me than the ego boost. I got a lot better after that.

LARRY MAZER Andy was even more tough on drummers. He didn't like the way Fred played and was like, "I don't want to fuck around, I gotta make a record, Fred can't cut it." So he used this guy, Jody Cortez, who was in Stone Fury, on that record. It was heartbreaking telling Fred.

FRED COURY I learned everything from him about being a producer, a composer, and drummer and playing for the song. Now I play on movies. I play on records. I play on video games. I think that all came through him. When you're beaten down, whether it be by a drill sergeant or whatever it is, you've got two choices. You can overcome it or you can just collapse.

LARRY MAZER The *Night Songs* album cover is how everybody looked in those days, the costume look. Everybody had the big hair, they had the long coats, the ripped-up this, the ripped-up that. Cinderella had done an independent single in 1984 for "Shake Me" and the photo was ten times worse! Totally glammed up and teased.

ERIC BRITTINGHAM We dressed and looked like how we thought a rock band should look. I remember reading reviews of our shows and people would write about getting past all of the hairspray and lipstick and, for one thing, we never wore any fucking lipstick!

MARK WEISS I had just done the Dokken *Under Lock and Key* album and I think they liked the way I lit it and the way I had the smoke and everything. I shot them in Philly during the day, and Tom goes, "Why are you shooting us in the daytime? It's called *Night Songs*," you know? And I said to him the famous words, "I shoot day for night." And he looked at me and goes, "I don't know what the fuck that is, but it sounds cool!"

TOM KEIFER There was another album cover that we submitted first, where "Night Songs" was written in water on a piece of glass, or the windshield of a car with light shining through it, and there was no picture of the band. And the label insisted on a band picture. I preferred the original cover because it had a really cool vibe, but the truth of the matter was that everybody, even Aerosmith, looked like that at the time. I don't think anybody at that time had a crystal ball saying, "You don't want to be too in sync with the times because you're going to end up stuck with this label that you don't want."

29

"THE POISON THING"

MARC CANTER Okay. So the Poison thing. I remember Slash was looking for a band to join—my best guess is it was maybe the fall of '84, when Axl was playing with L.A. Guns. And Poison knew about Slash because they used to gig with Hollywood Rose at the Troubadour. So they knew Slash was the real deal. They were friends, actually. Not Slash and Poison, but Slash and Matt Smith, who was Poison's original guitarist.

MATT SMITH My girlfriend came out to visit and when she went back home, we found out she was pregnant. We had a showcase with Atlantic Records, and they really liked us, so they asked us back for another one. We thought we were going to get signed, but then they passed. That's when I realized, Eh, maybe this isn't for me. So like eight months into her pregnancy, I told those guys, "I better go. This is no life for a kid and I've got to be a dad." I wasn't going to be an absentee dad.

BRET MICHAELS He said, "I am going to be a father and we are living like pigs. I can't do this. I need to go get a job and support my family." And he was right. We were living like pigs. We lived behind a dry cleaner's in a warehouse. It was a sad moment for us when he left.

RIKKI ROCKETT Matt was a badass motherfucker. I think he was a great guitar player, I loved his attitude, he was a good guy. And he was very true to his girlfriend. He never went out on her or anything like that. I found that very commendable. But we were like, "Man, we're in our early twenties, this is our time to fly. Let's just enjoy this. Let's make this work for us. Let's not get caught up where we can't work anymore. Let's make our work our pleasure." It was sad when he left, but it was probably the best thing for us at that time. I think we were stagnant.

SLASH I had been sort of scrounging around, looking for anything that was happening, just to get out there and play. So one day Matt called me up and said, "Poison's going to be auditioning guitarists. You should go out for it."

MARC CANTER Matt wanted Slash to take his job. But Slash was like, "Eh, I don't know. They've got all this makeup, they squirt Silly String . . ." Even though Hollywood Rose was a little glam, too. But Poison was over-the-top with it.

SLASH I really didn't like Poison. I didn't like that whole thing. But there was something exciting about them, and the thought of being able to get out there and start working the scene was enticing to me. I was willing to do whatever I could to break into it.

CHRIS WEBER I tried out for Poison, too. Tracii turned me on to those guys to get a gig. They were a local band at the time but they would sell out pretty good-sized shows.

TRACII GUNS I think I turned *all* those guys on to Poison. Chris and Slash and C.C. Because they knew who the Poison guys were, but they weren't friends with them. But I was. I always went to see them play even before they were really rolling. They were just cool guys. And they were a different band with Matt for sure. They were more Aerosmith–meets–Van Halen than they were New York Dolls–meets–Lady Clairol.

CHRIS WEBER I thought it would've been a good gig if I'd gotten it. I kinda looked like C.C. DeVille at the time. White hair straight up to the ceiling.

TRACII GUNS I knew C.C. because he was playing in a band called the Screamin' Mimi's at that time, who were a really cool, like, post–new wave rock band. They had their own thing, like, wearing fur coats on-stage, stuff like that. Not so much wearing women's clothes. And C.C. had a really cool Charvel with flames on it. That's all I saw. I was like, "Yeah, that dude rules!"

CHRIS WEBER I remember going to a rehearsal space and playing guitar with Bobby and Rikki. I can't remember if Bret was there. But it never ended up taking off.

MARC CANTER I actually drove Slash to a Poison gig at a place in Ana-heim called Radio City. This is still in '84, before Matt left. It was a sold-out gig, you couldn't get in there. The place was jam-packed. And I said to him, "Do it, because, look, they're selling out. You make a record with them, you play some gigs with them, somebody else will find you and you'll jump out. It's a stepping-stone." But there were little things that pissed Slash off, like he would have had to get up there and say, "Hi, my name is Slash!" during the part of the set where they introduce themselves.

RIKKI ROCKETT When we auditioned Slash he was like, "I don't want to do that."

MARC CANTER He went to a tryout and he bumbled his own tryout on pur-pose. He basically said, "Ah, it's not for me."

SLASH I played the shit out of those songs! And I got called back, twice. Then I was asked to come in a third time, which is when it got serious. And I remember as I was walking in that last time, C.C. was coming back the other way. We passed each other in the hall. So it came down to C.C. and me.

RIKKI ROCKETT C.C. brought in "Talk Dirty to Me." The arrangements and a lot of it changed, even some of the lyrics, but seventy percent of that song he laid out that day. He hit that first chord and I was like, "Fuck, that's 'Personality Crisis.'"

MATT SMITH I was at the auditions for both Slash and C.C. We'd jam. I was playing bass. It was pretty cool. I thought Slash was the guy. They should've picked him. Bret liked him, too.

BRET MICHAELS I got where Slash was coming from. But Bobby and Rikki saw it with C.C. It was one of our first arguments in the band. Because Slash fucking killed it. C.C. came in and barely learned our songs. He started playing his own stuff. He was like, "I've got these other songs! You gotta hear 'em!" We immediately butted heads.

RIKKI ROCKETT Can you really imagine Slash in Poison?

TRACII GUNS C.C., for good, bad, or whatever, back then he was a monster.

MARC CANTER Slash took one look at C.C. and he said to him, "You'll get the job." Because he was perfect. He was exactly the piece they were looking for.

SLASH He clearly fit the part better than I did. I mean, he came in with his hair all done up, he had all the right clothes and was wearing stiletto heels. I showed up looking the way I look now. And I also remember I had on a pair of moccasins. Because the Poison guys looked at me and asked, "What do you wear?" I was like, "This is . . . it," you know? And they said, "Well, do you have some different shoes?"

RIKKI ROCKETT C.C. was from Brooklyn. He loved the Dolls and Lou Reed and all that sort of stuff. I think he was frustrated in New York trying to make rock happen and we were frustrated in Pennsylvania trying to make rock happen. We all ended up converging on the West Coast, able to do what it is we wanted to do in the first place. I think that really drew us all together.

TRACII GUNS So once Axl and Izzy and I started doing Guns N' Roses, we got Rob Gardner and [bassist] Ole Beich, who had been playing in L.A. Guns for the past year. It was just kind of like, "Hey guys, we're going to do this new band now . . ." Our first show was at the Troubadour.

FLYER FOR TROUBADOUR GIG (March 26, 1985) *ITS ONLY ROCK N ROLL / L.A. GUNS HOLLYWOOD ROSE / PRESENTS THE BAND GUNS'N'ROSES*

ROB GARDNER We had a really good crowd. A new name, a new vibe. As a band we were really together.

TRACII GUNS Then Ole was the first to leave. And Ole was cool as shit. He was a Danish guy and he had played with Mercyful Fate. But he was like, "No, it's not metal enough . . ."

ROB GARDNER Ole was much more metal. And L.A. Guns was much more metal. But then once the change came around with Hollywood Rose there was a little more glam involved. And Ole didn't like wearing makeup and that kind of stuff. So then we replaced Ole with Duff, who had come down from Seattle and knew Izzy.

TRACII GUNS When Izzy was living with his girlfriend, Desi, I think it was on North Orange near Grauman's Chinese Theatre, Duff lived across the street from him. And one day Izzy called me up and he goes, "Hey, man, I'm friends with this guy, he plays with the Michael McMahon band. They play Top 40." And I'm like, "Top 40?" He goes, "Yeah, but this guy can play anything."

DUFF McKAGAN I had an apartment behind the Chinese Theatre that was, like, two hundred bucks a month. Super cheap. It was a crime-ridden little street. There was an alley behind it where drugs were sold. I knew none of this, but it didn't matter. I was nineteen. And Izzy moved in across the street. Izzy wasn't one of those long-hair guys I saw on the posters with the outfits, you know? And to be honest with you, neither was Slash or Steven. But one day I saw this Johnny Thunders–looking guy at the phone booth across the street and we started talking and he told me about this band he was putting together with his friend from Indiana, Axl. And I knew who that was. I'm like, "I've seen that guy!"

TRACII GUNS I'll never forget the first time I saw Duff. We pull up to our rehearsal space in the Valley at this guy Willie Basse's place. It was, like, nine in the morning, and Duff was sitting on the hood of a car drinking a Foster's Lager. I'd never seen anybody, not even my dad, drink a beer at nine in the morning. But he looked really cool, and when he plugged in and started playing he was legit, man. He could play anything from "YYZ" by Rush to "Richie Dagger's Crime" by the Germs. And that was a really good rehearsal because he had learned all our stuff. Izzy had shown him everything.

DUFF McKAGAN Rob was a good drummer. And Tracii was quite a guitar player. He was a shredder. And we played a couple shows at places like the Dancing Waters.

TRACII GUNS Then the next thing that happened was Rob left.

ROB GARDNER There was a lot of stuff going on. We were young, hormones were flying, there was drugs and everything else. But I'm not going to go into a lot of specifics. I don't feel I really need to. I'm not here to trash anyone.

TRACII GUNS Izzy kept suggesting Adler, but Axl was just like, "No, I don't want to play with that guy." Finally, Steven came down to rehearsal and it sounded great. And Axl's like, "Okay, fine."

MARC CANTER Duff booked gigs up north in Seattle, Oregon, places like that. The club scene he had passed through with other bands. And Izzy and Axl went, "Totally! Let's do it!" But Rob and Tracii were like, "There's no *way* we're doing that. Where are we gonna sleep? How are we gonna get there?" They came from homes. They lived in L.A., they went to school here. Their parents were here. They were situated. Whereas Axl and Izzy came from Indiana and their job was to quickly make it one way or the other. Axl and Izzy, I wouldn't say they were best friends but they had a special bond where they were part of a team. Both of them came out to L.A. with nowhere to live. They slept in the street or in someone's car or on a couch if they were lucky. I remember when I met Axl he didn't care where he slept. Sometimes he would even sleep in the stairwell at Tower Video where he worked—there was a little cubbyhole that you could kind of tuck behind and nobody would see you. And in 1984 his goal was to buy a gym membership. Not to have a place to work out, but to have a place to shower.

So for Axl and Izzy to go up north and do gigs, that's rock 'n' roll. They're gonna do it. They're gonna make it work.

ROB GARDNER They were saying, "We have these shows booked . . ." But we didn't have a reliable source of transportation and I was like, "Ah, it's kinda crazy to do it . . ." We had some junky old van, and I was worried it was gonna break down, which it did. They had to hitchhike back and everything. So I just made a decision that I didn't wanna go, and I ended up leaving the band. And I think Tracii was right behind me.

TRACII GUNS Okay, that is the stupidest thing I've ever heard in my life. And I think even Duff reiterated this story once. And I'm like, "What the fuck are you talking about?" And Rob wasn't even in the band when I left. So he has no idea. What happened was, Guns N' Roses were playing the Dancing Waters in San Pedro. And Izzy had called me and said, "Hey, if you get down there before I do make sure you put Axl's friend Michelle on the guest list." "Yeah, whatever, cool." So we get down there, and Izzy's there already, and Axl actually got down there early, too. And he starts unloading on me and Izzy, "Why isn't Michelle on the guest list?" He was just in a really bad mood and it kind of ruined the show for Izzy and I that night. But, you know, Izzy had a way of being very passive about those kinds of things. But I was just like, "This sucks. This is making me really unhappy." Then a few days later we played the Timbers club in Glendora, and that was the first time Axl was late to a show, and it was just waiting around, waiting around, waiting around.

So between then and our next rehearsal, which was on a Thursday, I had a lot of time to think, and I don't know, I just smelled trouble. I could see a very negative thing about to happen, and I didn't want to be involved in whatever that feeling was. Then on Thursday night I blew off rehearsal and I get a call from Izzy. "Dude, where were you?" I'm like, "Oh man, you know, the brakes on my Volkswagen, I need to get them fixed . . ." Some bullshit excuse. Then, finally, after like three or four days, Izzy and Axl called and Axl was flipping the fuck out, like, "What are you doing? What's your problem?" And I'm like, "Hey, you know . . . *this*. The way you're talking to me right now. I'm not into this."

So we're going back and forth and finally he goes, "Well, I'm just gonna call Slash." And I'm like, "That's a great idea!" You know, it'll be a perfect band. You guys can do what you wanna do and then you don't have the other chef in the kitchen. So I go, "I'll do my thing, don't worry about me." And they didn't. And they went and sold like fifty million records or something!

SLASH After the Poison thing, I joined this band called Black Sheep. Before me they had [future Racer X and Mr. Big shredder] Paul Gilbert, which is pretty funny given how different we are as guitarists. And it was at a Black Sheep gig that I started talking to Axl again. He told me he had had a falling out with Tracii and asked if I wanted to join the band. Izzy was already there, and so was Duff.

MARC CANTER So Slash was playing with Black Sheep, and even though his heart wasn't in it because they were a heavy metal band, he was capable of doing that gig. He played one show with them, at the Country Club, on May 31, 1985. And Izzy and Axl showed up. They were buzzing around and they said, "Hey, Tracii and Rob just left, we have a gig at the Troubadour next week, and then after that Duff has booked some gigs up north." And Slash already knew Duff. So they all knew each other and Slash was like, "Yeah, I'm gonna do it." I thought the best thing for his career would be to stay in Black Sheep because they were a bigger band. Plus there were no drug addicts in Black Sheep. But he quit Black Sheep and got Steven and they started playing with Guns N' Roses.

DUFF McKAGAN Our first rehearsal, we rented a room in Silverlake for, like, five bucks an hour. And Izzy and I took all of Steven's drums away from him—all the rack toms and all the double bass drums. So he just had a single kick and a snare. He was like, "Where's all my drums?" But it was literally one of those things where, from the first three chords, that A-G-D or whatever it was, it was, "Holy fuck!" We started playing and right away it had that warmth and that energy and that ferocity to it. It was like five swingin' dicks in a room, you know?

GINA BARSAMIAN They started with me on a weekday night. The first show was a Thursday.

FLYER FOR TROUBADOUR GIG (June 6, 1985) *A ROCK N ROLL BASH WHERE EVERYONES SMASHED*

MARC CANTER It was a really good gig, because now you've got the *Appetite for Destruction* lineup, and Steven's missing the double bass drum, so you can hear the vocals and the three ranges of Axl's voice, and everything's slower, not double time. And they're playing things like "Don't Cry" and Slash is whipping out this guitar solo that's the same one you hear on the record. I think I shot four rolls of film that night. Because everywhere I pointed the camera I was shooting rock stars.

SLASH It just happened, you know? The five of us got together and from that point on, Guns were the scourges of Hollywood. And we *hated* Poison!

PART III

KNOCK 'EM DEAD, KID

"Livin' in L.A. is so much-a . . . *fffuuuun!*" screeched Taime Downe, an outsider teen from Seattle who'd journeyed to Hollywood, remade himself as the platinum-maned, leather-and-lace-wrapped gypsy-god leader of Faster Pussycat, and summarily guzzled down all the women and booze the Sunset Strip could throw at him. It's a tale as old as time immemorial— or at least the 1960s, when the Whisky opened its doors, followed by the Roxy, Gazzarri's, the Rainbow, and the Starwood. By the mid '80s, all these clubs, along with the storied Troubadour, once a folkie hangout where James Taylor and Joni Mitchell rubbed shoulders, were catering to the throngs of hard rock fans and aspiring musicians who could not resist the gravitational pull of the Sunset Strip.

If life in Hollywood was frequently depicted as one big party (if it's Tuesday night in L.A., we suggest heading south on La Cienega to Taime and Riki Rachtman's "world-famous" Cathouse), that's because, for a lot of bands, it was. "It's a time that'll never happen again, in the history of music. It was just unadulterated fun. X-rated Disneyland, you know?" recalls Warrant's Joey Allen.

Nowhere was this more evident than in Penelope Spheeris' 1988 documentary, *The Decline of Western Civilization Part II: The Metal Years,* which captured the scene's winners and losers—and, in some cases, winners that sure looked a lot like losers—in stark reality. "It was kind of exaggerated and put a big exclamation point on some of the debauchery of the time," says Janet Gardner, whose all-female outfit, Vixen, were one of the up-and-coming acts presented alongside more established artists like Kiss, Aerosmith, Alice Cooper, and Poison, who were still buzzing from the massive success of their debut album. "There were some people looking like buffoons, but it did capture some rock 'n' roll attitude, for sure."

If partying came with the territory, most bands, regardless of their locale, were just as gung-ho when it came to the cutthroat business of booking the best gigs, securing the most fans, and grabbing the attention of the record labels who could make their rock dreams come true. "It was dog-eat-dog," says Guns N' Roses bassist Duff McKagan.

The primary form of hand-to-hand combat in L.A. involved posting and passing out flyers for your gig. Bands would print up hundreds, thousands, and sometimes even *tens* of thousands of flyers for a single show and carpet-bomb Sunset Boulevard with them, often ripping down and papering over one another's handiwork. By sunrise on a Saturday or Sunday morning, the sidewalks and streets of the Strip could resemble a paper-strewn, postapocalyptic war zone. "It was before the internet so that's how you did it," says Jetboy's Mickey Finn. "You went out there, you plastered."

30

"WHAT? A CHICK IN OUR BAND?"

ROXY PETRUCCI (drummer, Madam X, Vixen) My sister and I started Madam X around 1981 in Detroit. We were doing Zeppelin, Sabbath, Priest, Anvil, Van Halen, the real cool stuff—the deep cuts. Like, we did Van Halen's "Loss of Control" and "Tora! Tora!" We'd take those songs and make them even heavier, if that's possible.

MAXINE PETRUCCI (guitarist, Madam X) We were playing clubs all across the East Coast, Midwest, Southwest, and we worked our way to California. It was like a two-year deal.

ROXY PETRUCCI Any money we made went straight back into the band because we were self-contained. We had a PA, we had our own lights, we had a semi, we had a 1970-something Camaro, and we'd take turns sitting on that hump in the back. It was brutal, but we didn't care; we were having a blast.

BOBBY ROCK (drummer, Vinnie Vincent Invasion, Nelson) I was playing on the same circuit as Madam X. I used to go out and see them back in 1983. Roxy was playing her ass off back then. And don't forget that this wasn't just jumping up to play a forty-five-minute set. This was three to four hours a night.

MAXINE PETRUCCI In Texas I remember some guy was just screaming: *"That's not them really playing! That's not them really playing!"* And then he jumped on the stage to see if we were really plugged in. It was really strange. But it was like, Okay, I take that as a compliment. And a couple times we heard, "They must be transvestites. They're guys that became women." They couldn't accept the fact that we were really girls doing it. And we were two *little* girls. We're only like five-two!

ROXY PETRUCCI Rob Halford lived in Phoenix at the time and he'd occasionally go out to this club called Rockers where we were playing. He came backstage and he said, "Hey, do you mind if I sing with you guys?" We did "The Hellion," "Electric Eye"—six or seven Priest songs. Rob looked to his left and there's Maxine and he's smiling like, Look at this chick! Then he turned around and looked at me and he's like, And look at *this* chick!

MAXINE PETRUCCI We were spotted in L.A. by Bob Street, who worked for Jet Records. And he got Sharon Osbourne's father, Don Arden, who ran the label and at the time managed Black Sabbath, Lita Ford, and Electric Light Orchestra, to come to see us at the Troubadour. There was only a handful of people there, but I think Blackie Lawless and Chris Holmes from W.A.S.P. were two of them. Don heard us playing our original, "High in High School," along with all the covers we were doing. And he said, "I think you guys have a great song. I'd like to sign you." And we were like, "Yeah!" He put us in the studio with Rick Derringer producing. The record *We Reserve the Right* came out in '84.

ROXY PETRUCCI We were scheduled to play in Europe and we did. We played the Marquee, which was great. Ozzy showed up. We were supposed to play other places, too, but it just didn't happen.

MAXINE PETRUCCI Jet Records got into some sort of trouble with the IRS or accounting, I don't remember all the details, but basically the money ran out.

ROXY PETRUCCI I left Madam X and flew back to Michigan . . . and I wasn't doing shit. Then I got a call from Janet Gardner, who had tracked me down through an employee at Jet. Janet sent me the Vixen demo and I listened to it. I thought, Wow, this is really good. So I flew back out to L.A., we jammed, and I knew these girls were serious. They're good, they've got some good songs. What do I have to lose?

JANET GARDNER (singer, guitarist, Vixen) Before I joined Vixen, I was playing in a cover band and we were doing some crappy show in the San Fernando Valley. On one of our breaks, some girl comes up to me and goes, "I know this band that's looking for a singer that you would be perfect for. I know the manager. I'm gonna have him call you." I'm like, "Wow. They have a manager. That's pretty impressive!" He came to another show and said, "You'd be a good fit. Do you mind if they all come tomorrow?" The next night we were playing our show and I saw him but I didn't really see . . . I was expecting long-haired, guy-looking people. He came up to me and he goes, "I brought the band." I was like, "Really? I didn't see anybody." He goes, "Yeah, they're right over there." It was [Vixen guitarist] Jan Kuehnemund and a bunch of girls. I was like, "Oh . . . it's a girl band." He goes, "Yeah, but you have to keep an open mind." I said, "Well, of course, but I don't want to be in the Go-Go's."

SHARE ROSS (bassist, Vixen) I moved to L.A. in 1984 from Minnesota and was carving out a name for myself as a session player. I played with Australian pop singer Helen Reddy and was an on-call for the Drifters, the Temptations, the Coasters. I was also getting hired by all these bands and playing all over the Sunset Strip. Somewhere along the way Jan saw me play with a bunch of dudes at the Central, which is now the Viper Room. She came up to me afterwards and said, "Wow, you're a really good bass player. If you ever want to check out my band, Vixen, give me a holler." She wrote down her name and her number on a bar napkin, which I threw into my bag and promptly forgot about.

JANET GARDNER We started playing and touring, actually. We went out in an RV and went everywhere. Then at one point we were like, "We could do this forever or we could go home, make some new demos, and really hit the L.A. scene." Because the people were getting signed out of there, obviously.

ROXY PETRUCCI Around this time, David Lee Roth was auditioning drummers for his solo band and I went down and auditioned. I didn't even care if I got the gig. I just wanted the opportunity to jam with Billy Sheehan and Steve Vai, and I can say I did. Billy later told me that I was one of the top ten, which is pretty awesome. But Gregg Bissonette got the gig, as he should have.

JANET GARDNER Allen Kovac had managed Lita Ford at one point. There was that female-friendly vibe. So we sent him demos of what we were working on.

ALLEN KOVAC (manager, Vixen, L.A. Guns, Lita Ford) I just asked one question: "Can you guys play?" And when they said yes, I said, "This is awesome. There's no rock bands that are all girls." And I told them it's a terrible business for females.

SHARE ROSS Around 1986 I realized I was not in the right scene; I was in the session player's scene, not in the band scene. I started looking for bands to join and everybody that I talked to just laughed at me. "What? A chick in our band? Fuck off." And they would laugh at me on the phone, like openly. "Hey John! There's a chick on the phone who wants to be in our band!" They didn't even want to know. So I dug out Jan's phone number and picked up the phone. They had fired their bass player ten minutes prior to me calling.

JANET GARDNER We were starting to gain a really good following. The other bands would come see us. I remember one night Bret Michaels was there. Kevin DuBrow and Frankie Banali from Quiet Riot came a couple of times. One time Howard Leese from Heart was there. It was like, "I heard this chick band, whatever, *blah, blah, blah*. Let's go check it out." People were definitely showing their faces around us. But it was still hard to get a deal.

ROXY PETRUCCI Getting gigs was not a problem for Vixen. Getting a *record deal* was a problem for Vixen. And it wasn't because of the songs, it was "We already have a female artist." Allen Kovac ran into a lot of resistance. "We don't know how a girl band's gonna go over as far as their style of music" was another one.

SHARE ROSS "If they soften it and sound a lot more like the Bangles or the Go-Go's we would consider it." We also heard, "We would sign this if they would be willing to go onstage wearing lingerie and be little sex kittens."

JANET GARDNER We actually got a couple of reviews that talked about Roxy's boobs when she was playing drums. We were just too womanly. But we had the passion and the fire for it, so who cares?

31

"THE GIRLS WERE JUST, LIKE, MELTING"

MIKE TRAMP (singer, Mabel, Danish Lions, White Lion) In my local youth club in Denmark, I took part in theater and music. I just sat with an acoustic guitar and played some simple Bob Dylan songs around the campfire. Maybe half of the chords were wrong, but everybody was having a great time.

Then, when I was just fifteen and a half, I was asked to join a successful band called Mabel who were all ten years older than me. They had been a harder rock band but then suddenly decided to go light and have a Leif Garrett–looking singer. I asked my mom if I could leave school. She was basically in shock, but I think just because she was a divorced mother raising three boys in a rough neighborhood, she figured, What was there to lose? After a couple of years of touring all over Europe, we moved Mabel to Spain. The distortion had gotten turned back on the guitars because when we heard Van Halen's "Runnin' with the Devil" our jaw was dropped. We met an American at a discotheque in Madrid who said, "I'll be your manager and you can live in my house in New York." We sold everything we had and a month later we left. On the flight over, there were about three hundred American teenage girls that had been on a school excursion in Europe, and I was testing all kinds of names on them. By the time we landed, we were called Lion, which soon became Danish Lions.

VITO BRATTA I remember the night that I first saw Mike Tramp, I was in the dressing room at L'Amour's, this club in Brooklyn, just playing and playing. I was obsessed with the guitar. I would get to shows early and just practice.

EDDIE TRUNK (A&R, Megaforce Records; radio personality; author, *Eddie Trunk's Essential Hard Rock and Heavy Metal*) Vito was already kind of revered as a guitar player when he was in Dreamer.

MIKE TRAMP Danish Lions was playing with Dreamer at L'Amour, and about eleven o'clock at night, in through the door walks this guy with sunglasses on, real long black hair, and a broken guitar case with a Stratocaster hanging half out of it. I thought, What a fucking douchebag. We had these little practice amps and he says, "Man, can I plug into one of those?" And I say, "Yeah, let him plug in and make a fool out of himself." And he plugged in and just ripped through every Van Halen, every Randy Rhoads, every fucking solo that was ever great and I said, "This is a guy I need to play with."

VITO BRATTA When Mike walked into L'Amour that night, it was like a real major rock star just came in. People just spun their heads and were like, "Holy shit, is he somebody?" And the girls were just, like, melting. He was a beautiful person.

BRUNO RAVEL Like somebody off the cover of a romance novel.

MIKE TRAMP Vito and I formed White Lion and I was playing manager and fucking running around trying to knock on people's doors. I said to Vito, "I don't know where to go, I'm out." He said, "I might know someone." That's when he called Michael and George Parente, the owners of L'Amour. Vito got off the phone and said, "They need to hear some original songs." The next night Vito came over to where I was living in Queens. We just looked at each other and he started playing guitar and I started singing and the first song we wrote was "Broken Heart." Songwriting is one thing Vito and I have never, ever disagreed on—even for a second.

VITO BRATTA All you have to do is write a chord change, get Mike to listen to it, and he'll write that song with you. He's able to do that.

BRUNO RAVEL One day, I got to practice, and Vito, he was sitting in a chair in front of his amp noodling around, practicing. And I showed up and I walked up to Vito and I said, "Hey, Vito, Greg told me that you and Mike are writing for the record." I said, "I don't know if you're interested, but I got a ton of ideas. If you want me to show you any of them, I would be glad to sit down with you and maybe we could write something." He was like looking down at his guitar, and I remember he just stopped playing. And he looked up at me, and he said verbatim, he said, "You're the bass player. Play the bass." And then he looked back down at his guitar and continued noodling. That's when I knew it was time to move on.

EDDIE TRUNK The owners of L'Amour had a management company, Loud and Proud, that nurtured White Lion, Overkill, Tyketto, and Tora Tora. They would start putting these bands on as opening acts and bring them along slowly. White Lion got to the point where they could fill L'Amour before they even had a record deal. There was a great buzz on them. I mean, you had a great-looking lead singer that the girls loved and an incredible guitar player who was kind of like a new Eddie Van Halen. That combination was very powerful and those guys worked it to the hilt.

MIKE TRAMP Our managers sent us to Germany in January of '84 to make *Fight to Survive* because they'd done a deal with a producer and a studio, one of those "You guys come over, pay for your flights, you live in the studio, if you get a deal you pay me, if you don't, we're even" deals.

VITO BRATTA I've read people say that my playing improved and changed so much between *Fight to Survive* and our next album. But what happened was when we got to the studio they told me, "We need to get the bass and drum tracks down and they have to follow somebody, so play the guitar so that the bass and drummer can follow you. Then we'll go in later and we'll replace all the guitar parts." So I do that. And then they said, "Okay, we're gonna do the vocals. And then at the end we'll come in and redo all the guitar." Oh, wouldn't you know, at the end, it's like, "Guys, we took a little more time on the vocals, so we don't have time to redo the guitar." I was like, "You mean my first album is a guide track?"

MIKE TRAMP Two weeks after we got home we signed a record deal with Elektra Records. The wheels started turning with the album photo shoot and meetings with the record company, and then out of the blue one day at rehearsal, we get this phone call from our manager who said, "I've got good news and bad news." And this became something throughout our whole career they always would say. "Well, the bad news is Elektra has dropped you. The good news is you get to keep the money."

VITO BRATTA It was just crushing. And you don't ever get answers from these people. Maybe Elektra thought we were too corporate, like we weren't grassroots enough, which was ridiculous because we were paying our dues like crazy. It was one of those situations where it was better off if it didn't happen than to give it to me and then take it away. Because at that age, you think that record deals are something that only famous people get, not realizing that the reason they're famous is because they had a record deal, not the other way around.

GREG D'ANGELO (drummer, White Lion) The band rehearsed in the basement of L'Amour, and the funny thing was, the basement was also an open drain for water with a drastically pitched floor that these guys had to stand on. There were days when we would go to rehearsal and it would be raining, and there was water streaming in that floor. It was not pleasant.

JAMES LoMENZO (bassist, White Lion) The new bass player they had at the time, Dave Spitz, left to join Black Sabbath. I went to audition at L'Amour and I have to say I was a little disappointed when I saw that Nicky Capozzi was gone and that Greg was the new drummer. Not because I was even aware of whether he was a good or a bad drummer at all. I just thought Nicky was a great drummer. Anyway, we went through a couple of songs, and I found that I really liked what they were doing because it didn't sound anything like metal music to me. It sounded like pop music.

GREG D'ANGELO James played great and he had this giant Alembic bass. He was really a good complement to Mike in a lot of ways, particularly in his appearance. He had great hair.

MIKE TRAMP We had a third manager, Richard Sanders, who got us connected to JVC in Japan. He managed to do a licensing deal with them and Elektra Records and they did a major push on the band. So the band broke in Japan and through the underground in Europe. *Fight to Survive* starts being imported to record stores in New Jersey, Staten Island, and New York.

EDDIE TRUNK I started going out to the shows and watching them develop. I took them to Jon Zazula at Megaforce when I started doing A&R for the label and said, "I think these guys could hit, we should sign them." And he just didn't get it. I mean, Megaforce was Anthrax and Overkill.

GREG D'ANGELO People were paying upwards of a hundred bucks for a copy of this Japanese record. We had tried to buy the masters from Elektra, and they were not having it. Somehow, this guy in Pennsylvania, with this label called Grand Slamm, talked his way into getting the rights and he sold, I want to say, a hundred thousand copies.

MIKE TRAMP And suddenly we were an album band.

"PEOPLE DIDN'T KNOW WHETHER TO FUCK US OR FIGHT US"

VICKY HAMILTON Poison had a demo deal with Atlantic and Atlantic passed. The demo was okay but Poison is all about the show. If the executives did not see the show they didn't really get it, you know what I mean?

RIC BROWDE (producer, Poison, Faster Pussycat) They produced this demo that was truly hideous. It was just leaden . . . terrible. They wanted to sound like Kiss. I think the only song on there that made it to the first album was "#1 Bad Boy."

VICKY HAMILTON Bret got disheartened and he was like, "Well, then, we should take whatever deal we can get."

WES HEIN Vicky Hamilton was involved with Mötley Crüe when they were with us at Greenworld, and we had dealt with her with Stryper. And one day after we became Enigma she comes down and says, "I've got somebody bigger than Mötley Crüe. It's Poison." She was so passionate and she had a very good track record so I went and saw them at either the Troubadour or the Whisky, and they were great. I mean, the energy, the fun, the party atmosphere. And then the audience, which was just, you know, beautiful girls throwing themselves at them, and guys who were there because the girls were there, and everybody moving and everybody having fun, right? It wasn't a mosh pit, it wasn't fighting. It was people just, like, partying.

BILL HEIN I think what sold it was that the show was good—it was real showmanship. And we looked around at the audience . . . I was so used to going to metal shows where it was all dudes, right? You go to a Poison show and it was, "Wow, there's lots of girls here! And they're dressed up. This is a big night out!" That to me was the thing that clicked. And it didn't hurt that, you know, they could write hooky songs.

WES HEIN So we made an offer. And they wanted to be signed, but they also felt like, "We're going to be platinum." There was no question in their minds how big they were going to be. This was not ego. This was, in their opinion, matter-of-fact.

BILL HEIN I think we signed Poison for $25,000, which for us was a pretty big check to write. I know the first Stryper album, which was seven songs so it was kind of in between an EP and a full album, the recording budget was three grand.

BRET MICHAELS Who wouldn't want to get signed to a massive record deal? But here's the beautiful thing. We got signed for just enough money to make our record, right? But we got to keep our superstar royalty and we got to keep our publishing. That turned out to be amazingly great. It's like getting to own your house.

HOWIE HUBBERMAN (owner, Guitars R Us; manager, Poison) In 1985 I was running Guitars R Us on Sunset Boulevard. Poison came on my radar through Vicky Hamilton—she wanted out because she thought at that time Poison was losing their following. They used to sell out the Troubadour, now they were doing less people. So I bought her out for $4,000. Bret came to me and said, "It's over for us, man. We gotta figure how to do something different. We're not even selling out the Troubadour." And I go, "Look, it's just starting for you. We're not gonna play the Troubadour. We're gonna go to a place called the Country Club, which holds a thousand people, and we're gonna sell it out. I don't care what it takes."

RIC BROWDE I went down to a club in Reseda, California, a place called the Country Club, and I saw Poison play. And they sucked. They sucked horribly. But . . . the club held, I believe, something like 1,100 people. And I would say of the 1,100 people at the gig, 1,050 were girls. Who were *screaming*. And I was going, "Fuck. If anybody pulls this many girls, the guys are gonna follow."

KATHERINE TURMAN I kind of felt like you couldn't help but love Poison. The energy at the live shows was so contagious and I'd never seen anything like it, but of course I was, you know, eighteen or something. I went to see them a lot, and I had one friend, like an older accountant guy who looked like Bob Dylan, who hated them, but he always went 'cause he was like, "That's where I can see all the cute young girls."

MICHAEL SWEET Stryper did a show with Poison at the Country Club. That's the night Bret jumped off the stage and he broke his ribs and they took him to the hospital.

ROBERT SWEET I remember praying for him. "God, let this guy be okay."

HOWIE HUBBERMAN I would put $12,000 into a show that we'd get a $2,500 paycheck from, just to make sure it sold out the first couple times. And then it got wings of its own and, you know, it was on automatic pilot. We did twelve sold-out shows at the Country Club. We never turned back. Then they were in the studio with Ric Browde.

RIC BROWDE The funny thing is, musically I never was really that much into this type of music. But I had worked on a bunch of Ted Nugent albums so I was typecast as "You do heavy rock 'n' roll." The irony is the music that I'd listen to at home was all R&B and gospel—Marion Williams and Clara Ward and things like that.

But I knew Bruce, who you might know as C.C. And I think it was Bruce who approached me and said, "Hey, would you do this?"

HOWIE HUBBERMAN Ric Browde did as much polishing as he could in the studio and I think he did a stellar job.

RIC BROWDE We recorded *Look What the Cat Dragged In* at a studio on Melrose called Music Grinder. Stevie Nicks was in her worst drug period during this time—and why that is relevant is Stevie Nicks had booked out the Music Grinder. She had it on a lockout basis. But she was so fucked up on drugs that she never showed up. So I made a deal with the guy who ran Music Grinder that we would pay him $500 a day in cash under the condition that if Stevie Nicks ever got off her ass and showed up we had to get out of there. Of course, she never showed up.

BRET MICHAELS Ric had a different vision of what those songs were going to become and what he wanted to do with our music.

WES HEIN There were some strains in the studio. I think a producer feels like their role is to produce the album, right? In their opinion that's why they were hired. To come in and go, "You guys have never collectively done a record. I need to give you a sound. I need to bring that out." And when it works, of course it's great. But I think it was because they were so unique, and I think very sort of headstrong in many ways . . . There was a lot of friction.

RIC BROWDE Bret wanted to be Kiss and I thought they needed to be a lightweight bubblegum group. They didn't have the talent to be anything else. And Bret, you know, is to be commended because up to Poison I think the ability to carry a note and sing in tune had been a barrier to entry. Bret opened up that field wide open.

RIKKI ROCKETT Ric wanted "Talk Dirty to Me" to be four-on-the-floor. If you can imagine that. It would have sounded like "White Wedding" or something. It could have worked that way, I guess. It just wouldn't have worked for me.

RIC BROWDE I mean, Rikki, who is the nicest member of the band, couldn't play.

RIKKI ROCKETT As tensions rose by the end of the record, that's where we were about to record the vocals. Ric and Bret, they just weren't going to have it with each other. Of course, we were going to back Bret up and we did. I don't think we even talked to Ric after that.

HOWIE HUBBERMAN Actually they kicked Ric Browde out of the studio and Ric sued. Rightfully so. Because he had a right to be a part of the mix. But Enigma gave me strict instructions.

BRET MICHAELS And then we finished the entire record by ourselves with our engineer, Jim Faraci. So that's a gentle way of putting it.

RIC BROWDE The album ultimately cost $23,000. And a little bit over to get Michael Wagener, my friend, to mix the album with me.

MICHAEL WAGENER When they asked me to mix the Poison album, I was offered a choice between being paid $5,000 up front or taking one point on the record. I listened to the rough mixes and I just didn't hear what people wound up liking about this band. So I took the $5,000.

RIC BROWDE It was the worst deal he ever made. He'll tell you!

MICHAEL WAGENER Every time I see the guys now, they still make fun of me about that decision.

RIKKI ROCKETT I think *Look What the Cat Dragged In* sounds inspired. We were on fire. Even if we played some of the songs maybe too fast or some of it sounded adolescent at times. I think that added to the tension and the fun of that record. It should have been sounding adolescent and it did. It should have happened that way. I didn't want a prog-rock album by that point in my life. I wanted it to sound like we were playing a live show almost, you know what I mean?

BRET MICHAELS That was probably the most glam we ever got.

WES HEIN Without a doubt when the album cover came in, I remember the people in the art department kind of going, "Oh my god!" I think somebody made a comment that C.C. looked like Joan Rivers.

RIKKI ROCKETT Part of what it was, was that back at that time C.C. had an acne problem. Obviously he grew out of it, but at that time he did. I remember the Hein brothers going, "Don't worry about it, we've got an airbrush guy. We can make anything look good." It's like, "Well, that's good because I have bags under my eyes and Bret has this and Bobby has this . . ."

BRET MICHAELS I one thousand percent will never deny that the cover of *Look What the Cat Dragged In* is a great record cover, but I wasn't that excited about it at the time. I'm glad that I got overridden. I give Rikki much more credit for that.

BILL HEIN I loved the cover. We were a little independent label with a fraction of the funding of the labels we were competing against. At that point we were starting to have some pretty successful acts. We had Berlin. Stryper were starting to do well. Smithereens. So we were starting to compete with the majors at a certain level. But we still had to fight for recognition. We couldn't spend the dollars that Elektra or Geffen or Arista could. It was good to get people's attention.

RIKKI ROCKETT When you're on an Enigma budget, you don't necessarily have the top-rung airbrush guy. I think he may have done the wizard on my Dodge van, which I love by the way. So we're like, "Whoa, that's pretty heavily airbrushed, it almost looks animated, like anime." They're like, "Look, we just can't shell out the money to redo this. We can't do it." "Okay, well you know what? Let's go with this." We just went with it, like, "Fuck it." It shocked people.

"WILD" MICK BROWN I remember somebody brought the Poison *Look What the Cat Dragged In* album cover in and me and Michael Wagener and [Dokken bassist] Jeff Pilson and I think George, we were howling. We had never seen anything like it. It was just the funniest fucking thing. Like, "Look at this band!" And then we heard the music and we were like, "What the hell?" I thought, No way that band's ever gonna be popular. And now it's how many, twenty million records later? Jesus.

BRET MICHAELS The critics looked at Poison, from the day that we put out our first record, praying that we would be done. The problem that you have is this: Do I go to their house, do I smash their face in, do I beat them over the head with a bat? Which is inevitably what I'd really like to do.

NEIL ZLOZOWER I was meeting with the band at my studio about doing a photo shoot with them and we all got along great. It was like me and Van Halen, me and Mötley, me and whoever. As he's leaving, Bobby hands me the first album and I go, "Hey dude, who are these fucking hot-looking chicks on this album cover?" And Bobby's like, "That's us, you idiot." And I'm like, "That's you guys?" I go, "Damn. I thought it was fucking four hot-looking chicks."

C.C. DeVILLE (guitarist, Screamin' Mimi's, Poison) That whole androgynous thing was very cool, but you had to poke fun at yourself a little bit, because you didn't want to come off too strong. Because if you're growing up in Montana and you have a tractor, I'm not too sure that they're gonna get it. But if you show a lot of boobs in the video—you make sure that you show a lot of girls in the video, so that the guys that are chewing tobacco don't feel alienated.

RIKKI ROCKETT We got in so many fights I can't even begin to tell you. People didn't know whether to fuck us or fight us.

BILL HEIN If anybody saw the girls, their fans, how pretty their female fans were and how much in love, in *lust* their female fans were, they would set aside any notion of them looking girly.

HOWIE HUBBERMAN They would play a show where at the beginning of the show Bret had one girlfriend, Rikki had another. At the end of the show it was like a trading places situation.

NEIL ZLOZOWER Oh my god, did we have fun, me and the Poison guys. Back in '86, that was just like . . . I mean, that was all pre-AIDS and everything like that. It was just a big fuck fest.

KATHERINE TURMAN I interviewed Bret around the release of *Look What the Cat Dragged In,* and he hit on me at the end. He said, like, "Hey, you know, how about you come on the road? Just you and me a couple of nights, no one will know." And then I just said, you know, "Okay bye." I couldn't tell if he was kidding, or if it would have happened if I'd actually said yes!

HOWIE HUBBERMAN I was on the road for eight months with Poison just before and after the album came out. It was a crucial eight months. We went everywhere in the continental United States. We were playing the Bootleggers in Arizona, the Stone in San Francisco, the Cow Palace in Daly City. You know, shithole-to-decent places.

RIKKI ROCKETT Some of those early tours in the Winnebago were tough. We opened for Quiet Riot in clubs, and at that time, Kevin DuBrow and their tour manager were not the easiest people to work with. We had so many restrictions on us. A lot of the audiences were there to see Quiet Riot, they didn't give a damn who the opening act was. We had to prove ourselves night after night after night and we started to get used to that. We started to embrace that competitiveness.

FRANKIE BANALI They were like the new band and they were supporting us on the *QR III* tour. I felt really, really sorry for those guys because their rider was almost nothing. I mean literally there was no food or anything for them and we had so much. Every single day when the guys in Quiet Riot weren't looking, I'd get a big plastic bag and fill it up with drinks and food and stuff and drag it over to their dressing room.

RIKKI ROCKETT I have to say that Frankie Banali was the one that made it more than bearable for me.

HOWIE HUBBERMAN I think they got in a huge fight one day with Quiet Riot. And at that point, within two months it was a flip-flop and Quiet Riot would be happy to open up for Poison—if Poison would let them open up for them. And they wouldn't, because Bret got into it with Kevin DuBrow.

FRANKIE BANALI Things fell apart when they found out their record had passed some sales milestone and they decided to destroy the bathroom in that particular dressing room. And of course, Quiet Riot being the headliner, we were the ones that got charged back for the damage.

RIKKI ROCKETT We all go through things. There was some jealousy. They were on their way down, we were on our way up.

FRANKIE BANALI The next show we did—it might've been Minneapolis, but it was definitely somewhere where it was cold and snowing—as they walked offstage, our tour manager said, "Okay, fellas, the dressing room is this way." He opened up the door and he threw them out into the snow. And that caused some really, really bad vibes.

RIKKI ROCKETT We played one headlining show in Scottsdale, Arizona, where in the club it basically blew up. They told us we couldn't use our Silly String because it got on the mixing console. We're like, "We won't spray it on the console, we'll make sure it doesn't happen." Then they were like, "You can't have your confetti, you can't do this, you can't do that." Well, we decided to do it all. Of course, you tell Bret not to do something and he's right there on the console spraying it on the motherfucker. I think Bobby blew a confetti cannon right at the fucking sound guy.

HOWIE HUBBERMAN Both of the owners of the club got crazy drunk. They got so drunk they started a fight with the band. Also, Bret had to relieve himself on the side of the stage and he kinda did so very nonchalantly. And they got in a fight.

RIKKI ROCKETT They shut us down. The crowd rioted. It turned into a *Gunsmoke* episode where we were pounding the hell out of the whole bar. It was just a free-for-all. I remember Robbie Crane, who's now with Black Star Riders, bass teched for Bobby then, and he and I had our backs to each other just fending people off. Like, "You take this guy, I'll take that guy."

HOWIE HUBBERMAN Robbie actually beat up the bouncer. The police came, they took me aside, they said, "Look, these guys want to keep the backline for the damage that was done here." And I said, "Look at these guys from Poison. They're trying to tell you that these guys from *Poison* beat up the bouncers? You gotta be kidding me! Let us get our gear and go on to the next city." And the cops looked at us and said, "You guys get the hell outta here."

"HOW DO I GET A
RECORD DEAL?"

DON DOKKEN Anybody I met at that time, Poison and all those guys that were struggling on the Strip, I'd ask them, "Where're you from?" They're, like, from Ohio. Nobody was from L.A.

GREG STEELE (guitarist, Faster Pussycat) When I moved here, I thought, Fuck, this place is amazing! Because where I was from, I grew up in Northern California, a place called Foster City, and the scene . . . there wasn't a scene, actually. So I moved down to L.A. in August of '85. And I just thought it was amazing, all the music and stuff. And then I met Taime and he knew a lot of people and it just started from there.

TAIME DOWNE My birth name's Gustave Molvik, which is my dad's name and my grandfather's name. But I was kind of pissed at my dad so I just changed it. Taime, it was a nickname when I was little from my grandma, because she couldn't pronounce *je t'aime.* 'Cause she was Italian. But her assistant was French. She used to import clothes in Seattle from Paris, for, like, Bon Marché and Nordstrom and shit.

In high school I was in a band for a short period of time called the Bondage Boys. It was just fucking dirty . . . kinda glammy, makeup, like a mixture between the Misfits and Mötley. We were all just up in Seattle, underage, couldn't get into bars, trying to figure out what we were gonna do. We played a skating rink out in, fuck, what was it called? I can't remember. That's where I first got to be friends with Mike Starr from Alice in Chains. But I went to California when I was a kid a couple times and it was just always where I wanted to live. And then the whole scene with Mötley started, Ratt, all that stuff. I was a teenager, late teens, and I was like, "It's where you gotta be! Get in the clubs, get booze and get pussy!" When you're fucking eighteen that's all you wanna do—drink and fuck and play rock 'n' roll.

TRACII GUNS When Taime first came down from Seattle, I had met him somewhere . . . I don't remember where. But I had a girlfriend named Candy and I stayed at her house in Covina half the time and then half the time we stayed at my grandma's house. And Taime lived with me wherever I went for a little while. So he would stay at my grandma's or stay out in Covina with me.

TAIME DOWNE I came for a weekend excursion with some people, found a free place to live, we pulled a scam at the Palladium, scammed like eight tickets off the guest list, fuckin' sold 'em and found a free place to live that night. Had some cash, got to see Metallica. A good weekend. Been in L.A. ever since.

TRACII GUNS He was this real, like, glammy, alternative . . . you know, he could've went either way. He could've been in Poison or he could've been in Jane's Addiction. He had the two-tone black-and-white hair, he was skinny, he liked to wear fishnets onstage. He was into Specimen and these kind of avant-garde bands that weren't really great but the vibe was really cool. He really liked stuff like that. Same with Mick Cripps.

MICK CRIPPS (guitarist, L.A. Guns) I had just come over from London. I was living in England and I was playing in different bands with some of the guys from the London Quireboys—Griff and Spike and Nigel Mogg and all those guys. And the name of one of the bands I was playing in in England was Faster Pussycat, based on the Russ Meyer movie. So I came back to L.A., just to check out the scene, and I met Nickey Beat and Tracii and Axl and all those guys. And one of the other guys I met was Taime. I said, "Hey, you know, this is a great name for a band. Why don't you use it?" And he ran with it.

TRACII GUNS I remember Mick telling me that name. Because at first it was called Faster, Pussycat! Kill! Kill! Like the movie. And I was like, "That's a movie! You can't be in a band that's called the movie." And Mick would always use the excuse, "Well, Black Sabbath . . ."

MICK CRIPPS I was trying to figure out if I was gonna stay in L.A. or go back to England. And I got a job at a shop on Melrose called Let It Rock. We got all these great clothes from the King's Road. Johnson's suits and everything. We had a lot of music people coming in, like the guys from Stray Cats, Roy Orbison, big-name stars. A lot of people didn't have that stuff in L.A. A door or two doors down there was this gay porn theater on the corner, and they had converted it into a bar and a couple stores or something. And that's where Retail Slut was.

TAIME DOWNE I got a job at Retail Slut and doing lights at the Troubadour on the same day. In the meantime, I'm just meeting people all over, doing the social shit, ping-ponging, trying to get into clubs that I wasn't old enough to get into. Izzy was actually my first friend in L.A. And then I got to be friends with Axl through Izzy. We were at the Rainbow and I go, "Hey, who're you here with?" And he says, "I'm here with that guy over by the pay phone." And that was Axl. He had cool hair and a fuckin' pink biker jacket. All beat-up, punk rock. We just hit it off. And Tracii, I went to see him with Guns N' Roses at their first show, at the Troub, and that was right before I started working there. Then Mick started doing something with Tracii and I was already in the mindset with Faster. I liked the name. And I just started putting the shit together. I met Greg, he came into Retail Slut. He was like, "Yeah, I just moved here. I play guitar . . ." So I started shooting the shit with him and we exchanged numbers and we just started working on shit.

GREG STEELE He already had a bunch of guys that he wanted to get a band with, like Mark [Michals, drummer] and Brent [Muscat, guitarist]. We didn't have a bass player at the time. But he said, "Let's have a rehearsal." So we started rehearsing and we just kind of went from there. Really simple like that.

TAIME DOWNE We played a show at the Central, which is now the Viper Room. Our first show ever.

GREG STEELE It was a battle of the bands. There was not that many people there, but there was this dude . . . this guy who was dancing just like Axl does. And . . . it was Axl! I kinda thought the guy was just fucking around, making fun of us or something like that. But I guess he was kinda into it. And Axl knew Taime, and he was like, "Dude, we're playing"—I think they were playing the Whisky a few months later—"and I want you guys to open." He told Vicky, who was managing Guns at the time, "I want Faster to open." She was like, "I don't know . . ." He told her, "Fuck it, they're gonna open."

VICKY HAMILTON Axl was my roommate at the time. And he came in with a Faster Pussycat logo and said, "This is who I want to open up for us at the Whisky." And I'm like, "Well, we've already booked the Unforgiven." "Well, this is who I want."

TAIME DOWNE We played the show at the Central and then we did one at the Music Machine. And then our third show was at the Whisky with Guns N' Roses. And our fourth show was with Poison at the Country Club. I remember those because they were our first four shows. After that I have fucking no idea.

VICKY HAMILTON So I begrudgingly went to see Faster Pussycat. Taime was kind of a scenester then. He was working at Retail Slut. You know, everybody kind of knew him. I really didn't have any plans on managing them or anything like that but we became friends. He kept calling me: "How do I get a record deal?"

TAIME DOWNE I remember Izzy going, "Vicky's not managing us anymore, we kinda fired her. But she likes you guys." And anybody that liked us, we were like, "Cool!" Because we were fucking like a week old. I was like a little hustler back then trying to get everybody into our shit. I was pimpin' flyers and shit before we even had a full band, when I was working at Retail Slut during the day. We had a whole posse—Mick and other people down at Let It Rock, my buddy Jimmy, people at Flash Feet [of London], Jet Rag . . . we had a whole little scene down there on Melrose.

GREG STEELE I think at that show at the Whisky with Guns we threw a bunch of incense out. We kinda looked like gypsies onstage and we had incense burning and shit like that. And I remember throwing the incense out and burning people.

TAIME DOWNE We had it in, like, little tin cans onstage, and we'd kick 'em over. Fucking stupid shit we wouldn't do now, especially with the shit that happened with Great White and clubs burning down. But we wanted to be fucking dirty, Stones-y, gypsy, Hanoi . . . just the shit we grew up with. Pistols and Cheap Trick, whatever. We wanted to be degenerates but not super-complete fuckups, you know what I mean?

VICKY HAMILTON I took them to Peter Philbin at Elektra. I started that whole thing.

PETER PHILBIN Frankly, they were one of the worst bands I had ever heard. They were terrible. They couldn't play. They didn't have songs. I didn't care at all. Okay? I heard the music, I met the guys, I saw them play. I'm not interested. Have a nice day! I passed.

VICKY HAMILTON Well, I don't know if he actually said the word *pass*. But in his mind he passed.

PETER PHILBIN I passed on this band in no uncertain terms. The first time I met them, Vicky brought them up to my office. She wanted me to hear the music while they were there. Boy, that's always fun! And I heard it and I went, "Guys I have no interest in this. *I pass*." They were very clear that I passed.

VICKY HAMILTON At that point Faster Pussycat was really inconsistent. They either played a great show or a terrible show and there just, like, didn't seem to be any middle ground.

GREG STEELE We were out playing decent-sized gigs right off the bat and we sucked. So, you know, the first impression of people was like, "These guys fucking suck." And that first impression kind of sits with you. But the first few shows we had this guy on bass, he was just not into being in our kind of band. Basically didn't want to succeed at all. We wanted to succeed. We wanted to get signed. This guy was the opposite of all that. Then after that dissipated we got Kelly.

VICKY HAMILTON So I end up managing the band, and Kelly Nickels, the bass player . . . I had moved down into this house on Santa Monica Boulevard, and I had this housewarming party and all of Faster Pussycat came. They had a rehearsal later that night, and Taime and Kelly had ridden their motorcycles and I think Greg and Mark and Brent were in a car. And they left my party to go to a rehearsal. And then I get this call from Brent and he's, like, crying and freaking out. Kelly was involved in a hit-and-run accident and his leg got broken in several places below the knee.

HEIDI MARGOT RICHMAN (costume designer) Taime and I left the party and we were driving in my Jeep. We were literally right behind Kelly and we saw the whole thing happen. I'm pretty sure we were at Sunset and Highland, or we could've been at Hollywood Boulevard and Highland. But it was a huge mess. I hope you never have to see somebody lying anywhere, but in this case it was the middle of a huge intersection in Hollywood. He was laying there with his leg wide open.

TAIME DOWNE I held Kelly's leg together with my hands in the street. It was scary shit. We were kids, you know? It was fucked.

HEIDI MARGOT RICHMAN It's like, "Oh my god get the cops get the paramedics get whatever!" And then they took him to Hollywood Presbyterian on Vermont and Fountain.

VICKY HAMILTON I met Taime at the hospital. They wanted to amputate Kelly's leg, and they wanted to talk to a family member. I think somebody rifled through his apartment and finally found his parents' number and stuff. And I never knew that Kelly's last name was not really Nickels.

Taime and I were like, "What the hell's his real name?" It kinda saved his leg that we didn't know his real name. We're like, "We're not family. You can't, you know, take his leg off."

TAIME DOWNE I didn't want to kick him out of the band. But finally it was, "We need to get a record deal. We're young, and who knows if this opportunity will ever come back?" But we always remained friends, me and Kelly.

VICKY HAMILTON That's how Eric ended up in the band. I was at the same time managing Darling Cruel, and Eric was the bass player. So he ended up in Faster Pussycat.

ERIC STACY (bassist, Faster Pussycat) Originally I don't think they knew how long Kelly was going to be out. So it was, "Can you fill in for Kelly for a short time?" "Yeah, no problem." So I was doing double duty with Darling Cruel and Faster Pussycat. I played a show with Darling Cruel and had a few drinks and started partying and next thing I know it's like, "Oh, shit, I've got another show to do!"

TAIME DOWNE Eric was a better bass player. But Kelly was my buddy. I didn't really care about technique and any of that shit. But the label thought we were a better band with Eric in it.

ERIC STACY The first gig I did with them was at the Roxy. October '86. And the band had only been around since early '86. So it wasn't that long into it. And afterwards Peter Philbin came up.

PETER PHILBIN This is about five months after I had passed. I show up at the Roxy to see another band and, gee, guess what? They go on late. How shocking is that? And I'm there, and another A&R guy, a guy named Michael Goldstone, he was at Geffen Records, he's there to see the same band. I can't remember what band that was. And Michael says, "Let's go next door to the Rainbow and have a drink." And I go, "You know what? I'm gonna stay and see this other band." And that band was Faster Pussycat. I thought, Why not see how much these kids have grown up over the last five months?

So I watch their show and it's a lot better. And they have a song that I don't remember hearing before: "Got Your Number Off the Bathroom Wall." And the hook line is *"Boy I'm lucky I didn't use the other stall."* Wow. Now that's deep! Not about *my* life. Not about what I care about. But it's a cinematic lyric. I mean, you can visualize a lot. And I'm going, "These guys are actually doing something . . ." It's still not "I've found the future of rock 'n' roll." But I thought I should at least go backstage and say hi. So I go back and Ric Browde's there. And I know Ric. He's a viable guy who can make a record for nothing.

TAIME DOWNE Ric was cool. He did Poison's record.

RIC BROWDE Nobody believed that I had done Poison for $23,000. People just didn't think that that was possible. So Peter was talking to me, going, "Really, you didn't do the album for $23,000." And he said, "Well, I like Pussycat, I like the look. But I really don't think they can do anything. They really kind of suck." And I said, "Well, why don't you give me some demo money and let me make a demo with them?" He goes, "I'll give you $25,000." And I went, jokingly, "Why don't you give me fifty and I'll give you two albums?" You know, just being a brash asshole.

PETER PHILBIN Ric might have this memory of he told me he could make two albums for fifty grand. That's insane. They didn't have two albums' worth of songs! Two albums of what material? My memory is I went backstage at the Roxy to basically say, "You guys keep getting better." And Ric's there and Taime's going, "We're gonna make an independent record." I go, "Ric, how much is that going to be?" He says twenty-five grand. "Really? You can bring it all in for twenty-five grand?" Now my wheels are turning. I'm gonna do this for fun. I'm not serious. To quote Bruce Springsteen, "I'm not here on business, I'm only here for fun." So I say, "Guys, why don't we have lunch tomorrow?"

So the next day they come up to Elektra. This is like me going to Vegas. "Okay, here's what I'm gonna do. I'm gonna make you an offer. I'm gonna offer you seventy-five grand. And here's how that's gonna go. Twenty-five grand to make the record. There's five guys in the band, that'll be five grand for each of you. And then twenty-five grand for you to buy new instruments." Because if they had actual real gear, they might play better. And we make that deal.

TAIME DOWNE We're just like, "We don't know, we don't care." *Whatever.* I'm twenty-two and I'm on the same label as Mötley Crüe and the Doors and the fucking Cure. I was tickled.

PETER PHILBIN I think that for all the attitude I had about "Hey, I love Bob Dylan," and "Oh, I have such great taste," and *blah blah blah . . .* one thing I always understood is that rock 'n' roll should be fun. And I could see that Taime and Brent and Eric and Greg Steele and all these guys, they're out hustling girls, they're working the world. And they're having a great time doing it. And I'm going, God, if they've grown this far in five months, where are they going to be next year?

34

"OUR HERO IS GONNA FUCKING SPLIT HIS BRAINS OPEN IN FRONT OF US *RIGHT NOW!*"

TRACII GUNS After Rob Gardner was out of Guns N' Roses and they were auditioning drummers, before they got Steven Adler, we had Nickey Beat come down. He had played in the Weirdos and a version of the Germs and stuff like that. He had these real punk-rock anarchist values without being, you know, a harmful human being. But he wasn't right for Guns N' Roses.

But it was odd that after we played, I went outside with him into the parking lot and we're talking and I go, "Nickey, if for some reason this doesn't work out and I'm not in this band anymore, you're definitely the drummer I'd like to start something with someday." And so, lo and behold, I'm out of Guns N' Roses and the first person I call is Nickey. And he's like, "Yeah, yeah, sure, let's do it." We hung out for a couple days and then we went to see Guns N' Roses play at this frat party at UCLA. And Mick Cripps was at this party.

MICK CRIPPS Nickey Beat told me to go see this band Guns N' Roses. "They just got their new guitar player, Slash, and they're playing a frat party at

UCLA." Which was a fucking ridiculous place to play. So I go there and Axl's walking around with his chaps on, with his ass hangin' out. I was like, "This is hilarious!" That he had the balls to do that, right?

MARC CANTER Axl had *big* balls. And when I say that I mean *of steel*. To go out in a crowd like that? I can't imagine. But Axl did it. And he did it often. He had no issues at that frat party.

MICK CRIPPS I remember there was this grand piano in the frat house. And Axl's got his chaps on with nothing underneath but, like, a codpiece, and he sits down at the piano and starts playing an early version of "November Rain," I think it was. You can just imagine all the jocks at this frat party eyeing the guy with murder in their eyes. But Axl didn't give a fuck. He didn't suffer fools.

TRACII GUNS So at this party Nickey approaches Mick. "Hey, we need a bass player. Wanna be in this band?" And Mick Cripps was, like, the coolest-looking dude at the time in the scene. He was fresh off the boat from England and had a lot of vibe going on. So me and Nickey and Mick, we started this band. We didn't have a name. L.A. Guns was something that had already existed but I hadn't brought it up or anything. Then one day we're up at my grandma's house and there are all these old L.A. Guns posters laying around. And Mick says, "Well, since you have all these posters already, why don't we just call the band L.A. Guns?" And I go, "I've got a backdrop, too!"

TAIME DOWNE Mick and I had been playing a little bit and then he started doing stuff with Tracii. And that was fine. I was already in the mindset of doing Faster Pussycat. And I liked Tracii. So we all stayed friends and everything. Everyone was friends. All the Gn'R guys, Adler and Slash and shit. And Izzy was a really good friend, so . . .

TRACII GUNS I spent a lot of time with Izzy. And you know, he had a quiet way about him. Very convincing. We did some weird shit with women that we probably wouldn't have told our parents about. But it was great, man. A real eye-opening time.

MICK CRIPPS I think we were all helping each other find members for our bands. Later on, Kelly [Nickels], who was the bass player in Faster Pussycat and was in a horrific motorcycle accident, he wound up joining L.A. Guns.

TRACII GUNS I called Kelly when he was at home in New York in bed in, like, a half-body cast and I said, "Do you wanna be in L.A. Guns?" And he was like, "Ah, man, I was so hoping you were gonna ask me that!"

MICK CRIPPS There was a lot of rivalry but there was also a lot of unity and people helping each other out. Because it was a small scene and you didn't have the internet or any of those kind of means of marketing and stuff. It was all word of mouth and just getting out there and doing it.

BILLY ROWE There was only a handful of bands that I believe—that *a lot* of us believe—were really part of that scene at that time in the mid-'80s. Outside of Poison, it would be Guns N' Roses, L.A. Guns, Faster Pussycat, and Jetboy. And that's it. Those were the bands, and I'm sure all those guys would agree, that were the core of that next wave.

TRACII GUNS Before us you had Ratt and Mötley Crüe and W.A.S.P. and Great White, guys like that that are a little older and were in a way a part of the end of the '70s rock scene. What they did was they revived rock after punk had just stormed through L.A. So you had some viable rock bands that had record deals that were now leaving town. And the void was being filled by Poison and Guns N' Roses and L.A. Guns and Faster Pussycat and Jetboy, who were from San Francisco but they were a great band.

MICKEY FINN (singer, Jetboy) When we first moved to L.A., we were living in a hotel on Vine just down from Santa Monica. I don't know who picked it but it was ghetto as fuck—junkies and freaks and male prostitutes and trannies and stuff. There were multiple times where we woke up to the hotel literally being under siege, like helicopters flying over and you look out your window and cops with flak vests on have guys laid out facedown on the street with their hands handcuffed behind them. It was like, "Hey, welcome to L.A.! This is it!" It was a rough time.

TRACII GUNS It was definitely a turning point music-wise because everything became more rough around the edges, more blues-influenced, more junkie, more alternative. It wasn't just about looking like Mötley Crüe anymore. It was about injecting the Stones and the Dolls and the Germs and all these other influences into it. So what really happened is the quality of music, the diversity of music, got turned up in the scene. It got dirtier.

BILLY ROWE We all had our punk roots. I mean, Duff was punk, Mickey was punk. That's why we connected with Guns N' Roses big-time. We were all into Johnny Thunders, Lords of the New Church, the Dead Boys, Generation X, Hanoi Rocks. I mean, Hanoi Rocks was number one.

MICKEY FINN Poison definitely came from a different place. I don't think they were really turned on to, like, Hanoi Rocks. I'll explain it this way: When we met those guys they were kinda still stuck in their spandex pants and Capezio dance shoes look. Very Gazzarri's. But after the first year or so of meeting them and playing with them they were suddenly wearing creepers and string ties and bolo hats and they definitely incorporated more of that Hanoi Rocks element.

VICKY HAMILTON I think Poison looked up to Jetboy. They played some dates with them if I recall. And you know, Poison also idolized Hanoi Rocks. I got them on the Palace show with Hanoi Rocks and we sent out a press release and everything. And of course, that was the weekend that Vince Neil killed Razzle in a car accident. [On December 8, 1984, members of Hanoi Rocks were partying at Neil's house when Neil and Hanoi Rocks drummer Nicholas "Razzle" Dingley left to go on a beer run; on the way back the singer, inebriated, lost control of his car and collided with oncoming traffic, killing the twenty-four-year-old Dingley and severely injuring two passengers in another vehicle.] So that gig never happened.

BRYN BRIDENTHAL I know a guy who was a policeman on the beat there and apparently what actually happened was that Vince's passenger, who was Razzle, had a whole case of beer on his lap and the glass broke in the accident. He bled out.

MICHAEL MONROE (singer, Hanoi Rocks) Razzle was dead on arrival at the hospital. He was all smashed up. I'm glad that I wasn't there because I probably would have demanded to see him. It was our tour manager that went to identify him, and he never got over it . . . It was a horrible accident, really tragic, and I wouldn't wish it on anybody, especially the guy that was driving. I never blamed him. You can't blame somebody for an accident.

VINCE NEIL I wrote a $2.5 million check for vehicular manslaughter when Razzle died. I should have gone to prison. I definitely deserved to go to prison. But I did thirty days in jail and got laid, and drank beer, because that's the power of cash. That's fucked up.

NIKKI SIXX For us, it was kind of hard to grasp that somebody died in a car accident because Vince was drinking. We all drank and drove in the '80s. It's just what we did. We got lit up at home, we jumped in the car, we went down to Hollywood, we drank more, we grabbed a bunch of chicks, we got kicked out of a bar at two a.m., we went to a party, and then we got ourselves home. But when Razzle was killed, that was the first time we realized there was consequence to this. And it wasn't that you were gonna get in trouble—somebody died. Vince changed that day, and I don't think he's ever changed back.

MICKEY FINN When Razzle died and Hanoi broke up, that was devastating for all of us.

BILLY ROWE We were huge fans of Hanoi and we were going to open for them in San Francisco right prior to that happening. I have the ticket still.

GREG STEELE Warrant and all those Van Halen–type bands, they would play Gazzarri's. But Faster and Guns N' Roses and L.A. Guns, even though it was still rock 'n' roll, it was very different. And then you had Jane's Addiction, the Red Hot Chili Peppers, Tex and the Horseheads, that whole scene.

MICKEY FINN Perry Farrell [Jane's Addiction singer] was a little bit more of a freakish dude but Dave Navarro was always a rocker. He'd get right in there with Fernie [Rod, Jetboy bassist] and Billy and talk about Kiss and Aerosmith, classic stuff. He's a guitar player, man. He was a ripper.

DAVE NAVARRO (guitarist, Jane's Addiction) It was a little competitive but for the most part it was camaraderie. It was a healthy environment where they were your friends but . . . you wanted to crush 'em.

DUFF McKAGAN Guns N' Roses' first gigs, we were playing with bands like Social Distortion and Tex and the Horseheads and the Red Hot Chili Peppers. We were just trying to figure out, "Where the fuck do we fit into this whole thing?"

MICKEY FINN I remember partying up at the first Guns N' Roses house and being taught how to chase the dragon. Which, if you know anything about that, it's the act of smoking heroin out of a piece of foil, with a foil tube. I'd been way deep into many drugs, but I'd never got really deep into heroin. Luckily it was not something that really clicked with me long-term. But yeah, man, those were the days.

TRACII GUNS Weed was not a thing then in our music scene. It was more about cocaine and heroin. And there are no good, positive stories to tell about that. From 1984 to 1987, all the girls I hung out with were strung out on dope. I stayed away from the coke chicks. For some reason I liked the ones that did heroin. And it always led to heartbreak.

The funny thing is, at that time I was sober as a basketball. I didn't even drink beer. Nothing. I grew up in a Jewish neighborhood, all of that. I was not into any of that shit. But I was surrounded by it. I'm attracted to melancholy sad stuff, and at that time it was plentiful.

MICKEY FINN Heroin was huge at the time. And in L.A. it was easy to get. And cheap. And everybody worshipped the Stones. Everybody worshipped Johnny Thunders and the New York Dolls. In that light, being a junkie was a cool fuckin' thing. You walk around all sleazy and fucked up like Johnny Thunders!

BILLY ROWE I remember one time Jetboy and Guns N' Roses played with Johnny Thunders at Fender's Ballroom. And that was a highlight for all of us. But Thunders was a mess. He was pretty fucked up at that point.

TRACII GUNS I played guitar for Johnny Thunders one night in Long Beach. He was actually sober at the time. And right before we walked out of the dressing room he goes, "Watch this." And I looked at him and he just put the persona *on*. That's how glamorous it was in everybody's heads.

MICKEY FINN I mean, definitely there was a period where I was injecting drugs. It happened before and after shows at the Troubadour, the Roxy, the Scream. Todd [Crew, Jetboy bassist] got into it, too.

BILLY ROWE Mickey had his demons that he dealt with, and him and Todd connected in certain ways with that shit. But Todd was definitely going down and getting worse and worse.

MICKEY FINN All we do is rehearse and party. Every night you're going out to clubs and shows and events. There was sex in the bathrooms, drugs in the bathrooms, all the cliché stuff that went on that was super fun.

TRACII GUNS We did a video for our song "One More Reason," which is the thing that ultimately got us our record deal. We had this good song, and we had a manager named Alan Jones, a Welsh guy who had been the saxophone player in a band called Amen Corner. Their biggest thing was they toured a lot with Pink Floyd in the late '60s. And what happened was Bob Skoro at Polydor wanted to come see us play, so we set up a last-minute gig at the Troubadour. Warrant was playing, and they were really new. But they agreed to let us come on and do a half-hour set. So we went and did the set and Bob Skoro makes a beeline for me and goes, "I'm gonna do a deal with you guys."

That was a Wednesday. The following Monday, Alan Jones calls me. "Listen, Bob would love to give you guys a development deal." I'm like, "What's a development deal?" "Well, he gives you some money to demo up some more songs . . ." And I go, "That's not a record deal!"

But anyway, we follow through with demoing up some more songs, and now Polydor wants to sign us. So we go to their offices, which at the time were on Sunset near the Rainbow. And we're up there and Bob Skoro starts asking each guy some questions: "What do you want to get out of making records?" "How do you see yourself as a musician five years or ten years from now?" Everybody gives their spiel. And then he gets to our singer, Paul Black. He asks the question. And Paul just falls asleep. Like, right there on the couch. I had no idea what was going on. And then Bob Skoro goes, "Sorry, guys. I can't do this."

And just like that, it's over.

MICK CRIPPS I don't remember that.

TRACII GUNS I remember leaving the meeting, walking out with the guys, and I go, "What the fuck was that?" And they're like, "Well, you know, Paul's strung out." I'm going, "No. I *don't* know that Paul's strung out!" And they say, "Well, should we try to find another singer?"

MICK CRIPPS Alan knew this singer from a band called Girl. And that was Phil Lewis.

TRACII GUNS I said, "That's who I want to sing!" And Alan tells me, "He's not a great singer but he's really great onstage." And I go, "No—he's a *really* great singer." I have the Girl records, you know? I'm like, "Get him out here, now!" And Alan had him out here a week later. This was, like, the most unbelievable spoiled-brat musician story I could possibly conjure up. "I want this guy . . . now!" Because Guns N' Roses was solid. They got Slash and they were rollin'. And I had this band, we were gonna sign a deal . . . and we lost our singer. Now I'm getting fidgety. So we brought Phil out and we met at the Cat & Fiddle, which was a British pub on Sunset. I remember sitting there with him, and it's ninety degrees out and he has a leather jacket on. I think he had a couple hundred bucks and a little suitcase with a hair dryer and a pair of pants in it. Something ridiculous. He didn't think he was staying.

PHIL COLLEN (guitarist, Girl, Def Leppard) Girl was kind of a version of that glam thing already, before any of that stuff was going on in America. So it wasn't really much of a stretch for Phil to jump into that culture. He'd already been promoting it for years.

TRACII GUNS We did our first gig at the Whisky. It was a brand-new band. Now we have Phil Lewis. Now we have Kelly Nickels. Kelly sat on a stool with his crutches and played, but it didn't matter—the place was sold out. Then we did a Troubadour gig and Axl got up and sang a couple tunes with us, like a Zeppelin cover or something. And then after that, like the following week, Alan calls a meeting at the little shack I was living in. We were hoping to hear some good news from Bob Skoro. And Alan says, "I don't know how to say this to you, but they don't want to do the development deal." And me and Mick just look at each other, like, "Shit, man. Now what?" And in the next second Alan goes, "They just wanna go straight to the record deal." And that was it, man. The train was rollin'.

MICK CRIPPS God, within three weeks or so I think Jane's Addiction got signed to Warner Bros., Guns N' Roses got the deal with Geffen, and Taime's band got signed. We got signed, Jetboy, a couple other bands . . . The record companies just scooped everyone up.

BILLY ROWE Jetboy signed to Elektra around October of '86. And by '87 we were trying to write songs for the record and we really couldn't even continue rehearsing because Todd would just lie on the couch and pass out. We got to a point where we decided as a band that we needed to find another guy.

MICKEY FINN But it's not like we just said, "Later." We tried to get him into rehab. We got his parents involved. We tried to say, "Look, you're blowing this opportunity." I mean, being an alcoholic is one thing. When you start becoming a heroin addict and an alcoholic, you know, that's a double whammy that few people can balance out.

BILLY ROWE After Todd was out of the band our manager said, "If you could have any bass player, who would you want?" And I said, "Sami Yaffa." Simple as that. And our manager knew somebody in Sweden or Finland or something and she found the guy pretty quickly. And he accepted the offer.

MICKEY FINN People were like, "Oh my god, they got the guy from Hanoi Rocks!" And that was a big thing. It was like, "Fuck yeah!"

BILLY ROWE Once Sami joined Jetboy all the Hanoi Rocks guys—Mike Monroe, Andy McCoy, Nasty Suicide—started coming over to our place on Franklin Street. We had a pool there, and one time Mike, like he does onstage, he started climbing shit. He climbed up and got onto the second level of the apartment building, onto the railing. And then he got on top of the railing—I wanna say he either pulled himself up onto the roof or he balanced himself on the railing. And he fucking dove off into the pool. I remember we were all watching, like, "Wow, our hero is gonna fucking split his brains open in front of us *right now*!" But he just dove in and came out like it was fucking normal.

MICKEY FINN We were in Miami mixing our first record for Elektra, *Feel the Shake,* when we heard [that Todd Crew had died of a drug overdose]. It was a shock but also not a shock, you know? I wish we could've helped him. He was only twenty-three or something like that.

BILLY ROWE We got dropped before our record even came out. Peter Philbin, who had also signed Faster Pussycat, was not a guy who was really into our scene. Nor was Bob Krasnow, the president of Elektra. He was into, like, Tracy Chapman. So everything started going wrong for us. Eventually we wound up signing with MCA. *Feel the Shake* was originally set to be released the same month as *Appetite for Destruction,* but by the time our album finally came out it was already '88. The delay totally killed us.

MICKEY FINN We lost about a year of momentum. Meanwhile, Guns N' Roses is going out with Aerosmith, Poison is out with this band and that band . . . Everybody got good tours and they all went to the next level.

BILLY ROWE I think if our record came out when it should've things would be a lot different right now. We had everything on our side, you know? I can remember Tracii Guns saying to me one time, "Ah, man, out of all of us bands, I predict you guys will be the biggest. 'Cause you guys have *songs*." But it's interesting how things worked out.

MICKEY FINN We got some bad breaks and some of our peers got good breaks. But not many of them, really, when you look at it. As far as success and longevity, Guns N' Roses was really the band that broke through. Poison I guess would be second in line. And then, you know, L.A. Guns had some top songs. But for a lot of the rest of us, it fizzled out quick. And we were all kinda left scrambling, like, "What do we do now?"

35

INTERVIEW: ALAN NIVEN, GUNS N' ROSES AND GREAT WHITE MANAGER

Alan Niven signed Mötley Crüe to their first-ever recording contract with Greenworld, brought Dokken to Elektra Records, and helped to launch the Enigma label, later home to Stryper and Poison. But he truly made his name as a manager, working first with Great White and then signing on with Guns N' Roses after much entreaty by his old friend Tom Zutaut.

When Tom Zutaut first approached you about managing Guns N' Roses, you said you weren't interested. Why?

At that particular moment I had no intention, let alone a desire, to take on the responsibility of another project because I just managed to get Great White signed to Capitol after their abortive debut record on EMI. I wanted to completely focus my energy on making sure that possibilities and potentials of that band were better realized than they had been the first time 'round. So I told Tom, "Thank you, but I'm really not interested." Eventually Tom came back to me and said, "Niv, can I get you to think about this again?" Now, by this time, out of curiosity, I had done a little research on the band, and I looked him in the eye and I said, "Good fucking luck. You are out of your ever-loving fucking mind. This band is a disaster waiting to happen and it's probably happening even now as we're speaking. I pass."

What had you found out in your research that led you to feel that way?

That professionalism of any degree was not in their vocabulary. That a few of the members were rumored to have serious habits. That they were utterly destructive and uncontrollable. And that they had already pissed away their $75,000 cash advance [for signing with Geffen] on nothing except having a good time and Slash buying a few guitars.

But eventually you said yes.

Tommy came back and asked me a third time, and I remember clearly as yesterday him sitting in my little condo in the South Bay and going, "Niv, this could be the end of my career. I cannot get anybody to touch them or manage them." He actually said to me, "Would you at least pretend to manage?" He was that desperate. I said, "There's no fucking way in hell I'm going to do a thing like that. But for you I will go and talk to them and see where it goes." And that sort of started it.

So I think it was September of '86 that I signed a contract with the five individuals collectively known as Guns N' Roses. And once I did that, what I did not know is that [Geffen president] Eddie Rosenblatt turned 'round to Tom Zutaut and said I had three months to make it look feasible. Otherwise he was going to go ahead and drop the band like he wanted to already.

Needless to say, Guns N' Roses were not Geffen's top priority right off the bat.

No. Bryn Bridenthal liked them. But Bryn Bridenthal has a slightly wicked dark streak within her.

When did you first meet the band?

I first spent some conversational time with them at [Spencer Proffer's studio] Pasha when they were mixing the tracks that ended up being on [the 1986 EP] *Live ?!*@ Like a Suicide*. And then we were due to have a meeting, just myself and them, at their rental house in the Hollywood Hills. I rode my bike up there, and as I arrived there was a fairly well-known stripper coming out the front door. And just to the right of the front door was a smashed toilet. Which I thought was rather interesting and symbolic in many ways. I went inside and only Izzy and Slash were there. And Izzy proceeded to nod out at the table, which left just me and Slash. At which point Slash turned to me and said, "Come and see this." And he took me to his bedroom and showed me his fucking snake. I hate fucking snakes. Then he had me watch as he fed it a rabbit. My skin was crawling.

The *Appetite for Destruction* recording sessions have been fairly well chronicled by various band members. What was your impression of the process?

It was chaos all the time. We put them in a building that used to rent out apartments by the month. They destroyed it. I got them a cheap rental van. They destroyed that. I turned up to one of the studios we were doing overdubs in to see how Slash was doing with his guitars. I pulled up to park and there's a Gibson SG through the windscreen of the rental van. That's a message that even somebody as slow, dumb, and stupid as me can comprehend fairly quickly. "Oh, he's having problems with his sound!"

So it did not run smoothly, and it took a hell of a long time. And a ridiculous amount of money was spent on the record. *Appetite for Destruction* cost approximately $365,000. To have a debt of $365,000 before you spend a dime on a video or ask for tour support? And on top of that I'm looking at a band that is so against the grain that I know they're not going to get airplay. I developed insomnia during the recording of *Appetite for Destruction*. I would lay in bed at night going, "How the fuck am I going to dig my way out of this royalty hole?" Whereas the Great White record I was working on at the time, *Once Bitten,* I turned it in to Capitol for, I think, $115,000. And the label was blown away.

At first, Great White was actually the bigger of your two bands. How did Guns N' Roses feel about the fact that you were working so closely with another act?

Slash and Izzy were okay with it. Axl hated it. And I found it frustrating that he could not respect the fact that I'd had a relationship with that band for something like four or five years already, and that obviously I was not going to casually overturn the commitment that I had.

It also was disappointing that none of them really appreciated how much I hooked Guns N' Roses onto Great White's coattails in the very early days. For example, the "Welcome to the Jungle" video was only made with that storyboard and with that level of production because I coattailed it onto a Great White shoot for "Lady Red Light." We used the same director, Nigel Dick, and we used the same crew and the same equipment. I got four-day rentals and I could amortize the shortfall of what Geffen were prepared to put up to make "Jungle."

And as far as MTV, that Ritz show came about because MTV wanted to film Great White. I said, "Yeah, we'll come and do Great White, but my other band opens." This arrangement was made at the back end of '87. By the time we got to the show in February of '88, things had started to pop for Guns N' Roses and we switched them. Guns headlined.

Most people had not seen Guns N' Roses in concert at that point. But that Ritz performance, which MTV beamed into every home in America, really captured the power of the band as a live unit.

Some of the worst shows I've ever seen in my life were by Guns N' Roses. I mean, it could be catastrophic. But it could just as easily be sublime. That's because they weren't Def Leppard—I'll never forget seeing Def Leppard three times in a week and watching them put the same foot in the same place in every song. But what you should always be looking for is that magic of the moment. What is the definition of management? The definition of management is that you're obliged to supply the spontaneous on demand. And I'll tell you, when Guns N' Roses provided the spontaneous, it was fucking spontaneous. And it was magical.

36

"AND WE'VE GOT THE PICTURES TO PROVE IT"

PETER PHILBIN I was working at Elektra, and the guy who was head of Elektra, Bob Krasnow, was a great guy. Volatile, but a really strong music man. Bob had moved the company to New York, and I was still in the L.A. office. I was the lead executive. So Bob comes out to L.A. and we're having breakfast at the Polo Lounge. And he goes, "What d'ya got?" "Well, I'm looking at a band called Faster Pussycat." And Bob loves porno. He's well versed in Russ Meyer's soft-porn film *Faster, Pussycat! Kill! Kill!* And he goes, "Great name. Let me hear the music." And I go, "No." And he goes, "What do you mean?" And I go, "You're gonna hate it."

MIKE BONE After *Shout at the Devil* was such a big success, Doc McGhee came in to Elektra to renegotiate. 'Cause they had the typical shitty record deal. And Bob told him, "Look, I'm not gonna renegotiate with you on one big record. You give me two big records and I'll open the coffers for you." And they did *Theatre of Pain*. And then *Girls, Girls, Girls*. Okay. So after the second big record Doc comes in and renegotiates and he walks out with a lot of money. Bob was true to his word but had still never even seen the band play live. So we were headed to a WEA [Warner Elektra Atlantic] national sales meeting in Miami and I said, "Bob, on our way down why don't we go see Mötley Crüe? They're playing in Oklahoma City, we'll see 'em there, and then we'll go down to Miami the next day." And so he goes, "Okay."

So we get to Oklahoma City and Doc is there. Tom Zutaut is there. I think the head of the A&R department, Howard Thompson, is there. And Bob's complaining the whole night. Bob is not a person that likes being in heartland America! He's a New York and L.A. and San Francisco kind of guy. We get to Oklahoma City and it's, "Oh my god . . . who on earth would live here?"

PETER PHILBIN Bob Krasnow did drugs. This is well known and this is a guy I have a lot of affection for. Bob was like everything you wanted in the record industry. He was both a dream and a nightmare. But Bob was never a suit. Bob was never a corporate guy. I was a big fan of his. He passed away and I miss him.

MIKE BONE So the car picks us up and we go to the show. And Mötley, they're not even playing Oklahoma City. They're playing in a little town south of there—Norman, Oklahoma. There's a big basketball arena there that's part of the state college. I mean, it's fuckin' huge. We pull into this parking lot and about every third vehicle is a pickup truck. And Bob is still complaining—"Why am I here?"

BRAD HUNT Bob in Oklahoma City . . . I mean, Bob in *Cleveland* was, you know, an experience.

MIKE BONE So we go in and I say, "Bob, let's go look at the house." "Okay." We go up to the front and there's a merch table and they're selling T-shirts, hats, headbands, sweatshirts, panties, fingerless gloves . . . I mean, it's just crazy. And they're selling this stuff so fast that they have a giant cardboard box there, and the merch guys are just taking tens and twenties and throwing them into these big boxes. It's just *bangbangbangbang*. The idea is to get as much money out of that crowd as possible. I don't remember the merch numbers per head but it was astounding. And Bob saw that. He may not have had an affinity for the music, but when he saw the merch he was in.

Anyway, the band comes out, they play, the crowd goes crazy. And at that point I think the drum kit was doing something wild. It was, like, flipping over with Tommy Lee in it, there's a ton of pyro, the whole thing.

NIKKI SIXX With *Theatre of Pain* we figured out how to take the drum riser and have it lean all the way forward so you could actually get a view of what it looked like to watch Tommy play a drum solo. He wanted to be able to just slam it. What we did with lights, lasers, fire . . . that was different than everybody else. It became things that imprinted on your brain. You do it so people go, "*Holy fuck!*" There's room for "*Holy fuck!*" and nothing else.

MIKE BONE So then the show ends, the band goes backstage, and Bob and I give 'em a minute to dry off and then we go back there. And we're standing around chatting and one of the guys, I don't remember who it was, Vince or Nikki, he goes, "Look at this." And there's a door there that says DOG POUND on it. And he opens the door and on the other side is a room full of Oklahoma City's finest groupies. And we're not talking four or five of 'em, either. We're talking *a lot* of 'em. And as soon as the door opens they all perk up. They're smiling and waving. And these girls had all been preapproved and carded by [Mötley Crüe tour manager] Rich Fisher. There were no juveniles in there. I don't know what the age of consent was in Oklahoma City, but it was Rich Fisher's job to know that, state by state. And then the door is closed. And whoever it was, Vince or Nikki, he says, "Watch this." And he opens the door again, points at some girl, and she comes through. And he takes this girl into a bathroom stall, sits her on a toilet, and she proceeds to blow him in front of the whole room of people. And Bob looks at me and he goes, "Is it like this every night?" I say, "Yeah." And he goes, "I gotta come out and see more of these shows!"

PETER PHILBIN To Bob's credit, when I told him about Faster Pussycat, he said, "Great. Sign 'em." He liked laughs.

VICKY HAMILTON The Faster Pussycat deal stretched out a long time. It was a long time coming.

BRAD HUNT We had Mötley Crüe, we had Dokken, we had Metallica. And all of a sudden now we had Faster Pussycat.

RIC BROWDE The very first day that we started the album, we were recording at Amigo Studios, which was in North Hollywood. That's where the Poison album was mixed. We're in there getting a drum sound and the head of A&R at Elektra is there, and he's with another A&R guy, they're like the big shots that came in from New York. One of the guys I think signed Simply Red. And Peter Philbin's there. It's literally the first day. Maybe two hours into the session. And one of the A&R guys, he calls me over, and he calls Philbin over, and he just lays into us. He goes to Peter, "If you hadn't fucking given him all the money up front I would shut this fucking thing down right now. This is the biggest bunch of bozo bullshit I've ever seen. This is nothing but a con job. And you guys suck!"

PETER PHILBIN I mean, look, I honor Ric, because he was the perfect guy to be involved. But Ric isn't one of the great producers of the world. And Faster Pussycat can barely play. So I don't remember that conversation, but I'm not surprised.

ERIC STACY I know that when Elektra signed Faster Pussycat the expectations weren't "Oh, this is an amazing band that's gonna sell a lot of records!" I think the feeling was kind of like they'd be happy if we sold fifty thousand copies and they made a little money or broke even.

TAIME DOWNE It doesn't matter. We got a record done. It took us, like, three fucking weeks to do it. We were kids in a studio. I didn't know what all those knobs did. I do now. But I didn't know what-the-fuck back then. I was just like, "Is there a place for me to fuck bitches in here?"

RIC BROWDE We had five days to mix the album, so we were doing two songs a day. And the band would only come in and listen to the mixes. And I remember when we got to "Babylon," I was thinking, Ah, this song is gonna suck. Because it never really came together in the studio. If you strip it down it's a bad version of the Beastie Boys and not very good. So me and [engineer] Tim Bomba were working on a mix for "Babylon," and Taime came in with Brent and listened to it. And Riki Rachtman was in the room, too.

TAIME DOWNE Riki did the scratching on "Babylon." 'Cause Riki used to DJ.

RIC BROWDE So they're listening to it and they're kinda looking at each other. And I remember thinking, "Oh shit . . ." Because Taime had a very volatile temper. But I didn't hate him or anything. That's just who he was. He was a street kid. He was the only one of all the people I knew who were playing that street urchin angle who really was a street urchin. But anyway, we're listening and all of a sudden Taime starts smiling. Then he goes, "Play that again." And I'm like, "Fuck, he liked it!" And then everybody was just playing it for everybody, and I remember all these chicks came in and a couple of them started to have sex with the band. A bunch of the guys were on a couch with the girls and they're like, "Keep playing 'Babylon'!"

GREG STEELE Do I remember that? I wish I did. I'm pretty sure that probably happened. Because back then that would have happened.

TAIME DOWNE At that point all I wanted to do was bring girls in and have sex. We used to have contests and . . . no, I'm not going there. I don't want to be too much of a disgusting pig. But I was doing it the whole fucking time I was doing the record. I'd just always find a new room.

PETER PHILBIN The woman who was head of video at Elektra, Robin Sloane, she went out and got Russ Meyer to do Faster Pussycat's first video, for "Don't Change That Song."

ROBIN SLOANE Well, the band named itself after his movie, right? So it wasn't that difficult. He was happy to do it. It wasn't like he had a lot of work.

TAIME DOWNE He was an old codger but he was super fucking cool. And, you know, to have Russ Meyer make a little three-minute movie of me was pretty awesome. No one can take that away from me.

ROBIN SLOANE I would say that Russ had no sense of the music. And he wasn't really that familiar with the music video form. But he certainly knew how to film young voluptuous girls. I think the best thing about it was that we got some publicity.

PETER PHILBIN Did Russ Meyer like the band? Here's the real answer: I don't know. But there's a rule I have: When you hear "yes," quit negotiating. So Robin goes and gets Russ Meyer to make this video, and that's actually kind of interesting. MTV's never going to play it, but I still don't wanna be the guy who asks, "Hey, Russ, do you actually like this band?" I mean, shut the fuck up and say, "Nice meeting you. Can you sign a poster for me?" You know, you can really screw yourself up asking some girl who's already in the car, "Do you really wanna go out with me?"

TAIME DOWNE At that point in Russ' life I don't really know what he was into. I know he was still into big titties. Because he was like, "We're doing a casting, you've gotta come . . ." It was down in fucking Marina del Rey. I just remember hanging out and he's showing me all this stuff, going, "Ah, I saved these . . ." And there's Kitten Natividad's bra, fucking Haji's bra. I think I have them in a trunk with some photos up in Seattle.

ERIC STACY We were really hungry and we worked our asses off on that first record. We went out, we opened for Alice Cooper, we opened for David Lee Roth. We were out with Motörhead for a while. Y&T. Ace Frehley. We did the dinners and we did all the record store appearances. It was our blood, sweat, and tears that made that record sell 250,000 copies.

TAIME DOWNE Roth, we saw him like the first day, then we saw him on the last day. Alice Cooper we'd see all the time. But we did our own shit. We were kids in a candy store. We only played a half hour or so, and then the rest of the night was like, *whoooo!* We're on the bus doing the rock 'n' roll thing, livin' the dream at age twenty-two, you know what I mean?

GREG STEELE I remember the Alice Cooper audience was very much older people. And so they didn't like us too much. They were going, "What the fuck are these guys?" Alice Cooper was us when he started out but, you know, they didn't care. Whatever.

ERIC STACY Taime documented everything on tour in the early days. Even in the back lounge of the bus, which was where all the business went on, so to speak. If you climbed on top of the third bunk, there was this space where you could kind of see over the floor to the back lounge. Many a night you'd be back there with some girl or whatever, and all of a sudden you'd look up and there was a video camera lens sticking out of that space.

GREG STEELE We had some crazy-ass videos of crazy situations, absolutely.

TAIME DOWNE There was a lot of cameras snapping away. I remember going to the one-hour photo places in the malls, and little kids would be standing there watching our photos come down the belt thing and out the dispenser. And it'd be like, fucking pizza-on-pussy. Just stupid shit.

ERIC STACY On the first tour we had roommates in order to save money, and me and Taime would share a room. And I remember one night I met some chick and I brought her back and we were on my bed. I'm sitting up against the backboard and she's, like, facedown in front of me. I could see the whole room, and what she didn't see behind her was basically every piece of furniture moving by itself. The chair was moving closer and closer to the bed. Because Taime was behind the chair with his camera trying to get good angles. And then Brent came in, and Brent was behind the coffee table. Now he wants a better look. It was kind of funny because you'd just see this furniture moving all over the place.

TAIME DOWNE The back of one of our tour shirts at the time said "And We've Got the Pictures to Prove It."

ERIC STACY We always used to say to Taime, "Dude, one of these days you're gonna have to get rid of everything. Because you've got too much shit on all of us." But I think he realized to do anything with that stuff would be really fucked up.

TAIME DOWNE I have a couple photo albums from those tours with David Lee Roth and Alice Cooper. They're in that trunk up in Seattle. I told my mom, "Never open that." But yeah, it's all still there.

"THE HORNIEST BAND
IN L.A."

MAX ASHER There was a studio called Pitman Studios, right across the street from a newsstand called Centerfold, where Slash worked. We went and recorded the first Warrant demo there, and I still have a cassette. It was a three-song thing. We'd still never played a club gig.

JOSH LEWIS Adam and Max went to a few Black 'N Blue gigs, and there was this group of girls that were at these shows all the time, they loved Black 'N Blue. And one of them was Erik's girlfriend.

MAX ASHER I had a girlfriend that lived in the Valley, and we're at a stop sign and her friend Liz is at the other stop sign, and Erik Turner was in the car with her. My girlfriend says, "That's Liz's boyfriend, he's a guitar player," and I'm like, "Okay, whatever." Then we went to Liz's backyard party that weekend, and there was Erik again, so I said, "Hey, we've been thinking about adding a second guitarist. Do you want to come have a jam?"

JOSH LEWIS We played a few parties here and there, then we decided we would play our first show at the Troubadour. It was a Tuesday night, and I think we actually broke a record because it was all our high school friends.

JERRY DIXON (bassist, Risk, Warrant) My band Risk was on the bill at the Troubadour with Warrant. And this girl—this is sort of dumb—she was like, "Oh, you look like Matt Dillon. You have to stay and watch my friend Erik's band." I didn't even know who Matt Dillon was.

MAX ASHER My friend Gina told me, "Jerry wants to be in your band like nobody's business." And I was like, "Oh, well okay . . ." And I remember talking to Adam and Adam was like, "Dude, all you saw was girls in front of him the whole night. Girls loved him." It was kind of a no-brainer.

JOSH LEWIS We were with a girl who was dating Bret Michaels, and she called him and we got on the phone and said, "We want to play with you. We should do shows together." He was super cool. We opened for Poison at a lot of Troubadour gigs and we opened almost every single Country Club show they did until they were signed and out of L.A.

MAX ASHER We didn't have production right away, but the last year that I was in the band we had a guy named Val who was a really good carpenter. He built these massive Marshall cabinets on both sides of the stage where the actual cabinets would go inside.

JOSH LEWIS When we had our first headline show at the Troubadour, some girls decided they would rent a limousine for us, and they took us to the show in it. And I'll never forget, we drove up to the Troubadour and the line was all the way around the block.

MAX ASHER Our singer, Adam, was not happy with Josh's guitar playing and he was feeling like we weren't getting any stronger. There was another band that we used to play with that Adam really liked and thought their guitar player was great, and we hatched this idea that we could form this superband of those guys and us.

JOSH LEWIS We did our first out-of-town show in San Diego. And the next morning, Adam and Max pull us aside and they're like, "We're quitting the band. We're gonna start a band with the guys from Mickey Knight."

Me and Erik and Jerry drove home in Jerry's truck and everybody was crying.

JERRY DIXON We told Adam and Max, "We're going to keep the name Warrant." They were like, "All right, that's cool."

JOSH LEWIS Warrant played at least one show with Jani and Steven's band, Plain Jane.

JOHN MEZACAPPA Plain Jane's other guitarist, Paul Noble, was living in Woodland Hills. We all moved in and were sleeping in the living room on the floor. Paul and his wife and Jani had the bedrooms.

AL COLLINS Jani was really cranking the songs out.

JOHN MEZACAPPA We all had day jobs . . . except for Jani. Everybody kind of supported him because he was doing all the writing.

STEVEN SWEET Other than being broke, I loved L.A. because I fit in with all the other misfits. I came from a little town in Ohio where Bruce Springsteen was the hot musical ticket and I was the outsider. I was the kid with the long hair and the earring, and practically nobody else in my school was into the kind of music that I was into. So when I got to L.A., it was like, Oh my god! There were all these people that were like me, that came here from somewhere else and needed to get out. So I felt more at home there than any place since I was a kid.

AL COLLINS Honestly, I thought it would be a little bit easier than what it was. But once we got to L.A., we realized we really had to seriously buckle down and do some work. I remember Jani coming home one night and saying, "Man, I saw this band called Poison, and there was like maybe two guys in the audience. It was nothing but girls, and they were just killing it. We really need to go see this band and learn something."

STEVEN SWEET People put the label "glam" on it, but it was more of a look than a sound.

AL COLLINS We designed a stage show. We had a drum riser where the drums actually could revolve like 180 degrees. They had to stop and turn and go back the other direction, and there was a smoke machine underneath it.

JOHN MEZACAPPA I bought this drum riser from this other band that could turn 180 degrees. It kind of looked like a spaceship. The motors and the wheels that were put into it weren't really heavy enough to hold Steve and the drum kit, and there were a couple times where it started spinning and it stopped with Steven's back facing the crowd. People figured it was part of the show, but for us it was pretty embarrassing.

STEVEN SWEET Al Collins and Paul Noble were a little bit older than us. Meaning that they were in their thirties and we were in our twenties. And I think they wanted a little more security or a little bit more of a sure thing. When they left, we were resigned to just go back to Florida to regroup. We thought we could be a big fish in a small pond there.

JOHN MEZACAPPA Honestly, I never took the talk of moving home that seriously. I just kind of did what I did and said, "Hey, we can hang through this, and things are going to work." And they did work out.

JOSH LEWIS I just remember that Jerry and I saw Jani and we were like, "Wow, this guy, he's got balls." He went out in the audience and was singing to all these people that didn't even know him.

JERRY DIXON I think it was in a park and there was, like, thirty people there. I remember Jani climbing up this tree. He was up there singing and screaming like he was playing a stadium. I was like, "That guy's a star." When it came time when we had to find a singer and drummer, I said, "Who is that guy that climbed up that tree? I want that guy!"

ERIK TURNER (guitarist, Warrant) Jani and Steven lived in an apartment just down the street from Jerry and I, so he left a note on the door: "Hey, it's Jerry from Warrant. We need a singer. If you're interested, call us."

STEVEN SWEET We got together and played and it was great. We played "Down Boys," which was a song that Jani had just written, for the first time.

JOSH LEWIS We needed a writer, because none of us could write at the time. Jani could sing his ass off, he was confident. We pretty much let him have control of the band at that point.

STEVEN SWEET Warrant had already developed their flyering thing before Jani and I joined. "The Horniest Band in L.A." was one of their slogans. I wasn't always comfortable with everything that we chose to do, but you know . . .

JOSH LEWIS But then it kind of started getting a little more vulgar . . . We knew this girl who was a stripper and we were like, "Maybe she'll come up onstage at the Troubadour and she could sort of simulate giving Jani a blow job." We had these big walls in front of our amps that we could hide behind, it looked like a cowboy saloon or something, because that was when Bon Jovi's "Wanted Dead or Alive" was big. We were wearing cowboy hats and holsters and shit.

Anyway, Jerry is up there playing a bass riff and it's sexy-sounding. Then this girl comes up and starts sort of stripping. Then she gets on her knees in front of Jani, and while this is happening the lights are going down, and by the time anything could have happened, the lights were completely off, and the drums stop and Jani says, "I don't know, did she or didn't she?" All of a sudden you hear all these girls yelling, "You guys fucking suck! This is disgusting!" People were pissed.

JERRY DIXON I was flyering out on the Strip and a photographer who was about to shoot an ad for Capitol Records came up and said, "Hey man, we're shooting and we'd like to use you for it." We exchanged numbers and I did the photo shoot. It was funny, because it was a promotion for all the bands that Capitol had signed, like W.A.S.P. and Poison.

STEVEN SWEET This woman named Jamie Shoop who worked for Prince's management saw the ad in *BAM*. It was Jerry leaning up against a telephone pole flipping the camera off, wearing a motorcycle jacket, his hair long, and looking cute. And she goes, "I would love to get this young rocker-looking guy on a soap opera." She was also managing Luis Miguel at the time, who was a Mexican soap star and singing sensation.

JERRY DIXON Jamie tracked me down and called me. And I'm like, "No, I'm a musician. I've never acted or done anything like that ... But you gotta come see my band!"

JOSH LEWIS Then I got kicked out. I just wasn't ready. I didn't have the best equipment, I was kind of wild onstage, I'd sort of slam my guitar, guitars would be out of tune all the time ... I think Jani was just at a level of professionalism that I wasn't at at the time.

JOEY ALLEN (guitarist, Warrant) The way I got in Warrant was I lived in Hollywood, I was looking for a band, and I happened to be on the Sunset Strip one weekend partying and having fun and I was at Doheny and Sunset, right across from Gil Turner's liquor store. And lo and behold, Erik Turner walked up. And Erik and I had been in a band together two or three years prior. He said Warrant were looking for a lead guitar player, and I was looking for a band. You know, timing's everything, right?

So I went to a Warrant show at a backyard party somewhere out in the Valley and watched them, and what's funny is that Josh was hitting on my girlfriend and I was just sitting there laughing. 'Cause I'm like, "Dude, I'm about to take your gig!"

STEVEN SWEET Jamie Shoop somehow got Prince interested, because at the time he was looking for a young, white, long-haired rock band to sort of mold into his own Prince thing, kind of like he did with Apollonia 6 and Vanity 6.

JERRY DIXON She got Prince to put us in the studio with the producer Ed Cherney. That was the first time we actually were properly recorded, and we ended up using that demo to get signed.

JOEY ALLEN Prince liked the demo, but then he saw a live video of us at the Country Club. We were, you know, five guys in their early twenties with hormones raging . . .

STEVEN SWEET He thought, "Well, these guys aren't dancers, so they're not really what I'm looking for."

JERRY DIXON Everybody else was gone. Guns N' Roses and Van Halen and Mötley Crüe and Ratt and W.A.S.P. We were the only ones left in L.A. It got right to the end and it was like, "God, is this really not going to happen? Why can't we get a deal?"

BRET HARTMAN (executive, CBS Records, MCA Records) In 1987, before I was at CBS Records I was an intern at RCA. I'd go there from nine a.m. to two and then I'd take the bus down to Tower Records and work there from three to midnight. I had just moved from Seattle to L.A., and the second day I was at Tower I walked up to Gazzarri's on my lunch break, it was like three or four in the afternoon, and Warrant was soundchecking. So it was like the first band I saw. And they were already really huge. They had all the full-page ads in *BAM* and *Rock City News*, they had their flyers everywhere, they were selling out the Country Club on Friday and Saturday nights. But all the other labels had passed on them because they figured the market was already saturated and nothing was really going on beyond Poison.

STEVEN SWEET It was frustrating because we were selling out all the nights in places, and people were asking us, "Why aren't you guys signed yet?" But really, from the time that Jani and I joined together with the guys in Warrant, and the time that we got signed, it was only a matter of a couple years—a blink in time.

BRET HARTMAN Jani was such a great singer, they had great songs, and they were amazing live. And I was like, "They're not doing anything new but they're really good at what they do." And then the people from CBS Japan came and saw them at the Country Club and they really loved them, so

I went to Ron Oberman, the head of CBS, and got him on board. He brought in Beau Hill and Jani was down with that. Jani called all the shots.

JOEY ALLEN I don't know if Bret worked at CBS as an intern, I don't know if he had signing authority. But for all intents and purposes I would have to say that Bret Hartman–slash–Ron Oberman signed Warrant to CBS/Columbia. Absolutely.

BRET HARTMAN They were like the biggest band in L.A., you know? It was pretty much an easy picking right there. I mean it was like, "Why isn't this band signed yet?" But I'm fresh from Seattle so I had a fresh perspective. Where everybody else, maybe it just blurred together with all the other hair metal bands on the Strip and they couldn't tell the difference.

FLYER WARS

BRET MICHAELS There were flyer wars, let me say this. It was crazy. I'm talking parking-lot-knock-down-drag-out-fistfight material. Over *flyers*. Because that was your advertising. You either put your flyer up or no one knew you existed.

RIKKI ROCKETT It would get nasty sometimes. It really would.

CHRIS WEBER Back then, if you had a band in L.A. you spent your Friday and Saturday nights flyering for your next show. You would go to any of these copy places—and there were lots of copy places—and you would make two thousand copies of your flyer and you would go out with a staple gun and staple them on top of telephone poles all night long. Or you would go and stand out in front of whatever show was happening and you would pass them out to every single person walking out of the show. A lot of our time was all about promotion.

BRET HARTMAN Friday and Saturday nights on Sunset Boulevard there were, like, hundreds of hair metal bands handing out flyers. And hundreds of girls would come in from all over L.A. in high heels with their hair ratted out. It was just a crazy, magical time.

GINA ZAMPARELLI The flyer wars and the advertising, everybody had to be bigger than the next band. It was promotion that they learned how to do on their own. Nobody taught those guys. So there was a lot to be said about these bands' individual creativity.

MICK CRIPPS Well, you gotta remember this is an era before the home computer or cell phones. Cable TV was still in its infancy. So it was still like the 1970s, really. You had to do it all on your own, putting up pieces of paper on walls, putting ads in newspapers and things. It was very mechanical, put it that way. It was like horse-and-buggy!

GINA ZAMPARELLI The one thing I saw about Mötley Crüe was they understood overkill. They were, like, guerrilla marketers. I don't even know how many they made . . . ten thousand posters, thousands of flyers. Stickers everywhere.

NIKKI SIXX You know, as sad as it sounds, the concept of marketing has always intrigued me. Back in those days I would look at a telephone pole and think, That pole is covered with flyers on Friday, but on Saturday they're gone. So I would say to the other guys, "We have to get our flyers higher than everyone else's, because some guy who's making minimum wage to clean off that pole isn't going to climb a ladder just to get our shit down. So that will give us multiple impressions." And the band would look at me and go, "*What?*" We'd stand on each other's shoulders and get our flyers way up there. And they'd stay there for weeks.

LIZZIE GREY One time I was putting up these flyers and this guy in a black Mercedes pulls over and goes, "Hey man, you gotta put the flyer up higher. No one's gonna see it there." And it was David Lee Roth! He said, "You gotta make it so people can see that thing!"

DAVID LEE ROTH We had a list of fourteen high schools and junior high schools within driving distance, an hour in any direction. We would go out and wait for bad weather so we could have free run of the schools. In every outside locker we'd put a flyer in. We'd flyer the place. If you saw Aerosmith was playing the football stadium, great, that's perfect, we'll flyer them. You could get, I believe, four thousand flyers for forty bucks at the instant press and we would break into teams. Ultimately, we had little walkie-talkies because the police would stop one team from flyering cars, and you would know that that was happening so you'd go into overdrive on the other side of the stadium so you could flyer every car. This built up a tremendous following for Van Halen on a very, very grassroots level. On the flyers we'd write, "The People's Choice." I got it from Muhammad Ali fight posters.

RIKKI ROCKETT The reason we won that war most of the time is because C.C.'s parents owned a print shop—Barbara's Place. We had massive amounts of flyers and the ability to make more and more. We'd go out and party or whatever and hang out, hand out flyers and things like that, but then at two in the morning we'd come home and change into crappy clothes and go with a glue mat and start hitting everything that we could.

HOWIE HUBBERMAN Where bands would print up a thousand flyers, Poison would print up ten thousand flyers. And it was very cheap—for ten thousand flyers it might have cost me maybe two hundred bucks. *Maybe.* And the guys went out and worked the streets every night and got rid of all of them. On the Sunset Strip you would see wall-to-wall Poison flyers.

DUFF McKAGAN Poison wasn't my cup of tea. But they knew how to market themselves.

BOBBY DALL Not a day, not a moment went past that we weren't promoting, or stapling flyers or gluing flyers or knocking on doors or doing the hustle.

RIKKI ROCKETT Sometimes it was a conversation starter with chicks. You're like, "Oh, for sure they're going to come . . ."

SHARE ROSS Walking down the Strip you got flyered every two seconds. "Come see my band, come see my band, come see my band." Then you were trying to decide if the person you were talking to was definitely a guy as well. Like, I think that was a dude?

CHRIS WEBER You find some girls that you like or that like you and you sort of make them feel like, "Hey, I really want you to come to the show . . ." And then they get their girlfriends. You would try and make everybody feel a little bit special. That's how Poison and bands like that did it. They were nice to hang out with and friendly so they'd get a lot of girls coming to their shows, and those girls would get more girls. And then guys would come because the girls were going to the Poison show. And before you know it you have a thousand people at a gig.

JOEY ALLEN If you've got a thousand seats to sell, you put out four thousand flyers. And you've maybe already got a fan base with five hundred people so hopefully with those flyers you put out, four or five hundred more people come.

BRET HARTMAN Warrant had their flyers everywhere. And they also had that whole sex thing going on. It was kind of tongue-in-cheek and funny, though.

MAX ASHER I remember Poison had slogans, Guns always had slogans. The slogan thing was definitely big. I would say that Warrant got a lot deeper into that after my time in the band.

JOEY ALLEN There's so many childish things we came up with. "The Horniest Band This Side of Pluto." "$10 All You Can Eat."

BRET HARTMAN "If It's Not Love Use a Glove." "Sex Police." You know, like "Dream Police."

JOEY ALLEN Somebody in the band at one point or another would come up with an idea, we'd all laugh, and it'd go on a poster.

JERRY DIXON If we could make people want to slap us in the face, we knew we had a good flyer.

JOEY ALLEN I mean, a lot of people could look at it nowadays and go, "God, that's highly misogynistic." But I grew up with two older sisters and a mother. I've got a daughter. I love women to death. I'm a proponent of women's rights. It has nothing to do with that. It was just to get attention. You wish you could get it with just your music only, but at that time in life that wasn't the key to the kingdom, you know what I mean?

JOSH LEWIS L.A. is very grid-like, so we would map out the city and say, "Okay, we're gonna start at Vine, and we're gonna go from Hollywood down to Melrose." And we'd hit every single pole. Whenever we'd be like, "Should we hit that pole?" We'd go, "Well, do you want to sell out the show?" We did Vine, Highland, Crescent Heights—I mean all the way to the beach practically—which was miles and miles, but we would just do it. It was craziness.

MICKEY FINN Jetboy prided ourselves on being the flyer kings. When we hit it we hit it harder, bigger than anybody. Somebody posted half a wall? We would do two walls. We would just go crazy. We'd go out with wheat paste at two in the morning, three in the morning, we'd hit billboards and we'd hit street corners. That stems from our punk rock roots.

BILLY ROWE One time Izzy and I borrowed [songwriter and musician] West Arkeen's car and went out flyering. It was, like, an old El Camino with a cap on the top. And I can remember we got to a stop sign and fucking Axl's head pops up from the back. And he goes, "What's goin' on?" We had no idea he was even in the car. He was under a blanket sleeping.

MICKEY FINN Then we started doing ones where you'd print up, you know, a hundred flyers and then you put it together and it makes one giant ad. Like, next level, man.

DUFF McKAGAN People would try to fuck up your gear, poster a flyer over your flyers. I was like, "All right . . ." We all kind of had to put the fucking Vaseline underneath the eyes and get ready for the fight.

MAX ASHER I wish I still had a little phone message that I got from Duff McKagan on the Warrant Hotline number, which was just our personal phone number. We had gone over some Guns N' Roses posters because their show was already over and Duff called me and was like, "Hey, you little Warrant fuckers, this is Duff from Guns N' Roses and we're going to kick your asses if you go over any more of our shit!"

DUFF McKAGAN That sounds right. Warrant, they'd flyered over our stuff. And we'd just flyered the night before. It's not fucking cool, you know? And I think it happened one too many times.

JACK RUSSELL I remember driving down Sunset Boulevard and putting posters up—and just trying to get a nail into one of those telephone poles on Sunset Boulevard was an art, because it's almost solid metal. So we're pounding them in and I look behind us a couple blocks and there's Nikki Sixx on the back of a pickup truck, ripping our posters down and putting his up. So what do we do? We turn around, we go back behind him where he couldn't see us. We tore their posters down and put ours back up.

MICK CRIPPS In L.A. Guns we would *talk* about doing flyering, put it that way. Because we'd see these other—most of them not that good—bands putting flyers everywhere. And we'd talk about it, like, "Yeah, we should be out putting up flyers!" But we were all too fucking lazy to do that.

KRISTY "KRASH" MAJORS (guitarist, Pretty Boy Floyd) We used to do, I think, ten thousand flyers a show. If there was a big concert at the Forum or something, we would bring a couple people with us and we would hit every single car. And then you have the walls and telephone poles on the Strip, and just like with every other band, your flyers would get covered up two days later and then you'd go back out and cover up theirs.

STEVIE RACHELLE (singer, Tuff) We would pick up ten thousand flyers from a printer and at some point we would probably go through those and get another shipment. So we would do twenty thousand handbills and post them everywhere. Then we would go to Home Depot and buy these five-gallon pails of glue and paintbrushes, and then at, like, two in the morning we would put on old jeans and flannel shirts and work gloves and we would go out in a truck. And what we would do is we would literally go up to a telephone pole, take the paintbrush, dip it in the glue, and just coat the telephone pole with this super-sticky clear glue. And then one of the other guys would put up ten flyers, as high as you could go. If you're six foot tall you could reach up seven or eight feet. If there was a park bench, we'd pull it over, we'd paste them as high as we could. We'd coat the entire pole with the flyer. And if anybody else's flyer was on there, whether it was a pop band or a rock band or a rap band or another band from the Strip, we would just go right over it.

KRISTY "KRASH" MAJORS Every night was promoting night. Monday was at the Whisky for the No Bozo Jam. Tuesday was the Cathouse. Wednesday was Bordello. Thursday was someplace else. Friday and Saturday was the Strip and the Country Club. Sunday . . . I don't know where Sunday was. But we would just stand there and hand out flyers.

BRET HARTMAN Pretty Boy Floyd would be up and down on the Strip all night handing out flyers. And they took out huge ads in the magazines constantly. That was one of their tricks. It made them look bigger than they were by taking out these full-page ads in every issue of *Rock City News*. Because the magazines were really big, too. There was *Rock City News* and there was a few other fanzines, like *BAM*. People were just instantly becoming like rock stars in these magazines. And you could buy a full-page ad in *Rock City News* for, like, $200 or something. There was no internet so it was all flyers and word of mouth and fanzines and KNAC.

GINA ZAMPARELLI I think how promotion grew during the '80s, that's a story in itself. There were other papers, like the *Los Angeles Times,* but they were always too expensive. And a lot of these guys did not have money. They didn't have food. A lot of them were living in warehouses, in girls' apartments. But *BAM* was a magazine that was affordable. And then there was flyers and there was posters.

STEVIE RACHELLE Everybody's handing out flyers—pink and blue and orange and green and big and small and with tickets and buttons and stickers and everything else. And throughout the night a lot of it just ended up on the ground. So what would happen is every morning around four a.m. the city would have to hire some kind of crew to come and clean up the Strip. It looked like the end of a fair—there was just paper and cans and stickers and flyers everywhere. So much so that you couldn't see the sidewalk.

RIKKI ROCKETT For the most part we'd just nail everything that we could. I mean, we'd flyer dumpsters.

STEVIE RACHELLE I guess we were basically destroying property. Covering everything with our stupid flyers.

"IF THEY HAD CAMERAS BACK THEN, THAT WHOLE SCENE WOULD BE IN JAIL"

RIKI RACHTMAN (co-owner, the Cathouse; MTV VJ; *Headbangers Ball* host)
Dayle Gloria, as far as the underground clubs go, she was a big deal.
When I met her, she was the DJ at Seven Seas on Hollywood Boulevard,
which was kind of a seedy, hip, underground club. It was run by Ed Nash,
and we kept on hearing about all these Wonderland murders. But I didn't
really know what was going on.

DAYLE GLORIA (co-owner, Scream) You know who Ed Nash is, right? Okay,
so that was our boss. This was the guy who really started my career. And
if you watch the movie *Wonderland,* that's exactly how it was. [Nash,
who owned the Starwood and was a reputed organized crime figure, was
charged in connection with the brutal murder of four people at their
home at 8763 Wonderland Avenue in Laurel Canyon in 1981.] I was going
through the kitchen to go to the office and I would see people blindfolded
and handcuffed to a chair. And I would walk right through.

RIKI RACHTMAN So I came into this club, Seven Seas, I was like the new
kid. I didn't know what I was doing. And I got a gig there playing one
night and then I started to get a bigger and bigger following. I got to play
records, get loaded, and meet girls.

DAYLE GLORIA Me and another DJ there, Michael Stewart, would do all different kinds of music. But when it started to be a lot of Michael Jackson and all that kind of stupid dance music, we really wanted to open our place where we could play what was first called alternative music—Sisters of Mercy and Siouxsie and the Banshees and anything like that. So Michael and I went our own way because we had ideas for a different type of club. And that was Scream.

TAIME DOWNE The first Scream was downtown. I was good friends with Michael Stewart, and I've known Dayle since the early days. And I used to go to a lot of clubs when I first moved to L.A.—the fetish clubs and TVC15 and then Glam Slam. This was before there were any cool rock clubs.

DAYLE GLORIA Taime was the one who said, "You know, why don't you have bands instead of just playing music?" So we all talked about that and we went looking for a building and we found this place, it was called the Ebony Theater. It was in a really, really crappy neighborhood. We had Molotov cocktails being thrown at us. And the very first bill we ever did was with Jane's Addiction. And if I'm not mistaken it was the second show they ever did. Then we found a spot at the Embassy Hotel and that's when everything got real serious. We started there in June or July of '86. And that was the place. We had the first video room that any club ever had, we had the band room downstairs, there were different dance rooms, an outside patio, it was nuts. I mean, one thousand people, fifteen hundred people, two thousand. We got up to three thousand people. And here is my very first booking calendar: Guns N' Roses played on August fifteenth, 1986. Jane's Addiction on the twenty-second. Faster Pussycat on September fifth. Jane's on the twenty-sixth with Wall of Voodoo. The Chili Peppers played the fourteenth of November. It was really crazy.

TAIME DOWNE At that time Riki was DJ'ing and promoting at a club called Ice. It was more of a dance club. It was at the Probe on Highland, where the Cathouse later ended up.

RIKI RACHTMAN I met Taime . . . I was dating this mud wrestler, and we went to a party at some stripper's house. There weren't even that many people there. It was me, my friend Keith, these two chicks, and Taime. He was just this guy that a lot of people knew and he worked at Retail Slut. He was just about to start Faster Pussycat. But I thought he was just the coolest cat. And I was like, "Dude, come down to Ice, this club I'm DJ'ing." And he came down and he wasn't really into it because it was a bunch of rich snobby girls from the Valley dancing. But we hit it off right away.

TAIME DOWNE We just talked about doing a rock club together. He had DJ'd fucking Tommy Lee's wedding and shit before.

RIKI RACHTMAN I grew up in Hollywood. My parents were divorced and I lived with my mother, who was a schoolteacher. But my dad managed bands—Gary Puckett & the Union Gap; Lee Michaels, who had that song "Do You Know What I Mean"; Flash Cadillac & the Continental Kids; stuff like that. And my dad's girlfriend was Karen Black. So I was also around that lifestyle a little bit. And I knew a lot of people who were club DJs, and I used to help them carry records. Then I started DJ'ing clubs myself, and I was really good at it. I was playing hip-hop and dance music and new wave but, you know, I had long hair, I was a rocker. Izzy came and hung out with me in the DJ booth at one gig, and that was before Guns N' Roses even. At Ice I would DJ certain songs and then scratch, like, Mötley Crüe into it and do weird stuff like that. I did that one time at this huge club in L.A., and Tommy Lee was there with Heather Locklear. And Tommy came up and he goes, "Dude, you're so good! Would you DJ my wedding?" And I was like, "Fuck yes, I would!" 'Cause I loved Mötley Crüe.

Then when I met Taime, we started talking and I said, "Dude, I wanna do a club that's a dance club, but all we play is rock 'n' roll. Do you wanna help me out with it?" Because I knew that Taime knew a lot of people. So I took everything I knew from clubs, and he helped get a lot of girls to come down, and we just started from there.

TAIME DOWNE Riki and I put our brains together, and then I got a buddy of mine, Joseph Brooks, who was a DJ at TVC15 and the original Glam Slam and all the fetish clubs. We started over at Osko's.

JOSEPH BROOKS (DJ, the Cathouse, Scream) Osko's was this discotheque on La Cienega that was featured in a Donna Summer movie called *Thank God It's Friday*. It hadn't been updated since the '70s. When we started in there in '86 it looked exactly the same—mirrored walls, a ceiling that was all square mirrored tiles, and a DJ booth that was sort of perched over the dance floor in a very commanding way. It was like stepping back into a time machine. It looked like the inside of a big disco ball.

RIKI RACHTMAN You know in the movie *The Metal Years,* you see me and Taime saying the Cathouse was a place for us to get free drinks and meet strippers? That is *exactly* why it was opened. No other reason.

BILLY ROWE When Cathouse started, it was not well attended. You would walk in and there would be maybe a hundred people there. And it was a pretty big venue.

ERIC STACY It was basically just the guys in Guns N' Roses and Faster Pussycat and Jetboy and their girlfriends and a couple of their friends. It was just this little unknown place where the guys in the band hung out on Tuesday night.

RIKI RACHTMAN The first night there were like 150 people there. And it wasn't very good. But Gene Kirkland, who was a big rock photographer then, he was the first person in the door. And he walked in with Lita Ford. And I told the bartenders, "Give Lita anything she wants." I was stoked there was a rock celebrity in the place. Because at that time, Guns N' Roses, L.A. Guns, none of them were there yet. But Lita gets all fucked up and she winds up puking in the bathroom. Then when the night's over, everybody's coming up to me: "Dude, Riki, I'm sorry it didn't work out . . ." And I'm like, "Lita Ford puked in the bathroom." "Yeah, we know . . ." And I'm going, "You don't understand. *Lita Ford puked in the bathroom.*" I thought that was the baddest thing in the world.

DAYLE GLORIA Nobody was going to the Cathouse. It was really bad. I think at one point it was me, Taime, Nikki Sixx, and a couple other people. And all of a sudden on, like, the fifth week, it exploded and it was packed.

RIKI RACHTMAN We opened on September 23, 1986. I kept on promoting it and it would get a little bigger, a little bigger. And then December comes along, and by that time Faster Pussycat had played their first show. And they weren't very good at first. But Guns N' Roses, I thought Guns N' Roses were great. And they were about to release their first EP. And I was like, "Would you guys do a record release party at the Cathouse?" I talked to Steven and then I talked to Axl and they're like, "Yeah. And we'll even play acoustic." And this is before MTV ever thought of do-ing *Unplugged*. So then I asked L.A. Guns if they would do it and they said yes. I asked Jetboy and they said yes. Faster Pussycat said yes. So we just set up acoustic guitars on the floor and had all the bands play. And that night we had, like, five hundred people. It really put us on the map.

TRACII GUNS With the Cathouse you had the benefit of going to a place that was a really cool hang, like the Rainbow, except instead of sitting at a table with friends you're standing up, rocking out, there's beautiful, beautiful women everywhere . . . and there's bands playing, too!

ERIC STACY That was right at the same time the L.A. hard rock/glam re-vival thing was starting to bust open. So it was just like the perfect storm.

BILLY ROWE It was just sex, drugs, rock 'n' roll. It was as cliché as that. Everybody would be there. And there were tons of girls.

TAIME DOWNE We changed [the Faster Pussycat song] "Whorehouse" to "Cathouse." It was kind of about the Cathouse anyway, so I just figured when we do the record I'll fucking change it to that.

RIKI RACHTMAN All the girls were dressed like whores. But, when I say that, they were girls that owned businesses. They were girls that were doctors. They were girls that were attorneys. But they dressed like whores. And the reason was it was fun for them. Because they were women that were very independent. They were the furthest thing from bimbos. But they knew they could come to the Cathouse and dress sleazy and still have a fun time. That became the style to the point of *Women's Wear Daily*,

Sportswear International, California Apparel News, all the biggest fashion magazines were coming to the Cathouse talking about the fashion.

TAIME DOWNE It was just so much cool shit. Every week there'd be someone new that I'd get to meet. Billy Gibbons from ZZ Top would be there. Steven Tyler. The Hollywood Brat Pack fucking thing.

ERIC STACY You'd see Robert Downey Jr. there, Keanu Reeves, all those guys.

BILLY ROWE Crispin Glover used to pull up on his Pee Wee Herman bicycle and hang out in front. Steve Jones from the Sex Pistols, he'd always be there.

TAIME DOWNE Every week I'd stroll up to the club and fucking Jonesy would be outside, his chest hanging out and his tummy all thin and Robert Plant–lookin' . . . He'd be standing there just holding up the wall. And every chick that'd walk by, Jonesy would be like, "You fuck her? I bet you fucked her. I *know* you fucked her." And that's how I'd start my night at the club.

KATHERINE TURMAN I absolutely loved the Cathouse. I had a membership card. I'm not a person who enjoyed dancing, but the Cathouse was a place where you could go and sort of dance to rock and metal bands.

JOHNNY "DUKE" SIZEMORE (L.A. scenester; Cathouse regular) I'd be there every Tuesday and you'd always see Axl out on the dance floor.

RIKI RACHTMAN He would go out on the floor and dance by himself.

JOSEPH BROOKS Well, Cathouse was a lot of insecure guys and a lot of more secure women. And Axl, we had an extra chair in the DJ booth and he would come in and talk and hang out. And for the first hour or two, no guys would be dancing. Only girls would be dancing, and usually with each other. So to break the ice I knew the songs that would get Axl to jump up off his chair and go down on the dance floor. And he would dance like a demon. If I put on "Whole Lotta Rosie" by AC/DC I was pretty much guaranteed to get him out there. And I could keep him out there for an extended period of time if I played the right mix of songs. Anything by Queen. Anything by AC/DC. He would be out there kicking his heels up the whole time.

ERIC STACY It was maybe six months into the club when they moved to the address at 836 North Highland.

TAIME DOWNE We had to move it over to the Probe because the building we were in was falling apart. They were condemning it. We had no choice. The building's not even there now. It was torn down like a year after we moved.

ERIC STACY And when they did that, every Tuesday night there'd be maybe fifty Harleys parked out front on Highland. And when you go inside there was this set of thirty stairs to go up to the first bar or whatever, and you'd walk in and Slash would be, like, throwing up or falling down the stairs. And then you'd keep going up and they had this little roped-off VIP area above the dance floor and in there you'd see all these actors and rock guys sitting back there and doing blow, drinking. It was just a crazy, off-the-hook party. Joseph would play great music, from Hanoi Rocks to Bauhaus to the Cult. Chicks would wear nothing and everybody was fucked up.

TRACII GUNS I would watch all my friends just out of their minds getting on motorcycles at one forty-five, two in the morning, with girls on the backs of their bikes. And me just wondering if they were going to, you know, make it a block. Like, "Wow, what the fuck is gonna happen?"

JOSEPH BROOKS The Probe was another '70s discotheque.

RIKI RACHTMAN Scream was there on Mondays and Cathouse was there on Tuesdays.

DAYLE GLORIA Cathouse was more ripped jeans and big, big, big hair, while at Scream all the guys looked like [Echo and the Bunnymen front man]

Ian McCulloch and all the girls looked like Siouxsie Sioux. But everybody kind of intermingled. I mean, Taime was a real chameleon.

JOSEPH BROOKS I DJ'd at both clubs, and there was some crossover for sure. But I wouldn't play the Cure or Siouxsie at Cathouse.

TRACII GUNS Scream in downtown L.A. was where Guns N' Roses filmed "Welcome to the Jungle."

MICKEY FINN I can remember playing the Scream one time and Perry Farrell was so fucked up on acid. They were going on after us and he was backstage, curled up in a ball on a chair, holding his knees and bawling. And I remember going, "Damn, dude . . ." And an hour and a half later he's onstage just fucking killing it.

DAVE NAVARRO Scream was where I got my education as a professional musician. The shows were usually at, like, two in the morning at these really seedy downtown rented-out spaces, and in the early days you had to have a passcode to get into these things. It was like, "Swordfish," and then you get in. It was an exciting time for sure.

BILLY ROWE Everybody was drinking, doing lines of coke in the bathroom, flirting with girls in a way where if you did it now, you'd be behind bars, you know? If they had cameras back then, that whole scene would be in jail.

DAVE NAVARRO I'd go to the Cathouse to drink and meet girls. But we didn't play the Cathouse. That wasn't our scene.

KIM THAYIL (guitarist, Soundgarden) Chris [Cornell, Soundgarden front man] and I went and saw Guns N' Roses at the Cathouse. They hadn't gone gold yet, but I remember we went there with an A&R person from Geffen and they told us, "Their record's going to be gold next week." We're like, "Okay . . ." That didn't mean anything to us because we're just kids in a band.

The Cathouse, there was a lot of fucking Aqua Net and spandex and we thought that was kind of stupid and silly. But we're watching them play and Chris and I looked at each other like, "Fuck, these guys have some presence." It didn't seem rehearsed. It didn't seem scripted. It didn't seem assembled. They seemed like they were who they were and we loved it. And then we ended up touring with them like, four, five years later.

RIKI RACHTMAN We started getting a lot of the Sunset Strip bands. But to me that wasn't the Cathouse. Even though I don't have anything against, you know, Warrant, Warrant wasn't a Cathouse band.

JOEY ALLEN Did we go to the Cathouse? Absolutely. Went there many a night. That's where all the rock stars hung out, that's where all the pussy was, that's where all the drugs were. Sign this, suck that, snort this, that's what I remember. You'd wake up the next day going, "Fuck, what happened?"

JOSEPH BROOKS People would come into the DJ booth, have sex six inches from me, do drugs a foot away from me. I'm talking about rock celebrities getting blow jobs in the DJ booth. I'd be like, "Are you serious? Can you take that somewhere else?"

JOE LESTÉ (singer, Bang Tango) I mean, I don't want to be that guy, but you could easily go and say, "Oh, yeah, I just got a blow job in the corner by the stairwell over there." That happened all the time at the Cathouse.

RIKI RACHTMAN Crazy stories? The one that always stands out in my mind is Axl Rose chasing David Bowie down the street saying he was gonna kill him.

JOSEPH BROOKS This is when we were at the Probe. The security guards came up to me and they said, "Look, we have someone at the front door and we don't know where to put him in the club, we can't have him just walk around. He's a big celebrity. Can we put him in the DJ booth with you?" I go, "Who is this person?" They go, "David Bowie." I said, "Yeah, of course," but I was losing my mind. Because he was like my ultimate hero. And they brought him into the booth. He was there to see Guns N' Roses.

ALAN NIVEN If I remember correctly that was after we'd just come back from doing a Japanese tour. And the Cathouse had moved to a new location, and we went in to shoot a video for "It's So Easy" with Nigel Dick. It was a packed, intense night and Nigel and his DP got some great footage—probably some of the best live footage of the band in that period. And unfortunately, Axl decided that he was going to do a little bit of *Story of O* with [then girlfriend] Erin [Everly] to add in as concept footage. It was S&M, BDSM stuff. Blindfold and paddles and all kinds of things. You know, an entertaining way to make a Christmas card for the family. I told Axl we should just shelve it.

DUFF McKAGAN So we played a set, and we played "It's So Easy" three or four times. And something happened, I'm not sure exactly what, 'cause a lot was going on, but Axl, you know, that dude is the real deal. If he's pissed off he doesn't care who it is. It can be David Bowie and he won't get away with it. But I don't know what happened. Maybe Riki knows what happened.

RIKI RACHTMAN All I know is my security guard comes up to me and says, "Axl Rose is chasing David Bowie down the street." Okay. I didn't even know David Bowie was in the club. I would've loved to have met David Bowie!

ALAN NIVEN Bowie came to the live show, and if I remember correctly he was seen talking to Erin and that upset Axl. And the next thing you know is they were scuffling and screaming at each other on the pavement outside the club.

DUFF McKAGAN That was a new one. That was definitely a new level. And you know, like, Slash grew up with Bowie for a while. There was that connection. So not only was our singer chasing David Bowie down the street but it's also, like, Slash's mom's old boyfriend. So, yeah, that was one of the stranger happenings that I witnessed probably in my whole life.

RIKI RACHTMAN I stood there and I'm like . . . I just walked away. 'Cause there was nothing I could do.

KATHERINE TURMAN But an interesting thing about the Cathouse is that all the luminaries went there. I mean, if you were David Bowie, who I saw there, or Nikki Sixx or whatever, you weren't bombarded by fans. It was just a place where everyone could hang out. I'd even heard that Nikki was there, you know, the night that he OD'd.

NIKKI SIXX We went out to the Cathouse, and then back to Franklin Plaza [Apartments], where Slash and Steven [Adler] had rooms. We just kept taking it further, and it reached the breaking point for me. You take someone who hasn't slept, who's been on the road for almost a year, and whose health is falling apart, and mix that with heroin and pills and cocaine and tons of alcohol, and what happened kind of makes sense. My body just gave out.

RIKI RACHTMAN I just remember the night after because I went to Nikki's house and he had kind of a Christmas party. And Nikki had OD'd and he looked like shit. But I think he got high that night, too.

ERIC STACY Riki and Taime also had the whole merchandise thing. Axl Rose started wearing Cathouse shirts onstage with Guns N' Roses. Mötley was wearing Cathouse shirts. Obviously the Faster Pussycat guys. We would all wear them and spread the name all over the world.

TAIME DOWNE I was making more money off the club than I was with Faster Pussycat. I remember paying for shit for the band out of club money. That fucking paid the bills even after we got our record deal, because we didn't get no huge deal.

RIKI RACHTMAN There was one night before the club was open that Axl came by and brought the "Paradise City" video with him, and we sat in the DJ booth watching it. And he takes his jacket off in the video and he's wearing a Cathouse shirt. And I'm like, "I better order more shirts . . ." I still sell Cathouse shirts worldwide to this day.

And the thing was, as Guns N' Roses got bigger, they always took the Cathouse with them. They were always playing the club, they were always mentioning us in interviews, they were always wearing the T-shirts. I mean, Axl helped me get my job at MTV.

TAIME DOWNE Axl put in a good word for Riki at MTV and I just remember I kept telling Riki, "Go for it. Fucking do it." Then all of a sudden it was like, "I'm on MTV with Faster Pussycat, and we're being interviewed on *Headbangers Ball* by my old partner from the Cathouse!" It was great. Fucking cool.

40

"IT FELT LIKE BEATLEMANIA"

FRED COURY Cinderella's first arena tour was with David Lee Roth, and when we first met him, he was peeing in one of my road cases. It was great. It was awesome. I was like, "Wow, I'm never going to sell that road case." He couldn't have been nicer, but we started crossing him on the charts.

JEFF LaBAR The better our album did, the more restrictions they tried to put on us. At one point Tom was told that he was not allowed to speak in between songs. We pointed out how ridiculous that was, so then they said, "Okay, you're allowed to say the name of the city and the name of the song."

LARRY MAZER A couple of weeks in I'm starting to get phone calls from Dave's manager, saying, "We have a problem. Dave thinks that Tom is ripping off his raps." I said, "Wait a second." I said, "Guys, with all due respect to Tom, I can tell you right now what his raps are, and they're barely raps." "Hey, Houston, you having a good time?" "Hey, light up your lighters!" You've got David fucking Lee Roth, the greatest front man in the music business, and you're telling me that Tom Keifer is ripping off his raps?

FRED COURY But while all this was happening, Dave was inviting me to all of his after-show parties. The rest of the band wasn't allowed to come, just me, and I would go. It was called "Club Dave," and I would go every night.

STEVE VAI (guitarist, David Lee Roth, Whitesnake; solo artist) It was like Caligula from hell. Dave knew how to take fun really seriously. Every night the hospitality room was festooned with curtains and a gigantic stereo system with speakers that were like PAs. There were tables and tables of food and drink, and the techs and security guards during the show would go out and pull between fifty and sixty people, and ninety percent of them were girls in their underwear. Then he would invite all of the radio programmers and record company people and they'd get drunk and laid and they'd go on the radio the next day and talk about it. You know, Dave was very well crafted that way.

DAVID LEE ROTH My recreation director was named Paul. I had met him at a Club Med in Tahiti. He was entertainment director for the whole village. He would have theme nights, like Waffle House night, where we would come off the stage and he would have hired twelve bikini models from Hawaiian Tropic in Lakeland, Florida, and gone to the local Waffle House, rented uniforms, got menus. You walk in and there'd be two lines of girls in these sickening orange and green uniforms, like corn-dog waitresses. Or we would have Arabian nights and there would be sand all over the floor of the dressing room and he would have gone to a costume store in Omaha and come up with eight Scheherazade outfits. Everyone would show up on the bus later with glitter all over their jeans.

TOM KEIFER From the first arena tour with David Lee Roth we went straight to Bon Jovi. *Slippery When Wet* was taking off, and our record was going even bigger than it was when we were with David Lee Roth. It felt like Beatlemania.

JEFF LaBAR I'm like trying to envision right now what it was like looking out into the crowd. It felt like it was eighty percent chicks, but it had to be at least sixty to seventy percent chicks. And good-looking ones.

FRED COURY It was just hugeness. Everything's sold out, everything's multiple dates, seven nights in Detroit. It's just stupid huge. And to this date, nobody has treated us better than Bon Jovi did. They were just amazing, and we learned how to treat other bands like that. "You guys have enough lights?" "Yeah, we've got more than enough." "Okay, take more." "What?" "How's the sound, good? Want to come to a little birthday party?" "Yeah, we do." Jon would rent out a health club after, there'd be basketball and open bar or bowling, whatever it was.

LARRY MAZER Sam Kinison was everybody's idol back then. He was the comedian for all the metal bands and he used to come to all the shows.

JEFF LaBAR We had made friends with Sam real early in our career because our tour bus drivers were brothers and we were on tour at the same time and we kept crossing paths. So when the idea came up for Sam to be our crazy insane manager in the "Somebody Save Me" video, we were like, "Yeah, that would be awesome!"

LARRY MAZER So we're shooting in L.A. and it's during the Bon Jovi tour and call time was at nine in the morning. Everybody's there, the girls are there, the band's there, I'm there. And no Sam Kinison. Ten o'clock, no Sam Kinison. Eleven o'clock, no Sam Kinison. Everybody's freaking out.

JEFF LaBAR We had been partying in my room the night before. Last I saw Sam, he was crashed out on my bed. But when I woke up in the morning he was gone.

TOM KEIFER The whole concept was based around his character, him being this off-the-hook manager who was going to chase the Cinderella girls out of the studio. And he was gonna do a screaming and yelling routine and all.

LARRY MAZER In terms of the videos, it was just obvious: Your name is Cinderella, let's take it to the next degree. The head of video at Mercury Records at the time suggested this guy Mark Rezyka to be the director. We talked on the phone and I said, "You know, we want to do the Cinderella story, basically." They wrote this treatment based on that. Yeah. I think the "Shake Me" one is great, the setup, but I thought the "Nobody's Fool" video, which really carried out the whole, you know, the clock strikes midnight, girl running away turning into a pumpkin, was great.

JEFF LaBAR The girls who played the evil twins were different in all three videos. There was not one that overlapped.

LARRY MAZER No. It's the same girls for "Shake Me" and "Nobody's Fool," but "Somebody Save Me" was different girls.

JEFF LaBAR I went to the video shoot and Sam didn't.

LARRY MAZER Eric and I went in the other room and said, "What are we gonna do?" So basically we wrote the ending that you now see in the video, where the girls leave with the Bon Jovi guys. I found Jon Bon Jovi and I said, "Jon, listen, we have a problem." I told him the whole story and I said, "I have this idea for the ending, would you be willing to do it?" He says, "Yeah, anything I can do to help out."

JEFF LaBAR That was just them being nice guys. "Yeah, we'll come down and help you out." They were just the most amazing people on the planet to us at that time. You know, same label, same tour, guiding us along, teaching us the way.

TOM KEIFER That first record, the success of it and the tours we were on took us to a level of playing live that really felt great. I wanted us to stay there, and I knew that was dependent on the success of the records ultimately. So it was always in the back of my mind: If we want to keep doing this, which is the real payoff, playing these huge shows, we have to keep having successful records. So it's all connected, it's all interrelated.

41

GARDEN STATE MUSIC

JACK PONTI (producer, songwriter) Snake was living in my house and I remember him just being completely fucking despondent because he couldn't believe he got cut from Bon Jovi and he couldn't believe that he didn't get the Cinderella gig. And then he put together Skid Row with Jimmy Southworth—Rachel Bolan.

DAVE "SNAKE" SABO In 1986 I had this band with one of my dear friends that I grew up and went to school with, this guy Jimmy Yuhas, who played rhythm guitar. And we had a singer named Matt Fallon, who had been in Anthrax for half a minute. But we didn't have a bass player. Then I got a job at a music store in Toms River, New Jersey, which was like an hour and a half from where I lived. I had to take two buses to get there. And that's where I met Rachel Bolan. He walked into the music store and I was like, "This guy looks like a rock star!"

RACHEL BOLAN (bassist, Godsend, Skid Row) I was living in Toms River. And there were two music stores—there was Silverton Music, and that was right down the street from Garden State Music, where Snake worked. I never really asked him why he traveled an hour and a half to work at a music store. Probably so that he didn't have to cut his hair, I would imagine.

JACK PONTI Everybody hung out at the music store. I remember Snake behind the counter one day, and he has his fucking pants down while he was talking to these parents about renting a guitar or a violin or a trombone.

Skid Row in general was probably the most comedic fucking group of people.

DAVE "SNAKE" SABO By that time I had been networking so much that I had no fear. And so I approached Rachel and started just name-dropping as much as I possibly could.

RACHEL BOLAN He was a name-dropping motherfucker!

DAVE "SNAKE" SABO I was like, "Well, I've got this and that going on, and Bon Jovi are my best buds, and I know this A&R guy . . ." You know, like a total buffoon. Just bloviating. But I guess it left an impression.

RACHEL BOLAN The thing that really grabbed me was that this guy had the same passion and fire about making it that I did. He had a band together, and I had a band with Scotti Hill called Godsend.

DAVE "SNAKE" SABO We got to talking and he told me he was a bass player and he had his own band going on. And we realize he's the songwriter in his band and I'm the songwriter in my band. So I said, "My band rehearses in New Brunswick. Would you mind coming up?" And he goes, "Yeah. I just need some money for gas. I'm broke."

RACHEL BOLAN Godsend was kind of petering out at that time and so I was like, "All right, I'll come up and jam with you guys." And so I met up with Snake and we drove up to rehearsal. And I got in there and, you know, everyone was good players and all, but we rehearsed a few times and then one day on the way to practice I was like, "How do you feel about all these guys?" I guess it was kind of a dick move on my part but there was only one thing I wanted to do in life and that was be a musician. I didn't want to do construction anymore. And when Snake and I got together it just happened. Songs started coming out. I was still living with my folks at the time, and we'd write until six in the morning and then I'd get up and go to work.

DAVE "SNAKE" SABO Once we sat down and wrote together it was obvious that we were gonna do this together. And then we scrapped everybody in the band but Matt, the singer. And through [Bon Jovi keyboardist] David Bryan we got Rob Affuso to play drums.

ROB AFFUSO I had a girlfriend who was friends with David Bryan, and through that relationship I actually got an audition for Bon Jovi when "Runaway" was a hit on [New York radio station] WAPP. And Snake happened to be at that audition. But Jon ultimately decided to keep Tico [Torres]. I don't think it was about whether or not he wanted Tico, but rather whether or not Tico wanted to play with *him*. Because I think he was still with Franke and the Knockouts. But anyway, I did not get into Bon Jovi.

So then later on Snake is starting a band of his own and they have me come audition. They had a drummer at that time, and I don't know specifics but I think there were drug and alcohol issues. And so I actually went and auditioned in a basement on this other guy's drums, and I felt awful because I pretty much destroyed his drums. But a couple songs into it Snake and Rachel said, "Do you wanna do this?"

RACHEL BOLAN We ended up making a bunch of changes. And the next one was getting Scotti Hill in the band.

SCOTTI HILL (guitarist, Godsend, Skid Row) Rachel and I were good friends, and after our band Godsend broke up and he started jamming with Snake I moved back to Orange County, New York, where I had previously been living. But I would go down to Jersey on the weekends and just hang out with Rachel—we'd go to bars, sometimes I'd go to rehearsal with him. I remember when Rob joined the band. Then after they let the other guitar player, Jimmy Yuhas, go, Rachel was like, "Well, we need a guy. Come audition." They sent me a cassette with three songs on it. One was "Clock Strikes Midnight," which became "Midnight/Tornado" on the first Skid Row record. And "18 and Life" was in the works. They were a kick-ass band.

DAVE "SNAKE" SABO I loved Mötley Crüe. I loved Van Halen. But I also loved the New Wave of British Heavy Metal, and I was a fan of melodic bands like Boston. And then there was the local scene at CBGB and City Gardens in Trenton, and clubs in Philadelphia and Newark and Staten

Island and Asbury Park and Brooklyn and Long Island. There were original bands playing everywhere every night. It all had a big effect on me. So I had my influences and then Rachel had the punk influence and we met somewhere in the middle.

RACHEL BOLAN I was into Mötley Crüe but not heavily. My roots were wearing a Hefty bag as a shirt and spray-painting an anarchy symbol on it.

SCOTTI HILL I just knew I wasn't going to blow that audition. So I came down, I played rhythm, and I sang backups. And they asked me to join that night.

DAVE "SNAKE" SABO I remember Scotti joined the band in October of '86, because it was the same night that the ground ball went through Bill Buckner's legs in the World Series. Then two months later we were doing shows with Bon Jovi.

SCOTTI HILL As a matter of fact, I think my first gig with Skid Row was opening for Bon Jovi out in Bethlehem, Pennsylvania.

ROB AFFUSO This is before we were even signed.

DAVE "SNAKE" SABO We were lucky enough to be able to go out on three dates on the *Slippery When Wet* tour.

DOC McGHEE Dave Sabo was Jon Bon Jovi's best friend at that time. And then he had his band Skid Row and he would always bother me.

DAVE "SNAKE" SABO Look, the first time I met Doc, I went up the street to Jon's parents' house because Jon had invited me over. And we had a moment where it was just Doc and me out by their pool. And Doc's on a lounge chair and I'm like, This is my moment. I'm gonna lay this spiel on him. And I did: I'm the greatest guitar player in the world. I'm the coolest son of a bitch. I'm a rock star. I'm this, I'm that, *blah blah blah*. I couldn't have been more arrogant and egotistical. But in the nicest way possible!

And I'll give Doc props. He heard me out for, I don't know, maybe five or ten minutes. And when I ran out of breath and ran out of words he looked at me—and this is a true story—he looked at me and he goes, "That's great. You wanna go inside and get me a beer?"

RACHEL BOLAN So we wound up opening a few shows for Bon Jovi. I think it was two nights at Stabler Arena, and then the third show was supposed to be in Johnstown but something happened with production and we didn't play. We had been doing small clubs and then all of a sudden we have these gigs at, like, a five-thousand-seat venue. It was the coolest thing ever. Like, "Yeah, this is what I meant to do!"

ROB AFFUSO We were really excited but we were really nervous.

SCOTTI HILL Butterflies. Like, I can't believe I have a backstage pass around my neck! I can't believe we have a dressing room in this giant building! I can't believe we're going to play for all these people! The arena was probably only half full when we played, but it felt like being dropped into rock stardom. I can still feel it.

DAVE "SNAKE" SABO We were in the dressing room after the first or second show and Doc came in and he was like, "Yeah, the songs are great." Because we had done "Youth Gone Wild," we had done "18 and Life." But he says, "You need a new singer. This guy's not gonna cut it." So we basically fired Matt the next day. Well, not quite the next day . . .

SCOTTI HILL The last straw for us was a gig at Close Encounters in Sayreville. We got our gear onstage and Matt didn't show up. We're ready to play and the guy doesn't show up! So the gear got loaded back into the van. And then Matt shows up. And I remember Snake going after him in the parking lot. He was furious. We were *all* furious. I've got nothing against the dude. He just wasn't a good band guy.

DAVE "SNAKE" SABO We were opening for T.T. Quick. And Matt no-showed until after T.T. Quick was already on. And I went after him in the parking lot and he was running away from me. I was gonna kill him.

RACHEL BOLAN One day I walked into the music store and Snake says, "We're getting rid of Matt . . ." I was like, "All right." He goes, "Well, you accepted that pretty easily!"

DAVE "SNAKE" SABO Matt was good, don't get me wrong. He just wasn't great. He wasn't a star. We needed our David Lee Roth or our Axl Rose. We needed a *star*, you know?

42

INTERVIEW: DAVE "SNAKE" SABO OF SKID ROW

Before he auditioned for Cinderella and before he started Skid Row, Dave "Snake" Sabo was a self-described jock from Sayreville, New Jersey, and his good friend was Jon Bon Jovi.

How did you and Jon Bon Jovi first meet?

I was walking up the street to a friend's house and Jon was playing basketball outside of his house. I was probably ten or eleven and he was two or three years older than me. He had this weird blue basketball and I was a basketball freak, and I think I challenged him to a game or something like that. And we became very good friends. Not long after that he started playing guitar and I noticed how cool it was.

What led you to pick up a guitar yourself?

I went to go see Kiss at Madison Square Garden with Jon and a bunch of other people. It was December 16, 1977, and I was thirteen. And it changed my life completely. Up until that point it was all sports, predominately baseball and basketball. After seeing that concert I knew my immediate and distant future would be in music.

So I started teaching myself guitar and I loved it immediately. Then shortly thereafter I let Jon know, "Yeah, I started to play guitar, too." And Jon started teaching me a little. But he was still a beginner, so he suggested I go to his teacher, Al, who lived across the street diagonally from where Jon grew up. It progressed quickly and I had developed a huge fondness for all things hard rock and heavy metal. Jon and I became really close but we just had too different taste in music. He was leaning more toward Springsteen and Elton John and Southside Johnny, whereas I liked some of that stuff, too, but my taste went more toward the Aerosmiths and the Judas Priests of the world. So I had various bands and cover bands, and then he joined a band called the Rest. They ended up playing this big show at Freehold Raceway in New Jersey [in 1980], opening up for, I believe, Hall & Oates. Willie Nile was on the bill, too.

The guitarist in the Rest was Jack Ponti, who went on to be a successful songwriter in his own right.

Yes, exactly. I think I was about fifteen or sixteen when I went to go see them and it blew my mind. And Jon would take me to their rehearsals at the Fast Lane in Asbury Park, so I was getting a great education as well. Then I was working as an assistant bar manager at a club called Willy's [in Sayreville], which is now the Starland Ballroom, and Jon had written and recorded "Runaway" and sent it in to WAPP in New York for, like, a locals' contest. And if you won the contest they would put your single in rotation. They put out an album [*New York Rocks 1983*] with all the tracks on it—Twisted Sister was on there with "Shoot 'Em Down." And "Runaway" won the contest. So all of a sudden Jon had to put together a band to go play these shows that were part of the deal. He had David Bryan from a band he was in previously called Atlantic City Expressway. And he asked me, "Would you help me out?" "Yeah, of course, man."

This was basically an early iteration of what would become Bon Jovi.

We used to rehearse during the day at a banquet hall where they used to have wedding receptions for all the Polish people from Sayreville. There was no bass player and I knew Alec John Such from a club band called Phantom's Opera, who were one of the best club bands of that time. I contacted him and I was like, "Hey man, would you be into this?" And he said sure. He met Jon and Dave, got along great. Then Alec knew Tico, who at the time was playing with Franke and the Knockouts. So Tico came down and we got our band. I'm the little baby of the whole thing. I was nineteen when this whole thing was going down. We went out and played a bunch of shows.

What led to your exiting the band?

I was still working at Willy's as the assistant bar manager, and we had, like, a front lounge area where we would have bands come in and do some acoustic stuff, some covers. And one of the people that came in was Richie Sambora. He would do a bunch of covers, like Free and Bad Company, just really cool, soulful stuff. I was immediately enamored with this guy as a guitar player, as a singer and as a person. Alec knew Richie very, very well, so Richie was aware of what Alec was doing with Jon, and Alec had introduced Richie to Jon.

So after we were done with those six, seven, eight shows, Jon was like, "Okay, I'm gonna get serious now." And it was very obvious to me that I wasn't going to be a part of that band. First of all, Jon needed—and found—his Joe Perry to his Steven Tyler, or his Jimmy Page to his Robert Plant. I was not that guy. I wanted to be Eddie Van Halen or Randy Rhoads or whatever hotshot guitar player was out at the time. And Richie is more than capable of doing all that stuff, but he can sing amazingly, too. That's something I definitely couldn't do.

Were you disappointed when you were replaced?

When Jon was like, "Okay, I'm going to have Richie play guitar in my band," I wasn't shocked or hurt or anything. I loved playing with the guys and they're friends of mine. But it just wasn't my thing. It was his thing. Jon knew exactly what he wanted and he found it in Richie. And you know what? It was absolutely the right thing to do. So certainly no bitterness. I'm grateful for the time that I had. I got to watch the whole building process of it and watch it go from, you know, a club band to a record deal to getting a major manager to making a record to going on tour to making another record to more tours to making the biggest record [1986's *Slippery When Wet*] in a long, long time. All the while Jon and I remained dear friends. He was always like, "Man, I'll do whatever I can for you. Come along for the ride. Put together something great or become a part of something great, I'll help out any way I can."

And after three years, maybe four years. I put together Skid Row. And he held true to his promise.

"YOU MEAN SLASH COULDA PLAYED THE CHRIS HOLMES PART?"

ERIC STACY Our first records came out on almost the same day. *Appetite for Destruction* and *Faster Pussycat*. July of 1987.

RIC BROWDE I think Guns N' Roses entered the charts in the seventies. We entered at, like, eighty-six. Somewhere in that vicinity. And Philbin gets this call from Bob Krasnow, who goes, "Have you dropped Faster Pussycat yet?" And Peter is like, "No. Aren't you glad? They bumped into the charts at eighty-six. That's pretty cool!" And Krasnow says, "Drop them. They suck."

PETER PHILBIN No. That's wrong. But Bob and I did have many conversations about Faster Pussycat. And we actually had a falling out about it. Because after the band had sold a couple hundred thousand albums I was going, "Why are we arguing? We're making money!" But Bob, for better or for worse—and I loved him for it—he had an aesthetic. And if something didn't meet his aesthetic, he didn't want to be involved.

TAIME DOWNE The month after our album came out we did a week-and-a-half tour with Guns N' Roses in Europe—a couple shows in Germany, one in Amsterdam, and then like five in England.

ALAN NIVEN Taime had a decent relationship with Axl, so, you know, that's how that played out in terms of the convivial politics of the tour. But from my point of view I was led to believe from Geffen that we might have a chance of getting a little more support from WEA on our second trip over there if we had another WEA band on board. What I found interesting was Warren Entner, who was their manager [after Vicky Hamilton] and was glowing with his success earlier with Quiet Riot, had kind of persuaded the, um, cognoscenti of the companies in Germany and the UK that Faster Pussycat were the shit. You know, despite the fact that they were the opening band. Of course, come the day of the show, anybody could see that they were not superior to Guns N' Roses.

GREG STEELE Guns were ahead of us in popularity because they had been to England two months before. Plus, they had the label over there pushing the shit out of them. And our label was just like, not. But I remember that we had a fucking killer double-decker bus and they had a van. And they were fucking pissed.

ERIC STACY Even though we were friends in L.A. and we hung out at the Cathouse at the same time and stuff like that, the bands weren't, like, buddy-buddy best friends. We were both new bands on our first record. Everybody was just focused on working hard and trying to make it. But I think the feeling in Guns N' Roses was that they were like a better band than us. Better musicians. And I don't think that's wrong to say. Faster Pussycat were a different kind of band than Guns N' Roses.

ALAN NIVEN Bottom line is, go and see a Guns N' Roses/Faster Pussycat show. And you tell *me* which is the band.

GREG STEELE I know that there's been a couple things written in different books about a couple things that happened on that tour.

ERIC STACY There was a lot of partying going on, a lot of drinking going on. I remember we were in Hamburg, Germany, the first night and I took a walk down to the train station to try to find a pay phone to call America. And when I came walking back to the hotel I see . . . actually I didn't see it at first, I heard it. But our drummer Mark was up on the sixth-floor balcony of our hotel room, pulling the drunk rock star thing, you know like throwing all the furniture off the sixth-floor balcony and tossing it into the subway station down below, creating this huge commotion. So when I got back to the hotel, the manager of the hotel had our band manager at our door and he had Mark there and basically what he was saying was either this guy leaves the hotel now or I'm gonna call the cops and you guys can all get kicked out.

GREG STEELE It's like, Dude, who goes to another country and fucking causes so much trouble that you can't even get back into the hotel?

ERIC STACY So Mark basically just walked away with a bottle of vodka in his hand. And I guess he ran into the Guns N' Roses guys and then later they went up to one of Guns N' Roses' rooms. Mark was so fucked up that he passed out in one of the beds. And I guess Duff was trying to tell him, "Hey man, get the fuck out of the bed!" But Mark was just laying there, all drunk and shit. So finally Slash and Duff said, "Well, fuck this guy." They took him and wrapped him up in duct tape, covered him in shaving cream, and they were in the process of carrying him down the hall to the elevator and they were gonna toss him in the elevator and hit "Lobby" and just leave him there. And I guess he kind of came out of his drunken stupor and he got his hands loose and he just started wildly swinging. I think he hit Duff in the face.

ALAN NIVEN To my memory Duff and Slash took him down the elevator and dumped him in the street. And it was getting a bit cold. But I think he'd overstayed his welcome, shall we say.

TAIME DOWNE And that was the first fucking night! We were laughing about it the whole tour. It was funny as fuck.

GREG STEELE After I found out I was like, "Well, yeah, I would have done that, too." You're fucking drunk, you're high . . . I mean, we're trying to get somewhere as a band! And if you have a guy who's doing drugs all the time, you're only as strong as your weakest link. You fucking get sick of it after a while. Get your shit together, you know?

TAIME DOWNE At the beginning of the tour for the next album Mark had fucking heroin sent to him.

ERIC STACY Mark and I had been partying together on and off for like a year. And he had arranged to have something sent out to him on the road. So we played Kansas City one night and we had the next day off and then we were playing Omaha. And Mark wanted to get to Omaha and pick up that package. And I remember saying to him, "Dude, I wouldn't do that if I were you." But he was like, "No, I'm gonna go ahead with the road crew on their bus. See you in Omaha."

GREG STEELE We get to Omaha and our drummer's in jail and they took our bus driver with him. And it's "Ah, fuck . . ."

ERIC STACY We go to the venue to do soundcheck and Mark doesn't show up. So the tour manager called the hotel and he found out that Mark had gotten arrested. And then through association everybody started looking at me. But we gave Mark so many chances. We didn't wanna kick him out. He was our drummer. But by then it was like, You fucking idiot . . .

TAIME DOWNE They wanted to arrest the whole band at the hotel, but we weren't there. We had gone from Kansas City right to the venue. Thank god. Otherwise I would've fucking really killed Mark.

GREG STEELE Mark was a fucking total drug addict. In Germany the duct tape thing was one incident, and then Mark had another one later on.

ERIC STACY Two days later in Amsterdam Mark and Steven Adler and myself and one of the other guys in the band, I forget who, we were all running out the back door of a Holiday Inn and going out and partying, getting in trouble. Me and Steven went to a whorehouse together. That was back when both bands were at their wildest and craziest. That was just the way it was back then. Rock 'n' roll was still rock 'n' roll.

GREG STEELE My whole thing was I wanted to do music. I wanted to go on tour. That was the most important thing to me. I was like the only dude that wasn't getting drunk and high. I wanted to succeed. This is my dream. You know what I mean?

ERIC STACY Two days after we got back from Europe we shot our part for *The Decline of Western Civilization*. I think we got back on a Sunday and then that Tuesday we were at the Cathouse doing the interview and the live part.

PENELOPE SPHEERIS (director, *The Decline of Western Civilization Part II: The Metal Years*) I did the first *Decline*, about punk rock, and there was a certain, what shall I say? Well, you know what punk rock is—it's just that whole aggressive "everything sucks" attitude, and I was really attracted to that music at that point. And then time went by and everything went from, you know, no hair and combat boots to cowboy boots with jewelry on them and hair down to your waist. And there were *so* many people on Sunset Boulevard. Like, you couldn't even drive right around the Roxy and the Whisky. And I thought, What the hell is going on here? I'm actually more interested in documenting social behavior than I am in the music. But I used the music as a backdrop.

ERIC STACY As a matter of fact, in those early days of Faster I ended up hooking up with Penelope Spheeris' daughter, Anna. We dated for a while.

PENELOPE SPHEERIS Okay, so here's the deal. No parent wants to talk about who their daughter dated. But since we started this, what about the fact that my daughter went out with Nikki Sixx during that time. Okay? That was such a bummer. Eric is a very nice guy. Nikki? Ahh . . . no.

ERIC STACY So I would go and hang out at Anna's house, and one time I was playing demos for the first Faster Pussycat record and Penelope was saying how she really dug them. I wasn't sure if she was just being polite. But then she put one of our songs in a movie she was doing called *Dudes*. It starred Jon Cryer, and Flea was in it. If you ever see the movie, there's this scene where three punk rockers get in a fight at a bar, and the song that's playing in the background is "Bathroom Wall." So I guess she was really sincere when she said she liked what she heard. And then lo and behold, a year or two later we were being cast as one of the main bands for *The Metal Years*.

PENELOPE SPHEERIS Well, I loved the band. I loved the music.

STEVIE RACHELLE *Decline* was a big thing. It's kind of one of those cult classics that people still look at today. They talk about it. There's a lot of people on there that look stupid, meaning the younger bands that were like, "No, but I'm going to make it!" And I remember, as much as I might have been scattered or young and not knowing all the answers, I know we got asked some of those hard questions. But I also know that I was smart enough to not completely put my foot in my mouth, you know? *I'm going to be a star! I'm going to be bigger than Robert Plant or I'm going to kill myself!* We never said that.

JENNIFER PERRY (L.A.-based booking agent) You know Penelope Spheeris' movie *The Decline of the blah blah blah*? The singer in Odin made that big thing about, "If I'm not a rock star I'll kill myself." He's doing construction in Pasadena. Which is kind of funny.

JEFF DUNCAN For a while when I saw that movie I was like, "Oh, god, look at us." But Odin weren't too different from any other band on the Strip at the time. We just got filmed doing it. You watch that movie, and everybody in it is saying, "I'm gonna make it." Well, what if you don't? "I'm gonna." That was the mentality.

JANET GARDNER There was a lot of "Well, what's your backup plan?" "Well, we don't have one."

RIC BROWDE Remember the kid with the two-color hair, and Penelope goes, "What happens if you don't succeed?" "Well, I'm *gonna* succeed." Things like that? That guy was rehearsing right next to us when we were doing the Pussycat rehearsals. And he was just, like, trying to get anybody to come into his room. It was just, "Come play with me. I'm gonna be a star." I can't even remember what the guy's name was.

PENELOPE SPHEERIS Gabe? Gabriel? That guy's in jail now. He scammed a bunch of people down in Texas.

RIC BROWDE He would be in there with the door open, holding a guitar in front of a mirror. And making poses. You know, like while he was bending notes. And that was what L.A. was. You had bands like Odin. *O-din! O-din!* That was reality. All those bands, they were just like that. And it was damn fucking embarrassing. Penelope Spheeris captured it better than anybody. You know, Tuff, Warrant, all of them.

JOEY ALLEN We were shameless promoters. And I remember we wanted to get in that movie. I don't even think we had a record deal at the time. But it didn't matter to us. We were just like, "Yeah, we wanna do it!" I think we wanted to do it and we didn't get picked.

PENELOPE SPHEERIS Warrant wanted to be in it and I feel really bad that I didn't put them in it. Jani, he was a sweetheart. But I could only shoot so many bands, you know?

ALAN NIVEN In an empty club, during daylight hours, Penelope Spheeris tried to persuade me to involve my bands in her *Decline of All Aspects of Sanity* movie. And since neither appeared, I suppose something about Ms. Spheeris must have triggered my protective reluctance.

PENELOPE SPHEERIS We had the set all ready to go and Alan decided at the last minute he didn't want Guns N' Roses to do it. That's why I got Megadeth. So, thank you, Alan.

ALAN NIVEN Oh, damn, you mean Slash coulda played the Chris Holmes part?

PENELOPE SPHEERIS Chris Holmes, it's not my fault he was that drunk. I didn't want it to look like that, either. I told the cameraman, "We gotta set this up again and shoot something we can use. Because the guy was just a total fuckup and we didn't get anything. So when are we going to reschedule this?" And they said, "Well, we don't have enough money to shoot this again." So I went into the editing room and tried to cut it together and I was grimacing the whole time, going, "Oh, my god." And then it turns out to be the scene that everybody talks about in the film.

JAY JAY FRENCH I go to the Rainbow one night, and Chris Holmes is there. He's at the table, drunk as shit. I walk over and someone says, "Jay Jay, it's Chris Holmes." He puts his hand out, and as he puts his hand out he rolls off the table and falls facedown onto the floor. I'm looking at this scene, going, "Is this out of *Spiñal Tap*?" This was just too stupid. I said, "I don't need to meet people this stupid." I liked the guys from Ratt a lot more.

PENELOPE SPHEERIS I saw Chris in a bar [later on] and he said, "Hey, you fucking bitch! You owe me five hundred bucks!" He yells it across the bar. And I'm like, "Dude, you were too drunk to remember. We *paid* you."

RIKKI ROCKETT We had a lot of fun with that movie.

PENELOPE SPHEERIS I thought Poison were hilarious. C.C.'s so fucking funny. And Ozzy's hilarious. I tried to do a movie with Ozzy called *Shooting Stars* in the mid-'80s, before I did *The Metal Years,* and everybody that I went to for the money for the film, they would say, "He's not funny." I'd say, "Ozzy is hilarious. Could you please just listen to me? Ozzy is hilarious." Nobody would listen to me, you know?

SHARON OSBOURNE Penelope said, "Okay, Ozzy, you make breakfast and I'll interview you." And that's what happened. That was it. And that's what you got, you know, that's Ozzy.

PENELOPE SPHEERIS Well, if you've ever seen the first *Decline,* you've got Darby Crash making breakfast. If you've seen the third *Decline,* you've got Eyeball from the Resistance making breakfast. It's a common theme.

OZZY OSBOURNE I was fucked up when I did that.

PENELOPE SPHEERIS He put butter on the bacon!

SHARON OSBOURNE People always try and take something away from Ozzy. But there is nobody like him. Nobody. And when you see him, when he's at his purest like that, people are always, "No, that must be fake. That's really not Ozzy." Well, that's fucking Ozzy.

PENELOPE SPHEERIS I staged the orange juice thing. Common knowledge. But that's it.

OZZY OSBOURNE Penelope, I got on with her very well. She's a nice lady. A bit crazy, but we're all a bit crazy at times.

STEVIE RACHELLE My guess is the movie came out in the spring or summer of '88.

RIC BROWDE The movie debuted at the Cinerama Dome. It's that big, round theater in Hollywood. The kid with the two-color hair, he hired a limo to come to the movie. Because he thought he was gonna be a star. He was so sure he was gonna be a star. The look on his face when he saw that movie and realized what a klutz he was. At least he had a limo to go crawl into.

STEVIE RACHELLE I remember a couple guys from Poison were there. I know Gene [Simmons] was there. I'm pretty sure Dave Mustaine was there.

TAIME DOWNE I remember fucking Chris Holmes was there with his mom. It was fucking great. And the jokes were flying when Chris came on the screen . . . 'cause he's sitting there with his mom and shit, they were right in front of us. And we were right in the middle of the whole fucking theater.

LIZZY BORDEN (singer, Lizzy Borden) When you see Chris in the pool, it was fun and games, we were all laughing and having fun and no one was thinking about what this could end up being. But Chris is still alive, so it's all good.

GREG STEELE It was awesome just seeing yourself on a big screen like that, people laughing and stuff like, "This is cool!" I thought some of the local guys, I'd never even heard of any of those bands or seen any of those people. I didn't know where they found those people but they weren't part of the scene at all. I'd never seen those people in my life.

STEVIE RACHELLE The Wet Cherri guy, I mean, all of them at some point were on the Strip. Meaning, people would be hanging out and in a band. But those bands would last for like three or four shows and then somebody would go to jail or decide they were going to be a plumber or move back to Colorado or wherever they were from, you know?

RIKKI ROCKETT I don't think that most of the bands that were interviewed were that important for the scene at the time, quite frankly. I didn't think Odin was particularly important. So I think Penelope hit the mark in painting the spirit of that time, but she missed the mark of which artists to interview, in my opinion.

PENELOPE SPHEERIS The whole premise of *Decline,* in case nobody noticed, is the fact that the movies were made to spotlight unknown bands. And that's why unknown bands, relatively unknown bands, were performing. And the older guys that have already been established, like Poison and, you know, Ozzy and Aerosmith, those guys were just commenting on the time and *not* performing. It wasn't ever my intention to spotlight them. It was more about the unknown bands.

LIZZY BORDEN There was a massive big party across the street afterwards that everyone went to.

PENELOPE SPHEERIS The LAPD helicopters got real low on the party. Everybody's long hair was swishing around.

STEVIE RACHELLE At the party Penelope comes up to me and she goes, "Stevie, Gene Simmons wants to work with you." I go, "Huh?" She says, "I sat with Gene and as soon as you came up on the screen he said, 'Who is that?'" And she goes, "I told him, 'That's Stevie from the band Tuff,' and he was like, 'That kid's gonna be a star . . .'" But at this point Kiss was already kind of old and washed up and fifteen years removed from their height or whatever. So whether I was being arrogant or just stupid I was like, "Oh, that's great. Awesome. Whatever." You know? If she had said, "C.C. DeVille wants to work with you," I would've been fucking ecstatic.

ERIC STACY I could see how some people would watch it and go, "Oh, that's a joke." But you can't really say "That's a joke" about a movie that has Kiss and Alice Cooper and Aerosmith. So I felt it was a great thing to be a part of. To this day I think it's a great piece of rock 'n' roll cinema.

CHRISTINA APPLEGATE (actress) Originally, my character of Kelly Bundy on *Married with Children* was kind of like a tough little rebellious biker kind of chick. It kind of evolved, or devolved, if you want to call it that, after I saw this girl in this documentary [*Decline*] and I went oh my god, that's it. That's her. So we kind of changed her up to be sort of a product of the '80s, of this generation of girls that felt they needed to use their bodies to get further in the world, and the music was heavy metal. And there was a girl in the movie who had just won Miss Gazzarri's. And she was sitting there in, I believe, a white minidress, which I had never really seen anyone wear. And they asked her what she wanted to do after winning Miss Gazzarri's, and she said, "I want to continue with my modeling and my actressing." And I went, That's the best thing I've ever seen in my entire life. And literally the next day, I went to the wardrobe people and to everyone and I said, "We're changing this up."

PENELOPE SPHEERIS See, what I try to do, I don't make films like Michael Moore, where he's got an opinion and he wants to push it off on everybody else. My favorite documentarian is Frederick Wiseman, and if you don't know his work you should see it because the whole point is to not have an opinion about it. And with *Decline,* I didn't have an opinion about it. I was just showing you what was there. Because back then I was really one of the few people shooting it. So I wanted to document it and say, "This is what it was like." I did not mean to say it was good or bad. I just wanted to say, "There it is. You figure it out." And some people love it and some people hate it. They all have the right, you know?

LIZZY BORDEN When I talk to kids today about the movie, they really love it. And I'm like, "Okay, if you know some of these people who tried and failed and you know how hard it is, even if you climb to the top, you know, there's a big fall." I think it shows that. But it's interesting how the kids are perceiving that film now, I think that they're looking at it as a fun celebration, which is what I thought it was to begin with.

STEVIE RACHELLE I did go to a screening of it a few years ago, like a twenty-fifth anniversary screening. A bunch of us were there—Riki Rachtman, Penelope, Rikki Rockett, Nadir from London, one of the guys from Odin. There's, like, ten or eleven of us that were in the film, and at the end of it we went up and did a little panel and just talked about the movie. And people loved it. I still get little comments here and there online where people reach out and say something about it. That movie struck a chord with people. It definitely made an impact, you know?

44

"WE NEVER EVEN KNEW WE HAD MONEY IN OUR BANK ACCOUNTS"

VITO BRATTA We finally came up with enough material to make another White Lion record—pretty much all of the songs on *Pride*—and we said, "Let's go back to Germany and do this new album." That was in the summer of '86. We did it the same way we did *Fight to Survive*. Same producer. Same studio. Same everything. But when we came home, I said, "This is terrible. I hate this record." *Fight to Survive* was good for 1983, but by 1986 there were enough albums coming out like *Slippery When Wet* and *Night Songs* by Cinderella that it just didn't cut it. I think everybody agreed. But it was used to help us get signed to Atlantic.

JASON FLOM (executive, Atlantic Records) I went to Baltimore to see them the first time. It was '86 and it was the year before I went to rehab and I was just a fuckin' mess. So I made time to go see them in Baltimore and I was going to see this other band called Mannequin. And I was getting . . . I was trying to do the right amount of drugs to get myself out of the apartment and to an airport. I missed the flight and then I missed the next flight, and I missed the next flight. I ended up catching the last flight, which stopped in Pittsburgh, and I had to take a puddle jumper from Pittsburgh to Baltimore. I got there really late, as you can imagine. I'd been supposed to see the Mannequin guys first, and the managers were waiting at the airport for hours. But I didn't have time now because I had to go to the White Lion show. It was really an awkward situation because these guys were waiting for me at the airport and I was like, "Can you take me to White Lion?"

VITO BRATTA Jason Flom is twenty minutes away from us in New York City and he's gonna come to see us in Baltimore? Where we played like twice and there's twenty people in the place? I think he just liked to travel.

JAMES LoMENZO We came out, we jumped all over the place like idiots like we did in our superhero costumes, and I remember Jason actually right in front. It was obvious, because he so didn't belong there, and he had a girl or two under each arm, and he was basically using them for support. And the next day we were being signed to Atlantic Records.

JASON FLOM Those guys weren't really partiers but I ended up staying up late with them. And that was the night that I made the decision to sign them.

MIKE TRAMP We went to L.A. to record *Pride* with Michael Wagener. He's always been a band guy, and he just made us feel at home right away. This is the moment of White Lion that would never come again. The magic of the real first album. The one we love by every band.

MICHAEL WAGENER Vito and I hit it off. We were talking about the same things even in terms of cars and stuff like that, and we were shooting for the same thing. He played the solo to "Wait" in one take while we did the drums. I was sitting there and I was like, "Well, you're done with that solo!"

JASON FLOM *Pride* was dead on arrival and then one radio station in Minneapolis broke "Wait." It's a little miracle.

MIKE TRAMP When the video for "Wait" had come out, I think June or July, they would play it at like four in the morning. But one time they had played it at the right time and it got a serious response. Atlantic hadn't gotten a word of it, but they had heard that MTV was not going to put it on *Dial MTV*. I was up at Atlantic Records, this Danish boy with no real clue about how things work, but also fearless. And I picked up the phone and I called MTV, and I just kept getting turned on to another person, until finally I got some person that felt like they were in charge. And the following week, they added the video and it rose to the top.

VITO BRATTA I mean, when you show up at shows and people are just like, "God, that solo to 'Wait,' that solo to 'Wait . . .'" I'm like, "God almighty. I've written other songs!" And then you go onstage, and when it comes time to do that solo to "Wait," you freeze. I did that one time on CNN. We were playing some outdoor stadium in Texas and the cameraman from CNN goes, "I'm here to see your band but I love that solo to 'Wait.' So I'm telling you we're gonna go live right when you hit that solo." And I froze. First time ever, I didn't play the solo. I just stood there. And the guy's just shaking his head.

JAMES LoMENZO Mike's lyrics definitely did portray people being over-run somewhere else in the world and how we should be concerned about it. I'd tell the guys, "He's been living in Denmark. He's been looking at the world through a different lens." I actually appreciated that. I think it made me feel really comfortable to have somebody who's kind of think-ing a little bigger than the size of somebody's jeans. It definitely wasn't, "I'm gonna slide it in, right to the top."

MIKE TRAMP "When the Children Cry" has followed me ever since. Look at the lyrics. The lyrics are even more current today than they were back then.

JAMES LoMENZO That song put us in a place where even more people came out. And we could tour on our own merit and do theaters on our own. And that was a big deal.

VITO BRATTA The *Pride* tour consisted of three parts. The first part was Aerosmith, the *Permanent Vacation* tour. At one point, we had a higher-charting album than them. Then there was AC/DC, I think their *Blow Up Your Video* tour. And then it ended with Stryper in tertiary markets.

MIKE TRAMP We started in June, and we finished in November a year and a half later. We'd been to Japan, Europe . . . We'd played so many shows. We never even knew we had money in our bank accounts.

GREG D'ANGELO There were no drugs, no booze, no nothing. We were clean as the driven snow back then. At least, most of us were.

JAMES LoMENZO We were pretty much out there on the road just hitting it hard, and it could be exhausting. Especially when you're a little younger and you kind of play both sides against the middle. You know, you do your shows, and then you celebrate those shows.

VITO BRATTA The other guys could have a fun day off if they wanted to. They'd be knocking on my door, "Hey, you coming down to the pool?" No. I spent the entire time in my hotel room working on the next record. So at the end of the *Pride* tour, I had a cassette with the entire *Big Game* record demoed. But Mike Tramp never heard it.

PART IV

YOUTH GONE WILD

As the '80s wore on, the top tier of first- and second-wave hard rockers—Mötley Crüe, Ratt, Poison, and Guns N' Roses—were firmly established platinum sellers, as venerated by red-blooded American teens as Michael Jackson, Prince, Bruce Springsteen, or any pop star of the day. Others, like Quiet Riot and Twisted Sister, who had once been an inescapable presence on both radio and MTV, were unable to sustain their crossover success and were quickly fading into obscurity.

Big mainstream success begat, as it were, big everything else—the ever-glitzier clothes and higher hair, the bombastic stage productions, the overblown sonics and sentimentality of that eternal '80s rock touchstone, the power ballad. Crowds swelled and embraced a seemingly unending parade of new bands with open arms, and many of them—from Winger and Warrant to Skid Row and Nelson—landed almost immediately on arena stages and were presented with gold and platinum album plaques shortly thereafter. And while many MTV staffers were uneasy with the often crass male-adolescent fantasies depicted in so many hard rock and metal videos, the music and its associated imagery ultimately proved unflaggingly popular at the channel. "The Top 10 of *Dial MTV*, from what I recall, was almost always hair band videos," says then MTV vice president of music programming Rick Krim.

If it all started to look and sound a little bit the same to the casual MTV viewer, to the rock fans in the trenches there was an endless world of nuance between, say, Mötley Crüe and Dokken and Bon Jovi—even if they were, in fact, all being costumed by the very same designer.

So just how big were hard rock and metal? Big enough that, at the close of the decade, supermanager Doc McGhee could round up five of the genre's heaviest hitters—Ozzy, Scorpions, Mötley Crüe, Cinderella, and Skid Row—load 'em onto a booze-filled Boeing 757 headed straight to the heart of the Soviet Union, and have them usher in some glam metal glasnost in the form of the Moscow Music Peace Festival. The two back-to-back concerts at Central Lenin Stadium (capacity one hundred thousand) marked the first time Western hard rock and metal acts were permitted to play in the Soviet capital, and the event was beamed into households in dozens of countries and packaged for broadcast on MTV in America. Better yet, the Scorpions got a chart-topping power ballad out of the experience.

There was only one direction left for this music to go, and it wasn't up.

45

"YOU JUST SIGNED KIP WINGER!"

PAUL TAYLOR (keyboardist, Alice Cooper, Winger) My audition for Alice Cooper, I walked in, I literally had two days' notice. I got the call, like, "Hey, we need a guitar player/keyboard player/singer. We don't know anybody. Basically you're all we're auditioning." I had played with Nick Gilder, who did "Hot Child in the City," and I had toured with Aldo Nova for a year. Those were my only big professional things. But I came down and Alice walked up, and the first thing he said to me was "Hey, does your name start with a K?" I said, "No. I'm Paul." He goes, "Okay, you got the gig." What? He goes, "I already have a Kip, a Ken, and a Kane. I don't want any more *Ks*."

KIP WINGER (bassist, Alice Cooper; singer, bassist, Winger) I played on four songs on [1986's] *Constrictor,* and Kane suggested that I tell Alice that if they went on the road, I would like to do that.

KANE ROBERTS (guitarist, Alice Cooper) I met Kip and as soon as I heard him play I said to Alice, "You gotta get this guy on tour with you because, first of all, he's overloaded with talent. And he's a really good-looking guy, you know what I mean? So that's going to help since, you know, everybody's kinda swarthy in the band."

ALICE COOPER (solo artist) Well, Kane Roberts . . . Kane had Stallone's body and Jerry Lewis' brain. He was the most fun guy to work with because he made me laugh all the time. And he was this dominating character onstage.

KANE ROBERTS I was big instead of, like, a skinny, you know, glam guy. And I didn't drink, didn't do any of that stuff. That was a big deal. So Alice and I became really good friends and we were off and running.

PAUL TAYLOR I jumped in and joined the band for the Nightmare Returns tour. Those shows were crazy.

ALICE COOPER I saw bands like Mötley Crüe and Bon Jovi, and it was the era of the video, when everybody could be very theatrical and glamorous. All the bands looked really good. And there were some really good songs in that era. And the bands would give you a show. So I went, "Well, who does that remind you of? That's Alice Cooper!" All of those bands cop to it, though. I mean, they all were Alice Cooper fans.

KIP WINGER Alice had had a bad couple of years, he was coming out of rehab. He was trying to re-establish himself after, you know, being curled up in a fetal position in a hotel in Paris addicted to heroin. So I think the journey for him was just about, "Let's get back up onstage and try to resurrect who I am and what I was at the beginning of this."

PAUL TAYLOR It was full-bore. I mean, the shows were all about production. If a garbage-bag monster couldn't make it across the stage in time, Alice would go, "Ah, just cut that verse in half!" The music came second. It was more about, "When is the monster going to come in and chop so-and-so's head off?"

KIP WINGER But it was never about, "Let's catch up with these bands who were all influenced by me." Fuck no. He's Alice Cooper.

ALICE COOPER I heard about Kip Winger from one of my producers. He said, "I know this kid that plays bass that looks really good." We brought him into the studio and said, "Hey, why don't you come out and play bass with us?" I never realized Kip was as creative as he was. He was a black belt in karate. He could score a movie. He could score a symphony. He took ballet.

KIP WINGER I started taking ballet as a teenager because I had a girlfriend that didn't have any friends to do it with. But then I found I was really drawn to it. And that sparked my interest in classical guitar, and I started doing that and got really into baroque music and prog rock. But ballet, it's very athletic and very artistic and it suits my personality well, because it's outside of the norm. But I never was going to be a ballet dancer. I figured I had watched David Lee Roth as a kid, and I was just taking it one step further.

KANE ROBERTS He would do some spins onstage. But not, like, pirouettes and stuff. Although I did have to talk to him about not wearing a tutu. I'm kidding.

BEAU HILL Kip is truly a very gifted guy. And I wanted to help him as much as I could. So I would get Kip gigs. That's where the Alice Cooper thing came in.

KIP WINGER It all goes back to Beau Hill. I met him when I was sixteen and playing in a band with my brothers.

BEAU HILL The Wingerz were a band in Colorado.

KIP WINGER And Beau had a band called Airborne, they were on Columbia, and he was living in Denver. And my manager at the time was a radio DJ in Denver. He met Beau Hill backstage at a Heart concert at McNichols Arena and Beau was like, "I'd like to produce them." So we met Beau, he produced us when I was sixteen, and then he used us in the studio to do other stuff.

BEAU HILL We became incredibly tight, me and Kip and his two brothers. If you'll notice, Paul and Nate Winger sang on almost every record I ever did. They were great, great singers.

KIP WINGER When Beau moved from Denver to New York I followed him. He would hire me on projects when he could. He helped me immensely.

BEAU HILL When Kip came off the road with Alice Cooper, I had him work on a Fiona record.

KIP WINGER And then someone in Fiona's band brought in Reb Beach.

BEAU HILL I thought Reb was phenomenal. I introduced Reb to Kip and I said, "This could be the nucleus of a really great band." That's kind of how that happened.

REB BEACH (guitarist, Winger) It all started for me when I came to New York City. I had gone to Berklee, but I was only there for two semesters because rock was frowned upon at the time. It was, "You're holding the guitar the wrong way. You're holding the pick the wrong way." So I got in my car and drove away. I wound up getting a job as a singing waiter on the Bowery. It was a lobster restaurant right across the street from CBGB—they had one-pound lobsters for, like, $8.95. I was the only guy there who wasn't a Broadway hopeful. So I would kick the piano player out and just play Elton John and Billy Joel songs while everyone else was singing *Pippin* and *Cats*.

When I wasn't at work, I would hang around at music stores on Forty-Eighth Street like Manny's and Sam Ash, just playing guitar and talking with the people there. And I heard about this audition for Fiona. So I took a train way the hell out to Long Island, I started playing for one minute, and they said, "You got the gig." I wound up playing on the whole album [1986's *Beyond the Pale*], and Beau Hill was the producer. At the end of the sessions he came to me and said, "I don't want to insult you, but how does five hundred dollars sound?" I said, "Five hundred dollars? Oh my god!" That was the most amount of money I had ever held in my hand. Because I was surviving on Oodles of Noodles.

KIP WINGER Reb blew everyone away. He became the hotshot guy at Atlantic Studios. He was playing on a lot of these records.

REB BEACH Beau told other producers about me—I was easy to work with, I was a nice kid, and I did it for cheap. I wasn't in the union. You know, throw me some cash and I'd be happy. And so that's how I got all those sessions. [Producer] Arif Mardin used me on the Bee Gees. I did Howard Jones, I did Chaka Khan. I did Twisted Sister's *Love Is for Suckers* with Beau—I don't want to say the wrong thing about that, but some of the guitar performances were a bit wobbly, so I would come in and fix things here and there.

KIP WINGER I was doing a lot of solo demos at the time, trying to get signed as a solo artist. And when I saw Reb, I wanted him to play on some of my stuff.

REB BEACH When I met Kip, I'll never forget it. I was in the green room of Studio A at Atlantic Records, warming up. He came in and we hated each other. Just completely got off on the wrong foot. I totally didn't get his mild demeanor and his monotone voice. He just seemed to be totally full of himself. I thought he had such a lead singer attitude. But Kip had some really great stuff. Although it was a little bit . . . it was like progressive techno music. It was great music but it was missing something—a human characteristic. It was all drum machine and lots of sequencing and stuff. So Beau said, "Why don't you and Reb get together?"

KIP WINGER My music was a lot more progressive as a solo act. Peter Gabriel was my biggest influence. But Reb played on some of the demos, and he was great. And so when I went back to the Alice Cooper band I said to Paul, "Hey, I know this great guitar player, Reb Beach. Maybe the three of us could do a band."

PAUL TAYLOR Kip and I had been writing stuff together on that first Alice tour, just for fun. The first song we wrote was called "State of Emergency." But it was during that second tour [for Cooper's 1987 album, *Raise Your Fist and Yell*] where Kip kept going, "You know, I think I'm gonna quit Alice and go work on this and try and get us a deal." I remember telling him, "Dude, don't quit. Wait till we have something . . ." He said, "No, I'm pretty sure I can pull this off." So at some point he went to Alice: "I'm gonna try to go get me and Paul a deal." And Alice was always extremely supportive of everybody doing their own thing. So Alice said, "Go for it." And that's what we did.

KIP WINGER My feeling was, Once a sideman, always a sideman. I'm leaving. Plus, with Alice we had bands like Tesla and Megadeth opening for us, and I was thinking, Fuck, I could do this with two hands tied behind my back! Because I had been writing, like, Peter Gabriel music on my own. Stuff that was so much more complicated. But now I was seeing these bands and it was like, Wait a minute—you mean I could do what I did when I was sixteen years old and get a record deal? I'm outta here! So I left and went back to New York, and Reb and I made a pact to not take any outside work for six months. This was in '87.

BEAU HILL Kip and Reb moved in to my condo in Hoboken, NJ.

REB BEACH And either Beau or Kip knew a guy who had a Japanese management company called Amuse. And they had a place downtown on the West Side of Manhattan, and we would go into their back room where they stored all the boxes and record on a sixteen-track reel-to-reel Fostex. And the first day we wrote "Seventeen," "Time to Surrender," and one other song. *In one day.* And I remember walking out of that place kicking my heels just going, "Oh my god, I met a genius!" Because I had riffs, but I didn't know that these were songs. But Kip's a composer. He had studied this stuff. So everything came together really fast. We made demos— good-sounding demos—quickly.

PAUL TAYLOR It wasn't like we just walked into Atlantic and got signed. It was a long process. But I guess Atlantic had faith in Beau because he had already made some pretty successful Ratt records.

BEAU HILL Okay, so here's the way this worked. It's kind of a funny story. I took some songs to Doug Morris, and I played them and I said, "Listen, I would really like to bring this band to Atlantic." He listened to the demos and he said, "No. This is crap." So I went back to Kip and I said, "Doug didn't like these. Do some more." They'd write some more stuff and record it, and then I'd go back to Doug and I would change the name of the band. Just so that Doug wouldn't think I was still pitching the same guy over and over and over again.

KIP WINGER Call Your Doctor was one of 'em. I don't remember the others.

REB BEACH I thought Call Your Doctor was just the dumbest name ever. But, you know, Beau could sell you on anything.

BEAU HILL It was Sahara, and then it went to Call Your Doctor, and then I came up with something else. But it was just something to put on the cassette. We went back and forth and back and forth and back and forth. It was probably four or five submissions over the course of, like, a year.

KIP WINGER I mean, fuck, are you kidding me? Doug turned us down a gajillion times. He was like, "Don't play me another Kip Winger demo." I was fucking damaged goods. But the last time Beau went in, he played him "State of Emergency," and Doug said, "Well, that's pretty good . . ."

BEAU HILL I took "State of Emergency" to Doug and I said, "This is really incredible stuff. You have got to check this out." He listened to it and he went, "Wow, that is really something." I said, "Do you like it?" He said, "Yeah, I do." I said, "Will you sign it?" "Yeah, I'll sign it." And I walked around his desk and I stuck my hand out and I said, "So we have a deal, right?" He said, "Yeah." I said, "Thank you." And as I was walking out of the office Doug stopped me: "Wait a second—who did I just sign?" I said, "You just signed Kip Winger!" He goes, "You fucking prick." And he threw me out of his office.

KIP WINGER But we weren't directly on Atlantic. Beau had us on a production deal. That was a last-minute bait-and-switch that he did on us.

REB BEACH He got a cut of everything. He got part of the merch, he got fifteen percent as the manager, he got a huge amount of money and half the points on the record for being the producer. He got publishing. Just everything. So really I never made the kind of money that all the other bands that we later toured with were getting. And my wife would say, "Why is 'Wild' Mick Brown driving a Corvette?"

BEAU HILL I was participating on the publishing side and participating obviously on the production side, but without just being a complete money-grubbing person. And we got probably the world's smallest recording contract at that time. That's when there were a lot of big deals going on. But we had an embarrassingly small budget for the first record.

PAUL TAYLOR I don't remember who finally was like, "Let's just call the band Winger." Which was fine, you know?

KIP WINGER Doug was the one who said we should call it Winger. I hated it because I didn't want to be the namesake of the band. I wasn't into having it be like a Bon Jovi. But I asked Alice about it and he said, "That's a great band name!" When Alice said that I was like, "All right. Whatever." So we went with it, it worked, and it is what it is.

I still hate the name.

46

"MICHAEL JACKSON SAW THE VALUE IN POISON"

WES HEIN The first single from *Look What the Cat Dragged In* was "Cry Tough." The song went to AOR radio and it did just kind of okay and the video did not get much play on MTV. And the record stalled.

BILL HEIN I think we were at like 200,000 albums, something like that. And then Capitol became involved.

WES HEIN Enigma had a deal with Capitol Records where some of our artists were going to be distributed through Capitol's distribution system. There were two types of artists that would go through Capitol: one hundred percent pure Enigma artists, or, as was the case with Poison, joint-venture artists. And that meant Capitol would work it along with us.

BILL HEIN Capitol was ready for us to pull the plug and go to the second album. Like, "Look, you guys sold two hundred thousand albums. You should feel good. Why don't you guys go make another record?"

RIKKI ROCKETT We were told, "You're going to have to start thinking about the next record unless you can get another tour. Then we could support another single."

BILL HEIN I'm trying to think of Capitol's head of radio promotion; the guy had a cattle prod and he would chase people out of his office with it if he didn't like their opinion. He wasn't necessarily a bad promotion guy; that was the culture at the time. We wanted him to go out with "Talk Dirty to Me" and get the Capitol promotions team behind it. He was like, "No, this record's done. That's not a single. No one's going to play it. It's a weird little band."

RIKKI ROCKETT We worked really hard and got the Ratt tour. It was because of Ratt that we got to release "Talk Dirty to Me." Robbin Crosby was a big cheerleader for us.

WES HEIN Capitol as a label did not understand Poison. This is the label that thought Heart was a cool band. But one of the biggest exceptions was Tom Whalley. He got Poison.

TOM WHALLEY (executive, Capitol Records) The band had great ideas around how they wanted to image themselves and where they wanted to put themselves in the marketplace. They were a group of idea guys, right? Their presentation, all those bright greens and pinks, the idea of making things a party and vibrant—that was all coming out of them.

BILL HEIN Hair metal, whatever you want to call it . . . Poison certainly get a big chunk of the credit for creating not only the genre of the music but also the business model.

RIKKI ROCKETT For "Talk Dirty to Me" we had half the budget that we'd had for the "Cry Tough" video. So we told the directors not to worry about continuity. If you watch it, we're constantly changing clothes and guitars. It's like, "Look, this is a video, so what. Let everybody know it's a video. Let's have fun with that platform. Our main thing is we want people to smile and shake their ass when they see this." We really took advantage of what we had to work with.

BILL HEIN There was one weekend when we booked the A&M soundstage. That was a big expense for us. We did a Poison video on one day and a Stryper video the next. Big budgets for us on both of them.

RIKKI ROCKETT I only realized what we had accomplished with that video years later when I met Michael Jackson. I said, "Listen, I don't know if you know anything about our band, but I'm the drummer for Poison. I just wanted to say hi." He turns around and he goes, "Man, every time your video comes on, I sit down because you're having such a good time. I don't want to miss a second of it."

So if some dude says, "Oh, you guys suck," it's like, "Who fucking cares? Michael Jackson saw the value in Poison." How cool is that?

BILL HEIN "Talk Dirty to Me" was starting to get a genuine buzz. Our little promo team got that thing going and then Capitol came in on it and brought it home.

TOM WHALLEY The whole company rallied behind "Talk Dirty to Me" with the intention of breaking it through retail and touring and MTV and radio. And we were very successful at pop radio. At that time you could do that—you could take a song that you thought was a pop hit and just go right to Top 40 radio.

BILL HEIN The album went platinum . . . and then double platinum.

RIC BROWDE I remember that I was going to Doc McGhee's wedding—he chartered one of those Circle Line boats in Manhattan. And Derek Shulman, who signed Bon Jovi and Cinderella, he said, "You know, you just broke into the charts on Poison. Congratulations." I was like, "*What?*" I was flabbergasted. It was like *Springtime for Hitler.*

RIKKI ROCKETT We went back out and did the Ratt tour and stuff like that and when we came home, we had made a little bit of money. The first thing I ever bought myself was a red Toyota MR2. It was like a hot little two-seater semi–sports car. It definitely wasn't a Ferrari, but it was kinda cool. I never had anything like that growing up. I had a Ford Pinto and a '53 panel truck, you know? So that was pretty huge.

TOM WERMAN I liked Poison's presentation and I'd heard *Look What the Cat Dragged In* and I thought it was a reasonably well-produced album.

But I thought it was kind of one grade down from what I was doing. That it wasn't a first-rate production.

RIC BROWDE It's a piece of shit, that album. It sucks. Sonically, as a producer? It's the worst record ever. And I became known as a garbage producer because of it.

TOM WERMAN I met with Poison because Tom Whalley at Capitol called me. They had wanted Paul Stanley.

RIKKI ROCKETT Paul came out to the Texxas Jam to have a meeting with us. We sat down and we got along with him. I think we were all enamored that Paul Stanley was interested in Poison, but I'm not so sure that we were convinced it was the right move. I don't wanna say anything negative about him, but there were a few comments where I sort of felt like, I'm not sure if he's taking us seriously enough. But when Tom Werman wanted to step in it was like, "Okay, he's a real guy for sure. He's making real rock records out there." So it made a ton of sense for us.

TOM WERMAN We had a lunch meeting and I was sitting next to C.C., who asked me, "So, Mr. Werman"—which he called me in a friendly and cartoonish way—"Mr. Werman, I hear you do drugs!" C.C. DeVille asking me if I do drugs. And I said, "Well, yes, recreationally I do, but not in the studio. Work comes first."

RIKKI ROCKETT C.C. was a little bit of a bad influence, okay? Because he was actually doing things like that before we really got him in the band.

RIC BROWDE Bruce was doing stuff but it wasn't really bad in those days. He developed a cocaine problem as soon as there was some success.

C.C. DeVILLE All of a sudden, your real life exceeds your dreams, but then if you still kind of feel empty for something else, for whatever it is, well then the drugs come in.

TOM WHALLEY C.C. was probably the loosest cannon of them all. He was always overly amped as I remember. But his talent had a huge, huge impact on the songwriting.

TOM WERMAN He was loud and he was funny and he was all over the place. Very energetic. And so was his playing. He was more concerned with being as fast as Eddie Van Halen than with being creative. The solo for "Nothin' But a Good Time" took eight hours, partially because C.C. was constantly going back and forth to the bathroom. I assumed he was freebasing or doing something that had to do with inhaling cocaine, because it took him longer than it would to just go in and snort a couple of lines. That said, he was extremely cooperative . . . but definitely not all there.

RIKKI ROCKETT It did take an entire day. But it's a great solo!

TOM WERMAN Poison worked very hard. Especially Rikki Rockett. He would be the first to admit that he wasn't the greatest drummer in the world. But he enjoyed what he did and he stayed at it.

TOM WHALLEY The band was working *incredibly* hard. They were writing really, really good songs. They didn't have that kind of credibility that other bands were getting at the time in that world because of their pop sensibility, but then that's why I brought in Werman, right? You bring in Tom Werman and now it's more believable. It has a little more of a harder rock sensibility to it. Then you bring in managers who can really go connect at touring and deal with the promoters and all that stuff and now you've got that piece working. You connect at radio and you connect at MTV and you have an explosion and that's how it all happens.

"DIZZY" DEAN DAVIDSON Britny Fox opened up for Poison on the *Open Up and Say . . . Ahh!* tour. They were bigger than all the bands. Their tour was over-the-top. They had a number one single with "Every Rose Has Its Thorn," sold-out shows, marketing out the ass . . . It was a happy time.

RIKKI ROCKETT Capitol had Duran Duran, who were being marketed, like, very, very, very pop, you know what I mean? And I think there was a little bit of that marketing that went into Poison, whether we liked it or not, and we'd get upset about that. We'd be like, "Nah, this is just . . . it's a little pussified."

TOM WHALLEY With Poison, I don't know where the line begins of what is a pop band and what isn't a pop band, but it seemed that their whole approach to the music wasn't necessarily an aggressive approach. But at the same time you don't get the success that Poison had without some part of the rock audience buying in. And you could see that on the touring side, which I guess was more the male side of the audience.

BRYN BRIDENTHAL I was talking to Bobby Dall at the L.A. Forum after a Mötley Crüe show and he was all anti–Guns N' Roses. There was an article that Andy Secher ran in *Hit Parader* where Slash said that Poison was everything he hated about rock 'n' roll, that they were posers. Andy said to me, "Do you want me to take this out?" And I said, "Well, did he say it?" He said, "Yes." He had it on tape. I said, "Then let it play. It's true." Bobby was raging about it. What I did bad, I will admit, is that I had a big grin on my face when I talked to him. I thought this was just hysterical. I said, "Bobby, this isn't *Time* magazine for Christ's sake, it's the *Hit Parader*. I don't see how a band that sold two million records can feel so threatened by a band that hasn't even sold two hundred thousand." And he looked at me and he threw his beer in my face.

MITCH SCHNEIDER I went to meet Poison on the *Open Up and Say . . . Ahh!* tour because I was hired by their management as an independent publicist. Guns N' Roses was coming up on them and the group needed to harden its image. And as I'm going on the tour bus, I see all these beautiful women leaving, and I think Bret Michaels' opening line to me was "Oh, you can always feel free to have the ones that we don't." That was just Bret being a comedian. He told me about all the women he had in all the cities. We kind of joked about it and I said, "Well, I guess you have it written down in a black book?" He grinned at me, and I put out a press release that Poison had a sex computer, that in it the girls were all categorized by name, city, and type of sex acts they had done. And the line from Bret was "The only safe sex I practice is not falling out of bed."

"DIZZY" DEAN DAVIDSON The women on that tour were . . . It's like, Does Tiger Woods have an 8-iron in his golf bag? Yeah. Does a hobbyhorse have a wooden dick? Yeah.

LITA FORD (guitarist, the Runaways; solo artist) Poison would have their roadies pick them out of the audience and bring them backstage, so when they got offstage they would go into a room full of girls or women or whatever. Then they would take whoever they wanted out of this room. I thought it was disgusting. I don't know what they told the girls that went backstage . . . They were obviously into it and excited about it, but I just thought it was like a herd of cattle. I really did not hang out with those guys.

MITCH SCHNEIDER After the release went out, [journalist] Lisa Robinson proceeded to attack the band mercilessly in the *New York Post*. Then the group said to me later, about a few weeks in, "You know, Mitch, whenever we're going to radio stations now, we're noticing that some of the people don't even want to talk to us anymore." And I remember saying, "Well, mission accomplished."

TOM WHALLEY I don't know how much impact the critics had on the band. It has to, because when you're getting criticism like that it's going to show up somewhere in the day-to-day of the band. But I don't think it affected them to a large degree. I think that their belief in themselves, that belief in what they were trying to do, just created perseverance for them. Where the conviction to go accomplish something was just beyond the norm. I always had tremendous respect for that part of it.

RIC BROWDE All they need to be judged by from a historian's point of view is, they were successful. That's all that counts. At the end of the game it's, "Who's got the most toys?" They do.

47

"IF YOU PUT TITS ON HIM, HE COULD RUN FOR MISS TEXAS"

SCOTTI HILL After Matt Fallon was out of the band there was a long period of time where Skid Row didn't have a singer. I was working at Garden State Music with Snake and living at Snake's mom's house with him and Rob Affuso. And then we would rehearse in the garage at Rachel's parents' house. The typical day was: Wake up, drive to Toms River, go to work, go to rehearsal, go out, party, wake up, and do it again.

RACHEL BOLAN We went back to our jobs. I worked for the [New Jersey] *Aquarian Weekly.* I was a glorified paper boy. And I would pick up shifts at the music store with Scotti and Snake. It was bad enough when it was the two of them, but when it was the three of us there, it was bedlam. And we auditioned a bunch of guys over nine months' time, which seemed like ages.

DAVE "SNAKE" SABO We spent nine or ten months searching, putting ads in the back of *Metal Edge, Hit Parader,* things like that. And we had so many cassette tapes come in. We had people like Oni Logan [later of Lynch Mob] fly in, and he was really close but we just didn't click. We reached out to [future Mötley Crüe vocalist] John Corabi and he passed. We auditioned singer after singer after singer—three, four, five a week. And nothing. It was disastrous.

ROB AFFUSO At one point we decided we were gonna call the band This Blows and do a bunch of punk tunes and Rachel was gonna sing.

RACHEL BOLAN But what happened was there was a guy named Dave Feld who we were all friends with. He was working with Mark Weiss as his photo assistant. And one day he mentioned, "Hey man, if you guys are still looking for a singer, I saw this kid get up onstage at Mark Weiss' wedding . . ."

SCOTTI HILL Dave Feld was like, "This guy got up and jammed with Zakk." And we all knew Zakk.

ZAKK WYLDE I've known Dave and Rachel and Scotti since they worked at Garden State Music. When I went to Mark's wedding I had just gotten the gig with Ozzy. And Mark and Dave had helped me get that gig. That wedding was the first time I ever met Sebastian. And nothin' for nothin', he was the same guy he is now. Just without fame or money.

MARK WEISS I knew Sebastian because he had been singing for a band called Madam X.

MAXINE PETRUCCI In '85 or '86 Madam X needed a new singer, and there was this agent from Toronto, Shaun Pilot, that we met when we toured there at one point. He said, "I think I've got the right guy for you. He's got big hair and a great voice." We said, "Okay, send us a promo pack." So we got an envelope in the mail with a photo and a tape of Sebastian singing with [previous bands] Kid Wikkid and VO5.

CHRIS DOLIBER (bassist, Madam X) We pull this eight-by-ten out of a manila envelope and there's Sebastian with his hair up, a little like Michael Monroe, only a better-looking version of Michael Monroe, if you can imagine that. He was wearing some kind of black satin McDonald's jacket, like what maybe the employees would wear, but he rocked it out.

SEBASTIAN BACH (singer, Madam X, Skid Row) I think I was fifteen years old in that picture. That jacket . . . I didn't have any money. My mom was divorced from my dad. We were struggling. I didn't have a winter jacket. So I was in line at McDonald's in Toronto one day and I go to this chick behind the counter, "I love that jacket. Can I have that?" She looked around and nobody was looking and she goes, "Okay." And I just wore it.

The other thing about that jacket was that as a kid I worshipped David Lee Roth. I would read all his interviews, and he would say things like "A Big Mac's got all your three basic food groups. Vegetables, meat, whole grain . . . it's the perfect food." So I was like, "If Big Macs are cool with Dave, they're cool with me!"

CHRIS DOLIBER I looked at this photo and I said to myself, "No fucking way. Guys that look like that can't sing . . ." Because he was stunningly good-looking. Then we put the cassette in the player and it was like, "Holy shit, this kid can sing!"

MAXINE PETRUCCI So Sebastian joined the band and we went out on the road. We hit the East Coast, Canada, Texas, Louisiana, that sort of thing. He was with us for about a year, a year and a half. It felt longer.

CHRIS DOLIBER He didn't really have an off switch. Which was kind of annoying after a while. Like, "Geez, shut the fuck up!"

MAXINE PETRUCCI He would say to us, "You guys are just jealous because I'm prettier than you." Things like that. All the time.

CHRIS DOLIBER And onstage he was big and lanky and kind of in his own zone and not conscious of everybody else around him. Like, he would take the mic stand that had maybe a ten-pound cast-iron weight on the bottom of it and spin it around and whack you right in the shins. *Bam!* And it's like, "You motherfucker . . ." That's the kind of pain that brings you to your knees.

MAXINE PETRUCCI And what would happen was, he wouldn't last past three songs. He would blow his load.

SEBASTIAN BACH I had this this ear-piercing fucking scream back then. I can't even describe it—it was like the Mariah Carey note, but louder than that. It was earth-shattering. And Madam X would make me run out there and do it the first note of the show. I always tried to explain to them that it blew my fucking voice out. It was very stressful to me.

London studio shoot, Los Alamitos, California, 1980. From left: Nikki Sixx, Dane Rage, Michael White, Lizzie Grey *(© Don Adkins)*

Mötley Crüe at their first-ever studio shoot, Don Adkins's living room, Cerritos, California, April 1981. From left: Mick Mars, Nikki Sixx, Vince Neil, Tommy Lee *(© Don Adkins)*

Jake E. Lee and Stephen Pearcy of Ratt onstage at the Whisky a Go Go, opening for Mötley Crüe, Hollywood, California, 1982 (© Don Adkins)

Stryper performing at the Enigma Records warehouse for label employees, Torrance, California, 1983. From left: Robert Sweet, Michael Sweet (© Wesley Hein, Enigma Records)

(Above) W.A.S.P. light up the Troubadour, West Hollywood, California, January 1984. From left to right: Randy Piper, Blackie Lawless, Tony Richards, Chris Holmes (© Kevin Estrada)

Vince Neil and David Lee Roth at the Troubadour, prior to Roth introducing Mötley Crüe onstage, West Hollywood, California, New Year's Eve, 1981 (© Don Adkins)

Quiet Riot onstage, 1983. From left: Rudy Sarzo, Frankie Banali, Kevin DuBrow, Carlos Cavazo (© Mark Weiss)

Ratt onstage, 1984. From left: Juan Croucier, Robbin Crosby, Stephen Pearcy, Bobby Blotzer, Warren DeMartini (© Mark Weiss)

Twisted Sister on the set of the "I Wanna Rock" music video, Los Angeles, California, 1984. From left: Mark "The Animal" Mendoza, Eddie "Fingers" Ojeda, Dee Snider, A. J. Pero, Jay Jay French *(© Mark Weiss)*

Dokken, Los Angeles, California, 1984. From left: Jeff Pilson, Don Dokken, George Lynch, "Wild" Mick Brown *(© Mark Weiss)*

Poison's original lineup, backstage at the Roxy Theatre, Hollywood, California, 1985. From left: Rikki Rockett, Bobby Dall, Bret Michaels, Matt Smith (© *Don Adkins*)

Warrant early lineup, Max Asher's parents' house, Westwood, California, 1986. From left: Erik Turner, Jerry Dixon, Adam Shore, Max Asher, Josh Lewis (© *Cecil Brissette*)

Outtake from the cover shoot for Cinderella's *Night Songs*, Philadelphia, Pennsylvania, 1986. From left: Jeff LaBar, Tom Keifer, Eric Brittingham, Fred Coury *(© Mark Weiss)*

Lita Ford, Los Angeles, California, 1986 *(© Mark Weiss)*

Mötley Crüe in their *Theater of Pain*-era outfits, Los Angeles, California, 1985. From left: Nikki Sixx, Tommy Lee, Vince Neil, Mick Mars (© *Mark Weiss*)

Poison, Los Angeles, California, 1986. From left: Rikki Rockett, C.C. DeVille, Bobby Dall, Bret Michaels (© *Mark Weiss*)

(Above) Guns N' Roses, Los Angeles, California, 1986. From left: Steven Adler, Izzy Stradlin, Axl Rose, Duff McKagan, Slash (© Mark Weiss)

(Left) Faster Pussycat, 1987. From left: Brent Muscat, Eric Stacy, Taime Downe (in front), Mark Michals, Greg Steele (© Mark Weiss)

(Below) L.A. Guns, 1989. From left: Kelly Nickels, Mick Cripps, Phil Lewis, Tracii Guns, Steve Riley (© Mark Weiss)

Great White, 1988. From left: Jack Russell, Lorne Black, Mark Kendall, Audie Desbrow, Michael Lardie (© Mark Weiss)

Warrant, New York City, 1988. From left: Joey Allen, Steven Sweet, Jani Lane, Erik Turner, Jerry Dixon (© Mark Weiss)

Tracii Guns and Izzy Stradlin at the Palace, Los Angeles, California, 1988 (© Mark Weiss)

Kix, New York City, 1988. From left: Ronnie Younkins, Jimmy Chalfant, Steve Whiteman, Donnie Purnell, Brian "Damage" Forsythe (© Mark Weiss)

Skid Row, Los Angeles, California, 1991. From left: Rachel Bolan, Rob Affuso, Sebastian Bach, Dave "Snake" Sabo, Scotti Hill *(© Mark Weiss)*

Hanging in Moscow for the Moscow Music Peace Festival, August 1989. From left: David Bryan (Bon Jovi), Klaus Meine (Scorpions), Matthias Jabs (Scorpions), Zakk Wylde (Ozzy Osbourne), Dave "Snake" Sabo (Skid Row), Jon Bon Jovi *(© Mark Weiss)*

(Above) Vixen, 1989. From left: Share Ross, Roxy Petrucci, Janet Gardner, Jan Kuehnemund (© Mark Weiss)

(Left) Trixter's second-ever show, Paramus Roller Rink, Paramus, New Jersey, August 1984. From left: Pete Loran, Steve Brown (Courtesy of Steve Brown)

(Below) White Lion, New York City, 1989. From left: Greg D'Angelo, James LoMenzo, Vito Bratta, Mike Tramp (© Mark Weiss)

Winger, 1989. From left: Reb Beach, Paul Taylor, Kip Winger, Rod Morgenstein
(© Mark Weiss)

Tuff hang out on a rooftop on the Sunset Strip, Hollywood, California, 1989. From left: Michael Lean, Todd Chase, Stevie Rachelle, Jorge DeSaint *(Photo by William Hames, courtesy of RLS Entertainment, 2020)*

Lonn Friend (*center*) with Mötley Crüe on the *Dr. Feelgood* tour, Teterboro heliport, Teterboro, New Jersey, 1990 (*Courtesy of Lonn Friend*)

ixen backstage with headliners the Scorpions on the 989 Savage Amusement European tour. From left: Roxy etrucci, Francis Buchholz, Jan Kuehnemund, Klaus Meine, hare Ross (*Courtesy of Share Ross*)

Gunnar and Matthew Nelson, 1991
(© Mark Weiss)

(Left) Fleur Thiemeyer sketch of Nikki Sixx's *Shout at the Devil*-era outfit, with handwritten notes from Fleur and Nikki *(Courtesy of Fleur Thiemeyer)*

(Right) Mötley Crüe's Nikki Sixx onstage in *Shout at the Devil* outfit, the US Festival, San Bernardino, California, May 29, 1983 *(© Mark Weiss)*

(Left) Fleur Thiemeyer sketch of Ozzy Osbourne outfit *(Courtesy of Fleur Thiemeyer)*

(Right) Ozzy Osbourne in Fleur Thiemeyer–designed outfit, Los Angeles, California, 1985 *(© Mark Weiss)*

CHRIS DOLIBER The first song or two he'd be singing as hard as he could and then he would be flat. Because he'd be winded. And he would say, "Punch me, hit me, do whatever you have to do! Just make me great! When I'm flat, spit on me!" And I did—at his request.

MAXINE PETRUCCI Finally we told Sebastian, "This is just not working out. You need to go home." Well, he wouldn't. He didn't even have a phone number! So we took him to Mark's wedding. Mark had only invited me and Chris, but Sebastian really wanted to go. I'm sure he saw it as an opportunity.

MARK WEISS I got married at the Molly Pitcher Inn in Red Bank, New Jersey, in June 1987. I had my secretary invite almost anyone in my Rolodex that I got along with. So she said, "How about Madam X?" I mean, I had only done one shoot with them, but it was recently, that same year. So they were fresh in my mind. I'm like, "Yeah, they were fun and I had a good time with them, invite them."

CHRIS DOLIBER We sat in with the wedding band. We did some Zeppelin covers. I played bass, [Madam X's] Mark McConnell played drums, Zakk Wylde played guitar. And Sebastian sang.

MARK WEISS Then Sebastian called up Kevin DuBrow. And Kevin had told him, "Whatever you do, don't have me come up. I don't want to sing." But Sebastian kind of forced him. You know, put him on the spot. It was like a half-hour, forty-minute jam.

ZAKK WYLDE Sebastian got up there and knocked it out.

SEBASTIAN BACH I was doing that crazy scream, and when Zakk heard me do it he kept saying, "Do that again! Do that again!" It melted the fucking speakers.

MAXINE PETRUCCI They played a couple covers and he sang 'em great. He was always great for two or three songs. Superb. So everybody heard the great Sebastian.

SEBASTIAN BACH Dave Feld approached me and he said, "Hey, Jon's parents want you to come over and sit down." I was like, "Holy moly! Okay."

MARK WEISS I had invited the whole Bon Jovi band to the wedding, but they were on the road with Cinderella so they couldn't make it. But I was close with Jon's family, and so his parents came. I don't really know how they got to talking to Sebastian, because I was busy getting married, you know what I mean? But what I heard was that Sebastian befriended them.

SEBASTIAN BACH They sat me down and I said to Mr. Bongiovi, "Hey, nice to meet you. What's your favorite song by your son?" He said, "'Never Say Goodbye.'" I go, "That's cool. I like 'Let It Rock.'"

DAVE "SNAKE" SABO After the wedding I got word from Mr. and Mrs. Bongiovi: "There was this kid singing at Mark's wedding. Great voice, skinny, tall, good-looking . . ." The whole bit. So we talked to Dave Feld and Mark about it and we were able to get in contact with Sebastian, who I think was out of Madam X, and he was back up in Canada at this point. We sent him four songs: "18 and Life," "Rattlesnake Shake," "Youth Gone Wild," and one other that I forget the name of.

SEBASTIAN BACH When I put in their tape, "Youth Gone Wild" was on there and I liked it, but it didn't blow my mind. But the more I listened to it, I thought, I can fucking do something with this for sure . . . It sunk into my brain and the melodies would go around in my head, and that's pretty much the sign of a good song.

DAVE "SNAKE" SABO We made arrangements for him to come down to New Jersey to jam with us.

SCOTTI HILL The guy's in fucking Toronto, but we got our money together, got him a flight, and I picked him up at Newark airport and brought him back to Snake's house.

DAVE "SNAKE" SABO The first thing he does when he walks in the door, he goes, "Hey dude, how you doin'? I've got a nine-inch dick!" My mom is sitting right there and I'm like, "That's awesome. Just awesome . . ."

SEBASTIAN BACH They all still lived with their parents. I had lived in a couple different countries. I had been paying rent. I had a kid on the way with my girlfriend. It was a completely different scene for me.

SCOTTI HILL First impressions of Sebastian? High energy. *Super* high energy. He was all over the place. All over the house. Just, you know, pacing. Lots of elbows, very lanky and tall. He had a can of Aqua Net in his hand, and he was spraying his hair, it was going everywhere. The can runs out and he just tosses it behind him. Then we drank a bunch of beers and went out. And Sebastian got in a fight. *The first night.*

DAVE "SNAKE" SABO We went over to this club in Sayreville called Mingles. And Mingles had a big upstairs room and a smaller, more intimate downstairs room. We went downstairs to the smaller room and there was a band playing and we said, "You know, it'd be cool if we got up and jammed . . ." So we got onstage. I believe we did "Youth Gone Wild" and "18 and Life."

SCOTTI HILL Sebastian was great. He was on fire. He captivated the audience. He captivated *us.*

DAVE "SNAKE" SABO We played terribly.

RACHEL BOLAN We were all hammered.

SEBASTIAN BACH Inhaling beers.

DAVE "SNAKE" SABO But I believe it was Rachel that got on a mic and announced, "This is our new singer and we're Skid Row." And that was that. Then we proceed to get really, really drunk, and we were walking outside and I don't know what happened but next thing we know, Sebastian is fighting somebody.

SCOTTI HILL Maybe somebody elbowed somebody or bumped into somebody, just something stupid like that. And then it's like, "What the fuck is your problem?" One of those things. And that was it. Sebastian takes a swing at the guy.

DAVE "SNAKE" SABO He missed by a mile.

RACHEL BOLAN A big swing and a miss. And we were just like, "Dude, just chill. You're from Canada! You're in *Jersey*! You're gonna get your ass kicked!"

SEBASTIAN BACH Well, I don't remember that, because we drank more beers than I remember. I don't remember that at all.

SCOTTI HILL Everybody's breaking it up, tossing each other in the car, we're outta there!

ROB AFFUSO Then we went to a local White Castle. We go in, we're all hairsprayed up, you remember what the band looked like early on. Somebody calls us a bunch of fags, Sebastian turns around and swings at him, and that's it. All of us are fighting this group of guys and it rolls out into the White Castle parking lot. It was just a brawl. We wound up in the back of police cars. But nobody pressed any charges.

DAVE "SNAKE" SABO That was the infamous night where the five of us officially became Skid Row.

DOC McGHEE Getting Sebastian was the turning point for them. Because the songs were all there. And he was this six-foot-five guy, weighed maybe 120 pounds if he weighed that. And he had hair as tall as him. If you put tits on him, he could run for Miss Texas. He was a really good-looking kid. I started managing the band in probably '88.

SCOTTI HILL Doc and Jon Bon Jovi started courting all the labels.

JACK PONTI I was the one who called up Jason Flom at Atlantic. Because the second I met Sebastian, I was like, "Yeah, no shit!" Because Baz was an absolute rock star. You'd have to be in a fucking coma to not see that. I said to Jason, "Listen, this local band, they're starting to get their fucking shit together and Jon Bon Jovi's taking a very, very heavy interest in it." I said, "You better get on this Skid Row thing."

JASON FLOM I got a call one Friday night from Jack: "You should go see Skid Row tonight, they're playing in Newark." I didn't even really know Jack that well. But I decided to go to Newark. It was this club called Studio One. It was snowing, it was not a nice area at all. This was only the second show they'd ever done with Sebastian. So I walk in and they're playing "Youth Gone Wild." They're playing "18 and Life." And Sebastian was the best-looking guy ever. I was like, "This is the greatest fucking thing." I started going to see the band every time they played.

DAVE "SNAKE" SABO Jason was relentless, man. He was willing to do whatever he could to get our band on Atlantic.

RACHEL BOLAN One time he came to see us at the Airport Music Hall in Allentown, Pennsylvania, this old supermarket they turned into a venue. I think we were opening for White Lion. It was a snowstorm and Jason brought Ahmet Ertegun. They fly in on a helicopter, and they take a limo to the gig, which is basically on the other side of the parking lot.

JASON FLOM It was two stretch limos. And the club was across the street from the heliport. It was hilarious. And Ahmet was his usual self. He was having a lot of fun with girls around.

ROB AFFUSO We go onstage, we do our show, and when we come off we get escorted to this room. There's a bar set up, there's a couch, there's carpeting. We're like, "We're in the wrong room . . ." And then the double doors open up and Ahmet walks in. He has maybe five girls on each side of him. And he says, "Hello, gentlemen, I'm Ahmet Ertegun." And then he leaves the girls there and goes away.

RACHEL BOLAN That guy was classic.

JASON FLOM I was trying everything I could to get this band on Atlantic. And then finally Doc calls Ahmet one day and says, "Forget it. We're not doing it with you guys. We're signing with Geffen."

DOC McGHEE I gave it to David Geffen first because of Tom Zutaut. Because Tom was probably more responsible than anybody else for me getting Mötley Crüe. So I brought Skid Row to him. But he was not into it.

DAVE "SNAKE" SABO We did a showcase for Geffen at SIR Studios in New York. Tom Zutaut was there with John Kalodner.

SEBASTIAN BACH We get in this little tiny room, and Tom Zutaut's talking to somebody else. I say on the mic, "Hey guys, how's it going?" He looks at me and goes, "Shut up and sing."

DAVE "SNAKE" SABO We played nineteen songs. And then Tom says, "Well, I think you've got two songs."

SCOTTI HILL We did "Youth Gone Wild." We did "18 and Life." We did "I Remember You." I think the only one he liked was "Makin' a Mess."

JASON FLOM And the crazy thing was that Zutaut, at the time, was on one of the greatest rolls in the history of A&R. He had signed Dokken, Mötley Crüe, Guns N' Roses. He was a god at the time.

SCOTTI HILL And then Kalodner referred to us as Junkyard. He couldn't tell the two apart.

JASON FLOM It's like Babe Ruth missing a hanging curve ball. I still can't figure out how that happened. But everybody makes mistakes.

DAVE "SNAKE" SABO Truth be told, for a brief minute we were signed to Geffen. I remember after that showcase we were rehearsing down in Rachel's parents' garage in Toms River, and Doc called on the cordless phone. He was like, "Congratulations—you're on Geffen Records!" And it was so anticlimactic. It was terrible, man.

SCOTTI HILL We had a band meeting and we agreed unanimously: "We've gotta go with Jason." We got together with Doc and we said, "We feel like we're making a mistake." And we went with Atlantic and we got a label that absolutely fucking loved us.

48

"IF YOU LOOK AT THE CLOTHING, IT'S ALL PRETTY OUTRAGEOUS, INNIT?"

AL BANE When I styled a band I wanted everybody to have an individual look, right? But I wanted them all to kind of look "in character," if you will. So I would suggest that they imagine a fireman, a policeman, and a paramedic standing side by side. They all look like they're in uniform when they're in official capacity, but they don't all look like a squad of police officers. We would start with that kind of conversation and then I would say, "What is it that you want to present?"

HEIDI MARGOT RICHMAN For the baby bands, I mean a lot of them, even if they wanted to have a say, they didn't really have a say. But then from my standpoint, whatever their visual representation is has to be organic; it can't be something inauthentic. So for me the challenge sometimes was, "Okay, how are we gonna get you to look your very best and also be the most marketable, so I'm making the label and management happy but it's also gonna be authentic to you, the artist?"

RAY BROWN (costume designer) I don't like to call myself a designer . . . even though I am one. To me, the most important thing is if someone can create music they also have an idea of how they want to look onstage. It's not up to me to tell them how to dress. It's up to *them* to tell *me* how they want to dress, or how they see themselves onstage. And then I go ahead and translate what they've told me, no matter how, you know, incomprehensible it is.

FLEUR THIEMEYER (costume designer) You do sketches, you do variations, and you show them things and you start educating them. I sat and talked with Nikki about the look he wanted for *Shout at the Devil* and I said, "You mean like Vikings or Genghis Khan?" And Nikki goes, "Who's Genghis Khan?" So you start introducing them to things they may not have crossed.

LITA FORD I was living with Nikki Sixx at that time and I had him cut my hair. He chopped it off. I loved it, because my hair drove me nuts. It was so long, and it was so silky straight, and it was getting in the way of everything. He just gave me the Mötley Crüe haircut. I had to get away from that teenage girl, long pretty hair and tennis shoes thing I had in the Runaways. I grew into being a young woman. I wanted to attract attention as well as play guitar. I wore clothes that made people's jaws drop at that time. You put on a leather G-string and some boots up to your knees, and people are going to go, "Oh my god. Is this girl for real? Does she sleep upside down to make her hair a mess?"

RAY BROWN For *Theatre of Pain* I specifically remember Nikki saying that he wanted a black-and-white striped jumpsuit like he had seen Steven Tyler wearing. I convinced him that we should change it up to where it was like a two-piece thing with a longer jacket that kind of had all these points on the bottom of it. And it just evolved from there.

NEIL ZLOZOWER I shot the photos for *Theatre of Pain* and I thought it was like circus clothes. It looked like they were getting ready for Barnum & Bailey. Honestly, the clothes for *Shout at the Devil*, that was like *Mad Max, Road Warrior* shit. I mean, that was badass stuff.

FLEUR THIEMEYER When they were doing *Shout at the Devil* I lived on Ocean Avenue in Santa Monica and I said to the guys, "Come down to my place." I ran a whole lot of basic sketches off on a copy machine, just black and whites. I gave them, I think, four sketches each. They sat on the floor of my apartment with colored pencils and I said, "Color it the way you see it." Nikki did black and red because he wanted the power of blood. Mick Mars, his thing was blue, more somber. He really was this quiet one that sort of sat back and watched these other three monkeys perform.

RAY BROWN Vince Neil, in that same *Theatre of Pain* era, he had a pair of pink-and-white very see-through almost lacy pants that I made for him. He put them on and one of the other guys, I'm not sure which one, said, "Dude, you look like a fuckin' chick! Why don't you just put on a garter belt as well?" And we all looked at each other like, "Oh, that's a good idea, innit?" That was five years before Gaultier did it for Madonna.

NIKKI SIXX We were just rebelling against the fact that there were all these bad bands coming out of L.A. who were copping our look. There were all these awful new bands and we thought, Man, we're not responsible for this, are we? Well, let's change and totally throw a wrench in the thing. Let's dress in pink! I don't think that glam had ever really been embraced like that before.

AL BANE With Warrant we kind of built a cleaner sleazy look, if you will. Back then Poison was out there. L.A. Guns and Pretty Boy Floyd, all these bands were kind of competing against each other. And here comes Warrant. So what can we do? Well, we didn't do much different from what everybody else was doing—we just applied ourselves a little bit.

JOEY ALLEN Al Bane made all the really cool buckle-y stuff that Jani used to wear. In fact, he made the *Bad* jacket for Michael Jackson. And he pretty much, in my eyes, I mean you'd have to ask Al Bane, but he ripped that off from Jani.

AL BANE I gotta rewind the story a little bit. One day I get a phone call at my mom's house—"They're gonna send a car to come pick you up." I'm twenty, twenty-one years old, whatever. This limo pulls up, I get in, and we drive over to Universal Studios. They frisk me and we walk into this room. And way on the other end of this room is a stage. You can hear sound, there's lighting going on, it's a dress rehearsal. I have no idea for who. They make me wait in this little area and then these people drive up in little golf carts. I recognize one guy, it's Quincy Jones. And this guy in a robe, with a hood over his head, it's clear he's just gotten off the stage. They put him on a sitting pedestal, it looks like a wedding cake. Then they bring me up to approach the guy, and he pulls his hood off and it's freaking Michael Jackson! I'm looking at him going, "Oh my god." Then Michael Jackson reaches into his pocket and he brings out a crumpled-up Warrant flyer. And he goes [in high voice] "Are you Al Bane, the man with the leather?"

So Michael Jackson copied Warrant's look for *Bad*. Go look at the cover—the black cotton jacket with a bunch of belt buckles on it. Only with Warrant it was a cheap pin-star concho belt buckle thing instead of custom-made rhinestones, you know what I mean? It's Michael Jackson versus unsigned Warrant.

JOEY ALLEN So then we graduated to Heidi Richman.

HEIDI MARGOT RICHMAN I remember we sat down for our first creative meeting, just me and the band. I said, "Hey, I have this idea, what do you think?" And they were like, "Well, we have *this* idea, what do you think?" And we both said, "Wouldn't it be amazing to do all white leather and then have each guy's particular outfit really be a reflection of who and what they are?"

JOEY ALLEN To be honest with you I don't remember whose idea it was to wear [the outfits in the "Heaven" video]. All's I know is that they were leather, and to me it doesn't matter what color it is. If it's leather, it's leather. It smells like leather, it moves like leather. So to have white leather outfits with black on them, we didn't say to ourselves, "Wow, this is gonna be a Versace moment." You don't think anything but, It's leather, it's rock 'n' roll, it's a ballad, it's about heaven. Let's wear white. In retrospect maybe it wasn't a great idea. Who knows?

FLEUR THIEMEYER There was a fabric, I can't remember the name of it, but it came out of Japan and I think Ray Brown is probably the first person to use it. It looked like leather, it had the qualities of leather, but it was fully washable.

RAY BROWN It was a simulated leather but it was the best simulated leather I'd ever seen. And it was really expensive. I bought some of it and it just worked amazing. You could wash it in a washing machine, dry it in a dryer. All the pants I did for Guns N' Roses apart from Slash's were all out of that washable leather.

AL BANE One thing that happened with Michael Jackson was that after he pulled out that Warrant flyer, somebody says, "Go get the TV." They roll in a big 1970s TV on a fucking cart, like in your junior high school, they put a videotape in the VCR and . . . there's Warrant onstage! And Michael says, "They jump around like circus performers, and they can do it every day. Where my stuff is falling apart during one dress rehearsal." Michael goes through a half a song and the crotch is blown out on his pants. Meanwhile, the Warrant guys are doing everything they do and the pants are holding up every night. So what's the difference? Why can't Michael Jackson's clothes stay together and Warrant's did?

FLEUR THIEMEYER You put these people onstage, it's like you've put an electric shock through them. They just go ballistic. So the spandex or anything that had stretch in it, it allowed them to continue into this euphoric state of mind and not have to worry about, Oh, but what if I split them all?

KLAUS MEINE (singer, Scorpions) Those spandex, they were so comfortable! You could move around like crazy, which we did. You can move your little legs because it was so easy. It felt so good, you know?

STEVE BROWN (guitarist, Trixter) We recorded our first record next to where the Scorpions were making theirs, so we would see them every day. They would roll up in a van and they would be dressed in their stage clothes. Leather. They would wear leather pants to the studio. I would say, "How fucking crazy?" We were wearing, like, shorts and baseball hats.

FLEUR THIEMEYER We started making spandex for David Lee Roth because he did so many karate moves and high kicks and everything. And if something was to split or break, he would just lose it. You know, he would really . . . "What the hell!" That sort of shit. And so once this fabric was there and they could do things without any sort of being impeded in any way, you know, it gave them such a freedom onstage. If they wanted to do the splits they could.

RAY BROWN I remember Jon Bon Jovi and I sitting down and having a conversation about lace-front pants. And it was about, you know, if you go on tour and you gain or lose a little bit of weight, which can happen depending on what's going on, you can just adjust the front of them. And it got to the point where every hair band I could think of was calling up going, "I want some of those lace-front pants!"

LITA FORD Here's the story behind the torn jeans I wore in the "Kiss Me Deadly" and "Close My Eyes Forever" videos: I had been at Lemmy from Motörhead's house for three days. I was fucked up. I called my friend Patty and said, "Come and get me. There's no way I can drive." She picked me up, and we're driving down a side street. There was this electrician kid working on a telephone pole. I looked at his pants, and a little bell went off over my head. "I've got to have these pants." They were naturally shredded all the way down the front from him climbing the telephone poles. I said, "Dude, I'll give you a hundred bucks for those pants." He looks down at them, and he goes, "You're fucking kidding me, right?" I said, "No, man." I said, "I'll give you a hundred bucks for them." He goes to his car. He slips on a pair of shorts, and he goes, "I've got another pair at home. I live right around the corner. Do you want them, too?" I said, "Sure, I'll take them both."

I gave him two hundred bucks, and I got my first two pairs of holey jeans, which I took to Fleur Thiemeyer. She tricked them out by putting little pieces of leather and beads and stuff on the inside and stuff on the outside. My mother hated them. She goes, "Get in the house." I said, "Why, Mom?" "Just get in the house. I don't want the neighbors to see you in those jeans." Little did she know, they'd be all over MTV.

FRANKIE BANALI I can tell you for me personally, the tights came about because if you were traveling out on the road, you could wear them and then you could go back to your hotel room, stick 'em in the sink, water, Woolite, squeeze 'em out, and they'd be dry the next morning. It was out of necessity, not design.

FLEUR THIEMEYER David Lee Roth had all the argyle spandex pants— they'd be, like, red and white or red and black with stripes and all that. And one time his concept was he wanted me to make the same pants and a shirt for a monkey. So they came over to a studio I had on Santa Monica Boulevard. Now, the monkey standing up at full height would probably be a good three, three and a half feet tall. This wasn't a little monkey. So I get down on the floor and he's patting me on the head and I take a tape measure to try to get this monkey's inseam from underneath. From his scrotum, so to speak, to the floor. But every time I put my hand anywhere near that area, the monkey would grab my hand and throw it away. He got really pissed off. And Dave was just in hysterics.

DAVID LEE ROTH Pushing boundaries in terms of what [Van Halen] wore was never an ambition of ours, but it always seemed to be where we would end up.

FLEUR THIEMEYER I think the monkey got so upset he shit on the floor. So, you know, we ended up moving on.

SHARON OSBOURNE I'd used Fleur to do the clothes for Electric Light Orchestra. And then she did Ozzy.

FLEUR THIEMEYER Sharon realized that Ozzy's career needed a reboot. It needed to be different from Black Sabbath. But if you look at that album [1986's *The Ultimate Sin*], how much more commercial it is, you look at the "Shot in the Dark" video, it was very much a look of the time on MTV.

OZZY OSBOURNE People were saying I looked very camp and I did. I look back now and I go, "What the fuck was I thinking?" But it was what everyone was doing.

FLEUR THIEMEYER We used to laugh and say they were his Diana Ross gowns.

SHARON OSBOURNE It was all insanity. It was like Liberace.

FLEUR THIEMEYER Well, the funny thing is we used a place called the Design Studio in L.A. and they used to make Elvis' stuff and Liberace's stuff. The pattern we used for Ozzy's cape was from Liberace's cape.

SHARON OSBOURNE Looking back at it, Ozzy goes, "I never wore that." I'm like, "That's *you* in the fucking photo!" And he goes, "Thank god I was stoned."

GEORGE LYNCH Back then everybody used Ray Brown to make their clothes and style them. So we all wore the same outfits. Everybody from Mötley Crüe to Scorpions to Ratt to Dokken on down the line. Every single band. We all wore Ray Brown clothes. So we all kind of looked the same.

RAY BROWN What was the Dokken album where they had all that crazy clothing on the cover? *Under Lock and Key*? That was all mine. They really got a lot of flak about that.

MARK WEISS I'm the one that shot the photos. I think when they first saw 'em they were going, "What the fuck is this?"

DON DOKKEN You look at the album cover of *Under Lock and Key*, we're wearing these ridiculous outfits. I'm in blue! And Jeff's in red! And Mick's in purple! And George will be mauve! It's like, "Oh, fuck." And we spent a fortune on those clothes.

RAY BROWN I don't even remember how those designs came up. It was just a bunch of sketches that we had of these kind of weirdly shaped jackets. A little bit influenced possibly by the Duran Duran look, which was going on at the same time but on the other side of the world. But more flamboyant. And they said, "Yeah." They went for it.

"WILD" MICK BROWN Cliff Burnstein used to go, "God, why don't you guys just wear what you wear on the street? Because when you show up to do the videos that's when you look cool. And then they put you in all that crap, you've got so much makeup on and tiger spandex . . ." He hated all that shit.

CLIFF BURNSTEIN They were musicians, those guys. Lynch was an exceptional musician. But they were so part of that L.A. scene and it was so de rigueur to look like that and dress up like that. You know, it's hard to go against the grain.

"WILD" MICK BROWN We thought, No, you gotta do this. Gotta put more makeup on. And Burnstein would just go, "Fuck, I don't get it." But that's what was going on. And then we realized, "We can't keep up with this." Because as soon as your hair's big and you have enough makeup on, well, then that Ratt band comes out and they've got ten times more makeup! And then Mötley Crüe takes it to a whole new level, which was brilliant. And it's like, "Okay, how am I gonna win this one?"

EDDIE "FINGERS" OJEDA With Twisted it was almost like they prejudged you. It's like getting stereotyped or profiled—because you wear makeup you can't be good. You can't be serious players or have serious music.

DEE SNIDER At one point we did the "Have It Your Way" press kit, which was a picture of us with makeup and a picture of us without makeup. We were basically saying, "If this is a sticking point, sign us and we'll just be a denim-and-leather rock band."

EDDIE "FINGERS" OJEDA But I think it definitely helped us because it made it look like more of a show. It wasn't just a bunch of guys going up there in T-shirts and jeans rocking out, and I think that gave the audience more of a thrill. It turned into war paint after a while. It wasn't even glam.

FRANK HANNON (guitarist, Tesla) As far as Tesla goes, we were just wearing jeans and T-shirts and stuff. There were publicists and video directors that tried to doll us up a little bit and bring in makeup artists and stuff like that on a couple of our early videos, but it never really felt comfortable to us. In some ways we felt that, you know, being normal stopped us from getting on the covers of magazines. It was a little frustrating, but it didn't come natural to us to wear lipstick and pink spandex and stuff like that.

REB BEACH We always wanted to wear all the flashy clothes and pouf up our hair like everybody else. I remember having no money and being on welfare and watching MTV and seeing Britny Fox and going, "I can do that!"

"DIZZY" DEAN DAVIDSON For Britny Fox, I looked at the old Who. Remember the Who when they were in the '60s? With the ruffles? It was like the early Who, Paul Revere & the Raiders, Prince. It was more of a mod look and I ran with it.

BILLY CHILDS In the early days we had girls make the outfits for us who would do it for free. Dean had a sister that was invaluable to helping us out and making this shit work. 'Cause how do you dress like a Victorian-era dude? I don't know, you know? Oddly enough, it's actually more Edwardian than Victorian. But that's a whole 'nother story . . .

JEFF LaBAR Poison took it way further than anyone else. And they were gorgeous. I mean, seriously, the first time I saw the album cover [for *Look What the Cat Dragged In*] I was like, "Holy shit! These chicks are hot!" I think Cinderella did pretty much the same thing with the makeup and hair. We were just not as pretty.

NEIL ZLOZOWER Those bands, they were pretty boys. But there was no shortage of girls. I mean, you gotta understand, I used to always go out with the bad boys—Van Halen, Mötley, Poison, Ratt, Guns N' Roses. Those were the bands I liked hanging with, and every night there were billions of fucking girls that wanted to bone the guys.

FLEUR THIEMEYER The sexuality needed to appeal to both male and female in the audience, you know? Vince Neil, the girls were all over him like a rash. But the way he threw himself, the guys thought he was cool, too. It's very much a fine line. Because you don't want to look like a drag queen.

NEIL ZLOZOWER The prettier they looked at these photo shoots, the more chicks they had at the shows.

DON DOKKEN The Sunset Strip? I mean, the hair, the makeup, the spandex . . . you couldn't tell the chicks from the dudes.

TRACII GUNS None of the guys on the Strip were prettier than the girls. Except maybe [Enuff Z'Nuff drummer] Vikki Foxx. But he was from Chicago.

STEVIE RACHELLE When I first got to L.A. I went to Cherie Adams' Hair Magic on Robertson Boulevard. Michael [Lean, Tuff drummer] got me hair extensions. That was a necessary . . . my hair was like Leif Garrett's. It was barely to my shoulders. But a lot of guys went there. If you look there's old advertisements—I wanna say her ad was something like "Hair Extensions to the Stars."

DAVID COVERDALE (singer, Whitesnake) My hair in the "Still of the Night" video was actually a hairdressing accident. In those days it was a chemical rinse. I got it from [video director] Marty Callner's wife, Eliza, a stunningly beautiful woman. Just gorgeous. I said, "Do whatever you fucking want, baby." You know? So the day before the video shoot, I'd gone to Eliza to get a couple of highlights . . . and came out looking like a fucking beach boy! I said, "Put it back." And she said, "I can't—your hair will drop out." Because it was that kind of chemical shit. I went, "Ah, for fuck's sake." So I drove the old white Jag back to the Mondrian Hotel [in L.A.], where everybody—everybody—without exception went, "Oh my god, you look amazing!"

JAMES LoMENZO Mike Tramp took me to perm my hair, blond it up a little bit. It reminded me of one of those *Twilight Zone* episodes, because from my perspective after they processed my hair and washed it out, I had three heads come into my view and look at my head after they'd taken all the wrappings off. And one of them said to the other, "Yeah, that should loosen up in a few days." If you want to know what that means, take a look at the photo inside the White Lion *Pride* album cover and you'll see.

MIKE TRAMP I enjoyed dressing up onstage and I enjoyed having the long hair, but White Lion was a New York band from Italian families, and it's not who we were. But I ended up having a girlfriend of many years who was one of the biggest designers during the '80s for the biggest bands and stuff like that, and we had a lot of fun making these clothes . . .

FLEUR THIEMEYER I was married to Mike Tramp. And Michael had the stage presence, the character, the looks. He could wear anything, he could support it in his manner and in his physical abilities. But for a very, very, very long time, I did not tell people we were in a relationship, because then at certain times it comes out and they go, "Oh, yeah, just 'cause he's your boyfriend he gets everything." And it's like, "Oh, come on, please . . ." You start getting a bit of spitefulness coming out of people, and they've already got jealousy because, you know, the band's got a number two single on *Billboard* with "When the Children Cry."

ZAKK WYLDE I was sleeping with my hairdresser, who's now my wife. I still bang her whenever I get the opportunity, when the kids aren't rollin' around the house.

RIKKI ROCKETT Rock 'n' roll, like David Lee Roth said, "it's always been about haircuts and shoes." We were the next haircuts and shoes for a while.

NEIL ZLOZOWER I mean, honestly, you have a year and a half, two years between when the first Poison record came out and then Guns really sort of took off. All of a sudden the hairspray started coming down and all that shit.

FLEUR THIEMEYER Skid Row probably was the closest to a band that was not over-the-top in dress. But you had Sebastian, so, you know . . .

SCOTTI HILL Our first photo shoot in 1986, with Mark Weiss—very glam. It was just like, whatever was laying around. And lots of ripped-up denim.

RACHEL BOLAN I'll never forget, we were all sitting looking at the Polaroids at my parents' house. The phone rings and I pick it up. And I just hear, "Hey asshole!" I'm like, "Who the fuck is this?" And the voice says, "It's your worst fucking nightmare. What the fuck do you guys think you're doin', dressing like a bunch of chicks?" And I say again, "Who the fuck is this?" And it was Jon Bon Jovi. And he goes off on me. I'm paraphrasing but it was something like, "'Youth Gone Wild'? It's more like 'Chicks Gone Wild.'" Or something to that effect. He tore me a new asshole on the phone.

SCOTTI HILL I think from that day on everybody wanted to photograph us in front of a brick wall. At some point it was like, "No more brick walls!"

RAY BROWN I mean, when you look back on it, it was really, really fun . . . as long as you didn't think too much about what it was you were making. Some of the stuff was just nutty. You know that Alice Cooper jacket that had all the nails sticking out of it? When I shipped it to him, the FedEx guy cut his hands because the nails came right through the box.

FLEUR THIEMEYER At any given time, I could have four or five bands on the road, five people in each band, managers, labels . . . I could have forty people calling me every single day wanting this or wanting that. So it was just this nonstop production line and flying and traveling. You're trying to keep up, but you're also trying to come up with new scenes and new ideas. But the funny thing is they all wanted to be the same thing. They thought if they looked like Guns N' Roses, they would be as successful. But the singer isn't Axl Rose and the guitarist isn't Slash. I mean, there's a reason why these bands were successful, and why they sold ten million records compared to three.

HEIDI MARGOT RICHMAN Think of all the bands that were hopping in a van and flooding into L.A. and hooking up with a stripper so they had a place to live and try and figure it out. It was a massive ecosystem. And these guys, they were the ones who a lot of times would seek me out because they're like, "Oh, we want to look like Warrant," or "We want to be as glam as this, as hard as that."

RON KEEL Fashion killed us all. Because by '87 you had one guy, Ray Brown—great guy, fantastic talent. But he's making clothes for Mötley Crüe, Judas Priest, Keel . . . every band in the business was dressing up in Ray Brown costumes. So of course every band starts to look kind of similar. If you come from another planet and you look at Judas Priest and Warrant, you wouldn't know the difference 'cause they're all wearing Ray Brown clothes! So the fashion certainly got in the way. You can't build a lasting foundation on clothes and hair!

RAY BROWN Was there anything I thought was particularly outrageous? Well, if you look at the clothing, it's all pretty outrageous, innit?

JOEY ALLEN I think my white leather stuff's hanging up in a Hard Rock in Mexico somewhere.

49

"SAVING WHALES DOESN'T SELL ALBUMS; LEATHER PANTS DO"

MIKE TRAMP Everybody in White Lion was severely burned out. But a week after coming off the *Pride* tour—and I'm not bullshitting you—we end up in a deserted motel in Palm Springs and we're sitting in these bungalows with adjacent doors, and we sit and pull out ideas here and there. Then we meet and Vito says, "Check this out." Then I sing and then I go in the next room and I start working on some lyrics. And after four or five days, we actually end up coming out with ten or twelve songs.

VITO BRATTA I remember when he sang "Little Fighter" the first time, I said, "Mike, what's that about?" He goes, "A Greenpeace boat that the French government destroyed." I'm like, "You wrote a song about a boat?" I mean, we're coming off a multiplatinum record and our first single's about a boat?

MIKE TRAMP There's a famous quote also from John Kalodner that he says to Vito: "Man, tell Tramp that saving whales doesn't sell albums; leather pants do."

GREG D'ANGELO James, Vito, and I spent maybe two weeks in a rehearsal room in New York going through the arrangements for *Big Game*. But there was not a lot of work done as a band prior to making that record.

MIKE TRAMP As we neared the completion of the album, Jason Flom and Doug Morris come out to Amigo Studios in L.A. to hear the record. There's a song on *Big Game* called "Cry for Freedom," written about apartheid in South Africa, and the three other guys in the band have no fucking clue what that means. It was a haunting track in the studio when you played it loud, and that drumbeat could be U2 or whatever. Doug said, "Man, this is some of the most interesting stuff I heard since Led Zeppelin." We were told later that as they were driving back to the hotel, Doug Morris turned to Jason Flom and said, "Why are you letting them do this?"

GREG D'ANGELO James used to start that groove to "Radar Love" and we used to play along, and honestly for me, that's the highlight of that record. Not to take away from any of the other White Lion melodic stuff, but I don't think there's any other recording that we've done that captures what the band was really like live.

MIKE TRAMP "Radar Love" was actually shot the day after we finished a six-week tour with Ozzy Osbourne. At this point, we were a "special guest" with our own stage on top of his, and we were getting serious money.

VITO BRATTA Making the "Radar Love" video was like filming a whole movie.

MIKE TRAMP The director, Jean Pellerin, and us just wanted to do our version of *Vanishing Point*.

VITO BRATTA I had a Lamborghini like the one I'm in in the video, but it was in a dealership being stored under covers. The car in the video is from the movie *Rain Man*.

MIKE TRAMP That's actually me on the motorcycle going 120 miles an hour with no jacket and no helmet. Like a fucking idiot.

"SEND THE CHECK FOR THE NELSONS—THEY'RE READY"

GUNNAR NELSON Matthew and I were born and raised in Hollywood. We were born in '67, so we were there at the very epicenter of the birth of country rock at the Troubadour when our dad, Ricky Nelson, put together the Stone Canyon Band. At the Troubadour any night, you could see Linda Ronstadt's first band, the Stone Poneys, Jackson Browne, Buffalo Springfield . . . all that kind of stuff. That's what Matt and I grew up watching our father doing.

JACK PONTI Matt and Gunnar's life is unlike anything you or I could ever fathom. Their grandparents were Ozzie and Harriet. Their father was Ricky Nelson. Their uncle's Mark Harmon, you know, from that TV show *CSI*, whatever the fuck it is. Their aunt's Pam Dawber from *Mork & Mindy*. Their other uncle's Chuck Woolery from *Love Connection*. So they've just grown up around massive fame.

GUNNAR NELSON Matthew and I got our first instruments when we were six and seven and did our first recording session at eleven. We started playing the L.A. clubs when we were just twelve as Strange Agent.

MATTHEW NELSON (singer, bassist, Strange Agent, the Nelsons, Nelson) We hung out with punkers, new wavers, and rockabillies. That was our scene.

JOEY CATHCART (guitarist, Strange Agent, the Nelsons, Nelson) I met Matthew freshman year of high school. I bonded with him because he was the only guy in the class that had a blue tail. You remember rat tails? And he wore one of those jumpsuits like Sting used to wear. I was like, "Oh, that's an interesting guy." He was into new wave and so was I. We started talking at lunch about how we love music, and he said, "Hey, you should come up to my house sometime. My brother plays drums. I play bass. And since you play the guitar, maybe we can, you know, play some stuff." I said, "Sure."

GUNNAR NELSON We were playing five days a week on the same stages with the Knack, the Plimsouls, and the Go-Go's and all of those bands. It was a rough fucking scene.

MATTHEW NELSON Hanging out backstage with new wavers and power poppers, these guys, we're fifteen years younger than any of them, they're the scariest motherfuckers I've ever seen. I mean far scarier than any punkers or rivet heads, you know, metal guys. These were scary people that sang really happy songs, but they were all heroin addicts. They would do stuff like sabotage your gear before a show; cut your power cable or kick your amps to where they would blow a tube.

JOEY CATHCART Before Ricky Nelson died in 1985, we had already changed our name to the Nelsons. In fact, the last club date that we played before their dad died was at the Central, which later became the Viper Room, and he actually came. It was the night before he was leaving for his last tour. We saw him in the stairway. He was such a shy guy that he never came all the way into the club.

GUNNAR NELSON Our father died when we were eighteen years old. It was devastating. He was our best friend and our mom was a horrible excuse for a mother. She basically shot us out into the world. So when he died, it was literally like the rug was pulled out from under us, and we spent a year of our lives spending money we didn't have, impressing people that didn't matter, just trying to medicate over our grief. We were sleeping on friends' couches and living out of the trunk of a beat-up car.

MATTHEW NELSON Then we were asked to play *Saturday Night Live* in 1986, the night that Ron Reagan, Jr. was hosting.

JOEY CATHCART I thought we played great, and it was very fun. We all had a great time. I mean, it was like, "Woo, big-time!" There we were, eighteen, nineteen years old in New York City being treated like VIPs. Limos everywhere!

MATTHEW NELSON When you play *Saturday Night Live* and you're the only unsigned band ever to play it, you don't have to be a genius to think, Well, there might be something more freak show about this than "Hey, these guys are a really awesome talent and we really love them." On the way back, Gunnar, who had played drums all those years, just said, "Look, this isn't right and I wanna learn how to play guitar and come up front with you." And I'm sitting there freaking out, going, "But we're right there! We've been spending literally years doing this!" And he said, "I'm just telling you, it's what I really think we need to do. I wanna write some great songs and I'm gonna take a year to learn how to play guitar and I'm never gonna get off it."

GUNNAR NELSON I learned how to play guitar in a year of concentrated learning. I wanted to combine the country-rock vocalizing that I grew up with and the majesty and power of the guitar work that I heard with bands like the Scorpions, Dokken, and Boston.

MATTHEW NELSON And to his credit, he did it.

GUNNAR NELSON We put together a meeting with Marc Tanner, who had been a solo artist on A&M, because his publisher played us his demos and we liked almost all of them. Before you know it, all these songs started taking shape.

MATTHEW NELSON And we had some notable guys playing with us, like Vivian Campbell before he joined Whitesnake, and a great drummer named Andy Parker, who played for UFO. But a lot of players also just saw us as a meal ticket.

GUNNAR NELSON We shopped our demos to labels in New York and L.A. three times and were turned down by everyone before we got a development deal from John Kalodner at Geffen. We targeted him because he'd just done Aerosmith's *Pump,* the Whitesnake record, Cher, Peter Gabriel. This guy was unstoppable.

MATTHEW NELSON We figured he wasn't gonna get fired.

GUNNAR NELSON So here's what I learned about John Kalodner. First off, you'd make friends with the secretaries. Which was not hard for me and Matt, okay? John was famous for always wearing white suits like John Lennon, right? Now, occasionally, John wore a black suit. Nobody knew this, but that was the easiest way to tell that John was having a shitty day and he was in the worst mood ever. You never want to be around John when he was wearing his black suit. So I always called the secretary and asked, "What color suit is he wearing?" If it was a black suit, I'd reschedule.

We also realized that when we came in to play him demos, he had an attention span of three songs and that, moreover, he was going to shit-can two of them. Finally, Matthew and I figured out that John never remembered what he'd already heard! So since we had the twelve songs that we knew we wanted on the record, we took the next fourteen months going in and having meetings with John, acting like we were working on shit, and we'd play him three songs at a time. We would keep the one song that he approved aside and cycle the two rejected songs back in with another new song at another meeting.

JOHN KALODNER (executive, Geffen Records) In working with them as an A&R person, artists learn to hate you, because you are the only person in their life that criticizes them. You're the person who tells them no and you're the person that is always pushing them to do better and not gratifying them or kissing their ass. So when they're successful, they hate you and they feel contempt for you.

GUNNAR NELSON Okay, here's a typical John Kalodner criticism: "I fucking hate it." "John, what do you hate about it?" "You're the fucking musician, you figure it out!"

LARRY MAZER John Kalodner and I were very close friends, and after Asia broke up, the keyboardist Geoff Downes was going to do a solo thing and he didn't have a manager. So John said, "You should meet with Larry Mazer." And I was a huge Yes fan, I was a huge Buggles fan, I was a huge Asia fan, so I said, "Oh, absolutely." So I flew to London, and we're talking, and I said, "What are you doing?" He goes, "Well, I want to put something new together, but I've been doing some producing, some songwriting, and as a matter of fact John has been feeding me a couple projects, and one of them is this group, Nelson." I said, "Oh, who's that?" He goes, "Well, it's Ricky Nelson's kids." So he played me three songs and my head exploded. I immediately called Kalodner from the studio. I said, "John, why didn't you tell me about this?" He goes, "Well, they have managers." I said, "I don't care." I said, "I've got to be involved with this."

GUNNAR NELSON Matt and I had gotten to the point where we were down to our last sixteen dollars in the bank. We couldn't eat anymore. It had been about a year that we'd been courting John Kalodner, and he was still taking his time with us but no money, no commitment, nothing. We went to our managers and said, "Listen, we're desperate, we need this to go to the next level. He's not moving. We need to pressure him or do something." They said, "We're playing this politically. Don't go in there. Don't meet with him personally."

MATTHEW NELSON We rolled in there without an appointment and said to Kalodner, "Listen, we know that we could be blowing this, but we have a great song and we wanna play it for you and we have nothing to lose at this point." And we played "Love and Affection," which we had just written with Marc Tanner. And I remember John kinda getting this weird smile on his face. He was rocking his head through the whole thing and tapping his feet.

GUNNAR NELSON When it was done it was silence for, like, thirty seconds. Then he just reached over and called business affairs and said, "Send the check for the Nelsons—they're ready." Then he got off the phone and he goes, "I've been waiting for you guys to do something like that. For you to not listen to anybody. Because when you guys release this, everybody in the world is gonna want to tear you down. And I felt if you didn't have the balls to come in here and stand up to me, you certainly weren't gonna have the balls to go stand up to anybody else."

51

INTERVIEW: RICK KRIM, MTV EXECUTIVE

Rick Krim joined the staff of MTV in 1982, one year after the network's launch, and during his twelve-year tenure rose to become a vice president of music programming. He was instrumental in deciding which videos did and didn't make the cut during the hair band era and beyond.

What was MTV's attitude toward hard rock in the early days of the network?

I don't even think there was one. There was very little hard rock or metal getting played on the channel. At that time, it was bands like Duran Duran, Cyndi Lauper, and Culture Club that were really branded as "MTV." Also, it was a lot of UK acts. The Brits got it early on, whereas the American labels were more like, "Why should we pay for your programming by making videos and letting you air them for free?" But then MTV started breaking bands that weren't even on the radio, and that was the point where the American labels really started to see the potential value.

What was the first hard rock video that MTV really got behind?

Quiet Riot's "Cum On Feel the Noize." I'm sure there was stuff that was played before them, but that was the one that really broke through, the first real big hit from a band in that lane. Then came "We're Not Gonna Take It" by Twisted Sister.

The Twisted Sister videos had a story line that spanned several videos. Did bands like Cinderella subsequently pick up on that concept because it played well on the network?

Without a doubt. That stuff played better to the mass-appeal audience and probably to the female audience—unless, of course, the band was all cute guys, and then they could stare at them all day. But in general, it just made the videos a little more interesting. It was just fun. It hadn't gotten yet to the cliché of what the videos became—rain and smoke and cars—whatever the prop du jour was. And it wasn't misogynistic yet.

How did the staff react to how women were being portrayed in some of these videos? Was everyone just numb to it?

You did get numb to it, and I think living in a very, very pre-#MeToo era, when Tawny Kitaen was spread out over a car in a Whitesnake video, people thought that was sexy. I can't speak for the women who were working there, but nobody really voiced any real outrage. It's not like we sat in meetings and talked about it. Some people think Warrant's video for "Cherry Pie" is funny and silly, and other people are offended by it. That said, the Sam Kinison videos for "Wild Thing" and "Under My Thumb" stuck out. It was all these famous rockers standing around watching Jessica Hahn roll around on the ground, you had women on leashes, you had women feeding each other bananas, even spraying Reddi-Wip into their mouths. Those were a bit much for some people to handle and there was likely a larger discussion around them.

MTV had a standards and practices department that went through every video before it could air. Would you often require edits to a clip before accepting it?

I actually was the liaison for a long time with our standards and practices person, so I'm the guy that had to go sit with them every week and go through the proposed edits. I could either fight back or just accept it and relay that stuff to the labels. Every week there were little things, but as I recall, it was usually just "Edit this scene at 3:20" or "Take this one shot out—there's side-boobage." The labels generally just did it, because they wanted to be on the channel. Honestly, things like Nine Inch Nails' "Closer" or Pearl Jam's "Jeremy," where the original video has the kid sticking a gun in his mouth, were much more problematic.

What was your relationship like with the labels?

Me and John Canelli, who was my counterpart in the programming department, split all the labels between us. He had Geffen and Poly-Gram, so he had Guns N' Roses, Def Leppard, and Bon Jovi. I was the Elektra, Atlantic, Columbia, Epic guy, so I had Mötley Crüe, Skid Row, and whoever else was on those labels. We all had our big acts that we had relationships with. You were the liaison for all the business. Submitting videos went through us. The video promotion people at the labels would work us, and we would go into the weekly music meeting and represent those labels. We'd communicate their priorities, push for what they were pushing for. More often than not, we went out of our way to try to take care of people as best we could and to spread it around. We wanted to have good relationships with everybody. And yeah, there's always some barter going on; if you wanted to do something big with Guns N' Roses, then you would play the Junkyard video because it was also on Geffen. Nothing illegal or anything. It happens everywhere.

Was MTV fully enthralled with Guns N' Roses?

Guns N' Roses was awesome. I didn't even look at them as metal. Guns N' Roses was just this kick-ass, no-frills rock band. They weren't pretty boys, they were just rock. There was a purity to it that felt like, There's nothing contrived whatsoever about this. It was exciting to see that. People at the network were like, "Oh my god, this band, they're so fucking good!" Which I couldn't say for some bands that came around later on. A lot of bands that followed suit didn't feel quite as genuine.

Dial MTV, **where viewers called in and voted for their favorite videos every day, seems to have been incredibly important to a lot of the bands. Did hard rock groups just know how to mobilize their fans, or do you think the labels were hiring people to call in?**

I think some of the bands figured out how to get people in the phone banks. It seemed obvious when certain bands would be number one every day, and that didn't align with what was really going on in America. Britny Fox is the one that sticks in my brain. And Britny Fox was fine, but they were number one, like, every day. Not that they didn't deserve to be in the Top 10, but number one every day was pushing it. There's a long history in this business of trying to beat the system however you can do it, and I think they found a way and it worked for them. And others followed.

Did you have close personal relationships with any of the bands?

I got to be really friendly with the Mötley guys. I hung out with Tommy Lee a lot. I was really close with Kip Winger and I was golf buddies with the guys in Warrant. My whole thing was I genuinely liked the people in the bands I hung out with.

It must have been rough on these friendships when MTV stopped playing their videos.

Nobody ever likes giving people news they don't want to hear. That's never any fun, especially with people that you like and know. But I can't think of any example where I had a relationship damaged because all of a sudden it wasn't their day. At this point now, it's just fun to see these guys. I hadn't seen Nikki Sixx in a long time and ran into him last year. It was great to sit back and reminisce about those days, realizing what a great time it was and how much fun we had—and how much success.

52

"WE CALL THEM, UH, 'PANTY WETTERS'"

BRUNO RAVEL C.C. DeVille once said, "You come out with your rock songs, and then you put out your ballad, and then you buy a house." He was right.

BEN LIEMER (editor, *Circus* magazine) Everybody had to have their big power-pop power ballad, right? And you gotta drop your two heavy tracks first so you don't lose credibility. Understand? Then the power ballad comes six months down the marketing cycle because that's what's going to sustain the sales and break a band even bigger, get all the girls who aren't involved, and help sell out shows. But because the band came out rockin', the guys aren't turned off.

SHARON OSBOURNE Everything was the ballad. You always had to have those ballads.

MADELYN SCARPULLA (radio promotion, product manager, Mercury/PolyGram Records; manager, Kix) The Scorpions, that was a band for dudes. But then they would throw in a ballad.

KLAUS MEINE Scorpions was always about a powerful riff, but we would also go for the emotions with ballads like "Still Loving You." So of course we saw all these girls in front of the stage.

RUDOLF SCHENKER (guitarist, Scorpions) With "Still Loving You" we had a baby boom in France. Because making love and babies, the French people liked the slow songs very much.

MICHAEL WAGENER The women loved ballads and those were the people who bought the albums back then. They spent the money on it. And if it's a good ballad and it has emotion, then they loved it, and it paid the rent.

NIKKI SIXX "Home Sweet Home" for us was our "Dream On" or our "Stairway to Heaven." All of the bands that we loved always had that one song on their record and we liked that.

MICK MARS I believe that that was one of the first hard rock 'n' roll power ballads.

RICK KRIM "Home Sweet Home" introduced the concept of the power ballad. Every band had to have one, because that was the song that usually took them to the masses. You hit them over the head with the giant power ballad and get your double-platinum-record plaque, which wasn't hard to do at the time. If you had even a sniff of a hit, you had at least a gold record.

ROBIN SLOANE It was a hard rock ballad and we made this beautiful black-and-white video. And I think that sold a lot of records for the band and really made them an MTV staple.

TOM WERMAN Mötley was a big deal by then and they had to live up to their reputation and they were doing drugs big-time on *Theatre of Pain*. Tommy was dating Tawny Kitaen, so he was distracted, and obviously there are lots of distractions when you're stars . . .

NIKKI SIXX It came from a guitar figure that I had had since I was seventeen and had never really been able to flesh out. And then one night, we were leaving rehearsal to go up to the Whisky to have some drinks and then over to the Rainbow to do our usual shenanigans, and Tommy started mimicking the riff on the piano and adding his own flavor to it. Everything fell into place and we wrote the song in fifteen minutes.

TOM WERMAN I can't remember how we rearranged it because I can't remember the original, but I definitely orchestrated it.

NIKKI SIXX The record company was totally against us putting "Home Sweet Home" on there. They thought that since we had never done a ballad before, people would think that we were pussies. I was just like, "Look, we wrote this song and it's going on the album."

TOM KEIFER "Nobody's Fool" was originally a song that started off as a ballad and picked up into a double-time kind of thing in the tradition of "Stairway to Heaven." It was our producer Andy Johns' decision to change it when we were in pre-production for *Night Songs*.

JEFF LaBAR Andy thought that the original arrangement didn't make any sense. At first when somebody says something like that, it's always like, "What the fuck?" But in hindsight it was like, "Yeah, you're right, it's better this way." We added a bridge in the middle of it to break it up and then just totally took out the end section.

FRED COURY Andy Johns wanted to replace Tom on "Nobody's Fool." He said, "We have to get someone else to sing this."

MICHAEL WAGENER When you were doing a rock album in the mid-to-late '80s, you never considered the ballad to be *the* song, even though it always ended up being the moneymaker. In every case, I made all my money on ballads. But the guys weren't that focused on the ballads. They wanted to rock! The ballad was sometimes a necessary evil. "Okay, we've got nine songs . . . and the ballad."

VITO BRATTA "When the Children Cry" was written in the vein of "Dust in the Wind" by Kansas. Just guitar and vocals. Believe it or not, at that point we weren't really thinking of hit songs so we didn't look at that as a ballad. And believe it or not, we weren't that kind of band. We eventually *became* that kind of band being pushed by people, but we weren't gonna be the, you know, "Oh, I love you, you love me." But boy . . . were we driven in that direction.

MIKE TRAMP I sat and wrote most of "When the Children Cry" in Staten Island at my manager's house, where I lived. Vito came over later and I said, "Listen man, I got this here, let me play it for you." And he sort of converted it into what it became. The lyrics are even more current today than they were back then.

VITO BRATTA I remember at the time people were like, "Listen, you gotta have drums and bass."

JAMES LoMENZO That was the one that kind of put us in a place where even more people came out. We could tour on our own merit and fill theaters on our own. And that was a big deal.

SHARON OSBOURNE Ozzy had been working on "Close My Eyes Forever" and he goes, "I don't think this is for me," and yada yada.

OZZY OSBOURNE I started writing it when I was at Betty Ford [drug and alcohol rehab center]. Sharon was managing Lita Ford and I said, "I've got this song. Lita can have it if she wants."

SHARON OSBOURNE I'm like, "Please record the song with Lita." And Ozzy says, "Fuck off!" But he did it. And it was a huge fucking hit.

LITA FORD Sharon and Ozzy had come to visit me in the studio to bring me a housewarming gift—a big stuffed gorilla—and Ozzy and I ended up staying up all night. We played pool. We did drugs and drank alcohol. There was this little room off to the side of the control room, and it had guitars and keyboards. We went in, and we never came out. We just went in there and I started playing guitar and Ozzy started singing. The next thing you know, we had "Close My Eyes Forever" ninety-five percent written. There was one verse missing lyrically, which I went home and finished the next day.

SCOTTI HILL The ballads were getting cheesier and cheesier, sugarcoated, and the bands were just jumping on that. And it was such a deliberate thing. Rock 'n' roll wasn't a tough-guy thing anymore. It was fucking, you know, "Let's hold hands and swing on a fucking swing."

JOEY ALLEN Well, when nine hundred out of a thousand people in your crowd are women, they're not gonna like the heavy songs as much as they like, we call them, uh, "panty wetters." That's bad to say nowadays, but back then that's what we called 'em because they were the songs the chicks dug.

JERRY DIXON We were on the road for eighteen months, and it was weird back then because when our first record finally did come out, you really didn't have a gauge of the success other than your shows. The shows kept getting bigger and bigger and more people started showing up. When the radio machine kicked in, that transition was awesome. You turn the radio on and "Heaven" was on three stations at the same time, and you're like, "Holy shit, look at this."

MADELYN SCARPULLA Top 40 radio was the brass ring. The goal was to make sure to cover the base at rock radio with the rock songs and have those do really well. Then when the ballad came, you would have sold enough records in the market that the Top 40 station would already be aware of the band and give a flying shit.

TOM WERMAN You wanted to get on AM radio.

TAIME DOWNE We were Top 40 with "House of Pain," so it's like, knowing Casey Kasem was saying our fucking band name on AM radio somewhere was pretty fucking cool. We figured if the label wanted a ballad, we might as well write one, you know what I mean? So Greg wrote the music shit for "House of Pain" and I wrote the melodies and the lyrics.

GREG STEELE I always loved Lynyrd Skynyrd, and they had a song called "Tuesday's Gone." It's one of my favorite songs. And at that time I had a girlfriend who loved when I played acoustic guitar. So I literally wrote all the music to "House of Pain," using "Tuesday's Gone" as inspiration, in ten minutes and gave it to everybody. But Taime just wasn't into ballad stuff. It gave him writer's block. And so it took about a year and a half before he even came up with lyrics for it.

VICKY HAMILTON He wrote that song "House of Pain" about his father. His relationship with his father.

TAIME DOWNE It was hard writing something that personal. I changed the lyrics and shit, I don't know, a dozen times. Everything felt stupid. Just doin' a ballad alone, me and Greg were like, "Ah, cheesy shit . . ." But we fucking did it anyway.

TOM WERMAN With ballads, I used something that I self-deprecatingly call the "kitchen sink approach," which was to throw everything I could think of on there by the time the song was over. I love synth pads. I love string pads. I love pedal-tone notes that go through everything. They kind of hypnotize you and tug at your heartstrings. I love oohs and aahs and harmonies and I'm good at arranging them. Especially with "Every Rose Has Its Thorn" by Poison, it was a simple country song that Bret Michaels played in rehearsal, and I said, "Wow, that is a hit."

FRANK HANNON Bret Michaels, I have to hand it to him, man. Tesla toured with Poison in '87 and I remember watching him work on that song every day at soundcheck. He was strumming those chords and singing the lyric, walking around with a twelve-string acoustic backstage. On that tour everyone was really fucked up and partying except for him. He was pretty straight and really a hardworking guy, and he would chip away at developing that song. And it's a great fucking song. I mean, there's no doubt.

RIKKI ROCKETT The label didn't like the song. They were like, "Ah, this is too 'in the saddle.'"

BRET MICHAELS When we played "Every Rose" for our label and management, they told us it would end our career. They were like, "This song is not Poison. It starts with an acoustic guitar, and you've got this cowboy thing going on and it's just sad."

"DIZZY" DEAN DAVIDSON That song was like Kenny Chesney meets a rock band. If Tim McGraw did that right now, it'd be a hit all over again.

TOM WERMAN It was a country song. So I said, "We're going to arrange it . . . we're going to put strings in here and we're going to put in, like, Eagles oohs and aahs." And I remember someone saying, "I dunno, man, our fans may really beat us up for this." Because it was so sweet and not hard rock 'n' roll, which is what they all wanted to be. But it worked. It worked with all of them. It worked with "Don't Close Your Eyes" by Kix, and it worked with "The Ballad of Jayne" by L.A. Guns.

MICK CRIPPS I was a big Mott the Hoople fan, and "Ballad of Jayne" was basically based around being like that. Then me and the rest of the guys kicked it around and finished it. Kelly [Nickels, bass] and I weren't super happy with the lyrics and Kelly was watching some documentary on Jayne Mansfield. He was fascinated by the obvious, put it that way. And he wrote a new version about the tragic death of Jayne Mansfield. So that's how it became "The Ballad of Jayne." The version on the record is a little bit different from the demo, but the record company and producers wanted it to be more of a ballad.

ALLEN KOVAC Me and the A&R guy kept telling Tracii that would be the hit. Tracii didn't even like that song. He, of course, knows everything, and he never liked a song unless it was hard.

TRACII GUNS I bitched and moaned about "Ballad of Jayne" going on the *Cocked & Loaded* record. Because we were supposed to be a hard band. I always felt like, yeah, we could definitely have success with this song, but are we telling our male audience that we're not really metal? I kind of thought that we traded something for something at that point, you know what I mean?

MICK CRIPPS It was number one on MTV for, like, three weeks. Massive. I think we sold half a million records after that single came out.

TRACII GUNS Of course, when we got to our third record the label was like, "We need another 'Ballad of Jayne.'" I'm like, "No, man. We need another rocker like 'One More Reason to Die'!" I told Allen Kovac, "Allen, I think we're losing sight of what the band is." And Allen would say, "Yeah, don't lose sight of what you are, but remember that you wanted to be successful." So there was always that kind of push and pull.

DANA STRUM Slaughter really did write and record "Fly to the Angels" thinking it was more like a cool Led Zeppelin thing than an '80s rock ballad. It was kind of like our junior attempt to do something Zeppelin would do.

BRIAN BAKER (guitarist, Minor Threat, Junkyard) I was like, "Can we really call our ballad 'Simple Man'? That's a Skynyrd song!" And the answer is, "Yes, you can!" Apparently it doesn't matter.

CHRIS GATES (guitarist, Junkyard) For the "Simple Man" video, the one that never got played, they convinced us to hire this guy who had done power ballad videos for other people. And he had this concept and we're going, "We don't get it, but it's worked in the past. I guess we'll trust him." And they dragged us out to this Wild West set and hired a bunch of girls to sway rhythmically in front of us. And literally *none* of them would even talk to us when they weren't shooting. They wanted nothing to do with us. It was like, "Dude, we could've invited a bunch of pretty girls out here who *liked* us." Once again, we're reliving, like, junior high.

BRIAN BAKER The girl from, I think, *Melrose Place*? She was the woman who was shown the most for whatever reason, because she enjoyed simple men or she just really liked good western sets. I don't really know.

DAVID COVERDALE I mean what the fuck do the lyrics of "Here I Go Again" have to do with a beautiful woman rolling across a couple of Jaguars? It's madness! But it was eye-catching. And then when people got to see it, the music resonated, too. And radio was all over it. So, yeah, MTV just turned Whitesnake into a global phenomenon. It was immense. One time I looked at it and I went, "Wow, one video saved me from doing five years of tours."

NUNO BETTENCOURT (guitarist, Extreme) "More Than Words" put us on the map. It gave us power. It gave us success. It made it possible for us to keep pushing ahead. It changed everything. People recognize us, the mainstream knows who you are. I guess that's what having a hit feels like.

BRIAN "DAMAGE" FORSYTHE Atlantic Records thought that our album *Blow My Fuse* was done. We got informed that they were done with the tour support and that it was time to start thinking about the next record. There was no plan to make "Don't Close Your Eyes" a single.

STEVE WHITEMAN We played a show at Irvine Meadows [Amphitheater] in California with Great White. And after our set Great White's manager, Alan Niven, stopped us on the way offstage and said, "What's that ballad you guys play and why is that not a single?" And we said, "Don't ask us, ask Atlantic Records." So he called Doug Morris at Atlantic and said, "You're sitting on a hit single." The next week, we're flown to New York and we're shooting the video for "Don't Close Your Eyes."

BRIAN "DAMAGE" FORSYTHE A month later that song got released and it just took off.

STEVE WHITEMAN The song went huge, and that record is the only reason we were able to come back and still have a career. We did three tours on the strength of that single, and the people who saw us liked us. It gave us something to stand on. It gave us a legacy.

NUNO BETTENCOURT People always ask me the stupid question, "Was 'More Than Words' a blessing or a curse?" It can't be a curse. Anything that you write and that you create that becomes a hit is a blessing. Period.

53

"FUCKED IF I'M GONNA DO *THIS* EVERY NIGHT"

TOM KEIFER Even the heaviest songs on Cinderella records start with a lyric. Then the emotion of that lyric tells me whether it's a ballad or whether it's a heavy song. The melody and the lyric is what comes to me first always. And during the *Night Songs* tour, we were out experiencing things that we'd never experienced before. I'd barely left Philadelphia before those tours. So we're out living life, and different feelings and emotions, and I'm just writing them down.

LARRY MAZER Tom is a writing machine and he was on fire. I think *Long Cold Winter* is one of the defining records of that period. I think it's just, from beginning to end, one of the most brilliant records I've ever been involved with.

JEFF LaBAR When *Long Cold Winter* came out, it was like we got a little grittier, a little dirtier, looser.

TOM KEIFER It was pretty apparent to me that there was, like, a trend going on that was very flavor-of-the-day, and it was everything from the photography, to the imagery, to the clothing, to the sound of the records being very slick and processed. We started trying to steer the boat out of those waters after the first record. Because at the time it was still considered cool and hip, but the writing was on the wall to anyone who had half a brain that this was eventually going to become an anchor. If you look at the packaging for *Long Cold Winter*, the pictures on that were kind of more classic black-and-white. There was no picture on the cover. The sound started to get more organic, we were bringing in harmonicas and Dobros and pianos and trying to paint the picture production-wise more like the classic '70s records.

LARRY MAZER When *Long Cold Winter* came out, we did tours with Judas Priest and AC/DC and then we did arenas as headliners. It was a great show and we had a beautiful stage. The show started off with Tom standing on top of the speaker cabinets with his National guitar on a stand and a shroud over him. And we had this little intro tape and after that the shroud would go up and the spotlights would hit Tom and he would start the acoustic slide-guitar opening of "Fallin' Apart at the Seams" and play that by himself, and then he'd run down the steps and join the band.

Then in the middle of the set we had this elevator system that went up to the top of the arena, and Jeff would come out and do an acoustic guitar solo. And while he's doing that, Tom would go in this elevator and climb on a white baby grand piano that had an electric keyboard built into it, and basically when Jeff finished the guitar solo the opening chord of "Don't Know What You Got (Till It's Gone)" would start. Then Tom would lower down from the rafters on the piano and sing the first verse, and the piano was timed to hit the stage just as the drums kicked in going into the second verse. Then Tom would pick up his guitar and play the song out. That was the high point, and then for the encore we had these snow machines on the lighting truss and it would snow during "Long Cold Winter."

TOM KEIFER Before we started the tour we did production rehearsals in Louisville, Kentucky. They rolled all the trucks in and we had like two days of rehearsal in the arena before the opening night. That was the first time we ever did the thing where I came out of the sky playing piano. The first time I got on that, all the houselights were up so I could see the floor. I could see how high I was. And one of the rigging motors got locked up on the way down, so the platform started to tilt. Obviously the piano and the bench was bolted down but I wasn't, so I was white-knuckling on the piano. The rigger realized this and he stopped the motors, but it was sitting kind of cockeyed in the middle of the air. And the worst part was, you know, those guys sling around on those chains like Tarzan. So the way he got out to the piano was to jump from one chain onto the chain that was locked up, which started the whole thing swinging. I came down and I thought, "Fucked if I'm gonna do *this* every night."

JEFF LaBAR The amount of space you have to run around when you're headlining, it's like, "Ooh, this playground's big!" It's like the bigger amusement park as opposed to the carnival. I used to be very physical or acrobatic, I would run around a lot, and the bigger the stage the better for me. I would just run further and jump higher.

LARRY MAZER We sold three million copies of *Night Songs* and three million copies of *Long Cold Winter*. We even sold a million of *Heartbreak Station,* but we didn't become the bona fide arena sellout that Poison did, Ratt did, Bon Jovi did, Mötley Crüe did, whatever. I think because the guys were more like Dokken or Great White, more . . . not faceless, 'cause they certainly weren't faceless, but they didn't play up to that showbiz, Hollywood, tabloid thing. If you remember, Jon Bon Jovi started going out with Diane Lane, the actress, at that point. And obviously Tommy Lee was with what's-her-name. With Cinderella, unfortunately, because they never became rock stars in their own minds, they didn't develop that kind of lifestyle, and in a way that kept them from becoming even bigger. You never saw them hanging backstage at other bands' shows, you never saw them getting into car wrecks or whatever. Tom, even though he was a rock star, never played into the rock star thing. He lived with his wife in Cherry Hill, New Jersey, in a nice house a block from my office. We hung out every day.

54

"TOMMY LEE CAME TO OUR ROOM WITH A PLATE. AND HE HAD SHIT ON IT"

BEAU HILL I flew out to L.A. to see Warrant with their manager, Eddie Wenrick, who was working for Tom Hulett at the time. It was at the Country Club in the Valley. I walked in this place and there was, like, over two thousand kids all singing the words to "Heaven." That was it for me. As soon as I heard it, I said, "Yeah, I'm in. Let's go."

JERRY DIXON Beau despised "Heaven," which at the time was a mid-tempo rock song more like "Down Boys." We had to fight to keep that song on there. We were like, "Dude, this is our bread and butter live. This is our fan favorite." He's like, "Ah, I just don't hear it."

STEVEN SWEET He didn't like the song at all to begin with, so he said, "Let's just slow it down, see how it feels." And that's when it took on the big power-ballad feel.

BRET HARTMAN I think the guitar solos were played by some session guys, and then the band members had to learn how to play those improved guitar solos.

BEAU HILL We were in pre-production for *Dirty Rotten Filthy Stinking Rich* and I went to their manager, Eddie, and I said, "Look, we've got a problem with the guitar players, because we're in an era now where it's Eddie Van Halen and Warren DeMartini. These guys, they're sweet and they're good rhythm guitar players, but they can't play solos to save their souls. I'd like to consider bringing somebody else in to do it."

MIKE SLAMER (session guitarist) Beau Hill had produced my band Streets with Steve Walsh of Kansas, and we got along like a house on fire. I got a call from him saying, "I'm working with this band and it's sort of a touchy thing, but is there any chance that you could work with the guitar players for me?" So they would come up to the house and work on parts for the songs.

BEAU HILL It has been misreported a zillion times that I went in and recorded solos privately. I called a band meeting. Everybody sat there and I made my pitch. I said, "I think that we can do better with the solos if we bring in a guy." They listened and I don't think they liked it, but to their credit, they were gentlemen and they were businessmen, and they trusted me, I guess.

MIKE SLAMER Beau called me and said, "Look, how would you feel about doing the guitars on this record as a ghost player?" And I said, "If it's okay with the guys, then it's okay with me."

JOEY ALLEN Beau would take the shortest route possible. I mean, there are solos on *Dirty Rotten Filthy Stinking Rich* that are all me: "Big Talk," most of "Heaven." So, if you've got three-quarters of the solo, why don't you just work on the last ten seconds with the actual guitarist in the band? And it wasn't some consensual thing. It was more like, "This is what's gonna happen."

BEAU HILL The good part of the story is that these guys liked Mike so much that they started taking lessons from him before the record came out and he taught them the solos.

JOEY ALLEN I'm like, "Okay, if I need to get my shit together here, if I'm not good enough to play all the solos on this record, I'm gonna learn from this guy." I'd go over to Mike's house four or five days a week and sit down with him and say, "Teach me, man." And we got a great relationship out of it.

Look, I don't fault Mike Slamer for any of that. It's all on the producer. That was a bullshit move.

STEVEN SWEET We finished the record but it wasn't going to come out for like six months, so we got a little bit of money from the record company, got on a crappy outdated bus. Suddenly, you're playing all originals to crowds that have never heard a lick of your music. It was a little bit harrowing.

JOEY ALLEN The first tour was a co-headlining tour with D'Molls, who were on Atlantic. And we flip-flopped every night. Then we went back through with Britny Fox because they were on our label.

STEVEN SWEET We also opened a Paul Stanley solo tour. Funny thing is, he never spoke to us, not a word, until I think the last night where he just said, "Thanks." So we wound up playing in Hartford, Connecticut, and my dad and mom were living in Danbury at the time. I walk out of our dressing room and I see my dad down the hall, chatting up Paul Stanley. And I'm like, "He hasn't said a word to anybody in the band, and yet my dad is talking his ear off!" It was just crazy.

ERIK TURNER We lucked out in our first single, "Down Boys." MTV played the crap out of it and it got tons of ads at radio. The song was a hit. I don't remember where it landed in the single charts, somewhere in the Top 40.

STEVEN SWEET I remember we were in Cincinnati playing a club in a cold basement in December. And our manager walks in and says, "The record just went gold." And we were like, "This is what it feels like?"

BRET HARTMAN They went with "Down Boys" for the first single because they didn't want to go straight out with a ballad. But everybody knew that "Heaven" was going to be a huge hit. "Heaven" was probably the one that really sealed it.

JOHN MEZACAPPA Once "Heaven" came out, we couldn't even go to the mall without security.

STEVEN SWEET Jani just seemed like he was always trying to be on, always trying to put on a show for everybody. I think that's a lot of what got him in the end, that he felt like he had to act like he was cool to everybody. He would say things in interviews like, "I don't want to be one of those guys that just gets offstage and hides in his dressing room." Looking back on that now, I see that what he meant was "I'm not going to be one of those guys who actually takes care of his health and does the right thing for himself." So he felt the need to go out and show everybody that he's cool and that he's normal. But going out and drinking a gallon of tequila every night with everybody is not normal behavior.

JOHN MEZACAPPA Jani and I had an agreement that I was going to keep his ass grounded, and I did. If he was drinking too much, if he was getting too out there or getting too headstrong, then I was the one who could honestly tell him, "You know, you've got to chill out. This is a run that you've dreamt about your whole life, and we've got to stay focused." He wanted to be Mötley Crüe, he wanted to be the Rolling Stones, he wanted to be Pink Floyd. He wanted to be around forever.

ERIK TURNER Jani could have a hurtful sense of humor sometimes. He'd be joking around and say, "Warrant's my stepping-stone for my solo career." We're like, "If we didn't ask you to join our band, you'd be playing covers in Florida."

JOEY ALLEN We did the D'Molls tour, then we did the Britny Fox tour, then we did two weeks with Eddie Money at colleges on the East Coast. And god bless Eddie, love him to death, I think we broke him of his sobriety once. Then finally Mötley comes out with *Dr. Feelgood* and we did, I think, four, five, six months out of the gate with them.

JERRY DIXON When we went out with Mötley Crüe on the *Dr. Feelgood* tour it was like, "God, I can't even believe this!" You had to remember, I had never left California in my life. I'd never traveled, I'd never flown, I'd never done anything.

STEVEN SWEET It was just amazing to see how big everything was: the attitude, the presentation, the staging, the million-guy crew, and all the buses and the trucks. I felt like, if it doesn't go past this, at least I made it to a place where I'm in a league with this machine that I admire.

JOEY ALLEN I remember one time we fucking trashed our dressing room in some city. The next day we walked into our dressing room and there was no catering, no beer, there was nothing. And Tommy Lee came to our room with a plate. And he had shit on it. And he goes, "Here, I heard you guys were hungry. Here you go!" I don't know if they ended up paying the bill for us or if they got shit for it, but it was kind of like, "Don't do that." That's funny shit, right? Because it could've been, "Look, we're clipping ten minutes off your set," or "You don't get any lights or sound."

STEVEN SWEET Honestly, even though they were supposed to be sober, those guys in the Crüe never stopped partying. I just think they stopped doing heroin.

JOEY ALLEN There was a night, at the Cheetah in Atlanta maybe, we all went out, it was Vince, Tommy, myself . . . I don't think Nikki went out. And I remember T-Bone just going, "Dude! Dude! Order me a drink!" And I was like, "Fuck you, dude, you're sober!" But he kept at me, so I'd order him a drink and bring it to the bathroom and he'd come running in and have a shot of Jack. 'Cause there were handlers, you know?

55

"BON JOVI, JR."

JOEY ALLEN After our first record came out, it took us ten months to get an arena tour. We went out with D'Molls, we went out with Britny Fox. Finally we got the *Dr. Feelgood* tour with Mötley. But for the longest time Warrant couldn't get a big tour. And then here comes Skid Row, kickin' ass on the East Coast with their buddy Jon Bon Jovi! We weren't jealous. But we were definitely envious of their tour position.

RACHEL BOLAN Two days after *Skid Row* came out in January '89, we played the first show of the Bon Jovi *New Jersey* tour, at Reunion Arena in Dallas.

DAVE "SNAKE" SABO We were absolutely unknown. We didn't even have a big push yet at MTV. *Headbangers Ball* had maybe played the "Youth Gone Wild" video once or twice before the tour started. And then I remember in February we were playing a gig in Florida and I saw the video on during the actual daytime. It was like, "Wow . . ."

SCOTTI HILL I didn't start noticing anything until "18 and Life" dropped. They had *Dial MTV* back in those days, where you could call in and request your favorite video of the day. So we were covering the arenas with *Dial MTV* flyers, and "18 and Life" just smashed it. And then all hell broke loose.

RACHEL BOLAN We absolutely blew up. Once we got to "18 and Life" it just went nuts. We were everywhere.

DAVE "SNAKE" SABO But there were certain things we were up against. Because whenever you're helped by someone of note, like we were with Jon and the guys from Bon Jovi, there's a backlash that goes with that. There's the people who go, "Ah, they're just Bon Jovi, Jr . . ." We weren't naive about that. We knew we had to prove ourselves every night.

RACHEL BOLAN I always used to let shit like that just roll off my back. It was like, "You know what? They can say whatever they want. I know all the hard work we put into this."

ROB AFFUSO We could track our success because we could see the arenas were getting filled up earlier, prior to our set time. And our merchandise sales were starting to really increase until we were actually outselling Bon Jovi.

SEBASTIAN BACH I think it was Las Cruces, New Mexico—we outsold them in T-shirts at their own gig.

ROB AFFUSO Which didn't really go over too well—if you know anything about Jon, he's quite a businessman, so he wasn't happy about that. But he was still making money off us, so . . .

DOC McGHEE Jonny and Richie [Sambora] had their publishing company, Underground. That's what Skid Row was signed to.

SEBASTIAN BACH We signed a very shitty deal with him. But in his defense, who knew that we would make it?

ROB AFFUSO It was a co-publishing deal—he got it all, we got nothing.

DAVE "SNAKE" SABO I guess you could look at it like that. From an advance perspective, the deal wasn't generous at all. But when questioned about this I often say to people: "If you're in a position where you're being offered 130 shows on the biggest tour in the world as an absolute unknown entity outside of your hometown, what would *you* do?"

JACK PONTI And it's not like Jon just signed them to a production deal. Jon put a tremendous, tremendous amount of work into Skid Row. He was going to rehearsals and listening to every song they wrote and giving them advice. It wasn't just a passing interest.

SEBASTIAN BACH Jon Bon Jovi literally gave me the shirt off his back when I was a teenager. One day he brought me in his closet and goes, "Pick out whatever you want." I was like, "What?" I felt extremely lucky and fortunate to have the biggest rock star in the world bring me into his home and give me his clothes. I still have that fucking vest! So it wasn't all doom and gloom. We didn't hate each other.

SCOTTI HILL The deal didn't affect me as much as it did Snake and Rachel. And to some extent Sebastian. Because Snake and Rachel wrote the majority of the material. But flip that around—if that deal wasn't signed, we probably wouldn't have gotten signed to McGhee Entertainment. We wouldn't have gone on the *New Jersey* tour. None of this may have happened. So, you know, what're you gonna do?

ROB AFFUSO I do remember Richie relinquishing his part back to the band.

RACHEL BOLAN At one point Richie Sambora was just like, "You know what? Cross my name off this list. I've got more money than I know what to do with. I don't need to take any of your guys' money."

SCOTTI HILL I don't carry any grudges or any of that. But it wasn't a great deal for us. It was a great deal for people that already had money, that didn't really need money. But that's just how business rolls, man.

DOC McGHEE There was resentment. It was just one of those heated things that was a pent-up kind of thing. And Sebastian was saying stuff and it would get back to Jonny, and that would piss Jonny off and he would say something and it got to Sebastian. It just went on and on.

SEBASTIAN BACH My swearing got us in all sorts of trouble, because Bon Jovi had a lot of parents bringing little daughters to the shows. And I'd be up there going, "Fuck you and fuck off and fuck the cops and let's get stoned!" But you know, I would go see Mötley Crüe when I was young and Vince's first rap would be, "Hey, Toronto! Look at all the fucking pussy here tonight!" We would laugh our guts out at a rap like that. So in my mind I was just being funny. But mom and dad in Centerville, Iowa, they didn't think it was very funny.

SCOTTI HILL There was also prankster shit going on the whole tour. Occasionally the [Bon Jovi] band would come out, throw eggs at us or something like that. I remember Jon smashing a birthday cake in my face once.

DAVE "SNAKE" SABO I believe it was the second- or third-to-last show, and we got milk spilled on us before we went onstage.

SEBASTIAN BACH It got really ugly with Skid Row and Bon Jovi on that night.

SCOTTI HILL We were in Louisville, Kentucky, and we were on the way to the stage and we had to walk through a little curtain. And when Sebastian walked through the curtain, one of Jon's crew guys was there with a huge jug of ice-cold milk and he poured it over his head. And on this particular night, I think the second song in our set was "Piece of Me." Before the song breaks in, it's just bass and drums, and Sebastian's like, "All right, Jon Bon Jovi! Why don't you come get a *Piece. Of. Me!*" And what Jon hears from backstage, through the cement arena walls is, "Hey, Jon Bon Jovi! You're a *pussy!*"

DAVE "SNAKE" SABO Sebastian wasn't being malicious at all. It was taken the wrong way. I don't even know that Jon had any idea these hijinks were going on with the crew. Because he was completely removed from it. But apparently it got back to Jon that Sebastian had called him a pussy.

ROB AFFUSO I remember coming offstage and I was uneasy about the whole thing. But I didn't really expect Jon to go after Sebastian the way he did.

SCOTTI HILL We were all walking back toward our dressing room. I was right next to Sebastian. And Jon was standing on the ramp, like where they back the trucks down.

RACHEL BOLAN I actually passed Jon and I go, "What's up, dude?" But it was like he had blinders on. His jaw was set like he was about to go into a ring. I figured, "Maybe's he's got his show head on . . ."

SCOTTI HILL Jon was standing there by himself, tongue in cheek, kind of looking off into space. *Pissed*. And then I saw his brother and his dad maybe ten, fifteen, feet behind him.

DAVE "SNAKE" SABO And there was a security guy by the name of Fred Saunders, a couple other people. Jon had a look in his eye and I was like, "Oh, shit . . ."

FRED SAUNDERS Jon was vibratin'. He was pretty upset. But I think the road crew had kind of frenzied him up. Jon made such a snivel about the whole thing, and the road crew was all, "Yeah, yeah, Jon, I don't blame you!" So by the time Sebastian and Skid Row got offstage Jon was pretty fired up.

SCOTTI HILL So we walk past and Sebastian's like, "Ah, you got me . . ." Or something like that. Referring to the milk. And Jon goes, "You motherfucker!" And punches him in the face.

ROB AFFUSO It's like, "Oh, man, this is not good. You don't fight with the dude that's taking you out on a massive tour . . ."

SCOTTI HILL It's just elbows and fists flying all over the place. There's a lot of "fuck yous" and pointing of fingers and guys holding guys back.

FRED SAUNDERS They both got a couple pops off before production and tour managers and people broke it up. I got Sebastian away from Jon.

DAVE "SNAKE" SABO They pinned Sebastian up against the wall.

FRED SAUNDERS I remember telling him, "I'll kiss ya after I kill ya," or something like that. Because by the end of the tour Jon was getting a little "king of the throne." And rightly so, I might add. So when somebody finally challenged him, it was kinda cool.

SCOTTI HILL After that we were summoned to the production office. We got fucking ass-reamed. "You motherfuckers got no respect. I own your ass." I remember that. *"I. Own. Your. Ass."*

SEBASTIAN BACH I said, "What do you mean, you'll own me?" I didn't even know what the fuck he meant.

DAVE "SNAKE" SABO It was ugly. It stunk. Because we'd been doing this with each other for nine months, and we'd gone from being this absolutely unknown fart in the wind to a recognizable act. And Bon Jovi were a big part of that.

SCOTTI HILL Jon was very fair to us on that tour. And very good to us. But he was fucking pissed. He made a mistake with what he thought he heard, but he had had enough of our bullshit. You know, we were told not to swear during the show, and Sebastian was swearing; we were told not to do this or that and we would do it anyway. We were taking liberties. I think he had just fucking had enough. And so he was gonna throw his weight around a little bit.

DAVE "SNAKE" SABO But we were able to clear it all up. On the last night of the tour I believe we flew with Bon Jovi on their plane from Chicago back to New Jersey. So it ended well. But there still was some lingering sourness there.

MAXINE PETRUCCI Later on, this was '90, something like that, my sister Roxy was at SIR Studios rehearsing with Vixen. And Jon Bon Jovi's there, too. She walks by him and he says to her, "Are you the one that was in the band with Sebastian? Madam X?" She goes, "Ah, that's my sister, Maxine." And Jon says, "Well, you can tell her she can have him back!"

ROB AFFUSO Then we moved on to the Aerosmith tour.

DAVE "SNAKE" SABO The bottle incident happened in Springfield, Massachusetts.

ROB AFFUSO I did not see Sebastian get hit by the bottle. I *did* see him pick it up and throw it back and then jump into the audience. And I couldn't figure out if I should keep playing or if I should jump into the audience to protect my singer. I know that I didn't know exactly what was going on.

DAVE "SNAKE" SABO It happened really, really fast. Again, we're playing "Piece of Me" and I saw something out of the side of my left eye. And then I think I heard something hit the drums, which was the bottle. And Sebastian turned to me and I didn't know what it was immediately, but there was blood dripping down his face. I thought, Oh, it's ketchup or something like that. And then I saw him grab the bottle and I'm like, "Holy crap!" He whips the bottle into the crowd, and then he jumps in, feet first, after the bottle. And then Rachel jumps in shortly after. Obviously our crew guys are jumping in as well. And this happened in the space of, what? Seven seconds?

RACHEL BOLAN I would never whip a bottle into a crowd, let's just put it that way. Would I jump into the crowd and try to find the person? Absolutely. But I can't defend anyone for those actions. When you're at a general admission show your aim's not going to be very good, you know what I mean? But you know, it was what it was, a heat-of-the-moment type of thing.

SCOTTI HILL Good judgment in the heat of anger is really hard. So Sebastian got hit with that bottle, he picked it up, and he threw it back. And he hit the wrong person. And then he went in boots first and he trampled on some people's faces. After that there was word that the cops were waiting, so we figured we could just have the bus waiting and get out of there. I don't know whose brilliant idea that was.

ROB AFFUSO How are you supposed to hide with a tour bus?

SCOTTI HILL So we went from the stage to the bus and drove to another town, sat in the parking lot. And next thing I knew there were police cars outside. And they took Sebastian away to jail. And then the whole trial, money . . .

DAVE "SNAKE" SABO The worst part of it is that an audience member got hurt. That's always the worst part of it. No one should go to a show and walk away needing medical attention. That's the worst part of it. But the rest of it is, you know, lawsuits, people getting arrested, people having to pay out a lot of money. Not just one person but a lot of people. Responsible by association. And so it cost us all a bunch of money.

SCOTTI HILL Yeah, well, Sebastian got sued, of course. And management thought it would be only fair if the rest of the band contributed to the costs. And so, you know, I'm not gonna speak for anybody else but I coughed up fifteen grand and handed it over just because, hey, we're in a band together. You're a fucking irresponsible lunatic.

DAVE "SNAKE" SABO But that's the secondary aspect of it. At first the reports that were coming back were a girl got hit in the face, she had to go get hundreds of stitches. And luckily that number kept going down and kept going down and kept going down.

The bottle never should have been thrown onstage, obviously. No band member should ever be a target for anybody. That was just the most ridiculous thing in the world, that someone would come to a show and whip a bottle at a person in a band. But the bottom line was a person got hit with this bottle and had to get stitches in her face and there's no reason for that. There's no excuse for that. That retaliation, it's just unacceptable.

ROB AFFUSO So we had damage control around that. And shortly after, Sebastian wore that shirt that said "AIDS Kills Fags Dead."

RACHEL BOLAN That was another gem.

SCOTTI HILL The gay community was just fucking pissed. It was a stupid thing but you know, it's not like, "Hey man, let's hate gay people." It was just stupid fucking, "Huh, look at this shirt I got!"

RACHEL BOLAN I believe we were in Winnipeg and this kid gave it to him backstage. And then when the picture got in magazines I was just like,

"Well, that's his issue. Not mine." I have a lot of gay friends. It wasn't cool to me. It just wasn't cool. I didn't think it was funny.

SCOTTI HILL It was just a full-on nightmare for Sebastian. He had death threats. He had to move. People were like, "We're gonna burn down your house." It was hard for him, that whole thing. I think it was one of the few learning experiences that stuck.

JASON FLOM Sebastian didn't mean any harm to anybody. He was just a crazy fuckin' kid who was caught up in the whole moment, and that shirt that he wore was obviously politically insensitive to say the least, but he probably thought it was fun.

JACK PONTI He was almost like a Disney character. There was no malice. He just wanted to get out there and sing and you know, rock. I mean, that was Sebastian's premise in life. It's kinda like—and I don't mean this in a demeaning way—it's like when you have a big silly puppy. The puppy doesn't realize how big it is, that kind of thing. But whether or not their animosity or bad blood will let them admit it, those guys knew what they had when they got Sebastian.

SEBASTIAN BACH Well, you've got to also remember that one of the very first times I ever saw my band in print in a magazine was when Atlantic Records put an ad on the front of *Billboard*. It said *Skid Row—Meet the New Bad Boys of Rock*. Nobody asked me. I was a teenager. Nobody said, "Hey, is this cool, this ad?" I viscerally remember seeing that and thinking, Oh, really? Is that what you fucking want? I'll fucking give you that shit. Watch *this*.

DAVE "SNAKE" SABO That Aerosmith tour lasted seven months. And Aerosmith were heroes to me. And before that I had spent nine months out with Bon Jovi, guys that I loved dearly and admired and respected and looked up to. That tour had ended on somewhat of a sour note, and then we get to Aerosmith and all these incidents happen. The bottle. The T-shirt. People getting hurt. It was just like, "Ugh . . ."

SCOTTI HILL The incidents we're talking about are the incidents the public is aware of. But shit was going on all the time, you know? When Sebastian threw the bottle and went off the stage that night, that was just another night for me. I didn't raise an eyebrow. It was like, "Oh, Sebastian's in the crowd fighting somebody." You notice we kept playing. Because this shit was happening all the time. He's going after somebody in the crowd, or maybe he's going after somebody out by the bus, or maybe he's going after a crew member. I'm not gonna say the guy wasn't violent with people in the band, either. So, you know, I'm not a fan.

DAVE "SNAKE" SABO We always felt like we had our hands full. There was always tension, there was always the idea that this thing could explode violently at any moment . . . with brief respites of civility and calm. I say that jokingly, but it's half true.

SEBASTIAN BACH I felt that the more trouble I got in, the more I was living up to what people expected of me and what my record company expected of me. And also, the more trouble I got in, the more records we sold. I mean, it was almost like performance art in a really fucked-up way.

ROB AFFUSO Every time, with the bottle incident, with the T-shirt, our record sales would spike. It's ridiculous how that works. So on the one hand you hate it, but on the other hand you're selling, you know, twice the albums for that week. I wish it could have been different, but that's the way it was.

56

"IT WAS LIKE BEING ON A PLANE WITH TWO HUNDRED GREMLINS"

ROB TANNENBAUM (journalist; co-author, *I Want My MTV*) The Moscow Music Peace Festival, which featured Bon Jovi, Mötley Crüe, Ozzy Osbourne, Skid Row, the Scorpions, and a few Soviet bands, was Doc McGhee making the best of a very bad situation. In 1988, he was convicted of helping to import twenty tons of marijuana, which is a whole lot of marijuana. I mean, a *huge* amount of marijuana. He got a $15,000 fine and a suspended sentence of five years, and as one condition of his probation, he started the Make a Difference Foundation, which promoted anti-drug messages. Doc then found a way for him and his bands to personally benefit from running this anti-drug foundation, and the way he did that was by bringing them to Russia, where rock bands didn't exist. Russia was, except for China, the largest untapped market in the world, and Doc had to imagine, if all went well, that Bon Jovi would sell another fifteen million copies of *Slippery When Wet* there.

OZZY OSBOURNE Doc McGhee came around to my house and he says, "We're going to Moscow! I've got a private plane." And he asked me to this Moscow peace summit thing. They were just in that *perestroika* stage over there. Whatever that means.

DOC McGHEE Remember that the kids in the Soviet Union were being put in jail for listening to this music. They would trade cassette tapes on street corners and most of it was Black Sabbath and Scorpions, Deep Purple, stuff like that. They maybe got a little bit of Bon Jovi. Probably not. It didn't seem like it. But it was really just Ozzy and the Scorpions that were in Russia.

ROB TANNENBAUM Doc didn't have any delusions. He was taking them to Russia because he thought they could sell more records and make more money. He was a businessman and hair metal was a product. Like weed was a product.

RUDOLF SCHENKER The Moscow Music Peace Festival was organized by our manager, Doc McGhee, and Stas Namin, who was a big name in Russia—he was a music guy, and his uncle was the inventor of the MiG, the fighter jet. Also, his grandfather had been a leader in the Soviet Union. The two of them put this thing together.

KLAUS MEINE The whole Moscow Music Peace Festival was really like a Russian Woodstock. For us as a German band, with all the success we experienced in the United States, then to go to Russia, was a very emotional thing. Because our parents, their generation, they went to Russia fighting. And we came to Russia with guitars instead of guns.

RUDOLF SCHENKER One year before, we had played ten shows in Leningrad and now we were playing this festival together with Bon Jovi, Ozzy Osbourne, Cinderella, Skid Row, Mötley Crüe, and a few Russian bands like Gorky Park and Brigada S. You know, we had a much better chance to look into the Russian soul. We felt the whole situation was changing in the young generation. Playing the Peace Festival was for us a fantastic chance to see the changes from '88 to '89.

ROB TANNENBAUM Doc is a very genial guy. Welcoming, hilariously funny, and gregarious—until he's not. He's short and stout. He looks like a man to be reckoned with. You don't fuck with Doc.

MARK WEISS He's always chill. He's a listener, you know? He listens and then, behind closed doors, he acts.

DOC McGHEE We never had any permits or anything. Gorbachev and his people never said yes, never said no. Later on, it was told to me by people very close to him that that's exactly what it was. He wanted it to happen, but he couldn't condone it.

LARRY MAZER Obviously, Doc was in the news for the whole marijuana thing. The concert was part of the settlement.

SHARON OSBOURNE I think it was something about a car that was loaded down with drugs. I can't remember the deal. I don't know whether he was arrested in Florida or Arizona, some fucking state. But it looked good to the state that Doc is trying to do this, trying to do that. "Look at the good we're doing!" He got a gold star for fucking putting this show on.

TICO TORRES (drummer, Bon Jovi) It was an anti-drug thing and I think there was more drugs on that plane than in the whole country of Russia.

JEFF LaBAR That plane ride was the longest, funnest plane ride I've ever had.

ROB AFFUSO It was supposed to be alcohol- and drug-free. But we take off and everybody starts smoking joints, opening beers, it becomes a party.

ZAKK WYLDE We went from LAX to Newark, picked up a bunch of guys there, then went from Newark to Heathrow, then Heathrow to Moscow. So it's like thirty-plus hours of just boozin'.

KLAUS MEINE They picked us up in London. I don't know why we had to go to London to go to Moscow—they could have picked us up in Germany, dammit! But we were the last band that boarded the plane, and we got on and there were a lot of people drunk or drugged out or whatever. But there was a very special vibe.

DOC McGHEE It was "Make a Difference" . . . but then it was also a "Make a Different Drink" kind of thing, too. So, you know . . .

SHARON OSBOURNE Doc had some doctor that was traveling with us that had all the shit. It was like being on a plane with two hundred gremlins. And you know how you never put water on a gremlin? It was like, you never give these people alcohol. And the joke of it was, it was meant to be against drugs and drink, this whole festival. Because this was getting Doc a get-out-of-jail-free card. So anyway, we go and, Jesus Christ, the plane ride was a fucking nightmare because everybody was doing coke. Everybody was drinking.

DAVE "SNAKE" SABO I think the only people that were sober on that were Mötley Crüe. That's pretty crazy.

ZAKK WYLDE Ozzy was sober then, too, and mom [Sharon Osbourne] was with him. So he was on his best behavior.

OZZY OSBOURNE We got on the plane and it was like the bar in *Star Wars*. We were at the back and people were swinging on the bloody bins at the front, just crazy. We were supposed to be the sober American rock 'n' roll bands. I was sitting next to a journalist, I can't remember his name, but he turned to Sharon and he says, "Do you think there's alcohol on board?" I wet myself laughing. Everyone had gone to the duty-free shop and loaded up for the flight 'cause there wasn't any on the plane.

ROB AFFUSO Sebastian was just so hyper, you know? I was excited as well but he couldn't contain it. A couple hours before landing, Ozzy . . . it's pitch-black in the plane and he says to Sebastian, *"Do you ever shut the fuck up?"*

SHARON OSBOURNE Sebastian must have been the youngest one there. He was just a kid. And he was trying to keep up with the big boys and of course he couldn't. And so he was singing, singing, and, you know when you over-sing? It's like, "Shut the fuck up, kid. We all know you can sing. Now shut the fuck up!" And of course he wouldn't. Ozzy was going insane and going, "Put something in his fucking mouth so he can't sing!" And I remember Sebastian was laying full-out on the floor of the plane singing.

JEFF LaBAR Skid Row had roommates and not their own rooms. Sebastian was rooming with Rob and I think Rob kicked him out, so he spent the rest of the week with me.

MARK WEISS Before we got off the plane I went to everyone and I just screamed at them. I said, "Look, this is history in the making. I want to document this. This is the Beatles landing in America, you know?" I quickly ran in front of everybody and down the steps and I waited for them to come down. And as they walked down one at a time, I would snap their pictures.

RACHEL BOLAN We landed at what I believe was a military airport, so we never got a stamp on our passports, nothin'. We went in and it was basically like walking into someone's house.

JEFF LaBAR We're like, "Wait a minute—what the hell just happened here?" We just got off the plane into a 1950s movie. Everything was dark and dank and no color. It's like, "This is like a black-and-white movie."

RACHEL BOLAN Everything was just so dank and gray. And I mean, this hotel was decrepit, man. Turn on the lights and you'd see hundreds of cockroaches go run and hide, you know?

JEFF LaBAR A gigantic historic Moscow hotel from hell. They had terrible toilet paper, so Doc made sure we all had a lot of toilet paper. We brought so much with us. We brought our own doctor, we brought our own food, we brought our own catering, we brought our own toilet paper, we brought our own water . . . everything to sustain all the bands for a week.

WAYNE ISHAM (video director) All these bikers came and surrounded the hotel, and Ozzy was there and he had to come out and talk to them.

TICO TORRES They sat in the front and revved their bikes and kind of woke up most of the people that were in the hotel.

WAYNE ISHAM It was like in *Mad Max,* and Ozzy was the guy who speaks to all of them.

RACHEL BOLAN The KGB followed us everywhere, anywhere where there were cameras. Like, if you were filming a segment for MTV, the KGB would follow you around. And the militia was always not far behind.

JEFF LaBAR I remember seeing guys on the rooftops across the street watching us with binoculars.

SCOTTI HILL Randy Castillo, the drummer from Ozzy's band, was my running partner over there. I don't know how but we wound up in this stairwell in the hotel, and we came to the top and walked out into the hall and there was a room there, like a surveillance room. Like something out of a movie. And it was no secret that we were being watched, eavesdropped on, all that. And we were like, "Wow, this is like cloak-and-dagger shit." That got us all pumped up so we were like, "Let's go see what else we can find!" And we found another stairwell and we found our way up to a huge balcony with a beautiful view of Moscow. And you know of course we'd been drinking. And we kept going up and the stairwells kept getting more and more narrow. We got to the point where it was a ladder going straight up. And we popped through the top and we were in the tiny little bell tower of this giant hotel. There were four little windows up there, all the glass was broken up. And I remember there was just a folding chair. And we felt like the first guys on the moon.

JEFF LaBAR The dumbest thing I did was dropping my pants in Red Square.

KLAUS MEINE Skid Row, they were the first band on and Sebastian went out onstage and was just screaming, *"Hey motherfucker! Take this!"* You know? That was quite something.

ROB AFFUSO I never did a concert at eleven a.m. like that. And of course, we'd be up all night with everybody else in Moscow drinking. That made an eleven o'clock show kind of difficult. But we went out and did it.

SCOTTI HILL We played two days in a row. And the morning of the second show I remember our tour manager coming into the hotel room and putting Rob Affuso in the shower and shaking me out of bed. Because we weren't moving. But we had to get to the show. And I was hurtin', man. I was hurtin' real bad. So I get to the show, get changed, I'm walking to the stage and, you know, you feel it coming. You start sweating, you get that feeling in the back of your throat. And it's like, "Here it comes. I'm just gonna let it rip before I go up there." So I puke, and then I walk up the stairs to the stage and my guitar tech at the time, he puts out some water for me. He goes, "There's two glasses of water and one glass of vodka. See if you can guess which one the vodka's in." It's like, "You motherfucker!" But playing hungover was just how it was done for a long time.

WAYNE ISHAM It was so interesting, this dynamic between all the bands.

SHARON OSBOURNE Doc had promised everyone spots, you know? He'd be like, "Yeah, sure, you can play when it's dark." Fucking this and that. And so everybody had been going with the thought that they're going to close the show. And of course Bon Jovi closed the show. And with the greatest respect to Bon Jovi, the Russians had no fucking idea who he was. But it was being filmed for MTV, and MTV knew who he was.

WAYNE ISHAM There were a lot of egos because that's what it's all about. Poor Doc had to deal with all of them.

SHARON OSBOURNE All I can remember is Ozzy saying, "Tell Doc I'll just shut up and play where he wants me to play if he gives me coke!"

DOC McGHEE We were doing an MTV broadcast and MTV wanted Bon Jovi to be the headliner, because at that time they were the biggest rock band in the world. So then we had Ozzy, and he actually closed, and the

Scorpions were just before Bon Jovi. And in the broadcast we had to flip-flop it for MTV and Bon Jovi closed.

RACHEL BOLAN The fans kinda knew the Scorpions, but Black Sabbath was really big on the Soviet black market. So between every song of just about every band, until Ozzy got on and probably after he got off, everyone was just chanting, "Ozzy! Ozzy!" They didn't care about anyone that was there except for Ozzy. But they really enjoyed just having a full day of music, which is something that probably most of those people never did before.

STAS NAMIN (co-organizer, Moscow Music Peace Festival) When Ozzy Osbourne appeared, the fans bum-rushed the stage, and somebody even threw a bottle onstage. The guarding troops were ready to start suppression, and the festival had to be stopped. I asked the general to let me talk to the crowd and came onstage. I said, "You are humans, not pigs. Look around and block those who don't behave themselves properly. And now if you still want the festival to go on, back up three steps, sit down on the grass, and relax." And they did.

JEFF LaBAR It was like feeding starving children! It was unbelievable.

DAVE "SNAKE" SABO The experience was just unparalleled. To be a twenty-four-year-old kid in Moscow, where apparently they're supposed to be, you know, the devil, the enemy, all that stuff? And there you're in Lenin Stadium, playing in front of seventy-five thousand people, watching the Olympic torch get lit for the first time since the 1980 Olympics, when we boycotted them as a nation. It was wild, man.

ZAKK WYLDE I was mostly hanging out with Snake, getting blasted, and we were just laughing our asses off, going, "I can't believe we're here!" Compared to being in Jersey, with Dave working at Garden State Music and me playing guitar at home alone, it was pretty insane.

DAVE "SNAKE" SABO I'm not a political person by any stretch. But I could feel the enormity of the moment.

LARRY MAZER These kids had seen freedom for the first time and they were not gonna stand for this fucking communism thing at all. I came home and I said to my wife, "I'm telling you right now, the Soviet Union will be over within five years." But I was wrong. It was over in three.

PART V

THE LAST MILE

As commercial hard rock rounded the corner into the '90s, new bands like Nelson, fronted by the uber-photogenic twin sons of country music celebrity Ricky Nelson; Trixter, a group of fresh-faced New Jersey kids barely out of high school; and Winger, a supergroup consisting of seasoned sidemen and prog-rock refugees, were still getting record deals and releasing pop-flavored debut albums that kept the request lines at *Dial MTV* jammed at all hours of the day and night, especially if you knew how to game the system. "I had what we called the Boiler Room back in Denver, where we put ten telephones in an apartment building," confesses Kip Winger. "When 'Seventeen' came out, I paid people to call and request that fucker. We had ten people calling radio stations and MTV and *Headbangers Ball*. That's really how we climbed the charts, and then the public caught on."

Less-resourceful latecomers, like L.A.-based groups Bang Tango, Tuff, and Pretty Boy Floyd, had all the pieces in place for pop-metal success but still struggled to generate major excitement, even in the halls and conference rooms of the labels that had signed them. "There were so many songs that sounded the same at that time that you really had to stick out. And we didn't stick out," recalls Howard Benson, who produced all three of the aforementioned bands' debuts. "There wasn't anything on the Pretty Boy Floyd record like a 'Youth Gone Wild' or '18 and Life.' We handed it in to the label and I think the radio guys kind of yawned at it."

Meanwhile, on the East Coast a handful of gritty New York City bands like Law and Order, Spread Eagle, and the Throbs, who emerged from a tight-knit scene that encompassed clubs like L'Amour, the Cat Club, and Limelight, also managed to snag major-label deals but failed to capture the mainstream audience's imagination.

Even established acts like Cinderella struggled to maintain their momentum, falling victim to top-heavy marketing plans and a desire to evolve musically that did not necessarily conform with their fans' expectations or desires. "The songs on the *Heartbreak Station* record were so well crafted, and it wasn't caveman rock. It was something special," says Cinderella drummer Fred Coury. "It just wasn't the hard rock Cinderella that put the band on the map."

Of course, it wasn't just the bands who were outgrowing their fans. The opposite was also true, and it would prove to be a disastrous confluence of events.

57

"IS IT A GUN PROBLEM OR A BAT PROBLEM?"

LARRY MAZER Ratt and Guns and Mötley and Dokken and whatever, they all looked at each other. There was not a Rainbow-type place in Philadelphia or New York where people hung out. And New York never really developed a hair band scene—it was always more punk rock and that type of stuff. There was no Philly scene. If you look at Kix, from Maryland, or Twisted Sister, from Long Island, East Coast bands lived in their own world.

BILLY CHILDS There very much was a Philly scene, actually. But it was never really more than three or four clubs at the same time. Philly's a big sprawling area. It's not like L.A., where you have all these clubs clustered in one spot. From South Jersey up to, like, Philadelphia and the outlying suburbs, that's a pretty good reach, man. But I guess it was a smaller scene compared to some. You'd always run into the same thousand people.

EDDIE TRUNK Those were places where you would go and there would be people there no matter who was playing.

DAVE "SNAKE" SABO The scene was thriving. You had so many different clubs to play, down in Philadelphia and Trenton and Asbury Park and Newark and Staten Island and Long Island, New York City, Brooklyn. It was great. And those clubs had original bands every night. It was amazing to watch. There were bands making a living on the club circuit. And that's unheard of in this day and age. You weren't making a *good* living, but you were putting a couple bucks in your pocket playing your own music. It was really exciting.

MISSI CALLAZZO (DJ, WSOU; executive, Megaforce Records) There were other stations that had specialty shows, but when WSOU, which is the station at Seton Hall University, switched to an all-metal format in 1986, we were the only ones doing that. And I think that we definitely played a big part in bands like Skid Row and Winger and Kix getting their careers to the next level. It was like, where else can a record company get a major market radio station to support a developing artist and see if there's a spark when you put it in front of people?

SCOTTI HILL Our scene was very scattered out, from Westchester down to Jersey, Long Island, the tristate. There was no actual place to go and see people walking around on the street, like the Sunset Strip.

MARK WEISS No one actually wanted to go into Manhattan, you know? They wanted to go to the suburbs, where they could drive to gigs. That's where all the rock happened. We didn't like the city. You go to the city to go to Madison Square Garden.

MISSI CALLAZZO Skid Row had sold out the Birch Hill in Old Bridge Township, New Jersey, and L'Amour in Brooklyn.

SCOTTI HILL L'Amour was the epicenter of everything.

STEVE BROWN It was the big step for any band.

MISSI CALLAZZO George and Michael Parente, who owned L'Amour, they ran a good business. They were legit humans, you know what I mean? They managed White Lion. They managed Overkill.

BOBBY "BLITZ" ELLSWORTH (singer, Overkill) They were fun guys; local guys. If you're from here, you know that if you're not getting your balls busted, it means somebody doesn't like you. If everybody's being polite all the time to you, then it's probably that they don't like you. But if they bust your balls, there's a certain camaraderie with that.

DEE SNIDER One of the guys in Overkill told me that they came in to the management office because they had a problem on the road and the Parentes said, "Hold on—is it a gun problem or a bat problem?"

BOBBY "BLITZ" ELLSWORTH It wasn't a gun problem. They treated their bands as friends and wanted to do the best for them because the band's success would highlight their own success.

KEITH ROTH It had a very family-oriented kind of vibe; you'd see the same faces at L'Amour every week. The shows started really late, so I'd go home and get up at midnight by myself, get in the car at eighteen, and drive up there because I'd see my friends. And you'd grab at least one to take the ride home with you.

MISSI CALLAZZO After the show ended, the party would continue on the street. People would just, literally, hang in front of L'Amour until four a.m.

PHIL ALLOCCO (guitarist, Law and Order) L'Amour was a big venue for us because national acts would come through New York, and they would play with local unsigned bands as support. That was a great way for fans to get exposed to us before we signed to MCA. Kids would come, and when you can play a show in front of two thousand people or one thousand people and you get to work and play with a crowd like that . . . it really helped develop a band.

ROB DE LUCA (bassist, Spread Eagle) L'Amour was far from the East Village, where we lived, so we would go there to see shows, but that wasn't our hang. We always stayed in Manhattan, and it was a different place every night. Sunday was Limelight, Wednesday was the Cat Club, Tuesday was Danceteria, which had a heavy metal night. Then after all those places, you always went to the Scrap Bar on MacDougal Street to end the night.

PHIL ALLOCCO A scene really started to build in New York. It was kind of an eclectic group of bands. Circus of Power was one of the first bands that got signed. And then White Zombie, Raging Slab, Princess Pang, the Throbs . . . we could sell out clubs before we were signed, which is kind of unheard of today. We'd be playing L'Amour, Limelight, and the Cat Club in Manhattan. That one was interesting because whatever celebrities or bands were in town would be there. So, you would have Johnny Ramone or whoever in the audience and if you were a new band there, you might get a lot of people with their arms folded in front of you, just standing there. Whereas if you played L'Amour, people were jumping up and down.

EDDIE TRUNK The Cat Club was the closest thing we had in New York to the glammy thing in L.A. The guy who ran it was very androgynous. I think he was half Asian, half black, and he had a very strong look and he was cultivating this whole scene. In New Jersey there was Studio One, which I saw Skid Row and Trixter break out of.

STEVE BROWN We opened for Skid Row at Studio One. It was the first American show they ever did with Sebastian Bach and that was pretty much the night they got signed. And Trixter, we weren't far behind them.

BRUNO RAVEL Danger Danger first heard about Trixter when we were making the video for "Naughty Naughty." There was some girl that we were friendly with that was friendly with someone who knew them and she was like, "Hey, there's this new band, Trixter." And we just looked at them and said, "Oh, these young punks. Fuck them."

STEVE BROWN When we finally did a showcase, we played a club called Sanctuary in Manhattan. We opened up for Law and Order. It was kind of a weird pairing. They were like a dark city band, and here we are, fun, good-looking dudes. But it was that yin and yang that worked. The place was packed. This guy Steve Sinclair from Mechanic, MCA Records, came out to see us and he basically said, "This is the band that's going to make me a millionaire." He signed us within a month. That was May of 1989, and September of '89 we were on a plane out to L.A. to do our first record.

MISSI CALLAZZO New York was always . . . if there were men wearing any kind of makeup, it was definitely just more smudgy black around their eye. Their hair was more a mess because it was a mess, not because they were teasing it for three days before the show, you know what I mean?

ROB DE LUCA We looked at our music as street art, like subway graffiti. Some people think it's dirty and other people think it's beautiful. I personally think it's beautiful.

ANDY SECHER (editor, *Hit Parader* magazine) I think the East Coast bands, for whatever reason, had a little more substance to them than some of the West Coast bands, the L.A. bands.

PHIL ALLOCCO I always remember being very envious of bands who weren't from New York because it was easier to be a band in other places. To be a band in New York, the cost of living was so high. There is no room. It's hard to find a place you can make noise in, period. The terrain is very challenging to even put a band together.

ROB DE LUCA I mean, in Alphabet City, probably 30 percent of the buildings were empty, dilapidated. When you look at our video for "Switchblade Serenade," it was so easy to find locations that looked like that because there was just blocks and blocks of burned-out buildings.

STEVE WEST Everybody just wrote songs, put bands together, and got record deals on the East Coast. That's how it worked. There were no bands on the East Coast that were playing clubs, doing originals, and getting a huge record deal because they were the biggest draw in town like Mötley Crüe or Poison or Warrant had done in L.A.

ROB DE LUCA We were rehearsing at a place called Loho Studios, which was a low-level recording studio and a rehearsal space, and we also recorded our demos there. So we had this demo, we started sending it out, and people were reacting incredibly strongly to it. The labels start setting up appointments to come down and watch us rehearse. We had about maybe five or six songs and had shows booked but hadn't played one yet.

MCA came down and they said right away, "We want to sign this band, like, tomorrow." And we were like, "Holy fucking shit!" So then we canceled all the gigs we had and went right into recording and songwriting mode and pre-production.

BRUNO RAVEL Danger Danger started writing and recording and then just started submitting demos. We only submitted one demo, and we got interest from Lennie Petze at Epic. And so in a way, that's great, although sometimes I wish we had suffered a little more.

STEVE WEST Since the lineup we had on the demo had never played a show, Lennie said, "I need to see you guys play and make sure you're the guys on this tape." So they booked us at SIR, which is the big rehearsal studio in Manhattan that all the biggest acts in the world go to. And Lennie Petze sat down in a chair right in front of the stage by himself and we played five or six songs. And he said, "Okay, you're the guys. This is great." Whatever, the rest is history. It was interesting because he had done the same thing with Twisted Sister and he had actually walked out before they were even finished. So at least he didn't leave for us; he liked us and he signed us. And again, then we actually had to learn how to be a band, which was the opposite of all those West Coast bands that were already gelling and playing. We were just like, "Okay. Now we better figure it out!"

ROB DE LUCA Maybe we didn't make anywhere near as big a mark as the Hollywood scene, but there were a lot of bands here trying to get signed on the East Coast . . . and making it happen.

INTERVIEW: STEVE BROWN OF TRIXTER

One of the bands most closely associated with the tail end of the glam metal movement, Trixter, led by guitarist Steve Brown, enjoyed remarkable success with their 1990 self-titled debut album. The group's 1992 sophomore effort, Hear!, *was released two weeks after Nirvana's* Nevermind *and was virtually ignored.*

How old were you when you formed Trixter?

I was twelve years old. It was 1983 and I had started playing guitar in 1978. I discovered Kiss and two weeks later I told my mom that I wanted to be a guitar player. Then a couple months later I heard "Eruption" for the first time and I was just like, "What is this?" It hit me like a ton of bricks.

Trixter signed to MCA in 1989, when you were just eighteen. Did you manage to finish high school or were you too busy making music?

I did finish—by the skin of my pants. By sophomore year of high school I had long hair, I was a rock star. This was what I was doing. So I had pretty much given up on school. Luckily, my father was the vice principal, so he was able to sweet-talk some of the teachers.

Were you all still living at home?

We rehearsed in my mom and dad's house in Paramus. So we had all these record company people who wanted to sign us coming out there because we would rehearse all day long. My mom would make lunch, or we would order food and we'd drink ShopRite iced tea with them. That was part of the appeal—"Hey, you've gotta see these kids! They're real!"

The video for your first single, "Give It to Me Good," really leveraged that aspect of the band. You guys are rocking out in the garage and riding dirt bikes.

We had been out on the road supporting Stryper and Don Dokken, but when MTV added that video in September or early October of 1990, it fucking flew through the roof. It debuted at number eight on *Dial MTV*, and then the next day it was number one. And it was number one for thirteen weeks. That's when the phone calls started coming in: "You guys are going to go out for a week with Poison, and then you guys are going to go out for six months with the Scorpions. You're going to fucking play every arena throughout the country, multiple nights."

That must have blown your minds.

It was, like, the greatest thing in the world. The Poison run was our first arena tour. Muskegon, Michigan—Trixter, Slaughter, Poison. Sold-out ten-thousand-seat arena. We get there the day before. We go to the arena like Rocky—you remember how Rocky went to the arena before the fight? We go to check it out. "Holy shit, we're going to play this fucking place! It's going to be awesome!" Get there the next day, do soundcheck. Here it comes, man. We get onstage and destroy the place. First arena show, dude, and nothing went wrong. I'll never forget coming offstage that night. Bret Michaels is there. He's standing at our door, he's holding two bottles of champagne. We look in our dressing room and there's, like, fifteen strippers in there. And he goes, "Welcome to rock 'n' roll." There's a case of champagne, naked chicks everywhere. It was fucking unbelievable.

Did you spend a lot of money making your second record, *Hear!,* because the first album had been successful?

Totally. Jim Barton, our producer, was like, "Guys, I've got this great studio in Wisconsin. We can do the whole record for $150,000." It was the studio where Skid Row had made their first record and they were going out of business, so they were dying for bands. And I'm like, "Fuck that. I ain't going out to fucking Wisconsin to record a record! I want to make a fucking big-boy record! I want to be home. I want to be near my family. I want to fucking do this right." So I do my guitar tracks at Right Track in the city. Fifteen hundred bucks a day for the studio.

And then you finished the record in Los Angeles?

Jim was starting to get homesick, so he goes, "Hey guys, can we do the rest of the record in L.A.?" And we're like, "Fuck, yeah. Let's go to L.A. for a month!" So we get suites at Le Dufy Hotel in Hollywood. We each get a Mustang GT convertible to drive around in. We're living it. We're doing the thing. It was kind of like, here it is. We're going to fucking spend some money. We're going to do this like the big boys. You know? And as long as we don't spend two million bucks, we're going to be okay.

How much did you end up spending in total?

I think we spent six hundred grand on that record.

How about the videos?

We did a $250,000 video for "Road of a Thousand Dreams" with the guy who did Mötley Crüe's "Smokin' in the Boys Room." Big budget, cool video . . . but not that cool. We got the Kiss *Revenge* tour, but I knew there were going to be problems when the record came out and MTV didn't air our video. Our manager would be going, "Oh, they're going to add it next week." They didn't add it next week. We're a month into the Kiss tour and finally we get the call: "MTV's not playing your video." A year earlier we had played ARCO Arena in Sacramento with the Scorpions and sold it out, twenty-two thousand people. When we did it with Kiss, there were fifteen hundred people there.

Did you just want to pack it up and go home?

We had just signed a huge merchandising deal, so we had another eight months' touring we had to do. Luckily, we had a great booking agent, Mitch Rose at CAA, who saw the writing on the wall. He kept us in theaters, at festivals, fairs, made some money. We did ten months of touring on that where most bands would have gone home. The good news is the *Hear!* record did well in Japan, did well in Europe. So we got to go to Japan. But the final nail was we got an offer to do the Bon Jovi *Keep the Faith* European tour, but there was a catch—they wanted a $100,000 buy-on. The record company wasn't going to pay it, so they came to me and said, "Do you want to use your publishing money?" And I was like, "Fuck no." So that was a bummer. That was '93.

Looking back, are you bitter about how short a run Trixter had?

Look, I say it all the time. Every dream I ever had came true a thousand times over. Do I wish we came out two years earlier? Yeah, to get a little bit more of that wave. But we rode a nice wave. I just would have liked to have ridden a bigger one, and for a little bit longer.

59

"THE SCORPIONS WANTED US OFF THE TOUR AFTER THE FIRST NIGHT"

KIP WINGER So Reb and I were watching MTV every day during the first album and seeing all these Whitesnake videos and Def Leppard videos. And we said, "Okay, we'll just buy some concho shit and fuckin' perm our hair and do that thing." 'Cause everybody else was doing it.

REB BEACH Kip and I wanted to be rock stars, for sure. I was voted most likely to be a rock star in high school. And Kip has pictures of himself playing in a band when he was fourteen years old, and he's got a Rickenbacker bass that's bigger than he is. He used to lie and say that he was eighteen to play with his brothers. All he wanted to do was be a rock star.

KIP WINGER Actually I don't give a fuck about any of that. I just did what everybody else was doing [with the image]. It was a mistake, because our music sat outside the norms of quote-unquote '80s bands. So we could've just done jeans and T-shirts and been fine. We didn't push the threshold to a way higher level, but look under the hood and there was a hell of a lot more going on there than with most of those rock albums.

BEAU HILL They really were and are incredible musicians. And then they got Rod on drums . . .

REB BEACH Rod Morgenstein, of course, was in the Dixie Dregs.

PAUL TAYLOR Reb was a huge Dregs fans and couldn't believe Rod would even consider playing in a band like this. But we all wanted to add some kind of a progressive element to the thing.

BEAU HILL The first Winger record was relatively easy to make. I didn't have to do a hell of a lot of heavy lifting. All the rehearsals were really organized. When you're working with musicians of that caliber . . . I mean, what am I going to say to Rod Morgenstein? The biggest problem I had with Rod is that he's a jazz guy. So, he came in to do the record and he started playing really dumb.

REB BEACH Yeah, that happened. In "Seventeen," he was just playing everything as straight as possible. He did it as a challenge to be a real rock player. Because most jazz musicians suck at playing rock. Sorry, but it's true! So he was just really pulling back and concentrating on what we called at the time "fuck-shit drumming." Which is just kick-snare, you know?

BEAU HILL It was like AC/DC stuff, like, *boom . . . cha! Boom boom . . . cha!* But we wanted Rod to be Rod, all guns blazing.

PAUL TAYLOR We were like, "Dude, play anything you want!"

KIP WINGER Particularly on "Headed for a Heartbreak." At the end of "Headed" is where we went, "C'mon, do your thing! You're Rod Morgenstein! If we wanted your basic fuck-shit drummer we would've hired that guy." So we said, "Bring it!" And he did. Because Rod is Rod. He's no Lars Ulrich!

PAUL TAYLOR Once we released our record it wasn't like it just came out and went through the roof. Atlantic had to do some extra jumping through hoops to get it started.

KIP WINGER About a month in we had sold sixteen thousand records, which I thought was amazing. But the label was like, "Well, this isn't gonna do anything, so whatever . . ."

BEAU HILL Winger's agent, a guy who worked at the Agency Group, was such a fan of the band. He got them on the Scorpions tour, right out of the box. So Winger never played in clubs. They never did any of the normal stuff that normal bands do. The first gig they ever played was at some arena opening for the Scorpions.

REB BEACH And it was a complete disaster. Because we got out there and we had never played in front of an audience as a band. Rod Morgenstein was in the Dregs, I had been in a Top 40 band, and Kip had played with Alice Cooper. But we had never played together as Winger.

PAUL TAYLOR As a matter of fact, I had just met Rod two weeks earlier because I was out touring in Europe with Alice. I literally met Rod after the record was done. We rehearsed for a couple weeks and then just got thrown out on-stage with the Scorpions, opening for them in Peoria or something for thir-teen thousand people. All we could hear onstage was kick drum and Kip's voice. We got through the set and we just were praying that it sounded better out front. Which, evidently, it didn't. Our soundman said, "No, it sucked."

REB BEACH I remember my amp exploded. *Boom!* I had eight Kitty Hawks—they used to call 'em Shitty Hawks. And all eight blew up. And Kip hadn't been a front man in an arena before. So we get out there, Kip gets on the microphone with his monotone voice, and he's like, "Thank you very much. You people are great." Because Kip is a mild-mannered guy, you know?

KIP WINGER I was always in a band with my brothers where we all sang live. I didn't really know how to work a crowd in that way. So the Scorpi-ons wanted us off the tour after the first night.

REB BEACH But then Kip watched Klaus Meine and completely ripped him off the next night. *All riiiight peopllllle!!!* And we quickly were whipped into shape.

KIP WINGER We got it together and it was fine. And the Scorpions ended up taking us to Europe for three months later on. So we owe them a lot for getting us exposure in the early days.

PAUL TAYLOR Video-wise, Rick Krim at MTV was definitely a big help.

RICK KRIM When I was in college, my favorite band was the Dixie Dregs. And the drummer for the Dixie Dregs joined Winger.

REB BEACH And he got *Headbangers Ball* to play "Madalaine" at 2:55 a.m. on a Saturday. I stayed up and watched it. I was so excited!

KIP WINGER Well, first of all, Atlantic wasn't even going to give us a video. We had to audition to do a video, because videos were expensive. So we had set up a showcase in Hoboken, and these two people from the label came to see if we were good enough and visual enough to be in a video. So I'm jumping around like Peter Pan, because I studied ballet. And they went, "Okay, this'll be great." The budget was ninety thousand bucks for that "Madalaine" video.

REB BEACH And just from that one play at 2:55 a.m., radio got flooded. MTV was incredibly powerful.

PAUL TAYLOR Next was "Seventeen." And to this day, you know, to play the guitar riff to "Seventeen," just the riff, nobody plays it like Reb does. I've seen about ten different guys go, "Dude, how do you . . ." I remember when Kip first sent me a copy of that song. I was driving around Beverly Hills that day and I'm going, "Ah . . . I like the riff but I'm not sure about the lyrics . . ."

KIP WINGER It was a riff that Reb wrote. I stole the title from Kingdom Come. They had an album out and there's a song on their record called "17." So I stole the title and wrote a song.

PAUL TAYLOR Kip's thing was "Hey man, you know, the Beatles had a song about being seventeen . . ." And I was like, "All right, whatever." Of course, now we'd probably all look back and go, "Okay, we probably should call it something else . . ."

KIP WINGER People go, "Pedophilia . . ." But it's like, c'mon [quoting the Beatles' "I Saw Her Standing There"], "She was just seventeen." You know, whatever. I just happened to have a really big hit with that song. And then the one line I didn't write, that Beau wrote, was "Daddy says she's too young / but she's old enough for me." That was probably the line that did me in.

BEAU HILL Between the Scorpions and MTV, that really pushed the *Winger* album over the goalpost. The planets just lined up for us for some weird reason.

REB BEACH It felt like it would go on forever.

KIP WINGER We got some good touring out of our second record [1990's *In the Heart of the Young*], but the writing was on the wall before it came out. Bad timing. None of us were happy with that record anyway.

PAUL TAYLOR We tried to go a lot more progressive and the label was like, "We'll release it . . . but we're not gonna back it."

KIP WINGER They said, "You have no hits." And Beau told me, "They're not going to release anything but [the ballad] 'Miles Away.'"

REB BEACH So we said to the label, "Please just let us add a few songs. Give us a second." And we wrote "Easy Come Easy Go" and "Can't Get Enuff" in one day.

PAUL TAYLOR And they both had success, but by then we were into, what, 1990? So we were starting to all notice, like, wow, where's everybody at the shows? And where's our chart numbers? Of course we took it personally, but it was literally happening to everybody. I remember it finally hit home in Cincinnati. We had a night off and I went to see Extreme and Cinderella with David Lee Roth at the Riverbend [Music Center]. And it was half-full. And to me, David Lee Roth . . . the first time I saw Van Halen was at the Whisky, about a year before the first Van Halen record came out. And I became such a huge fan. So David Lee Roth was the ultimate rock star. And now the place is half-empty? I was like, "Whoa. Something's up." Because two years prior it would've been sold out.

REB BEACH If we had come out in '86, I'm sure I'd be a very rich man. But we came out in '89, right at the tail end. We didn't know it was gonna end. On the third album [1993's *Pull*] we were gonna get big publishing advances. If it had done well, I would've made a lot of money. And I banked on that. I figured, it's gotta do well! The last one sold a million and a half records. This one's gotta at least go *gold*. So I bought a new house and moved the whole fam to Florida. "C'mon, kids! We're moving to *Florida!*" I got a house on a lake with a pool, and you could jump from the pool right into the lake! It was incredible.

I was only there for eight months before I had to sell that house. That's how quickly it all went south.

60

"CHERRY PIE GUY"

STEVEN SWEET When Warrant got home from the *Dirty Rotten Filthy Stinking Rich* tour we went to Hawaii with Beau Hill for pre-production on the next record. But out of two weeks of unabashed partying and fun and just living the island life, we may have rehearsed two days.

JOEY ALLEN We had done literally sixteen months on the road and we were burned out. We thought we would go over to Hawaii and get some work done. And once we got over there, you know, sun, sand, surf . . . what are you gonna do?

STEVEN SWEET We had been opening our sets on the Mötley tour with "Uncle Tom's Cabin" because it was one of the heaviest songs that we had. And especially in front of Mötley's crowd it was a way to kick off our set and say, "Hey, we're compatible with Mötley as an opener." And people were into it.

JOHN MEZACAPPA "Uncle Tom's Cabin" was one of the songs that Jani actually wrote very, very early on. I probably heard that when I was twenty years old.

STEVEN SWEET Beau, he was a little bit more on autopilot the second time around. He was often preoccupied with other stuff. So we jokingly say that Jimmy Hoyson, who was the engineer, actually produced the record. He did a lot more hands-on work than Beau did.

JIMMY HOYSON (recording engineer, Warrant, Winger) It was at the time that Beau was involved with Jimmy Iovine and the creation of Interscope Records, so he was constantly on the phone. He definitely had his hands full.

JOEY ALLEN Beau actually pulled Winger into some of our sessions. We're paying the money for the studio, and after we would leave and go home after recording all day, he would bring Winger in to record. That's all you need to know about Beau Hill.

JIMMY HOYSON We had just finished Winger's second album, and when they turned it in they were told by the label that they didn't have any singles. So within the first couple of weeks of starting the Warrant album, Winger was coming into the studio at night to record "Easy Come Easy Go" and "Can't Get Enuff." It wasn't done out of malice or anything like that. It was just like, "Man, we gotta get this done!"

BEAU HILL We were almost finished with the record but hadn't delivered it yet. I went to Jani and I said, "I don't think we have a single." Again, it wasn't a conversation that I was looking forward to.

STEVEN SWEET I don't know that story. Donnie Ienner at Columbia heard the record and wanted another single, another song. He said he wanted it to sound like "Pour Some Sugar on Me" by Def Leppard.

BEAU HILL Jani said, "Okay." The next day, not even twenty-four hours later, he called me and he played me the "Cherry Pie" demo. Shortly before he passed away, Jani told me that he really regretted that song because he was known as the "Cherry Pie Guy." I got pissed and I said, "God, you fucking moron. You have written a rock anthem. That's like the Holy Grail. You'll have people singing the words to your song for the next forty years. Not only that, but you pulled one right out of your ass at the eleventh and a half hour. Are you out of your mind?" I hope I changed his mind a little bit.

HEIDI MARGOT RICHMAN What's that bromide where you have your whole career to make your first record, and then suddenly you're in the system and it ain't that way anymore? I think that was the hardest part for him, that there were so many cooks in the kitchen that had to sign off on stuff. It kind of became somewhat outside of his control, and he really wasn't gonna be able to change that.

JOEY ALLEN Jerry and I were in Denver at a celebrity golf tournament with Leslie Nielsen and a bunch of different celebrities, thinking our record was in the can. And I remember getting a call from Jani and him playing me the demo through the phone and saying that we needed to come home to L.A. to record.

STEVEN SWEET We actually went in and demoed it first at Sound City, in Studio A. And that's when Donnie was like, "Yeah this is it." So then we went back to Enterprise in Burbank, set everything up again, and tracked the song to its fullest. The guys from Danger Danger happened to be in town and they helped sing gang background vocals.

BEAU HILL Jani had C.C. DeVille come in to play the solo and I was really pissed at him for that. He did it for one reason and one reason only: to ingratiate himself with C.C. so that Warrant could go out with Poison on tour. I believe that got accomplished, but sitting in the studio with C.C. was the most painful experience of my life; C.C., on a good day, would never come up to my standards of something that I would want to put my name on and release to the public. But I bent over backwards to accommodate the greater good, if you will.

HUGH SYME (graphic artist, Bon Jovi, Whitesnake, Warrant, Slaughter) The cover photo was a pretty evident and shameless—yet one hopes, humorous—rendering of the band's album title.

HEIDI MARGOT RICHMAN A lot of people think the woman on the cover of the *Cherry Pie* album is Bobbie Brown. It's not. Bobbie didn't come along until the video. That was just a model that they plopped a wig on. I was there.

HUGH SYME Jani gave me his nod of approval for where I wanted to take the cover's look and feel. The roller skates, the drive-in waitress all played well to the airborne pie. Hence the '50s-era cherry-red car for the band photo session.

HEIDI MARGOT RICHMAN One of the inside photos of the *Cherry Pie* artwork shows the legs and roller skates of what's supposed to be the waitress from the cover, sticking out from behind the car door. It looks like she's blowing Erik. The woman who had been cast for that showed up and she had just gained a ton of weight. So they sent her packing and sure enough, the photographer, John Scarpati, said, "Heidi, we need you, we need you to do this." I was like, "Oh my god, you've got to be kidding me!" It is not the most dignified photo I've ever taken.

JOEY ALLEN When they were casting the "Cherry Pie" video, we were going through the model headshot books to pick out a girl. Jani was single at the time, so it was like him looking through a catalog for a girlfriend.

JOHN MEZACAPPA The moment Jani saw Bobbie Brown he just was absolutely infatuated. He told me straight up after the second day of the "Cherry Pie" video shoot that he was going to marry her. Everybody was like, "Dude, this is way out of your league." And I just remember him telling me that Christie Brinkley wasn't out of Billy Joel's league!

MARK WEISS Jani was smitten. That's all he thought about. I was there when he got her flowers. He's like, "Mark, take some pictures when I give her these flowers." He was courting her, you know?

HEIDI MARGOT RICHMAN The shoot took three days. The director, Jeff Stein, was a perfectionist, and don't forget, the technology wasn't what it is now.

JOHN MEZACAPPA The shots from above where you see Steve hitting his drums and they're all cherry pies? Those are actually cherry pies that had to be replaced for every take!

JOEY ALLEN In the long run, I think Jani's relationship with Bobbie caused more damage to the band than egos or anything. Jani left a tour of Europe with David Lee Roth because he heard that Bobbie was driving around in his Mercedes with some guy in a local L.A. band, which she was. They were both promiscuous and infidels and one infidel meets another infidel and you can imagine the fireworks that brings on.

HEIDI MARGOT RICHMAN Because he was sort of having trouble wrapping his head around this creative direction, perhaps feeling like he'd lost control, what he could do instead was spend all his time with Bobbie. We had these reclining . . . they were maybe like barber chairs or something, that were in the makeup/wardrobe space of the studio where we shot. Basically, he spent the whole time when he wasn't shooting in one of those chairs with his arms around her. They didn't talk, they didn't do anything.

JOEY ALLEN When the record came out, we went on the road opening for Poison on their *Flesh & Blood* tour, which was great until the very last day. Even though "Cherry Pie" was a hit, we were still fired up to kick ass every single night, while they might have been a little burned out. We had two or three weeks left of the tour and were playing a show somewhere in Montana and they boarded up portions of the stage that they didn't want us using. I broke a guitar over one of the barricades. We were just pissed, like, "What the fuck?" You can't just dump some, you know, totalitarian "You can't go there!" on a bunch of twenty-seven, twenty-eight-year-old guys that are in a rock band. And when we walked offstage, Scotty Ross, who was Poison's tour manager, told us that it was over.

STEVEN SWEET After that we started headlining arenas and theaters with Trixter and Firehouse opening. We were firing on all cylinders. I think that was sort of the ultimate for us at that point.

STEVE BROWN It was called the Blood, Sweat & Beers tour. The Warrant guys were fucking party animals. They were like Mötley Crüe junior. But they knew how to handle it, I guess. Jani would smoke and drink tequila during the show, but the guy never fucking fucked up. He was unbelievable. Like, I'd be sitting there going, "This guy's fucking amazing. How is he doing it?" I don't know how those guys would be able to get onstage some of the nights. Because I know what we were doing with them the night before and we only had to play for forty-five minutes. They had to play for two hours! Then at the end of the show, all three bands would come out and do "(You Gotta) Fight for Your Right (to Party)" by the Beastie Boys.

STEVEN SWEET Jani would ask somebody in the crowd, "What's the happening rock bar in town? Because as soon as we're done here, we're going to go over there and continue the party." And we would do that. We'd go to whatever the local place was and whoever owned that bar was ready for something, because people would show up.

STEVE BROWN They would make a deal that Jani would announce that the bands were going to go hang out at the bar as long as we could drink for free. Before we'd get there there'd already be a thousand people there, so the place would make a shitload of money. They would have a fenced-out area for us and we would just party, play pool, and do whatever else. It was like that for five months!

61

INTERVIEW: BRIAN BAKER OF JUNKYARD

Brian Baker spent much of the '80s in the DIY punk world, playing in the seminal straight-edge D.C. hardcore act Minor Threat and later the Meatmen and Dag Nasty. But by 1988 the guitarist was living in L.A. and looking for his next musical act. A chance encounter at a Hollywood 7-Eleven with guitarist Chris Gates, an alumnus of Austin, Texas, punk mainstays Big Boys, led to an invitation from Gates to join his latest project, the sleazy, boogie biker-rock outfit Junkyard. The group had just signed a deal with Geffen Records and were poised to record their debut album, Junkyard, *with Tom Werman. Today Baker plays lead guitar with punk legends Bad Religion.*

You joined Junkyard after the band had already signed to Geffen Records. How was that?

It was awesome. All of a sudden I was in a band on a major label about to record their debut LP. That was just like, "Fuck! Here we are!" I think I was making a couple hundred dollars a week and I was . . . it was not exactly the gravy train, but to me, it was just this insane new world. I'd never seen anything like it. You're at a top-of-the-line studio in Los Angeles with this hit maker. You're hitting a buzzer and a gate's opening. I mean, *fuck*. You're driving your four-dollar car and you're parking it next to your producer's Porsche. And "What do you want for lunch? We're getting sushi." I mean, what the fuck? The equipment and the scale of it, I'd never seen anything like it. It was the big leagues.

Did you feel a lot of pressure to perform because of how much money was being spent?

I was really just doing my thing and excited to be there. I didn't feel under pressure to perform or this is all going to be ripped away from me. I really wasn't thinking like that. I wouldn't call it cocky but I was like, I know what I'm fucking doing. And by the way, I have blond bleached hair and I'm twenty-one. I'm kicking ass. I'm wearing too much jewelry. I'm dating the receptionist, I just met her. I have access to a woman without a mohawk.

You guys all wore matching biker vests. Was that a true representation of an outlaw lifestyle or something that a stylist thought up?

The vest was not a costume. We wore those vests all day. That was it. It's like, "You're in the band, here's your vest." It was real. We lived in a shitty house in the back part of Hollywood, and Chris and Clay [Anthony, bass] and Pat [Muzingo, drums] were definitely into drugs. David [Roach, vocals] and I were basically more drunks who would take drugs if they were there. But we weren't really drug guys. I think the lifestyle fed into the band, particularly our live show. We were just fucking *way* not slick. We were very, very angular and sloppy. Not pro. Well, that's a bad way to characterize it. But it was definitely, like, anything can happen. It was chaotic.

Given that, what do you think Geffen saw in the band?

We were like a cred band. It's proving that the label has vision and is doing something interesting. Like, "Look, we've got this!" It showed the breadth of knowledge of the genius A&R staff to be able to find these plucky ex–punk rockers who were doing this thing that isn't really a standard thing. Junkyard was kind of an outlier. It wasn't a Whisky or Roxy band. We were running this other separate program.

In the punk world you did most of your touring in a van. Was part of being in the "big leagues" getting to tour in a bus?

I'd been in a van for seven years, basically. I mean, Chris and I, more than anybody else, really had done that. We had slept on the floor of the fucking apartment with vermin and ten other dudes in sleeping bags. We had run out of gas in the van three thousand miles from home. We'd done all of this shit, hard. And the bus is an entirely different thing. You're not driving. You're drunk. You have a bed. You have something to show women that you matter. So this was just like . . . amazing. You want to pinch yourself. Is this really happening still?

What was life on the road like?

We weren't really a "We're going to the titty bar" band. As a matter of fact, we had a tour manager who kept trying to get us to go to the titty bar. We called him "Titty Bar." I don't even remember his fucking name. It was just Titty Bar. Even back then, I'm like, "I really don't think human trafficking is that sexy." I'm not saying we *never* went to one, but again, it wasn't really . . . there was still some punk going on in us, I think. And we just were taking the ride in our own way. But I get it—you're in Kansas and you've played their biggest non-shed venue. And you're done and you're young and you're drunk. Of course you're going to go to the titty bar because it's like, "All hail the musicians!" So it's continuing your show. The glow is still on and you're eating up all of this. You want it all.

Neither "Hollywood" nor "Simple Man," the two singles from your first album, were popular enough for the record to go gold. Were you disappointed or even worried that you'd get dropped?

Back then, going gold was the gauge of whether you got to open the next door. I don't know what we were, but I think we kind of petered out at, like, three hundred thousand copies, which is now amazing to think about. We just didn't quite get there. And a lot of bands did. A lot of terrible bands. Like Danger Danger. I mean, fuck. *Fuck*. What are we doing out here?

What did you do after Junkyard?

I went to work at a pool hall and a rehearsal studio where Weezer and the Goo Goo Dolls practiced. I was a people person. I was friends with all these people. I was still kind of in the mix and I was thought of as a pretty good guitar player. I was keeping the brand alive. I also formed a band called Careless that sounded a lot like the Goo Goo Dolls and later Replacements and stuff that I liked to listen to. Even throughout this Junkyard thing, I didn't sit around listening to Bang Tango. I liked good music. So I put together a bunch of local guys who had all almost made it, who were really good players, and we made this band that was okay. It was almost good enough, but wasn't.

62

WHAT COMES AROUND GOES AROUND

STEVIE RACHELLE When I was eighteen, I saw Van Halen, Mötley Crüe, and Ratt all within about a five-month period. This was 1984. That changed everything—I became obsessed with '80s heavy metal. I started buying all the magazines—*Circus, Hit Parader,* anything that had Mötley Crüe and Ratt in it. And everything I read in these magazines was about the Whisky a Go Go, the Sunset Strip, Hollywood, the Troubadour, the Roxy Theatre. It all started painting this picture. So fast-forward three years, I'm twenty-one years old and I'm on the Sunset Strip. And the first time I walk into the Whisky I think, Wow, this is really small! The same thing rang true for the Troubadour and the Roxy and the Rainbow. All these places were just tiny little clubs. I'm comparing them to the neighborhood beer bars that were in Oshkosh.

JOE LESTÉ I moved up to L.A. from San Diego and it was mind-blowing. It was basically like walking into Disneyland for the first time—you see all the lights and all the glamour and all the people walking around in all these outfits. You've got Mickey, Minnie, all of 'em. I was in shock for a while until I got used to it.

STEVIE RACHELLE I can tell you I arrived here on a Thursday. June 25, 1987. I had a girl I knew from Milwaukee who picked me up. And the very next night some guys in her building said, "We'll take you to Hollywood."

And we went to the Troubadour. I was probably in there for not more than five minutes . . . I might have been in the building not more than *twenty feet* . . . and two or three girls came up to me and said, "You look like Bret Michaels from Poison!"

KRISTY "KRASH" MAJORS I was playing around in some bands in New York City and a friend in L.A. kept sending me magazines like *BAM* and *Rock City News*. It just seemed like there were a gazillion bands and everybody was getting signed out of Los Angeles. Whereas in New York we had a small little scene and it was impossible to get a record deal. So I packed up everything I had and drove across the country. I set up a few auditions before I came out, and one of them was with Pretty Boy Floyd.

STEVIE RACHELLE I first saw a flyer for Tuff in Wisconsin. It had four squares on it: *George, lead guitar. Todd, bass. Michael, drums.* And then it said *Lead singer* and it was an empty square. And in that square was where they wrote *Wanted: Bret Michaels /David Lee Roth /Vince Neil* . . . I think it said Robin Zander and Billy Idol as well.

MARK KNIGHT (guitarist, Bang Tango) Bang Tango got together in 1988. Joe came up with the name. On the way home from work one day he saw a sign that said BANG and then another one that said TANGO. I'm like, "Well, it's kind of Ted Nugent–ish, I guess."

JOE LESTÉ We played anywhere we possibly could. We played the Whisky, of course, we played the Roxy. We played shows with Warrant, L.A. Guns, Faster Pussycat . . . a lot of Strip bands like that. Pretty much all of 'em.

STEVIE RACHELLE My first show with Tuff was at the Roxy, opening for Warrant. It was a pay-to-play show. We were second slot. Pair-A-Dice— and when I say that I have to discern it wasn't Paradise, like, with palm trees, who were another band on the Strip at the time—were third. And then Warrant were the headliners. I didn't even know who Warrant was, other than that everyone was saying they were the hottest band around, and that Jani was a superstar. I remember Michael [Lean, Tuff drummer] telling me, "Your competition is Jani Lane of Warrant and KK [Kent

Kleven] of Taz. Those are the two hottest bands and the two hottest singers on the Strip."

KRISTY "KRASH" MAJORS Pretty Boy Floyd did the Roxy, Gazzarri's, the Country Club . . . I think those were pretty much the places we played. We never played the Whisky. We never played the Troubadour.

STEVIE RACHELLE The Troubadour, one night I walked in the door and met this girl—I couldn't even tell you what her name was but I remember she was from Alaska. I had never met anybody from Alaska in my entire life! She was absolutely beautiful. Probably nineteen. Visiting L.A. with her family. She liked rock so she went to the Troubadour because she knew that was one of the clubs that rock bands played at. Within ten or fifteen minutes I took her outside, we went behind the club where the valet guys park the cars, and we ended up having sex against a wall. When it was done we walked back in the club and I never saw her again. That was not that unique.

MARK KNIGHT I was born and raised in L.A. I watched Mötley Crüe do their two nights at the Whisky when I was in high school. But by '87 the only way to describe the Strip would be . . . it was like the Rose Parade or New Year's Eve. Every night was just a complete spectacle. Every club was packed. And there'd be five hundred or a thousand people walking the streets, passing out flyers, promoting their bands.

STEVIE RACHELLE The clubs were at capacity so people would just stand outside Gazzarri's or the Whisky or the Roxy. And all these places are within about a two-block stretch. So there were hundreds, if not thousands, of people crammed into this area, and maybe a hundred bands or more promoting their shows.

BRET HARTMAN Pretty much all the clubs back then—the Whisky, Roxy, Gazzarri's, the Troubadour, the Country Club—they were all doing pay-to-play. 'Cause a lot of these bands were moving here from all over the country and they were doing anything they could to get exposure. So the clubs would have the headliner and then there'd be three opening bands. And they'd give 'em two hundred tickets at five dollars each and then the bands could sell the tickets for, like, ten dollars each, so they could make their money up front. Bands would spend all day long going around Hollywood delivering tickets because they didn't have jobs anyway.

STEVIE RACHELLE I never thought pay-to-play was a bad thing. I looked at it like this: There were thousands of bands and tens of thousands of musicians. If a hundred of those bands say, "Okay, we want to open for Warrant," well, *we* want that slot! We want to play in front of that crowd! So the club says, "You guys can play second. But you have to sell fifty tickets at twelve dollars apiece." What is that, six hundred bucks? So we say okay. And we agree contractually that by soundcheck on the day of the show we will have six hundred bucks to give to the club.

BRET HARTMAN And the bands that didn't have money to buy the tickets, they'd hook up with strippers at, like, the Seventh Veil. A lot of these strippers were paying for the tickets and the ads in the magazines.

STEVIE RACHELLE Some of these girls, maybe they came from good families and their parents gave them some spending money. Some of them were strippers making five hundred dollars, seven hundred dollars a night. And they saw the bands struggling, five guys all living in one rehearsal space or a one-bedroom apartment, and they're like, "Hey, we'll take you to Carl's Jr.! We'll buy you groceries! We'll get you a new pair of cowboy boots for the show!" I think at one point or another most guys did take advantage of those girls.

KRISTY "KRASH" MAJORS "You wanna hang out? Bring a pizza over!"

STEVIE RACHELLE Looking back on it as a grown man now, I couldn't imagine saying to a girl, "Would you pay my rent?"

BRET HARTMAN It was just hustle, hustle, hustle. Get all the girls you can to come to the show and create this illusion with smoke and mirrors that you have this big fan base.

STEVIE RACHELLE Within one to three square miles on a Friday or Saturday night there was probably fifty to seventy-five bands playing. So to try to get all these people to come and watch you at nine thirty to ten fifteen, it was competitive. It was like, "He has a bigger drum set! They have a faster guitarist! They have more Marshall stacks! That singer's hair is bigger!" There was so much competition between the bands to try to draw those people. You had to play great, and you had to look great.

JOE LESTÉ As far as our look, I don't know, we had this sort of "tipsy gypsy" thing going on.

MARK KNIGHT I worked at a big thrift shop on Melrose called Aardvark's. Taime [Downe] was right down the road at Retail Slut. And then there was Lip Service, all that stuff. Guns N' Roses took that Melrose look and kind of accentuated it. Jetboy, too. As opposed to, like, Warrant and Poison and all those bands who were more like the spandex-type vibe.

KRISTY "KRASH" MAJORS It's kind of funny that people say Pretty Boy Floyd were the glammiest band. Because we were more like Kiss and Alice Cooper and early Mötley Crüe. We even used to do Mötley Crüe's "Toast of the Town" live. And we wore leather, while other bands were out there wearing a whole bunch of colors and looking like Poison.

STEVIE RACHELLE At one point, people started saying I was trying to have surgery to look more like Bret Michaels, which was ridiculous. I mean, we have a similar background. He's a couple years older than me but he's from a small town in Pennsylvania and I'm from a small town in Wisconsin. We both have German heritage. We both had, sadly, thinning dirty-blond hair. But we were cute guys, you know?

KRISTY "KRASH" MAJORS Bret Hartman, I used to constantly see him around when we were promoting and flyering and this and that.

JOE LESTÉ He found Bang Tango before anybody.

BRET HARTMAN I signed Warrant to CBS in 1988. Then I went to MCA and I was going to sign Bang Tango but they got scooped up by Mechanic.

JOE LESTÉ We got signed within, like, six months of being a band. Really.

BRET HARTMAN There started to be a frenzy of signings. So then it's like, Pretty Boy Floyd is next . . .

KRISTY "KRASH" MAJORS We only played about ten shows before we got signed.

BRET HARTMAN I saw them playing at the Roxy one time and they had super-poppy songs but they were really extreme. They had the red flashing lights, they had the smoke bombs, they had the dry ice, they had the big hair, the leather . . . they were definitely more extreme than anything else on the Strip. I mean, Tuff was pretty extreme, but they probably didn't have the songs as much as Pretty Boy Floyd did. And Pretty Boy Floyd worshipped Mötley Crüe. I went to their rehearsal space once and their whole practice room was just Mötley Crüe posters. You figure, "Well, if they can do half as good as Mötley Crüe . . ."

KRISTY "KRASH" MAJORS Vinnie [Chas], our bass player, had been in a cover band with Jerry Cantrell from Alice in Chains before he played in Pretty Boy Floyd.

JERRY CANTRELL (guitarist, Alice in Chains) That was in Tacoma, which is where I was born. Vinnie was a friend of mine from about the middle of high school. He and I formed a band, and we had a couple gigs at, like, a roller-skating rink and a VFW hall. We would jam in a fucking storage unit. Then we moved to Dallas and we had a band called Sinister. It wasn't anything big but it was fun.

JOE LESTÉ Bang Tango recorded our first album, *Psycho Café,* in San Marcos, Texas, with Howard Benson.

HOWARD BENSON (producer, Bang Tango, Pretty Boy Floyd, Tuff) I had worked at this studio in Texas called the Fire Station. And Bang Tango, to me they sounded like Billy Idol with, like, funk grooves. Yet they were styled as a hair band. So I thought to myself, Why don't I take this Hollywood hair band to San Marcos, where we can get away from all the craziness and make a record? And, boy, the first night there, with me, a rookie producer? I had never seen anything like it.

JOE LESTÉ Well, how far did Howard go with this? I remember one night we're in the studio with the lights out and, you know, I mean, I feel awful saying this because it's a different time now. But we're all standing there and this roadie of ours, he has this girl on all fours and he's paddling the hell out of her with a ping-pong paddle. And she was a rather large girl . . .

HOWARD BENSON They started picking up girls from, I think it was Texas State University, and it was chaos. We were walking down the street to a pizza parlor and these girls come up and they go, "Who are you guys?" "We're Bang Tango!" They go, "You're gonna be huge!" Like, before they even heard a note. It was crazy. And the thing went on all night long. Drinking. Partying. I think they threw a girl through a plate-glass window into a pool. I'm not kidding.

JOE LESTÉ I don't know anything about that . . .

MARK KNIGHT The first or second night we were there, our roadie and a couple of the guys in the band, they corralled these girls, brought them back to the studio. We played music for 'em, they danced, they did all this crazy stuff. They came back to our room where the whole band was in, like, a condo, and it just got completely out of control. We ended up trashing the place, breaking the entire front window out of the condo.

HOWARD BENSON I remember going over there the next morning and I see the broken glass and I go, "What happened here?" They said, "Well, we didn't like this girl so we just tossed her out through the window."

MARK KNIGHT Really, it was just a tennis shoe that went through the window. I made up the rest of the story on the spot.

HOWARD BENSON After Bang Tango I did Pretty Boy Floyd.

KRISTY "KRASH" MAJORS Actually, the Bang Tango record sounds a lot better than our record, *Leather Boyz with Electric Toyz*. I think if you look at Howard's discography, I think we're the only album that he excludes.

HOWARD BENSON I used to try to hide it on my résumé. But once I had a lot of hit records I thought, Ah, fuck it. And I put it back on there. And now it's sorta a record that people like for some reason. I don't know why.

KRISTY "KRASH" MAJORS Obviously Howard's got a massive ego right now. [Benson went on to produce multiplatinum records for My Chemical Romance, All-American Rejects, and others.] But back then Howard was a new guy and he was pretty much begging to do the album. I wanted, like, Michael Wagener or Beau Hill or someone like that. But they were busy.

HOWARD BENSON You want to compete with the stuff that guys like Tom Werman and Michael Wagener are doing. And you're just like, How do I do it? And so you're hearing rumors—"Oh, they triple-tracked the singer from Poison." And you know, Kristy Majors, he could play. But the bass player was barely able to play a note and the singer was just all over the place. And we didn't have Auto-Tune back then. So we had to do quadruple tracking just to make a melody.

KRISTY "KRASH" MAJORS I wanted the record to sound more like a street record, a little heavier. And I think Howard tried to make it sound more on the pop element. He wanted to make us sound like the New Kids on the Block of rock 'n' roll or something.

HOWARD BENSON Hair metal, to me, it was like pop music except we had guitars in it. And these were just poppy party songs. The label was like, "What's the single?" We said, "Well, we're gonna go with 'Rock and Roll (Is Gonna Set the Night on Fire).'"

KRISTY "KRASH" MAJORS That video, it was like over $100,000. It's crazy the amount of money they spent back then.

BRET HARTMAN There was a huge soundstage and these huge letters spelling out PRETTY BOY FLOYD behind them. And they brought in these six-foot-tall light rings—that's a light that's round and when you shine it on people it just makes them *glow*. We had caterers, grips, cameras that are on those train tracks. It's like a three-day, thirty- or forty-person operation. These record labels were spending crazy money on these videos you would see once or twice on *Headbangers Ball*. It was ridiculous.

STEVIE RACHELLE Tuff's label put, like, fifty grand into our "I Hate Kissing You Good-Bye" video. But by the time we got signed it was the summer of 1990. Did it feel too late? I mean, yes and no. Looking back after the fact, we could've said, "Fuck! We were too late!" But at the time, no one really could have foreseen these bands from Seattle were going to change the landscape.

HOWARD BENSON I did a band called Tuff. They looked like Poison . . . I couldn't even remember what the bands looked like after a while. They were just all looking exactly the same. They all had headbands on, they all had long hair, all poofed up with hairspray, it was nuts.

STEVIE RACHELLE By the time we got signed, we're meeting with Howard Benson and we're playing him all these songs we had written and half of them were from 1988, 1989. Meanwhile, we were about twelve, fourteen months into hearing Skid Row, which is a band that had some hair band qualities, but they also had some heavy metal qualities. And their singer looks like, you know, Cindy Crawford. And he can sing his ass off! But we sold almost a hundred thousand records. Because the ballad ["I Hate Kissing You Good-Bye"] started getting some play.

HOWARD BENSON I would say that album [*What Comes Around Goes Around*] was one of the better projects I worked on at that time. And that singer, Stevie Rachelle, worked really hard. But they came so late in the process. They didn't stand a chance. They could've literally made *Sgt. Pepper's* and it wouldn't have sold. It wouldn't have mattered at that point. They would have had to reinvent themselves. A lot of bands actually tried to. They tried to look like Stone Temple Pilots, they tried to change their look. But, no.

STEVIE RACHELLE The week our video came out we were one of three adds on MTV. It was us, Metallica's "Enter Sandman," and, like, a Kid 'n Play video. Eventually we made it to number three on *Dial MTV*. It was "Enter Sandman" and, I think, "Don't Cry" by Guns N' Roses that were ahead of us. But this was September 1991. The video at number nine or ten? "Smells Like Teen Spirit."

HOWARD BENSON Pretty Boy Floyd, I don't even know what happened to them after we did that record. They got dropped. I did try to make a second record with Bang Tango, but they didn't want to make it with me because I told them their songs sucked. Then they hired me for the third record but by that time it was over. We had no chance. It was '92, '93. I remember going, "This record's never going to come out. We're gonna compete with Nirvana?" And what happened was we handed the record in and the manager calls me up: "I have bad news." I said, "The record's not coming out." He goes, "How'd you know?" I said, "I sorta figured! Where were we gonna sell this thing?" You know? Like, to *who*?

"IT WAS A TOTAL SCENE OUT OF *GUNSLINGER* OR SOMETHING"

STEVE VAI When the '80s came along, the shift was more towards the rock star thing. Entertainment. But at the same time there was a desire to play the shit out of the instrument. We loved playing instruments.

ZAKK WYLDE The '80s were an amazing time for guitar.

VITO BRATTA It was a really strange time period, because no matter what new band came out, everybody waited for the solo. "Let me see who the guitar player is." It was just one after another. Reb Beach. Nuno Bettencourt. This one. That one. Whoever.

BRAD TOLINSKI (editor-in-chief, *Guitar World* magazine; co-author, *Play It Loud: An Epic History of the Style, Sound, and Revolution of the Electric Guitar*) Eddie Van Halen was ground zero for the modern era. If you want to pull it backwards, it was like Elvis and the Beatles . . . Everyone knew that they were the kings, and everyone else just lived their life around that. Even amongst all the players, people like Reb Beach or Vito Bratta or Nuno Bettencourt, who might have actually had a better technical command of the instrument, they all acknowledged that it was really Eddie's world, and everything revolved around that.

NUNO BETTENCOURT The Bettencourt soup has a bit of a sprinkle of Eddie, it's got some Al Di Meola, it's got some Prince, it's got some Brian May, it's got Zeppelin. It's my soup. It's not anyone else's. But you also wanna compete. You wanna go in there and take those guys down . . . in a friendly way.

VITO BRATTA The first time I ever met Nuno, Extreme were opening for us in Boston. And we're playing this club. Half the club was a rock club, the other half was, like, a banquet hall. We were backstage, which was the banquet hall with the sliding glass doors closed. I'm there, I've got my guitar with a little practice amp, and Nuno's about twenty feet away, and he's got a guitar and a practice amp. And he's staring at me and I'm staring at him. It was a total scene out of *Gunslinger* or something.

BRAD TOLINSKI The interesting or sad or weird thing about shred guitar is that for years and years, rock 'n' roll was primarily rooted in this idea of deep personal emotional self-expression and the trauma of the black experience. And soloing was supposed be this sort of anguished cry—that's what Eric Clapton and all the British Invasion guitar players were trying to replicate. But I don't think American kids could relate to that for even a second. And there's no reason why they should have. So what did the guitar become? It became this sort of extension of what high school kids were into—it became sports. Or because the guitar players tended not to be as extroverted as the singers, it became this idea of doing well at homework or achieving the American dream, where if you worked hard enough, you could become rich and famous. You could be the best and the brightest and have the brightest white smile.

STEPHEN QUADROS Here's a story: At the Snow house we had one phone that all the guys would get calls on. This is 1979, 1980. So one day I answer the phone and there's this girl on the other end and she says, "Can I speak with Carlos [Cavazo]?" And I said, "Karen?" She says, "Hi, Stephen." This is a girl I used to hang out with, date, whatever. She's really cute, too. I said, "Um, I think Carlos is taking a nap. What is it?" She goes, "Well . . ." and there's this big uncomfortable pause. I say again, "What is it?" And she says, "Well, I'm calling for George." "George? George Lynch?" She says, "Yeah. I'm calling for George Lynch. George wants to challenge Carlos to a guitar battle."

VITO BRATTA It was just so perfect. Nuno and I didn't even say hello to each other. We didn't wave, 'cause that was, you know . . . guys don't do that. He's just sitting there doing all his warm-ups, and I'm like, "Oh, yeah?" And then I do my warm-ups. If I ever run into him again, I'm gonna ask him if he remembers that.

NUNO BETTENCOURT Umm, okay. I'm not sure if I remember that but it's definitely possible. I mean, it would have happened but I don't know if his perception would be my perception. But I think Vito's a great, talented guitar player, without a doubt.

STEPHEN QUADROS So I say to this girl, "Okay, have George call me." And I hang up the phone. Within five minutes the phone rings. It's George. I go, "Hey, George. What's the deal?" He says, "I wanna challenge Carlos to a guitar battle." He wanted to do it at a Snow gig, while Snow was playing! He'd get up onstage and play guitar against Carlos. And I said, "No, no, no. That's not gonna happen." I told him, "You go get a following. And when you get a following and Snow opens for you, then we'll do a guitar battle." And that was the end of that.

CARLOS CAVAZO There was competition. Who could have the biggest hair. Who could have the loudest guitars. Who could bring the hottest chicks down. It was definitely a competition, but a friendly competition.

GEORGE LYNCH It was an interesting scene at that time. And there was a lot of really good guitar players.

JAKE E. LEE Before I moved to L.A. I asked everybody, "Okay, who are the hottest guitar players in L.A.?" And George was one. "You have to see George Lynch. You have to see Carlos Cavazo." And I had heard Randy Rhoads. In San Diego I was the hotshot guitar player. I was the man. But I would go up to L.A. and catch shows and be like, Fuck, is everybody in L.A. a fucking awesome guitar player?

WARREN DeMARTINI Jake had that thing where he elevated any band he was in. I saw him in different bands in San Diego and it was always an event. Like, this guy is going to be huge. He was already in that league of the people we were listening to on records. And I can't say that about anyone else.

RON KEEL People call it hair metal, but how can you take a guitar player the caliber of Jake E. Lee and put him in the hair metal category? Dude's amazing! That's music, man! It's like Elvis or Bach or Beethoven. But you call it hair metal? That's not giving the musicians enough credit.

JERRY CANTRELL I love the guitar players of that era. George Lynch and fucking Warren DeMartini . . . so many great guitar players. I loved a lot of that stuff.

RON KEEL I heard a cassette recording of Yngwie Malmsteen on January 1, 1983, at Mike Varney's apartment and I thought he was the best guitar player I'd ever heard. And we called him and he was very hungry to come to America and make a career. It wasn't too long before he showed up in L.A. and we made that historic Steeler album together.

YNGWIE MALMSTEEN (guitarist, Steeler; solo artist) I had a very heavy classical influence. In Europe they didn't really give a shit about that, but as soon as I came to America, where the classical music is not as ingrained in society as it was where I came from, and I played 120 decibels through Marshall stacks, people fucking freaked out.

RON KEEL Yngwie would wake up in the morning at the "Steeler Mansion" and, still laying down, he would reach out with his right hand, grab a Strat, pull it into bed with him, and start playing. Then he would get up and go to the kitchen, and with his right hand he's pouring his cereal into a bowl, and with his left hand he's still doing all that Yngwie stuff. Then he's pouring the milk into the bowl. Then he's got a spoon and he's eating his cereal. But that left hand is still doing the Yngwie thing, man. He's still playing.

MARK SLAUGHTER (singer, Vinnie Vincent Invasion, Slaughter) Vinnie Vincent thought of himself as Yngwie Malmsteen. He even hired Yngwie's manager as his manager. He was getting more and more into wanting to be a guitar virtuoso. And Vinnie was an incredibly fast player, incredibly great technique. But it's about songs. Vinnie just wanted to frickin' . . . his foot was on the gas, you know?

DANA STRUM If you want a guy that can play at those speeds and do those kind of things and that's your cup of tea, Vinnie has a unique type of style and he was a standout guy that did that, for sure. But it was all so over-the-top.

MARK SLAUGHTER He'd start the show with a twenty-minute guitar solo. Before we even hit the stage.

TRACII GUNS Our first record, L.A. Guns opened for the Vinnie Vincent Invasion. We did places like Harpos in Detroit. But it didn't last. Vinnie was not a nice guy and he would stand there onstage and play guitar for two hours during soundcheck and not let us soundcheck. Shit like that. And my guys were feisty motherfuckers, you know? Shit went down and we got sent home.

STEVE VAI Some of the extreme players in the '80s, guys like Yngwie and Eddie, it takes a whole lifetime of intense focus to be able to play like that.

SLASH When Van Halen first came out in 1978, I hadn't picked up the guitar yet but I was really listening to stuff. And I was like, "Wow, that's fucking awesome!" But it wasn't one of those things where I tried to emulate it. It was just one of those cool things where you listen to it and you go, "God, that's fuckin' bitchin'!"

BRIAN "DAMAGE" FORSYTHE I remember I learned Van Halen's "Eruption" at one point, just to figure out what Eddie was doing, because it was so mind-boggling. But it wasn't our thing and I knew it. The interesting thing was there was a song that didn't make it on the first Kix record called "Rock and Roll Man." It was kind of a lame-ish song, but I did do a little . . . It wasn't fancy like Eddie Van Halen, but it was finger tapping in the solo. And I hate to admit that, because I always say, "I've never done that." But I have.

FRANK HANNON George Lynch and Eddie Van Halen and all those guys, I realized that I really couldn't keep up with them. And so I just went back to writing more song-oriented stuff.

LITA FORD Eddie Van Halen told me one time, "I am not a fucking rock star." He said, "But you are a rock star. What the fuck are you doing? Why are you fucking around? Just fucking do it." When someone tells you, "It's okay. You can do it," it depends on who that person is and what you're doing. I think if my mother had said the same thing, it wouldn't have had the same impact, but coming from Edward Van Halen, it was real. Nobody was taking me seriously as a guitar player because it was before our time: "Girls don't play electric heavy metal guitar." They might have played blues or they might have played bass or they were a singer, but they didn't play heavy metal guitar. I thought, I do. I want to prove to the world that it's me playing guitar. Because nobody believed me. That's why I insisted that I be the only guitar player in my first solo band. I wanted to put that in people's faces by there being no other guitar players onstage to look at. Within three months of doing that, I was out playing shows and I got signed.

But let me tell you, even after that, when we did TV shows, I'd be playing the solo and the cameraman would pan over to the bass player, because he's a guy. It was absolutely ridiculous.

KEITH ROTH Before Zakk Wylde joined Ozzy, he was in a band called Zyris that played at a bar where I worked in New Jersey called Close Encounters. Between sets he'd be downstairs with his Les Paul jamming to the Allman Brothers and Zeppelin. He would nurse maybe one Heineken the whole night. It was all about his playing.

DAVE "SNAKE" SABO As an eighteen-year-old kid Zakk would come into Garden State Music where I worked and just destroy. *Humbly* destroy. He was very quiet at the time and he would pick up a classical guitar and he'd do these fingerpicking pieces. Then he'd go over and play something on the piano. Then he'd pick up a Les Paul and just go berserk.

SCOTTI HILL He'd sit down at the store and just burn it up. And Snake and I would look at each other and giggle. We loved it.

BRAD TOLINSKI The musical content that some of the guitar players were bringing to the table was often superior to the actual songs that they were playing in. George Lynch was a really talented guitar player, but I thought that Dokken wrote the most clichéd, hackneyed songs ever. I had to interview George Lynch once around a Dokken live album, and I just remember fast-forwarding through the songs to listen to the solos.

REB BEACH "Headed for a Heartbreak" was the one that definitely showed the other musicians that I was a good musician. Players of all ilks would come up and go, "Man, that 'Headed for a Heartbreak' solo is just smokin'!" But I felt like anyone that played over that song was gonna sound good. It's just made for that sort of longing guitar sound with long notes, you know? Even if you suck you sound pretty okay over that riff.

FRANK HANNON It was fun to learn new techniques at that time. It seemed like guitar was still blooming and a lot of things were being discovered— hammer-ons and pull-offs and whammy bar techniques and arpeggios, all that stuff. So we would discover a new trick on the guitar and then just try to put it in a song, for sure.

REB BEACH We opened for Bon Jovi and I couldn't believe it when Richie Sambora yelled my name. "Hey, Reb!" I turned around and there was Richie Sambora. And he walked up to me and he said, "You are the luckiest guitar player in rock." And I said, "Why is that, *Richie Sambora*?" And he said, "Man, have you ever heard any of my solos? They're this long. But you've got the longest solo on MTV, on radio, of all time."

DAVE "SNAKE" SABO In Skid Row the song always came first. And then the song would dictate to us what we needed to do as far as the soloing. It's not that we didn't pay attention to all the shredders that were out there, it's just that, at least from a personal standpoint, the Yngwies of the world were way above my pay grade. And Scotti, his solos were always the sing-along solos in the sense that they were so melodic and beautiful. But it's not because Scotti can't shred. Scotti can play anything.

SCOTTI HILL The solo in "18 and Life," my original ending was something more melodic. But I played it and I was asked by Michael Wagener, who produced the *Skid Row* record, "Can you give me something fast at the end?"

PHIL COLLEN There was a time, a place, it would usually be four to eight bars and anything more than that and it would start becoming indulgent. You would have to really make it work in that context so as not to fuck the song up. And that's where I heard everyone fall off the cliff. They'd go, "Oh, I can show how great I am." And you go, "You know, it's a shitty song, it's a shitty band, and now you just proved that you're a shitty guitarist!"

BRAD TOLINSKI White Lion is another great example. Mike Tramp as a singer was maybe mediocre at best. I could see his appeal—you could barely look at him because he was so handsome—but the songs were fundamentally terrible. But Vito Bratta's guitar parts were almost always engrossing.

FRANK HANNON Tesla toured with Poison, and C.C. DeVille would always give me shit—"You play like an old man!" That's a C.C. DeVille quote. I think he meant it as a compliment, really. Because he was, like, totally just crazy squirrelly guitar playing, you know?

ACE FREHLEY (guitarist, Kiss, Frehley's Comet; solo artist) I could play as fast as the other guys. But, you know, my favorite solos are the ones that you can hum. Speed metal just doesn't do it for me. Because the melody gets lost in all the screaming and the superfast solos and stuff.

MICK MARS Everybody and their mother was playing all scales. "Oh, I'm a great guitar player now!" And everybody's playing the same lick over and over and over.

TOM WERMAN Mick Mars was a really good rhythm guitar player. I thought he was very, very underappreciated.

MICK MARS Was I kinda overlooked or put in a different category? Yes. My schooling, I don't know how to read music. It came from how I felt about the song and following the melody of the song. Playing something that fit and something that was memorable. It has a melody line to it, not just a barrage of notes. And because I didn't play all the scales or do this or that, you know, people thought that I was this crap guitar player. But it's okay.

BRAD TOLINSKI Guitarists personalizing their instruments was always popular in country music, and then in the '60s you had people like the Beatles, Eric Clapton, and Jimmy Page painting on their guitars. But when Van Halen appeared with his striped "Frankenstein" strat, I think that it really established this idea that your instrument should make a bold visual statement. That coupled with the rise of upstart guitar companies like Charvel, Kramer, and Jackson, who were jazzed about creating wild new "pointy" guitar shapes and actually interested in catering to the hair bands, really opened up the floodgates. A guitarist could order an axe with virtually anything painted on it—which, if you're twenty-two and horny, just might be a Trojan condom wrapper . . . or something even less tasteful.

JOEY ALLEN I had a Felix the Cat guitar where he's flipping you off, and his bag of tricks was a guitar and a bra hanging off. Erik [Turner] had a Trojan guitar. He had a money guitar—"In Sex We Trust." Everything was ramped up to this sexual innuendo level. Good times, man.

WARREN DeMARTINI My Bomber guitar was clip art from a Gary Moore album jacket, *Corridors of Power*. On the back of that there's a picture of Gary with a flight jacket on and there's Japanese characters going straight up and down. Charvel just copied that. Skip ahead two years in Japan and I'm doing an interview and they're like, "Why does it say 'London' on your guitar?" And I realized, man, that was a reckless thing to do. Because I didn't even know what the letters said. They could have said anything. I mean, can you imagine?

JOEY ALLEN I had a Jackson guitar that when I'd flip it over an arrow pointed to my member and it said, "Suck This." Where that came from, I don't know. I know that Richie Sambora did it as well. I don't know who did it first.

BRAD TOLINSKI You could look at 1990 like the end of it, but it certainly didn't feel like it then. The height of it was when Steve Vai put out his solo record and then was hired by Whitesnake for untold money to come play for them. Steve was considered the king, and one of the bigger bands in the world hired him for all this money, he had the solo record out, he was in a movie . . . It looked for all intents and purposes like this was a trend that was going to go on for a very, very long time.

PHIL COLLEN When Nirvana came along they actually did something very different and it caused a big effect. It was a really cool thing, especially with guitar. It was like, this isn't an Olympic sport. It's about appreciating and enjoying the instrument for its purity. I thought Kurt Cobain actually did more for guitar than a lot of these '80s shredders, because they actually missed the point. What he was doing was a bit more kind of real.

BRAD TOLINSKI Slash more so than Kurt Cobain was the end of the whole shredder thing. Hair metal was about the pomp and majesty, and Slash brought it back into a sort of Keith Richards attitude.

PHIL COLLEN I loved Slash's playing. Guns N' Roses had some really killer songs, and Slash was always on it.

SLASH I hated that whole sort of whammy bar thing that caught the whole fucking country by storm so that every band was doing it, everybody was ripping Eddie off. My roots all came from a different place.

BRAD TOLINSKI And in terms of the guitar-playing audience, it's no wonder that they would somewhat breathe a sigh of relief when Slash came in. I think there was a little bit of a sense of alienation that these guys were getting so complicated that they were almost turning off their fan base.

VITO BRATTA When the whole grunge thing happened I was told by people, "You know what your problem is? You play too well." I'm like, "Okay . . ." Explain what I'm supposed to do with that comment.

GEORGE LYNCH It wasn't like most of us had incredible farsighted vision. It was pretty myopic reasoning, watching what every other band was doing and the way they were dressing and the songs they were writing and the sounds they were getting and the way they were shredding. And it unfortunately worked its way to an apex, and we backed ourselves into a corner and there was no place to go. Because you could only play so fast and then what does it really matter? And then the whole thing falls apart and Nirvana comes along and says it all with one nasty, dirty, attitude note. You go, "Ah, that's rock 'n' roll!"

"THE GIRLFRIENDS AND WIVES DIDN'T WANT US THERE"

ALLEN KOVAC I had Richard Marx and Thomas Dolby at EMI and ultimately, I asked the label to trust me about signing Vixen. That I would make a great record, and that this would be a great project. They were having a lot of success with me and they said, "Okay, fine. We'll trust you."

JANET GARDNER It was all about "It's got to be radio-friendly." We were a live band who were just used to going out there and kicking ass, so it was a bit of an eye-opener. But when I heard some of the songs the label wanted us to do, I got it because some of our stuff was a little heavier, a little more basic. We understood it and we wanted them to push it, so we didn't fight a lot. In hindsight, there was stuff that we were right about. But you know what? We learned a lot and we needed to learn a lot. It worked out great and I can't complain.

ROXY PETRUCCI Even when the record was done, they weren't sure we had the single. That's when Richard Marx came in with "Edge of a Broken Heart."

JANET GARDNER There had been a lot of talk before about us working with Richard, so it wasn't a surprise. I was like, "Yeah. Cool." He had a melody and some chords and a guitar riff in his head. He was like, "*Dunt, da. Da,* *da, da, da, da, da.*" Jan fumbled around, tried to find what he was looking for. When I went in to record it, there were no lyrics yet. Fee Waybill from the Tubes showed up with the lyrics. I literally had no rehearsal. I'm at Capitol Studios, with Richard Marx on the other side of the glass. Woo-hoo. Yeah, I'm not nervous *at all* . . .

SHARE ROSS We were up for tours and then we wouldn't get them because the girlfriends and wives didn't want us there.

JANET GARDNER Don't flatter yourself, honey. We don't want your rock star dude. We know what they do, and we don't want them.

ROXY PETRUCCI We started out doing theaters with Eddie Money and then our first arena tour was with the Scorpions. They were very respectful to us, which was pretty awesome. Our first night they said, "Welcome to the big show." And they had flowers in our dressing room with a card that said, "Love, the Scorpions." I can still to this day remember looking out of the curtains and just seeing thousands of people. "Holy shit! I've got to go to the bathroom!"

JANET GARDNER It was a little nerve-racking and sometimes for the first couple of songs, it was like, "Oh, god. Oh, shit. Oh, they're not buying it. They don't like it." By the end, ninety-nine percent of the time we were getting big roars at the end of the songs, so it was working.

ROXY PETRUCCI We went from Scorpions to Ozzy with White Lion to Deep Purple. It was just like bam, bam, bam. We'd be out three or four months with each one.

JANET GARDNER Ozzy was really complimentary to me. He was really super nice. He was like, "I admire your consistency. Every night you're hitting every note." That was really sweet. That made me feel great. Ozzy Osbourne just told me I'm doing a good job!

SHARE ROSS We were very intense about always doing the best that we could, and I think all of us appreciated our positions of getting to perform from the point of view of being a fan. What if this person in the audience, it's the only time they're ever going to see us play? We better not suck that night because we got so fucked-up the night before.

ROXY PETRUCCI We were in France, in Paris, and we're hanging out in the bar and Allen called and said, "Hey, your record went gold today." We were like, "What?!" That called for shots.

JANET GARDNER I think that record companies underestimated the fact that we would get a lot of good female fans. Because the genre—Bon Jovi and stuff—they had a lot of female fans. It was when metal became female-friendly.

SHARE ROSS We kind of didn't know which end was up by the time we came back from that tour. I was married and then I got divorced and Janet's longtime relationship ended. We both ended up living in a hotel.

JANET GARDNER We did not come back rich at all. We knew that a lot of money was being spent and that a lot of money had to be recouped before we would make any money because those videos were not cheap. The making of the album was not cheap. It wasn't that surprising, but it was disappointing. It was like, "Well, we're almost famous, but we're still flat broke."

SHARE ROSS For the second record, *Rev It Up*, we were all adamant. "Okay, this is how this is going to happen. We're going to write or co-write everything on the record, we're going to work with only one producer." Et cetera, et cetera, et cetera. And it was really fun. We had a blast doing it and I think the second record is fantastic.

ROXY PETRUCCI The band started to divide to Janet and Share, me and Jan. Jan and I were writing together; Janet and Share were writing together. The *Rev It Up* record came together fine. It was after that.

JANET GARDNER We were in Europe touring with Deep Purple thinking that our record was being worked in the States. We got home and it was kind of like...nothing was happening. EMI dropped the ball. They went, "Well, you know, that's how it goes."

ALLEN KOVAC I had come to an impasse with Sal Licata at EMI while I was trying to renegotiate Richard Marx's deal. So I went to the chairman of EMI Global, Jim Fifield. Sal was so pissed off that a guy went over his head that Richard Marx, Thomas Dolby, and Vixen are dropped. Well, they weren't really dropped; Fifield has already made an agreement with me that we'd put it out on Capitol. Richard Marx put a record out on Capitol and so did Thomas Dolby...Vixen probably would have put out a record, too.

ROXY PETRUCCI We lost our deal and the band started not getting along and we ended up imploding. I think some egos got out of hand, mine included. We all thought we were the shit. The direction of the music for the next record, if there was gonna be one, was up for debate. I think we were lost.

SHARE ROSS It was like a big chip fell, which was EMI, and then all these other chips started to fall apart. Then Nirvana's starting to take off, you're just questioning everything. At that moment, looking back on it, we should have stayed united and I remember Roxy saying to me, "We should really unite." I was like, "Fuck you, what do you fucking know?" Egomaniacal child that I was.

JANET GARDNER It was one of those things where everybody kind of dug their heels in. And if any one of us, literally, would have backed off our position, it could have changed things. But all four of us stood our ground.

ROXY PETRUCCI Instead of taking a break, which is what we should have done, we ended up breaking up.

ALLEN KOVAC Janet and Share were approached by John Kalodner, who wanted to create a Heart-type band. He was gonna put three guys around them.

JANET GARDNER Share and I found a couple other players and put together a band, made some demos, and somehow it got shopped to John Kalodner.

We met with him and he said, "Yeah, I really like what you're doing. I'd like to hear more." So we did the demo deal.

SHARE ROSS I had nothing. I was working for five bucks an hour under the table, cash.

JANET GARDNER Definitely we were flat broke. I didn't know what to do. I was scouring for any kind of little demo jobs or jingles or anything that I could do to get by for another couple weeks.

SHARE ROSS At the end of the day, Kalodner wasn't interested. He wanted to try and get Lita Ford so it could become a supergroup. He changed his MO.

JANET GARDNER Ultimately, I just went home and became a normal person. Yeah, it wasn't as thrilling and as exciting and as invigorating, but I still had a pretty good life and great memories. I wouldn't trade those for anything.

"CHACHI'S BUMMING EVERYBODY OUT"

TOM KEIFER *Heartbreak Station* was kind of an effort for Cinderella to step away even more from the slick '80s production and get back to all the great music from the '70s that I grew up on, like the Stones and Zeppelin. When they made those records, they didn't go in and track all the drums in one studio with the same sound and then overdub everything from the ground up. A lot of tracks were recorded in different locations, and they all have different characters to them as a result. So that was the goal. For songs like "Shelter Me" or "Love's Got Me Doin' Time," we wanted a tighter, more '70s R&B vibe, so we did those down in Louisiana, outside of New Orleans. We also wanted that classic "Tumbling Dice" gospel background vocal on "Shelter Me," and the studio found us some local girls who were amazing. And we supplemented in the way my heroes the Stones did, where they'd bring in other players and stuff for a particular feel that they wanted. We were trying to grow the landscape and the color of the songs in a way that we weren't hip to when we made the first record.

FRED COURY It's definitely a great way to make a record, because you get the vibe of the city and you just have a good time. But it can be a little distracting. I remember that we were in Miami and we were supposed to show up at the studio at eleven in the morning or something. Jeff and I, walking on the beach to the studio, found some Jet Ski guy who was like, "Hey, you guys want to go on the Jet Ski? I don't charge you." In the ocean? Jet Ski? That could be kind of fun. We didn't show up until maybe five p.m., sunburned and so tired, like, "Oh, we've got to play?" We didn't do anything that day. I think we went to dinner.

JEFF LaBAR We record loud, and for some reason that would always put me to sleep. We had a Polaroid camera sitting around the studio, so there was a succession of pictures of me sleeping throughout the making of that record and they would write captions on them like "Jeff working out his solo for 'Heartbreak Station.'" "Jeff contemplating the world's problems." Shit like that.

JOHN JANSEN (producer, Britny Fox, Cinderella) We did part of the record in Philadelphia, and in those days, I used to seek out the best restaurants, 'cause I like food and wine. So I found this French restaurant, one of these places where if you don't come with a jacket they put a size 56 long on you. But I invited the band. I said, "You wanna go eat at this French restaurant? It'll be good, I'm buying. Just so you know, you should wear a sport jacket or something." So Jeff shows up in this black suit, and all over it, as if with a stamp, is "Fuck." It has like one hundred and twenty "Fucks" on it. And I go, "Oh great." I think they made him take it off and put another jacket on. Of course, when he went to the men's room, he still had his "Fuck" pants on.

LARRY MAZER We delivered the record, everybody loved it, and I went to the marketing meeting and I said, "Look, here's what I want to do. Because we recorded this record all over and it's got this bluesy-type feel, I want to do this party and I want to launch the record in New Orleans." So we rented a riverboat called the *Natchez* on the Mississippi River. They flew in two hundred journalists from all over the world, the party cost a quarter of a million dollars. We did a three-hour cruise and then we moored in the middle of the Mississippi and had a fireworks barge that did a fifteen-minute fireworks display that ended with the Cinderella logo being blasted into the air.

MADELYN SCARPULLA They spent a lot of money making that record and setting it up, but Cinderella could just never get over that hump into mega-sales like Bon Jovi and Def Leppard did.

LARRY MAZER For the "Shelter Me" video, we hired Jeff Stein, who had done the *Kids Are Alright* movie for the Who. He was friendly with Little Richard and got him to be in it. We also needed a girl for the scoreboard in the video, so Jeff Stein was in the bank one day and sees this gorgeous blonde and says, "Hey, I'm a video director, I'm doing this video shoot." She was like, "Oh, I'm a struggling actress. I just got my first TV show, called *Home Improvement*." He said, "Would you like to be in a video?" And she said, "Yeah." And that was Pamela Anderson. At the time she was dating Scott Baio, from *Happy Days,* and he came to the shoot to make sure nobody was gonna hit on his girlfriend. And at one point I walked up to her and said, "Hey, you know what? Chachi's bumming everybody out, can you tell him to calm the fuck down?"

TOM KEIFER "Shelter Me" came out and it was, I think, the highest-charting rock track we had in terms of crossing over to the Top 40. Usually, only ballads got over to Top 40 but the rock tracks didn't. But it didn't get that high. It crept up to like thirty-six on the pop charts.

LARRY MAZER If I could do it over again, I probably would have led with "The More Things Change" to lock in the Cinderella core audience because, looking back at it now, even though it went to number one at rock and also went on Top 40 radio, "Shelter Me" was such a departure that you could sort of feel their audience was not buying in completely. But it was still a big hit, and we booked a European tour.

ROSS HALFIN I'll tell you how they fucked up their career. They were about to be massive in England and the Gulf War broke out. They played these shows in Nottingham, London, sold out, and they were about to go to Europe and they were like, "We're going home." And I was like, "Why?" "Well, we could get bombed by Sudan." I'm like, "Sudan's going to bomb Munich?"

LARRY MAZER The tour is completely sold out—ten dates in the UK and then a full European tour. We land in England in January to start the tour and that day the Gulf War starts. So we're at Hammersmith Odeon the first night, and Tom is losing his mind 'cause then we're supposed to go to

Germany. I showed him a map and said, "Here's Kuwait, here's Europe, here's England. Scud missiles can't go that far."

Anyway, for whatever reason, the poison then starts spreading to the crew and now the crew guys are freaking out. So the morning of the second Hammersmith show, they had a band vote/crew vote and they voted to go home. I said, "Guys, this is terrible." "We don't care, we're going home." So we rented a plane, it cost us a hundred grand in cash, and we had a police escort take us to this military airfield and we flew home.

MADELYN SCARPULLA We went straight from the arena to the airport. And I remember that I had banged my knee into a ramp or something backstage when I was running to do something, and that the pressure on the plane made it swell up and almost explode out of my jeans. The stewardess kept bringing me bags of ice but nobody else seemed to care. Eric, Jeff, and Fred were against coming home, and everyone was having their own private drama about canceling the tour. It was a very morose flight.

LARRY MAZER So this was January 20, 1991. We land in Philadelphia, January 21, 1991, and the next day the Gulf War ended.

TOM KEIFER Actually, there's a bit of backstory to this: The previous time we had been in Europe, we had tickets on hold for the Pan Am 103 plane that exploded over Lockerbie, Scotland, but didn't end up using them. So terrorism was a little close to our hearts at the time. When things started feeling weird and we had military coming in with bomb dogs and all this at every show, that experience from before was in the back of our minds, and it wasn't hard to make the call. A lot of artists were coming home at the time, so I don't have any regrets over that.

LARRY MAZER Before we went to Europe, we had a meeting in my office to start planning the American tour. At that point Mötley had had the big *Girls, Girls, Girls* stage with Tommy in the cage and right away it was, "We gotta beat them." I said, "What for? You're Cinderella, they're Mötley Crüe. They need that stage to get over because they can't just rely on the songs. We can." I fought tooth and nail and I lost. Tom was like, "We gotta be big, we gotta be big."

JEFF LaBAR The thing that made the production so huge was the stage itself. Bands don't usually take their own stage. They take stuff to put on top of the stages, but arenas have their own stage. We brought our own fucking stage that took up three trucks. It was designed to look like an old porch. Like, the ego ramp stairs were all jagged and looked like old planks of wood, and our backdrops looked like a swamp with the Spanish moss hanging from them. The drum riser also was all jagged planks of wood, and behind it was a Cinderella logo that had about six hundred lights in it, I think. Or maybe it was six thousand. The logo was on hydraulics, so it could lay flat or be pushed up so the crowd could see it behind the drum riser, and it would light up and had pyro around the edges.

We all started out under the stage, and the drum riser would come up slowly as the Cinderella logo was burning into the back of the stage. And then, at the end of the intro tape, it would just be a big bang, big pyro explosions, and they'd throw us up onstage from underneath. It looked like we just appeared out of nowhere because pyro would go off right in front of each of us.

LARRY MAZER The tour started in Madison and the ticket sales were terrible. By the third show, promoters were getting killed and it was costing us a ton of money. We had a meeting and we basically sent the stage home and cut everything down.

"IT WAS LIKE, 'FA-AN-NU-NO-NU-SH-ABBA-ABBA'"

MATTHEW NELSON We were out promoting the *After the Rain* album for five months before it was even released. We went out to all these radio stations and kind of overtook their morning shows—introduced ourselves and sang and played. This was right after the whole Milli Vanilli scandal, so we were definitely guilty until proven innocent. We went out with two acoustic guitars and our voices because we had to show people we were for real.

LARRY MAZER The buzz started building in the industry. So the first thing that happened was my friend Jody Gerson, who was at EMI Publishing, said, "Hey, I want to be involved with this." And I said, "Well, I want a lot of money." She goes, "What do you want?" I said, "I want a million dollars." And she said, "*Really?*" Luckily, her boss was Charles Koppelman, who had signed Wilson Phillips to SBK Records, a subsidiary of EMI. So he's sitting there going, "Wait a minute, I have Wilson Phillips, and I can also get Nelson? This could be amazing!" So he gave me a million dollars. And then right after that, Dell Furano at Winterland Productions called and said, "Larry, I'm feeling a real buzz on this thing. We'd like to be the merchandiser." I said, "Great. I want a million-dollar advance." And he said, "You got it." So before the record even came out, I made them two million dollars.

GUNNAR NELSON I don't know how Larry Mazer did it, but he also got us on as the guest VJs on *Dial MTV* in place of Daisy Fuentes for the week before our record dropped. This is before *MTV Unplugged* or anything like that. People are not used to seeing people do shit live. We went in there with a couple of acoustics, we ripped on each other, and then we would do snippets of songs in and out of the commercial breaks. That's what did it: Geffen sold out of their first pressing of fifty thousand copies in two hours. They spent two weeks trying to catch up.

MATTHEW NELSON The directors of the "Love and Affection" video were Jim Yukich and Paul Flattery, and they had done a lot of work with Phil Collins. They came in with storyboards and said, "When we're shooting this, you're going to see snow coming down and you're going to be singing backwards. But when we reverse the film in post, the snow is going to be falling up and your mouths are going to be going in the right direction. So we're going to write out what you have to sing phonetically and you're going to have to learn it." So it was like, "*fa-an-nu-no-nu-sh-abba-abba.*" It was the weirdest thing ever.

BOBBY ROCK The directors were like, "Wait a minute, if they're playing, they've gotta be playing the shit backwards so that when we roll forward, the drumsticks will be coming off of the drums at precisely the time that the listener is hearing the drum being hit." And same with the fingers on the guitar neck and all of that. So we had to learn how to play it all backwards. When the video came out, it always cracked me up because people—especially the harder rock guys—would say, "Oh, look at these faggots." And I'd think to myself, If they only knew what we had to do. You gotta be able to really play to do that on camera. That level of musicianship is like some Frank Zappa–type shit!

GUNNAR NELSON We had very strong images, I can't say that we didn't. There's a little bit of, I guess you could call it a glam element. But we never wore makeup and we never had big hair. And where everybody else was kind of black leather and all that kind of stuff, we made a counterstatement with our fashion. It was color, it was different. And we got a lot of shit for it. But the truth is we really wanted people to pay attention. The whole thing was "Love us or hate us, here we are." We polarized and it worked.

JACK PONTI The desire to be taken serious was important to them, but they'll be the first to tell you, because they're pretty self-effacing, that their biggest mistake was allowing the image to get out of hand the way it did. I think if they have any regret, that's probably it. "Fuck, why did we let that happen?"

BOBBY ROCK The first time that we were all out in public was when we did an in-store at the Sherman Oaks Mall. The record's out, it's going through the roof. That was the first time that I saw, up close and personal, what this shit was like. I mean, girls, like, tears rolling down their faces and just hyperventilating. I think there was three thousand kids at this thing. And when they all start pushing, it's like, "Wait a minute, now. Somebody's about to get crushed." The police closed it down.

MATTHEW NELSON We did in-store autograph things that would last . . . I think our record was thirteen hours. It got to a point where I couldn't go anywhere with my brother for about a year. Because when you walk around a mall on a day off, you just look like, "Look at that loser that looks like one of the Nelsons." What are you trying to do, right? But when you go with your brother, they call the cops because you started a riot.

LARRY MAZER The week of their twenty-third birthdays, which was September 20, 1990, "Love and Affection" was number one on the *Billboard* Hot 100 chart.

MATTHEW NELSON We had the number one song in the country and nobody would take us out on tour. Like, literally nobody.

LARRY MAZER For whatever reason, none of the hair bands would take them. They thought there was a credibility issue because it was such a pop thing, with that video with the long coats and the long blond hair and the twins . . .

GUNNAR NELSON Larry came to us and said, "No one's giving you a tour. I've exhausted all my possibilities, and now you've got two options. Either you stay home, or you do it yourself. You're gonna have to spend all of your own money 'cause Geffen's already told me that they're not gonna give you any tour support. You're gonna have to spend your own publishing advance so that you can get on the road and start building your live story. Because people see the 'Love and Affection' video and they don't think it's a real live band." We decided we were gonna start with a fifty-two-date theater-headlining tour. We put the tickets out on sale and they didn't sell. We were really bummed.

MATTHEW NELSON We tried to do a headlining theater tour when "Love and Affection" was happening and we put tickets out and it didn't sell well. I said, "Look, my gut is that the first video didn't really put across the point that we're a great live band. So whatever we do for our next video, let's have a live element in it so people know that if they come to see us, they're going to see a rock show." And so when we did the "After the Rain" video there was still a concept, but the meat and potatoes was us playing live. It was actually at the old L.A. zoo—lion cages all lit up and stuff. After the video came out, we sold out forty-five cities in five minutes. So it really is the theater of the mind. People just have to know what you're selling them. It was a great tour and we had Enuff Z'Nuff as our opener. We had a lot of fun.

BOBBY ROCK That tour was insane. The only thing I can compare it to is those early films that you'd see of the Beatles where girls are just losing their minds. And what you don't get from the footage that you get when you're actually in the venue, like in front of it, is how loud it is. Like when something hits your eardrums so loud that you get that almost rattling in your eardrum or whatever it is. And it was like that every night. As soon as we were on the side of the stage the lights would go out and that shriek would happen. And it would not really let up. We had to upgrade the sound system on two different occasions through the course of that tour. Like, actually bring in more shit, more cabinets, more power and all that to get the music over the sound of the screaming.

JOEY CATHCART The configuration of the stage was such that the audience was right next to me, and I remember a girl grabbing my hair—and I had a lot of hair at that time—and she wouldn't let go. I finally had to beat her off with my fist and I felt really bad because I don't want to do that, but she was going to pull this chunk of hair out of my head. So, yeah, it was nuts. And there were all the nutty fans, you know, that think they're married to Matthew and Gunnar. I was telling our road manager, "This may seem funny to you guys, but these boys are scared because they're being told that they have made these girls pregnant and that they are aborting the babies because 'our spirit child still lives with us, Matthew, and he loves you.'"

DONNIE VIE (singer, Enuff Z'Nuff) We opened for Nelson on that tour, and it was all twelve- or thirteen-year-old little girls all dolled up like strippers and shit. We had a song called "In the Groove," and one night I decided to jump down off the lift and walk into the audience. I just got torn to shreds. I mean, handfuls of my hair ripped out and my shirt and everything gone. Almost my pants—I was holding on to my pants. That's when I used to wear one of those Sid Vicious necklaces with the lock and the dog-collar shit, and I almost got choked to death and hung. I was screaming on the mic, yelling for my bodyguard instead of singing the words. *"Ahh! Help me!"*

BOBBY ROCK You could, at any given time, just crack your hotel room door open six inches, peer out in the hallway, and just wait. One minute, two minutes, three minutes, whatever, and there would be different girls in twos or threes, just roaming up and down the halls, trying to see if they could figure out which rooms we were in. And at that point, it was just "Hey, what're you guys doin'? Wanna come hang?" Boom.

LARRY MAZER It was tough being married, managing that band. As tough as it was managing Kiss during that period, with Nelson it was like *Penthouse,* you know? It was like a *Penthouse* magazine show every day of the week. And those guys, they took advantage of it, let me tell you.

JACK PONTI One of Gunnar's greatest moments was when he was engaged, and he comes off the tour on Christmas Eve and his girlfriend picks him up. They're driving to her parents' house and she nonchalantly says to him, "Gunnar, did you ever cheat on me on tour?" And Gunnar goes, "Yep." Just like that! Now there's complete silence till they get to her parents' house. She goes crazy, Gunnar runs upstairs, and he's locked in the bedroom. He calls me up and goes, "Dude . . . help me!" I said, "What did you admit it for?" And he goes, "Well, she asked."

GUNNAR NELSON I think we had already sold like five million records, and Larry had us go out with Cinderella, who he also managed. He told us, "Look, you know, no one takes you seriously, they don't think you're rock, it's gonna be great for your career," *yada yada yada*. What he didn't tell us is that we were gonna have to basically change everything about ourselves just to be able to survive out there. You know, we'd have to go out there and we'd have to rock and we'd have to be tough and we'd have to be doing all this stuff. So we went from an audience full of chicks that came to see just us and loved us unconditionally to Cinderella's audience, who were mostly dudes that wanted to fucking kill us.

MATTHEW NELSON The other band on the bill was Lynch Mob, and I remember George Lynch walking up to me on day one and me doing the whole, "Hey, I'm a huge fan of yours, George." And he said, "Fuck you. I'm not getting tour support because you motherfuckers are on the tour." And then he walked away. I thought, Well, that didn't go well . . .

ROSS HALFIN Tom Keifer from Cinderella said to me, "I'll give you $200 if you ask Nelson if they're gay." I was on the Nelson bus and I said, "Which one's the queer one?" And they're like, "What?" I said, "One of you's a homosexual, right?" And they were like, "Keep this guy away from us!" Keifer was like crying laughing. He had a great sense of humor.

LARRY MAZER The Cinderella tour wasn't that long because it was not doing great business. I booked another month's worth of dates, they didn't do great, they did okay. We did Radio City, and it was two-thirds full. It wasn't the same. For whatever reason, the heat was off.

GUNNAR NELSON I needed a break. I wasted down to 119 pounds. I mean, we would run the equivalent of six miles a night onstage. I'd been doing it for over a year, my hair was bleached absolutely shock white from the lights above us.

MATTHEW NELSON We were almost six feet tall and I was 123 pounds. We were emaciated. My poor brother was having tons of problems, emotional problems, vocal problems. It turned out his voice doctor had put him on some pills to help with his throat, which happened to be uppers. I remember I literally had to pull him off of a ledge because he wanted to jump out of a hotel window when we were on tour. He was so freaked out. He said, "I can't take it anymore." He was just fried out.

67

"YOU'RE GONNA LOSE HALF YOUR AUDIENCE"

SEBASTIAN BACH After the success of *Skid Row* we felt freedom. I was fucking twenty-one, I had bought an incredible house, and I had all these platinum records from the first album on my wall. I said to myself, "Hey dude, now you've got to do that again!" It was like, "I'm not losing my fucking house. I want more platinum records!"

SCOTTI HILL There was a lot of anticipation for *Slave to the Grind*.

SEBASTIAN BACH "Youth Gone Wild" was a hit song, and "Piece of Me" was a video hit on MTV, but our giant smash hits were "18 and Life" and "I Remember You." Which . . . we considered them ballads. We were young and full of piss and vinegar, and we didn't want to be known as a ballad band. So we went as heavy as we could for the next record.

DAVE "SNAKE" SABO I remember Jason Flom saying to me about *Slave to the Grind*, "It's one of my favorite albums ever. But you're gonna lose half your audience." And I was like, "What?" He goes, "I'm not telling you that you should write one, but there's not an 'I Remember You' on there. So you're gonna lose a lot of the females."

JASON FLOM That first album was obviously great. And the second one was even better. Although ultimately it didn't sell as well because it didn't really have songs for girls.

SEBASTIAN BACH I remember walking into Atlantic the week before *Slave to the Grind* came out, and I went to Ahmet Ertegun's office. He goes, "Hey, Sebastian! It sure looks like we're going to sell a lot of copies . . ." I say, "Yeah." He goes, "The first week, anyways."

SCOTTI HILL People were anticipating it, so everybody got it as soon as it came out. And there it was: number one. I wasn't expecting that. It was an awesome feeling. I remember waking up in a hotel and having our tour manager come in, going, "*Slave to the Grind* is the number one album on *Billboard*." It was like, "Holy shit!"

RACHEL BOLAN The beginning of the *Slave to the Grind* tour is when we went out with Guns N' Roses on their *Use Your Illusion* tour. And neither of our albums were out yet. I was never really a Guns fan but I had fun on that tour.

DUFF McKAGAN They'd just done that second record and it was a little harder, right? Like, "Monkey Business" and all that stuff. I think they wanted to get out from under the shadow of Jon Bon Jovi. So they were going through their own thing. And they were good guys. Baz is hilarious. They were fun to tour with.

SEBASTIAN BACH Was there ever a moment when we pushed it too far? The first thing that comes to mind is the night that we played with Guns in Toronto, at CNE [Grandstand]. We had to drive back to America after, and we had so much blow that we had to fucking do it all. I'm not going to tell you who did it with me, but we were on the bus, we get near the Canadian border and we still have so much that we have to throw it out. But we don't want to throw it out. So we went to a go-kart track. And I was so fucking high that I thought it would be a good idea to go in the opposite direction from everybody else on the track. I thought that would be hilarious. So I was flooring my go-kart with parents with their kids coming the opposite way. At, like, eleven in the morning. That was a moment that I never repeated in my life and never will. But that was a moment.

RACHEL BOLAN Izzy Stradlin was there for most of the tour. He wasn't there for the whole time we were out though, 'cause Gilby [Clarke] came in at some point. But Izzy was clean. I remember when we played in Toronto, it was an outdoor gig, and he had his own bus with a trailer filled with different BMX bikes and stuff.

SCOTTI HILL He had go-karts, dune buggies, motorcycles, all kinds of shit.

RACHEL BOLAN I walked by him and he was washing this trials bike that he must have been riding somewhere earlier that day. I was fascinated by those things. So I went up to him, like, "Dude, you've got a trials bike!"

DUFF McKAGAN He entered some trials contest in Kentucky and won. He was doing all kinds of cool shit.

RACHEL BOLAN And Izzy was the quiet guy. He never really hung. But we got to talking, and we talked for about an hour. Very cool. Then I go into the dressing room later and I see Duff and I'm like, "Izzy's a really cool dude! We talked for an hour." Duff looks at me and asks, "How long?" "Like an hour." And he goes, "Dude, I don't think over the past year Izzy has talked to us collectively as a band for an hour!"

ALAN NIVEN Izzy went through a terrible period of cocaine excess. Tin foil went up on the windows. He triple-locked his door. He wouldn't talk to anybody. He wouldn't come out. What's that saying about the road of excess? It leads to the palace of wisdom? That's if you don't end up in the fucking ditch on the fucking way. And believe you me, vehicles left the road quite frequently. But Izzy found wisdom. He got sober.

SCOTTI HILL We were at the St. Louis show for the riot. That was fucking crazy.

RACHEL BOLAN We were backstage and we heard Guns stop playing. But you couldn't really hear anything going on yet. Then their tour manager came in and he tapped me on the shoulder and he said, "Get your guys, get on your bus, and get the fuck out of here." And I'm thinking, "Oh, no. What did somebody say?" But he had a look of urgency on his face and he goes, "Do it now!" The buses were already started.

SCOTTI HILL Our bus was actually moving when I jumped on. The door was open and we were all jumping in while it was rolling. Got a quick head count and then, *boom!* Pedal to the metal.

RACHEL BOLAN We're peeling out and we see just cop car after cop car coming in the other direction. Then we're on the highway and I look out the windshield of our bus and I go, "Is that Izzy's bus in front of us?" 'Cause I saw the trailer with all the motocross stickers on it. And the bus driver goes, "Yeah."

SCOTTI HILL I think we drove to Illinois—the next gig might have been there. We checked in to a hotel and went to sleep. We turned on CNN the next morning and it was like, "Holy fuck!"

RACHEL BOLAN CNN's showing a map of the United States and then it zooms in on Missouri. And over St. Louis it has, like, a cartoon explosion. A *kapow!* type of thing. And it says, RIOT AT GUNS N' ROSES CONCERT.

SKY MAGAZINE, SEPTEMBER 1991 *At a St. Louis stadium Axl Rose jumped into the audience to snatch a camera from a fan, sparking off a riot that caused $200,000 worth of damage and injured more than 60 people.*

ROB AFFUSO Things started to spiral out of control with us when we were touring with Guns N' Roses and Sebastian started hanging out with Axl. Sebastian would watch Axl and listen to his words and, you know, one day he comes into rehearsal and it's, "Well, this ain't a fucking song until I say it's a song!" Guess where he heard that from? But the thing you have to remember is, Axl Rose owns Guns N' Roses, right? Sebastian Bach did not own Skid Row. He's one-fifth of the team.

LONN FRIEND (editor, *RIP* magazine; journalist; author, *Life on Planet Rock, Sweet Demotion*) Sebastian called my office during *Slave to the Grind* and he said, "Dude, I wanna be on the cover of *RIP* holding a broken bottle." And I said, "Okay." He wanted to be shot that way because he believed they had made a truly heavy record and he didn't want a pinup photo on the cover. I went, "I can accommodate that sensibility."

SCOTTI HILL I can remember doing a *RIP* magazine photo shoot in L.A. and Lonn put on the *Nevermind* record. I don't think any of us had heard Nirvana. Maybe Rachel had. I was like, "Wow, this is fucking cool!" Didn't think anything of it and went on with life after that.

LONN FRIEND I said, "I want you guys to listen to this fuckin' record." And Sebastian lost his mind. He goes, "We gotta take these guys out on tour with us!"

DAVE "SNAKE" SABO We reached out to Nirvana to tour with us after the Guns N' Roses tour. And they declined because they said that we were homophobic. True story.

DANNY GOLDBERG (manager, Nirvana) I don't remember Kurt saying anything about Skid Row, or the name ever coming up. I definitely remember him talking about Axl Rose. But you know, I'm sure he wouldn't have opened for somebody who made an anti-gay statement.

DAVE "SNAKE" SABO This was before we got Pantera.

SCOTTI HILL I remember one particular day we were on a tour break and I was painting my kitchen and listening to WSOU. And "Cowboys from Hell" came on. I had never heard Pantera before. And I was like, "What the fuck is this? This is nuts." I came back to the band and told them about it: "Listen to this. These fucking guys are incredible." One thing led to another and we wound up touring together.

SEBASTIAN BACH At the time when we hired Pantera it wasn't like we were throwing down the gauntlet. They were unknown. We hadn't even seen them live. Their album *Vulgar Display of Power* didn't come out until about a month into the tour.

DAVE "SNAKE" SABO I think it was pretty amazing that Dime ["Dimebag" Darrell, Pantera guitarist] and Phil [Anselmo, Pantera singer] and those guys even agreed to go out on the road with us. Because most people perceived us as a hair band. We got away from that a little bit with the Guns N' Roses tour and the *Slave to the Grind* record, but you don't know if people's opinions are really changed or not.

SCOTTI HILL And the partying with those guys was another level. People would say, "Didn't you get bad hangovers?" But after a while it's like, your whole life is a bad hangover.

DAVE "SNAKE" SABO You'd be up until five in the morning drinking Black Tooth Grins [Crown Royal and Seagram's 7 with Coke] and everything that you could get your hands on. I remember one night in the Midwest we came back to our shitty motel and Dime's door is open and him and Vinnie [Paul, Pantera drummer] and the guys have chicken wire and papier-mâché all over the place. The room is completely ruined. They're making these giant pot leafs, five or six feet high, and the plan is they're gonna wheel these things out onstage on dollies. And then Phil's gonna have a joint that's, like, three feet long, with a smoke bomb at the end of it so it's billowing out smoke. And they did it! It was the fucking funniest thing.

SEBASTIAN BACH Some nights they were very, very hard to follow. But they were one of the first great bands of the '90s and so it was cool to watch them get big right before our eyes.

DAVE "SNAKE" SABO A lot of our fans got eaten up along the way. A lot of those young girls that were standing there in front of the stage waiting for Sebastian to come out were shocked when they had to sit through Pantera—and the mosh pit that came along with them. The general admission shows were fucking crazy.

RACHEL BOLAN And our demographic changed drastically. We went probably from 65 percent women at the shows to, like, 35 percent.

PART VI

SHUT UP, BEAVIS

It's become a rock history truism that grunge killed hair metal. But did it? Really?

One thing's for sure, even if an argument can be made—and it has been, many, many times—for grunge as the proverbial nail in the '80s hard rock coffin, it was only one factor that helped seal the genre's fate. As many of the style's artists and industry players attest to in these very pages, the writing was already on the (bathroom) wall well before Kurt Cobain popped up on MTV in a tattered puke-green-and-brown tee and declared, "Here we are now."

Some of the rot, it's worth noting, came from within. A headline in the July 2, 1989, edition of the *Los Angeles Times* screamed GN'R SOUND-ALIKES DRAIN THE SCENE ALONG SUNSET.

"Nobody was really coming up with anything valuable at the end," Tracii Guns says of the acts that flooded the scene in its final days. "It was just, 'This is what's happening so this is what we're gonna do.'"

At the same time, the industry was gorging itself on hard rock to the point of bursting. "By the end of the decade every label had five to twenty hair metal bands," says A&R man Bret Hartman. "It was just overkill as far as what people could buy and what could get on the radio and what could get on MTV."

He continues, "In '89 and '90, MCA hired four or five A&R guys and told us each to sign three bands. So there's like fifteen bands we're putting out in a year and a half. And that's every label. So you had Extreme over here, Living Colour over there. Guy Mann-Dude and Steelheart and Spread Eagle. And then you had all your existing bands, like Mötley Crüe and Poison and Bon Jovi and Ratt and W.A.S.P. and Y&T . . . There were just so many acts."

What's more, some of those existing bands were now hobbled by a degree of internal dysfunction that proved fatal to their careers—and in a few instances, to band members themselves.

And what to make of the case of poor Winger? Lars Ulrich may have landed the first blow to the band's cred when he was shown using a picture of Kip Winger as a dartboard in Metallica's video for the song "Nothing Else Matters." But who would have guessed that the knockout punch would come from a cartoon character, namely the whiny, bed-wetting loser Stewart in the hit MTV show *Beavis and Butt-Head*, a walking punchline who was always depicted wearing a Winger T-shirt?

"We were the best band to pick on," acknowledges Winger guitarist Reb Beach. "I mean, if I were to choose I would've picked on us, too. Because we were professing to be excellent musicians, and yet we were up there as *froofy* as could be."

"People had enough of the hairspray and the big hair and the spandex," Don Dokken says simply. "They had enough. And then grunge came in, and it was the antithesis of Mötley Crüe."

And so, perhaps, the death of the scene was less the result of a coordinated attack from the Northwest than a matter of recognizing that, as the Crüe themselves once sang, it was "time for change."

Jerry Cantrell, whose band, Alice in Chains, is recognized as one of those responsible for the carnage, concurs. "I don't think anything really killed anything else," he says. "And it doesn't make me feel good to be used as an example for killing something or stopping somebody's career, because I don't think we did that.

"You're only shiny and new once, and then it's on to the next thing," Cantrell reasons. "It happened to us, too. And that's totally okay. That's the way it's fucking supposed to be."

68

"38 GUNS N' ROSES, 20 RATTS, 14 WARRANTS . . ."

STEVIE RACHELLE By the late '80s I think bands started running out of names. You had Bang Tango and Bang Gang and Dangerous Toys and Electric Boys and Pretty Boy Floyd. There were multiple Wild Sides, there was Paradise and Pair-A-Dice. I remember it got to the point where bands had to start using, you know Queeny Blast Pop and Juicy Miss Lucy and Back Alley Sally—the names got longer because all the one-word names and two-word names were taken. Then you had David Lee Roth and Vince Neil and Bret Michaels and Jani Lane and now Ted Poley and Stevie Rachelle and Drew Hannah . . . another blond singer with a headband on. It just became saturated. And the Strip was even worse. Whatever you saw on *Headbangers Ball* or in *Metal Edge,* there were *hundreds* of those bands in Hollywood.

OZZY OSBOURNE Every band, the singer had blond hair and the band had dark hair, it was kind of like a uniform.

TRACII GUNS I remember going to see friends' bands and being like, "Man, you guys are just like Poison. You guys are like this weird Junkyard-meets-Jetboy." Where if you really look at Junkyard and Jetboy and Faster and L.A. Guns and Guns N' Roses, it was like, "We all love Mötley Crüe, but we love this other stuff, too." It was this crossbreeding thing and adding a new angle to it, whereas at the end nobody was really adding a new angle. But even Pretty Boy Floyd had a song I liked. A ballad. But it was too late.

RIKKI ROCKETT It was kinda like, "No, this nest is full. We don't need more of that."

RON KEEL How much spaghetti can you possibly eat in a week? The fans had enough. They're gonna go pick something else off the menu.

JACK RUSSELL All of a sudden you have 38 Guns N' Roses, 20 Ratts, 14 Warrants, 12 Great Whites . . . It was like, "Come on, really?" And it was a carbon copy, you know? Lesser and lesser than the original. And then the bottom fell out.

RON KEEL The emphasis was put on two things: fashion and sex. Everybody called it cock rock, right? It's about how promiscuous you can be and how many conquests you can notch on your barrel. Well, all of a sudden in the mid-'80s sex became deadly because AIDS was a huge epidemic. All of a sudden you sing about that, you're an idiot! Why would you wanna go out and screw six chicks a night and your odds of dying increase exponentially? Everybody loves sex, everybody wants sex, everybody needs sex, but you gotta sing about real life, love, heartbreak, drinkin' beer . . . You just can't sing about "Bang Bang," "Let's Put the X in Sex," the list goes on.

CLIFF BURNSTEIN If you were a little intelligent at that point, you would go, "God, this stuff is absolute shit!" How much makeup, how big can the hair get, how many scantily clad young girls are going to be hanging around . . . What does this have to do with the music that I really like?

RUDOLF SCHENKER Longer hair, more colorful stage clothes. Left arm a girl, right arm a girl, great cars. Guitar player playing faster than hell. Everything was too flashy. And also us, we were a little bit overdressed.

OZZY OSBOURNE In the mid-'80s I said to Sharon, "This is gonna last forever." And she said, "Wait until 1990."

JAMES LoMENZO I could see the writing on the wall for any number of reasons. Our relationship with MTV—I could see they were struggling to figure out how to keep us in there.

LONN FRIEND MTV, they just stuck a knife in it. Because they couldn't get the exposure anymore. Just a year or two before, the Top 10 *Billboard* charts were Scorpions and Def Leppard and Whitesnake... All those bands were ruling the charts, selling millions of albums. Then, you know, it's gone.

RICK KRIM We had the thing called "Buzz Bin" or "Buzz Clip"—it was called different things in different years—where we'd pick a video each week to really put our stamp of approval on and get behind. And there was a week where it was either going to be Thunder or Alice in Chains.

JAY JAY FRENCH Thunder were on Geffen—that was the latest hair band jet that was supposed to take off. Album cost a million bucks. Band looked perfectly coiffed. Everything was ready to go.

RICK KRIM We were looking at that and Alice in Chains' "Man in the Box," which came before "Smells Like Teen Spirit." And we decided as a group, and I literally remember this meeting, it was a very intense discussion, and we decided we're going to go with "Man in the Box." I think that was the changing of the guard right there. We were like, "There's been enough, we've done our thing, we recognize this new thing coming." It just felt like it was time. We've got to keep the train moving forward.

JERRY CANTRELL You know, I get the slant. And the slant is "That shit needed to be killed. 'Cause it was fucking stupid." And like, I'm not gonna say that, you know? And I'm not gonna say that we were so much cooler and that's why we fucking took over. I don't think anybody had some big master plan of how it was gonna go. It just kind of organically did. It was a cultural shift.

KIM THAYIL We were never motivated to damage another genre. We were motivated to advance ourselves.

HEIDI MARGOT RICHMAN Peter Fletcher was the product manager at Columbia for both Warrant and Alice in Chains. So I get this phone call from him one day and he says, "I have an interesting request for you . . . but it pays well." He said, "Layne Staley [Alice in Chains lead singer] is obsessed with the costumes for Warrant and the costuming in general for the 'Heaven' video, and he's especially obsessed with the Joey costume. Can you re-create the Joey jacket?"

STEVE BROWN I thought it was kind of sad the way that a lot of the grunge bands turned on us. Because all those bands—let's not forget, Pantera, Alice in Chains—all those guys were hair metal, hard rock bands. They were all Van Halen, Def Leppard fans, you know? Alice in Chains opened up for Poison. The same time that we were out, they came out after Trixter on the Poison tour in '91. So it was kind of funny how all the bands kind of changed their tune a little bit. I was like, "Dude, a couple months ago you were pounding beers in our dressing room. Now you're slagging us in the press?"

JERRY CANTRELL We always had the attitude that we would play with anybody. I just wanted to get on a fucking stage. I didn't care if it was with fucking Poison or Warrant or Iggy Pop or fucking Slayer and Megadeth. Whatever.

BRET MICHAELS I was the sole instigator of calling and getting Alice in Chains to play a bunch of Northwest dates with us. This was '91. They came onstage and we did a Kiss song together. "Rock and Roll All Nite." It was amazing.

KIM THAYIL I remember [Green River, Mother Love Bone, and Pearl Jam bassist] Jeff Ament was really into that first Poison album. He turned us on to that.

JERRY CANTRELL We opened for Helix and fucking Extreme. And fucking Great White for god's sake. We got signed fucking opening up for Great White on a fucking racetrack out in fucking eastern Washington.

LARRY MAZER I went to a meeting at DGC Records, and in every office in every department it was advance cassettes of the Nirvana album playing. All they wanted to talk about was Nirvana.

MATTHEW NELSON I was in the parking lot of Geffen Records on my way in to have a meeting about our next record, and Tony Bird, an A&R guy there that was big with the whole Seattle thing saw me and said, "What, you're still here?"

DANNY GOLDBERG Axl Rose apparently had heard the *Nevermind* tape, and he wore a Nirvana hat in a Guns N' Roses video.

JIM MERLIS (publicist, Geffen Records) Lisa Gladfelter, Nirvana's first publicist at their label, had worked with hair metal bands, so she brought them to the people she knew.

KATHERINE TURMAN She sent me the advance cassette of *Nevermind*. And she's like, "I don't know what this is, but I think it's gonna be big."

LONN FRIEND Nirvana came to my office at *RIP* and I had all these pictures on my wall. One of them was me pinching Metallica's butts at the . . . *And Justice for All* photo sessions. And another one was Alice Cooper and me in a bathtub. Oh, and there's a Queensrÿche photo that Ross Halfin insisted on taking of me naked just wearing a towel with Chris DeGarmo and Geoff Tate. So there were a lot of pictures. And Kurt apparently fixated on these *Hustler* kind of images. Even though Dave [Grohl, Nirvana drummer] and Krist [Novoselic, Nirvana bassist] had a great time at that lunch, Kurt didn't get me, he didn't get my vibe, he thought I was kind of a clown.

NEIL ZLOZOWER I was asked to shoot Nirvana once. I had to bring my gear backstage at the L.A. Sports Arena. I probably brought four hundred dollars' worth of film. I get to the gig and I look around to see what I could do within the parameters and the boundaries of what I was given to work with. Kurt comes out and I'm like, "Oh, hey, Kurt, how's it going? Look, I just want to let you know I'm really fast and painless, I've been doing this for twenty, twenty-five years. So look, we're gonna shoot here, then we're going to move ten feet over here, then we're going to move ten feet over there . . ." And now all of the sudden he's like, "*Gidodo gadagideo dooda gagaga.*" I'm like, "What the fuck planet is this guy on?"

So then the other guys come out and we get to the first location. We start shooting. And they're just sitting there talking to each other. The tall guy, he's turned around looking at Kurt and Dave, and he's talking to them so I get the back of his head. So I'm like, "Guys, look here." They were ignoring me. I pop off a frame and the guys are still talking. So I pop off another frame. Then I'm like, "Guys come on. Look in the lens." And this is my big-format Mamiya camera, which is only ten shots on a roll. Finally, they look at me for about three or four shots and then they start talking to each other again. So after literally ten shots, I was like, This ain't fucking happening. Fuck this shit. I say, "Okay, guys. We're done." And they look at me like, "We're done?" I'm like, "Yeah. See you guys in the next world. Bye, bye! Adios! Nice knowing you." And I just packed up and left.

ROSS HALFIN When Nirvana came along, someone played me "Teen Spirit." I started laughing. I thought it was fucking rubbish.

BRIAN BAKER I remember very clearly when I heard "Smells Like Teen Spirit" for the first time. I was in my car at Vine and Hollywood Boulevard. I just had an AM/FM radio and I heard it and I immediately knew that this was a whole new thing that was going to be huge. I really was blown away by how great it was. The elements were just all perfect and they sounded like everything, if that makes any sense.

HOWARD BENSON I remember that day, too. I remember exactly where I was—in the studio with Little Caesar. I turned on MTV and I saw the video for "Smells Like Teen Spirit" and all I thought was, I'm so fucked.

I knew we were screwed. And it was sort of like, as a producer, there's nothing you can do.

MICHAEL WAGENER When I heard "Smells Like Teen Spirit" I went, "Shit, that's a great song." It was noisy and it wasn't played that well and it was not in tune that well, but I knew that it was a great song and that it was going to have a big influence. And it did. I got out of audio for a while.

69

"WE SAID, 'FUCK IT,' AND HUNG IT UP"

BRAD TOLINSKI Grunge didn't kill all of the hair metal bands. Some of them did it to themselves.

VITO BRATTA It always cracks me up when people say that Nirvana killed us. As a matter of fact, I'm going to look it up, 'cause I want to give you the right dates here. Okay: "*Nevermind* is the second studio album by American rock band Nirvana, released on September twenty-fourth, 1991." And White Lion broke up on September third.

JAMES LoMENZO It was becoming apparent that White Lion needed to be bigger and wiser and more pop-oriented for our next record. Richie Zito had produced those Heart and Cheap Trick records at the time and given them a second life. Especially after *Big Game*, we needed something to put us in that pantheon. It was time to start moving, and that was where Richie Zito came in.

VITO BRATTA I'm like, "This is gonna be a huge thing for us." And then it was actually our worst record.

MIKE TRAMP Somehow the day "Broken Heart" got released as a single, half of Atlantic's promotion department went on vacation. The song died, and the video died. Then we come into New York and we play a sold-out show at the new Ritz, but nobody from the record company showed up. Actually, I think Jason Flom was there, but he was hanging out more like just doing these stupid Italian jokes with Vito. "Yeah, *wassup?*" The next day while we were still in New York I went up to Atlantic Records and asked for Doug Morris. The secretary didn't know who I was so she said, "I don't think he's available." And I said, "You tell him Sebastian Bach is here." Doug Morris came out and I turned around and walked out.

JAMES LoMENZO We finished the *Mane Attraction* tour in Europe and we were going to continue in the States. I essentially told the guys, "You know, we've got to make this more equitable. And I think we should do that with our drummer as well. If that can be accomplished, then I have an incentive to keep going." And a decision was made, and basically it was like, "Well, we'll take care of one of you, but not the other." I decided I'd had enough of doing it.

MIKE TRAMP They want to renegotiate and Vito just says no.

GREG D'ANGELO It always comes down to money.

VITO BRATTA The mistake that we made is that we should have went on a hiatus instead of just saying, "Okay, we're broken up and that's it. I never want to see you again."

MIKE TRAMP Two nights later we were playing at an amusement park up in Boston or Rhode Island, and the power cut off and Vito and I are standing behind the stage. And somehow I just reached out and said to Vito, "Vito, it's the final show. I'm calling it off." Vito just said, "Okay." And we did not speak about this for almost twenty years.

ERIK TURNER I think on the first two Warrant records we got a lot of love from the fans, but Jani didn't get a lot of love or respect from his peers. And so when it came time to do *Dog Eat Dog* in 1992, he wanted to write a record that his peers would find undeniable. "Hey, I'm a songwriter. I can write great songs that aren't all about chicks and stuff like that." He started listening to bands like Mother Love Bone around that time as well. So maybe he saw something coming that the rest of us didn't.

JOEY ALLEN There were a bunch of songs that he had written for the third record which were poppier. One of them was called "Pop Music." That could have been another "Cherry Pie" for certain because it was that type of song, but we sabotaged it in the studio because the rest of the music was so dark and different for Warrant. In hindsight maybe we should have kept with the formula we had and done *Cherry Pie 2*. Who knows.

MICHAEL WAGENER *Dog Eat Dog* was a great record and it didn't get what it deserved because it got pushed aside. We just made the record *they* always wanted to make, because they were forced a little bit to make more poppy records than they would have.

JOEY ALLEN For *Dog Eat Dog* we got offered tours from a lot of different bands and I know Kiss was one of them, but we opted to go out on our own. The tour went from, like, four semis and arenas down to two semis and theaters pretty rapidly. And by the time we rolled around to the Carolinas, Jani's drinking had gotten pretty heavy. And at the time Vince Neil had just left Mötley and gotten a big advance from Warner Bros. to do a solo record. His wife back then, Sharise, and Bobbie Brown were hanging out quite a bit. Jani said he got sick and said he had to go to a doctor and have his voice looked at, but instead of going back to L.A. to look at his voice he went down to Baton Rouge to hang out with his wife and party. Then we all rode the bus from North Carolina down to Dallas and got on a plane to go home, thinking that our boy was at home being seen by a doctor.

Well, the next day we went in, met with our manager, and he told us that Jani wanted to leave the band and do a solo run. Some of us were starting families, and we had a huge merchandising contract that we had all gotten big advances from that we needed to play thirty-five more shows to fulfill, and the company turned around and sued us. Then Columbia dropped us. They had record number four coming up and they had a huge advance they were gonna have to pay us millions of dollars for.

We could've gone in, made it for about half, and put the rest of the money in our pockets. But Jani bailed, and then he turned around and called Columbia and said, "Hey, I wanna do a solo record." But he had pissed them off so bad that they said, "We're not interested."

JERRY DIXON I think I was twenty-five?

LARRY MAZER *Heartbreak Station* limped to a million sales and then I said, "Well, look, let's put out 'The More Things Change' and recapture the pure Cinderella." But at that point Nirvana was smoking and it was like . . . What could you do? Then to put us into complete blackness, Tom calls me and goes, "I can't sing."

TOM KEIFER The voice problem started overnight. And unbeknownst to me at the time, it had nothing to do with singing or the touring schedule. I never really studied voice but I was using it properly. They say it's important if you're gonna scream that you scream properly. I had figured that out, because we were playing night after night. And ultimately what it ended up being was a neurological problem: I had a partial paralysis of my left vocal cord, which can be caused by flu or common cold viruses lodging themselves in the nerve that controls that vocal cord, and it just degenerates. It can also be caused by general anesthesia if you have surgery. I was told I would never sing again.

LARRY MAZER It took Tom three years to get his voice back, and then we made *Still Climbing*, which has some really good Cinderella songs but isn't the album that the others were as far as beginning to end. But at that point, it was obvious that the train had left the station, so to speak.

JEFF LaBAR I really like that record and I think it's our best-sounding one. It was sort of wasted at the time that we put it out.

ERIC BRITTINGHAM The *Still Climbing* tour, which was in 1995, was a disaster. We were playing to, like, nobody. It was the height of the grunge era. When we played Seattle, the radio station was so anti-'80s that it would not even sell advertising to us for our show. It was crazy. I think that we played to, like, fifty people. We had some good shows, but they were few and far between, so when it was over, the label dropped us and we said, "Fuck it," and hung it up.

ROB AFFUSO When *Subhuman Race* came out in 1995 Skid Row started touring and we didn't have the support. We had been the darlings of Atlantic Records, we were the priority band for years and years, and all of a sudden we weren't. Hootie and the Blowfish were. If we weren't fighting amongst ourselves, I think there may have been a much better chance to survive that and keep moving on.

SCOTTI HILL At that point there was just a lot of bad energy between Baz and the rest of us.

RACHEL BOLAN The hill got too big to climb. And it was the musical climate that really was the final nail. We weren't having fun with each other anymore, we were doing shitty tours, people just weren't accepting us.

SCOTTI HILL We showed up that first day of the *Subhuman Race* tour and we had to cut our budget. We went from a really nice bus to a really shit bus. I remember showing up to the hotel and there are homeless people in the lobby. I was like, "Whoa, this is different . . ." A few steps backwards. And those shows were really, really poorly attended. The shows in the States, there was nobody there.

SEBASTIAN BACH I can just tell you that we tried to play bigger venues at the start of that tour and we didn't sell them out, so we moved to smaller venues but we sold those out. We sold out, what the fuck is the place in Hollywood? The Palladium. It was packed. It was fucking outstanding. So we did very well at mid-level places all over the world. But to be honest with you, by the time the *Subhuman Race* tour was over I was exhausted.

SCOTTI HILL Everybody's not getting along at this point. Everybody's got their ideas of what they wanna do. And then all of a sudden there's no audience for it anymore and you're fucking miserable. Why go on?

RACHEL BOLAN And then that phone call happened and Snake was like, "I'm done with this shit."

DAVE "SNAKE" SABO It was Christmas and I had a family gathering at my house. The phone rings and I let the machine pick it up. And there was just this rant from Sebastian that was so expletive-filled and demeaning. It was a man who sounded like he was losing his mind. I could see the look in my family's eyes, like, What was *that*? You know? "Don't worry about it! It's all good!" I got up and I called Doc, I called Rachel. And I said, "I'm not playing in a band with that guy again."

SCOTTI HILL This was over some sort of offer to tour with Kiss [which Bach wanted to do but the band ultimately declined]. So when Baz called Snake's house that day and left a message on his answering machine, his family's sitting at the table and he's got this guy just fucking cursing up and down, calling him every name in the book. That ridiculous verbal abuse was just the last straw for Snake.

RACHEL BOLAN It wasn't a Kiss tour. It was a Kiss *show*. But there was really no point in doing it, you know? Me personally, Kiss was one of my all-time favorite bands, and I could have driven there and driven home that night. But I just didn't care. But to this day I don't regret that decision at all. I always said, "If I'm not having fun I'm not gonna fucking do it." If it becomes a job that I wanna quit? I'm gonna fucking quit.

ROB AFFUSO Basically Snake got us all together, said, "Well, Rachel and I were talking and we just feel we really don't want to go on with Sebastian and we think it's time that we kick him out of the band. Let's take a vote." I mean it's kinda silly taking a vote with four people, but I was the only one that didn't want him out of the band. Even though he and I were the ones that fought the most.

SCOTTI HILL I think it was three years maybe that I sat at home and didn't do anything. I played with guitars, I bought a bit of recording equipment. But aside from that, nothing. You're just kind of shell-shocked from the whole experience. Rising and falling. And when we fell, man, we fell fast and hard. As most bands did in those days.

SEBASTIAN BACH I kind of turned the phone off and enjoyed time with my family at my big, gigantic house. I was okay. I just didn't really pay attention. I've always been good at compartmentalization.

SCOTTI HILL We got back together [in 1999] with [new singer] Johnny Solinger . . . and did a Kiss tour.

RACHEL BOLAN Pretty ironic. But it was awesome!

STEPHEN PEARCY Everything was way copacetic with Ratt until, like, '87. Then everything got a little weird. And I can't blame it on our addictions. We were led around, we had to do an eight-month, nine-month tour, two hundred and forty dates a year, and then have, what, a couple weeks off and go in and start writing a new record. And when we got in the studio, Beau Hill was just cracking that whip, man. *Crack crack crack*. Then it was back out on the road. And it got to be longer and longer. Then we started getting introduced to other drugs and situations and things, to just kind of deal with the stress and shit. Everybody was at fault, depending on what chemical they were into.

WARREN DeMARTINI I think in our case it was just the direction of the business—is the glass half-empty or half-full kind of stuff. I really think it was stuff like that because creatively, you know, I think we were doing good work. It was the other twenty-three hours where we couldn't really seem to manage.

STEPHEN PEARCY It was pretty much just beating ourselves up and nobody really making sure we had rest. There was no rest for the wicked, man. We'd be a mess when we got back from tour.

MARSHALL BERLE When Robbin [Crosby] got sick and things sort of went sideways, that was the end of that. It ended. It was a period of time and it's not there anymore. I've seen it before.

NEIL ZLOZOWER I knew Robbin liked doing junk, but he always seemed to be in control. It wasn't like he was always dozing off or anything like that.

WARREN DeMARTINI The whole *Detonator* recording process in 1990 and then the video process was when it was clear that this was not something Robbin could handle anymore. And with Robbin, and I think with that kind of thing in general, like, people get pretty good at hiding it for a long time, you know, and then they have a harder time continuing to hide it.

BEAU HILL If somebody is a junkie from the first day you meet them, then that sort of establishes the baseline. My understanding is that Robbin was using when I met him.

WARREN DeMARTINI So by the time we were recording *Detonator* and doing the videos it was at that point where, you know, like, he's not supposed to be doing this, but he wasn't able to hide that he was doing it. And that's when I realized, Wow, this is something that has taken over. It was something that I was lucky enough not to get involved in.

BEAU HILL I completely lost touch with Robbin for years. Then I got a call from one of our assistant engineers at Atlantic and he said, "Do you know what's happened to Robbin?" And I said no. He said, "He's in the hospital and here's his number." I called him and he was at a convalescent home.

So I went over there to see him. It was quite bizarre. He had nothing. He was morbidly obese. I'm going to say, without exaggerating, he was four hundred–plus pounds. He was so big that he could not get out of bed to go to the bathroom. If you just sort of cut out a little circle around his nose and his eyes and his mouth, that was the only thing that looked like him. The rest just was Jabba the Hutt. It was bizarre.

That was not a good day for me because I remember thinking when I walked out of the hospital, because Robbin was talking about, "Yeah, I've got my guitars here and I'm working on a solo album and all this," and I was just, You're not ever walking out of here, ever. About six or seven days after I saw him, I got the call that he had passed. [Crosby died on June 6, 2002, after a long battle with AIDS and drug addiction. He was forty-two.]

JOEY ALLEN On our 2008 reunion tour with Jani it was a sober backstage. I mean, if you were on our guest list they would take your alcohol away from you. We had AA meetings backstage. We really tried to help him as much as we could. Even though no matter what we did he found a way around it. Addicts . . .

HEIDI MARGOT RICHMAN For all of his amazing, amazing, really strong personality traits, Jani had so many demons and a lot of self-sabotage in him.

JOEY ALLEN That was why we made the decision during the reunion tour to stop doing the reunion tour. He just wasn't healthy. And the last thing we wanted to do was wake up one morning to go to soundcheck and knock on his door and the guy's not answering.

EDDIE TRUNK We taped an episode of *That Metal Show* with Jani about a week before he died. He had been going through a lot. He was in and out with Warrant and not doing well, and they were having some rough shows with him trying to hold it together. But he came on the show, and he was wonderful. He didn't seem impaired in any way. He was really grateful that I had him on, he was really grateful that we treated him with respect, and it wasn't like, "Oh, here comes the 'Cherry Pie' dude," and all that. When he passed away, I had a ton of people say to me, "Hey, did you notice anything? Was he off or in bad shape when you saw him?" And I said no. And it's true, he seemed fine. The only thing I really remembered about him is that he had kind of given me a hug and he was very, very thin. He felt very frail.

BEAU HILL Jani called me shortly before he died . . . I hadn't talked to the guy in probably eight years. I knew peripherally all the crazy shit that he was going through, and he's trying to get on a game show on TV [Lane appeared on the VH1 series *Celebrity Fit Club*] or whatever silly stuff he was doing. He called me and it was one of those weird calls where it was like I hadn't seen him since yesterday. It wasn't awkward. He was as lucid as you could possibly imagine. He told me about his new girlfriend and that he was getting ready to get married. Very optimistic, just as warm and cordial as you could possibly imagine.

Then two days later my phone starts erupting and everybody that I hadn't spoken to in months and months or years and years is calling me going, "Did you hear about Jani?"

JOEY ALLEN Warrant was on the road with Robert [current Warrant vocalist Robert Mason] in North Dakota and my phone rang and it was Jeff Blando, who plays in Slaughter now and with Vince Neil. And I answered it, like, "Hey, what're you doin'?" You know, just laughing. And he goes, "I'm so sorry, I'm so sorry . . ." And I hadn't . . . we hadn't heard yet. It literally had probably happened within the hour. [On August 11, 2011, Lane, age forty-seven, was found dead in a Comfort Inn motel room near his home in Los Angeles; the cause of death was later determined to be acute alcohol poisoning.] We were all sitting there at a band dinner on a night off and it just sucked. It still sucks. It *sucks*. And who it really sucks for is his family. His kids, his two beautiful daughters, his brother and sisters. It just . . . it didn't have to be that way.

RIKKI ROCKETT Poison was so not on the same page at that point in time. We were not communicating correctly.

BRET MICHAELS C.C. was getting fucked up and I was drinking. He's high but I'm drunk. We were having rows; he slammed me, I slammed him. We kept having really stupid arguments—stuff like his guitar was too loud for me to hear myself sing . . . We just couldn't get it straightened out. I called it our "substance egos." We had just been on tour way too long. Everyone was paranoid and down.

RIKKI ROCKETT Then at the 1991 MTV Music Video Awards we went into the wrong song—the one we were gonna do for the commercial break as opposed to what we were supposed to play live. That's what happened. Everybody starts blaming each other, and pretty soon it's a fistfight. And that's national TV. Our manager always used to tell us, he's like, "Don't do TV." He goes, "You build something up for thirty years and blow it in five seconds." And he was right, you know?

MICHAEL SWEET We started drinking right as Stryper started rehearsing for *Against the Law*. So this is about 1990. You know, one guy brought a six-pack into rehearsal and everybody went, "Oh, yeah, I'll have a beer!" And the next day at rehearsal it's a twelve-pack. It just kinda progressed and started spiraling out of control, so to speak. So by the time we were making *Against the Law* we were drinking in the studio—and I mean getting *drunk,* you know? Not just having a drink or two but by the end of the session we were all hammered. It wasn't anything to be proud of, certainly. But it's very easy to fall into that trap.

ROBERT SWEET I watched myself go from being incredibly successful and then a couple of years later to not having a band, right? It was hard on everybody, but, you know, that happens every day, unfortunately.

MICHAEL SWEET I left because of the hypocrisy. There was a lot of guilt on my side because of the fact that for a few years we had been going up onstage and telling people about God and then after the show going to the bar and getting drunk with them. I got sick of that. I just felt like, You know what? I don't wanna do this anymore. I'm not saying that the other guys *did* want to do it, I'm just saying that I wanted to get my life in order. I had a son and a daughter being born in '91, and I just wanted to change my life and not be a fake and a phony and a hypocrite. That was the priority to me. So that's why I left.

FRANKIE BANALI With us, we had Kevin DuBrow, and I really fucking loved Kevin [DuBrow passed away from a cocaine overdose in 2007. He was fifty-two], but Kevin's biggest fault was the fact that he was the most honest person I've ever known in my entire life. And what I mean by that is whatever he thought about something, he said it. The difference is that, you know, he used to say it in his apartment, and all of a sudden he was saying it to the world.

CARLOS CAVAZO Even the guys in Ratt told me one time they pulled into some town and some kid comes up to them, "Yeah, Quiet Riot was just here. Kevin DuBrow says ya'll suck!"

FRANKIE BANALI I tried to explain to Kevin, but he wouldn't listen. "If you're a Quiet Riot fan, there's a nine out of ten chance you're going to be a fan of a number of other rock bands in the same genre. And if you start picking at those bands, then the fans are going to have to make a choice."

CARLOS CAVAZO Kevin, we all know that he had a drug problem. And I'm not trying to place blame on him because we were all doing it. But I think he may have said a few wrong things because he had a cocaine hangover, an alcohol hangover. Whatever. But I think he said a few wrong things and then it started putting a crack in the band. I saw it all falling apart. I saw it a million miles away. I knew it was gonna happen.

DEE SNIDER We did different things. DuBrow had his mouth. He shot off his mouth a lot and turned his audience off. My actions turned the core audience off. I misread the room so badly. I thought releasing "Leader of the Pack" [as the first single from 1985's *Come Out and Play,* the follow-up to *Stay Hungry*] was the slickest move I could fucking make. But I remember when [MTV VJ] Mark Goodman introduced it as "Twisted Sister's latest cartoon video." I was like, "What? Did you say 'cartoon'?" I went, "Holy fuck . . ."

JAY JAY FRENCH The band crashed and burned in '87. We crashed and burned well before hair metal crashed and burned at the foot of grunge.

DEE SNIDER I'm angry seeing that I'm not in what's going on. It's going on, I should be in the thick of things.

CARLOS CAVAZO We could've gone a lot further. You know, there's no reason in the world we shouldn't be up there with Bon Jovi and Def Leppard and Mötley Crüe right now. We were then. We were right up there with them. But it just started a downhill spiral. We were not prepared.

FRANKIE BANALI Even back then, I was very aware that maybe ten percent make it, and maybe one percent of that ten percent sustain a long career. So it never affected me in any way. Music changes, tastes change. Maybe if Kevin hadn't said some of the things he said, things would have been different. But I can't really blame any one thing or any one person for how it went down. I had no idea the band was even going to be as successful as we were.

JAY JAY FRENCH On the one hand, you're praying for your success. On the other hand, you're always like, How's it gonna fail?

70

"I DON'T THINK NIRVANA EVER WANTED TO KILL ANYONE'S CAREER"

JIM MERLIS No one in the Geffen camp ever, *ever* imagined that Nirvana was going to get so big. Because it wasn't music that was designed to be particularly commercial. When something like that happens, it throws everything into chaos and you lose control of things. They literally had to stop pressing albums by other artists because the plants had to make more *Nevermind* CDs.

DANNY GOLDBERG I don't think Nirvana ever wanted to kill anyone's career. There was just . . . there was a yearning from a new generation for new stars.

MATTHEW NELSON I remember reading that article in *Rolling Stone* where Cobain says . . . you know, they asked him about what's it like being on the same label as Nelson, and he said, "We burn effigies of them before every show."

JIM MERLIS I think that Kurt certainly had issues with the misogyny in hair metal, but he also didn't like some of the music . . . I mean, I think he probably had a visceral hatred of it a little bit? He did not want to be part of it.

BRYN BRIDENTHAL I had to explain that Guns had become everything that Nirvana was against. They'd become corporate. Axl just didn't understand that Nirvana was the anti-Guns.

DANNY GOLDBERG There was a cultural contrast and honestly, as one of Nirvana's managers, I loved that contrast because it imaged Nirvana as something special to their fans and differentiated them from other bands. Kurt was passionate about gay rights, and Axl Rose referred to people in one of his lyrics as "faggots."

DUFF McKAGAN I think, really, Axl was bummed because he was a fucking Nirvana fan, you know? But he couldn't get away from being Axl Rose at that time.

CLIFF BURNSTEIN My partner, Peter Mensch, and I had Def Leppard, who were supporting *Adrenalize,* at the MTV Music Video Awards in September 1992. As I recall it was Def Leppard, Bryan Adams, who had the hit from the *Robin Hood* soundtrack, Pearl Jam, the Red Hot Chili Peppers, and Guns N' Roses. And as me and Peter walked around, the enmity between the Nirvanas and that group of bands and the Def Leppard and Guns N' Roses contingent was so palpable. It was, like, hatred.

DANNY GOLDBERG A week before the MTV Awards, Axl Rose had said at a concert that Kurt and Courtney Love should go to jail, that Kurt was a degenerate and his wife was a degenerate because of what he'd read in a *Vanity Fair* article. It was devastating to Kurt and Courtney. It threatened their custody of their daughter. Their daughter, Frances, was, like, a month old or something and was with them. They had her at the show.

DUFF McKAGAN There was that whole kind of fracas there. But you know what that was? That was a bunch of drunk fucking idiots.

DANNY GOLDBERG We were sitting at a table in catering, and then Axl and a couple of bodyguards and his girlfriend at the time, Stephanie Seymour, were at the next table. So Courtney says, "Hey, Axl, you want to be godfather to our baby?" And Stephanie Seymour looks over to her and says,

"Are you a model?" And without missing a beat Courtney says, "Are you a rocket scientist?" At that point Axl comes over to the table with a body-guard and says to Kurt, "Hey man, if you don't shut your woman up, I'm gonna put you down to the pavement." Kurt was rattled by it. Axl was physically bigger than him. Axl had bodyguards. There was a little bit of shoving, I think, later between other members of the band and Krist.

DUFF McKAGAN I got into it a bit with Novoselic . . .

DANNY GOLDBERG Kurt was telling the story about Axl Rose threatening him for months. It was a great story because it differentiated the guy who talks about shutting up a woman and the one who wants to empower them. The guy who threatens violence and the guy who doesn't.

CLIFF BURNSTEIN This was a generational shift. Literally when Peter and I left that night after those MTV Awards, we said, "Our future is basically done if we don't get out of what we're doing." As soon as we got back to New York we started calling people and saying, "We're not just heavy metal guys. We can talk to you about all kinds of music." Like, "I signed Pere Ubu. Give me a fucking break." So a lawyer named Rosemary Carroll called us and said, "Screaming Trees have signed to Epic. Would you be interested in managing them?" It got us over the chasm.

71

"ALL OF A SUDDEN YOU WERE RADIOACTIVE"

ANDY SECHER And within a year hair metal had been wiped off the face of the earth by Nirvana, Pearl Jam, Soundgarden, Alice in Chains. Did not see it coming. Should have. One of my few regrets. But, yeah, I was putting Warrant and people like that on the cover of *Hit Parader* when I should have had Nirvana on the cover.

JAY JAY FRENCH I think a lot of hair metal bands would like to think there was a conspiracy against them. The labels must be sitting in a room and going, "We don't want this kind of music anymore." I say, since when is capitalism and fucking people over to make money a conspiracy?

GREG STEELE We went to New York and met with Elektra when they were setting up everything for the Faster Pussycat *Whipped!* record. All the people that worked there were like, "We're gonna push the shit out of this, it's gonna be great, we've got so many plans for this . . ." We did a video for a song called "The Body Thief" on a Friday and Saturday. And by Monday they dropped us.

TAIME DOWNE Kiss was the last tour we did on that record. We'd be in cities and there'd be no Elektra reps at the gigs when we're playing an arena tour. There wasn't anybody. So we knew something was going down. For us it was like, it was just a matter of time. We weren't surprised by anything.

JANET GARDNER All of a sudden, we were the school nerds. I mean, no shit. It was pretty ugly. Luckily, I am blessed with a super-supportive family, really good friends. I did not have any inkling of like, oh, maybe I'll drink myself to death, or anything like that. It was always like, well, there are other things in life, and so I did other things in life.

LITA FORD I left the music industry. The people turned into bank tellers. They weren't rock stars anymore. It was, dude, you should be pumping gas or something. You just don't look right. You don't sound right. There's nothing special about anything you're doing. This was just my thought. I loved Alice in Chains. I loved the whole Pearl Jam thing. That whole change didn't last long, but that whole changeover, it was awesome. Then it went into the deep end of it and that's when I left. I got married and got pregnant, moved to a deserted island.

KIP WINGER The thing that makes me different is that I was personally attacked. You know, it wasn't like I was Slaughter and I was one of the many bands that just went away due to the era. It's that I was personally attacked by Metallica and by *Beavis and Butt-Head*.

RICK KRIM The problem? Kip was a good-looking guy, and he pranced around with his bass, and he let his chest hair show, which worked to his advantage. But next thing you know, Metallica's throwing darts at him, and *Beavis and Butt-Head* have their nerdy kid, Stewart, wearing a Winger shirt.

REB BEACH We were on tour for *Pull,* selling a thousand tickets a night in theaters. It was going really well. And this guy came on the bus and he said, "I gotta show you guys something." We were driving down the road and he put in a *Beavis and Butt-Head* video. And when they hung that kid by his underwear on the tree in his Winger T-shirt, we all just looked at each other. I remember going, "Oh no, this could be all over. Jeez, I hope it's not all over." Well, it was all over. *Boom!* The day after it aired nobody bought Winger tickets anymore. We had to cancel the tour.

RICK KRIM I'm sure it bummed Kip out. I'm sure that other stuff bummed him out, bands poking fun at him.

KIP WINGER Metallica, they had my poster in their video for "Nothing Else Matters," throwing darts at it. Now, they're a very powerful act. And they were basically telling their fans that I suck. It was an attack on me. *Personally.* So they can live with that.

REB BEACH It was Kip that was getting picked on. I didn't get that kind of ridicule as much as he did. You know, Kip got laughed at walking into a McDonald's. I felt bad for him.

RICK KRIM He became the poster child for the people who didn't like this, who thought these bands were bullshit. But musicianship-wise, I'd put Winger up against any other band that was out at the time.

KIP WINGER I mean, c'mon. Lars [Ulrich] . . . everybody knows Lars is not an amazing drummer. He's no Rod Morgenstein. It's a fuckin' joke. So, whatever. I'm not a bullying, slag-off-other-musicians-to-try-to-prop-yourself-up person. That's what they are. Or maybe they were. But it's all spilt milk. The way I came back from that was to get a Grammy nomination for Best Classical Composition. So fuck them, you know?

JOEY ALLEN We were at a Sony Grammy party in L.A. right after *Dog Eat Dog* came out. Donnie Ienner is there, Mariah Carey is there, Tommy Mottola is there, everyone is there. It's like '92 and Seattle is starting to come out and Pearl Jam's record, *Ten*, is just killer. So I had a few drinks in me and I bumped into Rick Krim and I pulled every credit card in my wallet out and all the cash I had and put it in my hand and said, "Please play my video!" He looked at me and said, "I wish I could, but it's not up to me." Up until then, it was a good relationship between MTV and Warrant.

KATHERINE TURMAN Even Mötley couldn't survive. They split with Vince and put out a strong album with John Corabi, a superior singer and charismatic front man, but no one cared. Even using the same team—Bob Rock, who produced their massive hit, *Dr. Feelgood*, five years previously, they weren't able to make the record fly. I'm sure Mötley thought it would be like Sammy Hagar joining Van Halen: a new lease on their career and a bunch of multiplatinum albums and radio hits. But nope.

NIKKI SIXX When the album came out, I remember *Rolling Stone* saying, "This should be the album of the year—unfortunately it's by Mötley Crüe." That was our experience of the '90s. There was some good music in the '90s, but I didn't think the bands were very sexy. Soundgarden had some really cool riffs, and obviously Nirvana had a really iconic figurehead with Kurt Cobain. But nothing had that "let's go in the bathroom and have a quickie" feel to it.

KIM THAYIL You know, I love the song "Dr. Feelgood."

HOWARD BENSON At the time did it seem like such a massive change? Well, you know, it's a very interesting thing. I have an alternate theory that I sometimes throw around. There's another thing that happened in 1991, 1992, that people don't remember and that was the advent of SoundScan. So we didn't really know what was selling up until that moment. And I remember the chart that came out at the end of 1991, the chart the week before had had hair bands at the top. The next week, it was this guy at the top of the chart named Garth Brooks. And nobody knew who he was, you know? But he was actually selling. And we weren't. And all this stuff was being made up by the record companies. The numbers were being juiced up and there was no way to keep track of anything. It was all promotion. So we didn't know how much this stuff was selling. We just thought it was selling. SoundScan leveled the playing field. All of a sudden you were like, "Whoa, we're not selling any hair bands!" I don't know if that had anything to do with it or not. But I sometimes wonder, if that hadn't happened . . .

TOM WERMAN I remember thinking during the mid-'80s that I could, if I wanted to, keep doing this for the rest of my life. And I was wrong.

BEAU HILL I had no idea that my name, Beau Hill, would be synonymous with nuclear waste at that point. The shift was unpredictable and very unpleasant, because anything that touched any hair band in any way—production, songwriting, whatever—all of a sudden you were radioactive and nobody is going to answer your phone call and nobody is going to do anything.

BRET HARTMAN There was probably a hundred hair metal bands that got let go between 1991 and 1992 just because they'd gotten one album or two and, you know, it costs $150,000 to make the album, $100,000 to make the video, the label gave them money to tour . . . Most of these bands were in debt for like, four or five hundred thousand dollars. And so the labels didn't want to spend any more on them.

"DIZZY" DEAN DAVIDSON Britny Fox's A&R guy, like all the guys on the floor, was let go. People were packing their boxes up when I was there at Mercury, like their office supplies, and I'm like, "What's going on?" And a person let me know. They said, "Well, every single label in California and New York, where all the hubs are, are cleaning up their label because of this new music that's coming in." Which was Pearl Jam, Soundgarden, Nirvana, Stone Temple Pilots, the list goes on, Blind Melon, like, all of them. And they were getting people in the offices that were younger and knew that music . . . You could see it.

EDDIE "FINGERS" OJEDA I mean, with Nirvana and bands like that, I liked them. I get it. But it's like having the table set for Thanksgiving, and then you sit down to eat and everybody takes the food away.

"DIZZY" DEAN DAVIDSON I see a guy in the record label dressed with leggings with combat boots and oily hair and I go, "We're doomed."

EDDIE "FINGERS" OJEDA It's kind of funny because it was just this costuming in a different way, but instead of dressing up, they would dress down. You want to look homeless or just wear the weirdest shit that you could find.

JAY JAY FRENCH When "Smells Like Teen Spirit" came out, the whole thing changed. I sat back and said, "Okay, these things happen in the cyclical nature of the music industry. The Beatles came, wiped out everything before." Punk comes, I said, "Okay, fine, this is another thing." Now grunge is in. The problem with it was that when I was going to see bands, just because friends of mine would say, "Come and see this band," all of a sudden everyone cut their hair and is wearing plaid shirts. I'm saying to myself, "Boy, the scene never changes. These are the wannabes."

TOM KEIFER Every decade, every generation of music has a look. The one that took over from the '80s became ultimately a bigger pose than the '80s. If you didn't have your flannel shirt and Doc Martens . . . It was just a different pose. But somehow that was a credible one.

FRED COURY Grunge didn't kill our music. We all did. Winger put out *Pull,* which was a different thing for them. Warrant put out a hard rock record with "Machine Gun" on it, great song. Everybody did great work. Warrant was on their way to being a Journey, with the ballad and Jani's voice. They were on their way to be pop superstars. The issue is, and this is just my opinion, of course, but the issue is, everybody alienated their fans at the same time. Warrant puts out a hard rock record, no big ballads like normally. Skid Row put out a heavy metal record practically. Ratt put out whatever the heck that was, their worst record. Everybody did something completely different than what their fans were used to.

TAIME DOWNE I went to Chicago and I did Pigface. Kept busy learning different shit. Took the time to learn how to work with computers and gear. Learned how to track. Learned what the fucking knobs meant on a fucking console. Before I didn't know what the fuck—I just wanted a couch to fuck pussy.

RON KEEL We lost our European deal. And you think, That's all right, I'll get another deal. Then we lost our Japanese deal. Then you lose your U.S. deal. Then you go through the personnel changes. I went on with a band called Fair Game for a couple years until finally I had nothing left except a guitar and a story to tell. And I went to the desert and I made a campfire and I sat there with that guitar and started pouring my heart out. And it came out as country music.

TAIME DOWNE You gotta fucking move with the fucking punches. Do something different. Shit always changes.

GUNNAR NELSON Our record label, DGC, was ground zero for grunge. So we came home and all the employees had shifted over to flannel-wearing nineteen-year-olds who fucking hated us.

MATTHEW NELSON We went from being the heroes to being the zeros over-night, and we were heavily leveraged by the time we were done. But hon-estly, if somebody asked me right now, "Okay, you're going to sacrifice your life, like completely, and you'll get like three years. You're going to be a huge superstar, you're going to have amazing experiences, girls will be throwing themselves at you, it'll be amazing, amazing, amazing. But at the end of it you're going to be worse off financially, by a long shot. You'll be paying it off for years. Are you going to do it?"

The answer for me? "Yeah. Absolutely."

PART VII

EPILOGUE

When Tom Keifer came up with the line "Don't know what you got till it's gone," he surely didn't realize he was being prophetic. Sure, the '90s *sucked* for most of the artists we've chronicled here. But soon enough, fans both young and old started to pine for the groups that had rocked the '80s in such grand style. Keifer and Cinderella, Poison, Skid Row, Kix, and many others reemerged from the shadows, while Guns N' Roses, with Axl, Slash, and Duff back together, and Mötley Crüe, once again with Vince Neil out front, returned to the road and arguably experienced some of the greatest success of their careers. Today the bands fill clubs, theaters, arenas, and, yes, even stadiums, with the loud and proud anthems that were the fist-pumping soundtrack to a bygone era.

"THIS IS WHAT WE DO"

SCOTTI HILL There was a time in the '90s where it felt like as soon as you walked out of the house, people were going to throw rocks at you. You were just *hated*.

TRACII GUNS I didn't do anything for a year. I shaved my head, wore a pair of shorts, walked around in the sand in Venice, and smoked weed. I mean, I could afford to do that, but I had no income.

BRIAN "DAMAGE" FORSYTHE I moved to L.A. Everything sort of went downhill as far as drugs and alcohol, and so I kind of did a nosedive. But I look back at the '90s and I was constantly playing in different bands—I even went out at one point and auditioned for the Wallflowers and almost got the gig. But it was a blessing in disguise that I didn't get the gig because there's no way I could've held it together at that point.

MATTHEW NELSON We really couldn't work for a couple of years. Around '96, '97, Gunnar and I went out with a couple of acoustic guitars and opened for America. Then we went out with Air Supply . . . I've never seen a more ravenous fan base than Air Supply's, by the way. Like full-on fainting girls.

LONN FRIEND The '90s were taken over by Pearl Jam and Nine Inch Nails and the music that came out of industrial and grunge and alternative . . . the more "serious" kind of existential rock. They owned radio and they became the big touring bands, and the bands that built the movement of the '80s, of the Sunset Strip scene, they felt completely disenfranchised.

SHARE ROSS From '93 to the end of the decade I definitely did *not* lead with the fact that I had been the bass player in Vixen.

BRIAN "DAMAGE" FORSYTHE People would ask me who I played for, and I'd just say whoever I was playing for at the moment. Like, if it was the Purple Gang, the blues band that I was in, I would just say, "Yeah, I play in a blues band called the Purple Gang." I would never bring up Kix.

EDDIE TRUNK It was brutal. A lot of bands didn't even attempt to try to go out to play, because they just knew they weren't going to get taken seriously. They weren't going to be able to sell tickets, and economically it didn't make any sense. There were some bands that tried to stick it out and tried to get heavier, tried to get tougher, change their look, change their sound, but there were also a lot of bands that just folded their tent and said, "We're going to ride this out and we'll come back up for air when there's an opportunity."

TOM KEIFER It was amazing to see how an era where there was actually a lot of great music—and there was some that wasn't, admittedly, but I think that's any era—the whole thing was just dismissed. Not by the fans but by the tastemakers, I guess.

EDDIE TRUNK I think everybody took the same level of hit, meaning, say, just for the sake of argument, seventy-five percent of the fan base went away. If you're Bon Jovi and your average draw is twenty thousand and you take a seventy-five percent hit, you're still playing to a respectable amount of people. But if you're Warrant and your average draw was one thousand people as a headliner—and I'm just throwing out numbers— you take a seventy-five percent hit, you're playing to two hundred and fifty people.

LONN FRIEND What kept a lot of the bands alive during the '90s was to simply get out there and play. Play smaller venues, play different cities that they may have missed the first time or their second or third time around. Go overseas, where the fans have longer memories.

EDDIE TRUNK There were bands that went and realized, "Hey, we actually might be getting killed in America right now, but I can go to Australia or Europe or South America and actually still be a rock star and do really well." Scorpions is certainly one of the bands that could do that.

RUDOLF SCHENKER When these grunge and alternative people came in, we didn't fight with them and try to make it—we went to Asia and Russia and played in big stadiums. We went to Malaysia and Jakarta and Indonesia. We went twenty times platinum in Thailand and ten times in Korea. And there we didn't have to fight. We had our other playground, and then later on we came back without any kind of harm.

KATHERINE TURMAN The Bon Jovis and the Guns N' Roses were still out there in arenas and stadiums. But the other bands, the Ratts, the Faster Pussycats, even though they weren't front and center on MTV or in the magazines, they still carried on, just in a slightly smaller world.

ALEX GROSSI (booking agent, Vince Neil, Slaughter, Vixen, Kix, Faster Pussycat, Nelson; guitarist, Quiet Riot) I think the secret of '80s metal is that it never went away; the media just stopped covering it for a decade. A lot of the bands still stayed together even though they were playing small clubs, because what else are you gonna do when you're wired to do a certain thing for a living? You're like, "Well, I don't want to work at Walmart, so yeah, let's go on tour."

DANA STRUM Anyone that was willing to give it a go, keep trying, had any integrity, and was reasonably good at what they did would've found a way. I mean, by '94-ish, when the managers were quitting, the agents were quitting, at that point I was so hands-on from the beginning of Slaughter anyway, I thought, What have these people done other than run the minute the shit hit the fan? Their loyalty was to the commission they were earning. And my loyalty was to the music we made.

SCOTTI HILL When Skid Row started up again in 1999, we were back in small clubs and we were getting really low guarantees and we were in a van and we were sucking it up, man, because that's what we wanted to do. When people think of us, and they think of the videos and all that, they don't realize the fucking gutter we dragged ourselves through *after* all that. It's one thing to be out there in a van driving around, but when you're doing that after you've had multiple buses and three-truck tours and being very popular and making good money? Now you're in a sleeping bag in the back of a van for a couple of years . . . which seemed like forever. But eventually it started to get a little more popular and a little more popular.

RACHEL BOLAN People just want memories. And it's the type of rock that, I don't wanna say it's lighthearted, but it's just, like, fun. And people wanna go out and have a good time. I see that rising to the surface again, which is a really cool thing.

EDDIE TRUNK Poison, when they're active, they would certainly be one of the bigger ones.

RIKKI ROCKETT When Poison came back in 2000 and started touring again, I felt like the girls were even more . . . they knew what they wanted more because they were a little bit older now. Do you know what I'm saying? Back in the day, there were a lot of girls that were nineteen and twenty. They didn't know what the hell they were doing. Most of us don't even know who we are until we're thirty.

BRIAN "DAMAGE" FORSYTHE In 2003, Kix booked a couple of reunion holiday shows in Baltimore. We didn't know what was going to happen, and it was huge. They sold out immediately. So we thought, Wow, that was cool. Let's do it again.

EDDIE TRUNK I think a really big moment was in 2007, when there was a rock festival launched outside of Tulsa called Rocklahoma, which still exists to this day. Now it's just a festival with a variety of rock bands, but when it was launched the idea for it was for it to be the Woodstock for '80s rock. So the very first Rocklahoma was headlined by Poison and had every '80s band on it you could imagine, from Warrant to Winger to Kix to Slaughter. It was a three-day event. The idea was "Hey, there's a lot of people out there that love this stuff. They've been marginalized. They've been told it's not cool, whatever. We're going to change that and we want to have a big event to celebrate and say, 'It's cool, it's okay,' and let's have fun." That first year drew somewhere between ten and fifteen thousand people a day, which given that it was in the middle of nowhere in Oklahoma, is very good.

BRIAN "DAMAGE" FORSYTHE Kix did the holiday shows for a couple of years and then I started thinking, Maybe we could go with this . . . And that's when I started looking around at booking agents and I started noticing bands like Warrant and Great White. They were still doing it, but they were doing like the fly-date thing.

JOEY ALLEN In the rock 'n' roll world, back in the old days, you'd have seven days a week, right? And Monday, Tuesday, Wednesday, and Sunday are always kind of tough sells because everybody needs to get up and go to work and do what they do. So nowadays what happens is those Fridays and Saturdays are what we do. And we do them at state fairs, casinos, clubs, all the events. We get on a plane and we go do a gig, and then Sunday I'm flying home, I get in the pool with my kid and have some fun. Then Friday morning, five a.m., I'm up, I'm ready to go, and I'm working again.

SCOTTI HILL It's two lives. It's really crazy, man. You're out there doing a rock 'n' roll thing on the weekend and playing for lots of people and big crowds. And then, you know, Monday morning, *boom*! I'm in daddy mode, walking my son to school.

SHARE ROSS I don't even travel with a bass. I'm, "Have strap, will rock."

MARK SLAUGHTER I come from Las Vegas, and I met Tony Orlando once and he told me, "Listen, you're gonna be in casinos." I was like, "*What?*" And guess what? The man was exactly right. If you look at my schedule,

I do fly dates into casinos, do some shows, fly home. No different than Tony Orlando.

MADELYN SCARPULLA Constant touring, that's a grueling thing to do for a guy who's in between fifty and sixty years old. The weekend gigs are comfortable. This is for grown-ups. And you know who's a grown-up? The bands are grown-ups and the fans are grown-ups.

JACK RUSSELL When you're in your fifties, you got a wife at home that you love, you don't want to be on the road on a tour bus smelling people's socks, people's farts in the middle of the night. It's like, "Ah, dude . . . really?"

KATHERINE TURMAN When Twisted Sister came back, there was still a lot of call for those big hits. They had really authentic songs—and humor, of course. And also, you know, visually, Dee Snider was in even better shape than he was in the early days. They aged really well.

EDDIE "FINGERS" OJEDA When people see some of our old videos, especially young kids, they say, "Wow, I wish I was there for that!" That's why the whole retro thing became so big for us. When we got back together, we were bigger than we ever were. Most of the festivals when we played in Europe, these huge festivals for forty, fifty, sixty, seventy, eighty thousand people, we weren't the fifth or sixth band—we were *headlining*. And back in the '80s in those big festivals, we were never the headliners.

JAY JAY FRENCH We didn't succumb to the stupidity of making a new record, which nobody would have bought to begin with. We kept ourselves out of the marketplace, we drove the price up astronomically. We just played ten to fifteen shows per year—cherry-picked them, biggest festivals and greatest exposure—then went home. I can't think of a better scenario for us. I don't know how it works for everybody else, but for Twisted, it was perfectly done.

EDDIE "FINGERS" OJEDA It's almost like we went back to the '80s, but better.

ALEX GROSSI All the bands from the '80s are out touring now because the people who grew up on this music now have jobs and make real money and in some cases are the CEOs of big companies. They can afford to have Vince Neil play at their company's Christmas party for two hundred grand, or they can afford to drop fifteen hundred dollars to go on a Monsters of Rock cruise and do the VIP meet-and-greet.

MADELYN SCARPULLA It's what we refer to as the Gold Card crowd. They buy tickets in the front row and VIP experiences. They buy beer and merch. And they come back the next year.

LONN FRIEND It's not cheap going on the Monsters of Rock cruise. That's a four-figure investment! But you get the lifestyle experience. This is what's really important—you're not just getting on a boat to see bands. You get to drink like it's 1989. You get to hang out with your kin, and it's a sisterhood and a brotherhood. You get to share stories. And it sells out every year.

It's the same with the M3 Rock Festival in Maryland. It's in its tenth or eleventh year, they've got thirty thousand people coming. And you're gonna be there with thousands of the like-minded who don't give a shit about hits or popularity or visibility or whether something's bleak or blazing. They just want to be in the room with the music that made them happy, that gave them purpose. They still have memories of, you know, that was the first time they got laid. That was the first time they got drunk at a show. That was the first time they fell in love with a guitar. These groups mean so much as far as the historical memory to fans.

GUNNAR NELSON I'm actually bringing more money home to my family now, not being on MTV, not being in a number one band, not being on Geffen. I'm not touring with forty-five people and twelve trucks. But I own my own stuff. And by rolling into a gig with four duffle bags and a three-piece band, I'm bringing home a lot more money. Back in the day, every night I was out there playing I was in the red fifteen grand a night. It's weird because you sit there and you're playing for twenty thousand people and you're going "How in the world can this be going in the red fifteen thousand dollars a day?"

TRACII GUNS Money's a weird thing to talk about, but yeah, I'm doing good. I'm doing fine. Live, L.A. Guns makes about three times the amount of money we ever made in the past. Ever. That coupled with, you know, really nice merchandise sales and a combination of everything that comes in the mailbox from all the records and things I've made over the years, plus we get recording advances from our label, Frontiers. It just seems like there's more income streams.

KIP WINGER We're getting fees as much as we ever got. Winger played Japan last year with Alice Cooper. We got paid the same amount we got paid in our heyday. I think it all just came back because when new generations started rediscovering the music they're like, "Wow, this is good music." The grunge era didn't last very long and the people that really loved it weren't as fanatical as the '80s fans. So the '80s fans played all our music for their kids and now all their kids love it. And there was a bigness to it and the personalities were bigger than life. There was an anonymity to grunge music that kind of inoculated it from being a personality-based thing. Okay, Kurt Cobain and Chris Cornell, that's it. Those are the only two people from that era anybody remembers. They're both dead. But from our era you've got fuckin' Poison, Winger, Warrant . . . Well, Jani's dead but, you know, fuck, the list is endless.

VINCE NEIL All those grunge bands have been gone for a long time, there's maybe like two bands that stuck around. All it was, was the exact same thing that happened in the early '80s: a bunch of one-hit wonders came out and then in the '90s the same thing happened—just a couple good bands and the rest are one-hit wonders and it just goes on from there. That's when bands break up; they're not around for thirty years like Mötley Crüe.

LONN FRIEND Mötley Crüe is such an interesting story because they peaked with *Dr. Feelgood,* which is like thirty years ago. They peaked on *record.* But touring . . . that's a different story. Especially that "final tour" [in 2014 and 2015], where they were really delivering great shows. They took the performance, the visuals, the interaction with the audience, the animation of Tommy and Nikki onstage, they took that really to the pinnacle, to the highest level.

NIKKI SIXX The band always prided itself—even when we were a club band—on pushing it as far as we could push it. If you look back to 1981 at shows at the Whisky, we played them like they were stadium shows, but they were only to 250 people. It's just what we do.

KATHERINE TURMAN That "final" tour was, I don't know, two years, maybe more. And I think it was more successful than they ever imagined. And that success was not assured. But with the excitement and the theatrics, with Nikki's flamethrower bass and Tommy's drums on a rollercoaster, you know, it really made them a shit-ton of money. And it was super interesting when *The Dirt* [the Netflix biopic based on the 2001 Mötley Crüe autobiography of the same name] movie came out how crazy everybody who loved that music went.

BRAD TOLINSKI What's also interesting about audiences for bands like Mötley Crüe and Guns N' Roses, and even some of the lower-tier acts, it's not just fifty-year-old guys reliving the past. They have new fans in their teens, in their twenties, in their thirties, who truly dig the music. I mean, Guns N' Roses have made something like half a billion dollars on their most recent tour. You see their T-shirts on everyone.

KATHERINE TURMAN It was really a great thing for rock 'n' roll when Guns N' Roses came back, almost reunited—as long as it's Slash and Duff on either side of Axl, I think the world is happy. They have a genuine group of new fans, twenty-somethings and thirty-somethings who aren't looking back but who are going to the shows and saying, "Wow, this isn't just a pale imitation of what they were in the '80s. This delivers."

SHARE ROSS Young kids today, they show up with their parents and they're like, "I love you guys and you're my idols and you're the reason I want to play music." Holy crap! It's amazing.

SCOTTI HILL There are kids who've heard so much about it that they're just like, "Man, I wish I was a teenager in 1985. I wish I could've experienced *that*." Just like when I was a kid I was like, "I wish I was a teenager during Woodstock." You've got a lot of these kids trying to live it, and they look like we did. When I first started noticing them in the early 2000s I was like, "Wow, that almost looks funny. It looks like they're wearing costumes."

TRACII GUNS There's also a lot of guys my age, that come out all dressed up, reliving the day, which is interesting. But I mean, as long as people come, I don't care who they are. And the older fans are slightly larger now, so it makes the room look even fuller.

LONN FRIEND This "rock 'n' roll is coming back" bullshit that I've been hearing forever . . . rock 'n' roll will never come back 'cause it's never gone away. Rock 'n' roll goes through peaks and valleys of genre, affectation, and popularity . . .

EDDIE TRUNK It just keeps turning over. And I think, circling all the way back to the beginning, that's one of the biggest reasons why this stuff is able to get a fighting chance again, because you've seen younger people turn up because they've heard about these bands from their parents or whatever and they want to see them. Now, whether anyone in the current lineup of the band is in that video they watched from the '80s is a different question . . .

LONN FRIEND It's almost laughable that some of these groups are going out with their original names with one band member. You know, Faster Pussycat, essentially it's just Taime and . . . players. But it's almost irrelevant to fans.

EDDIE TRUNK I think a lot of people don't know or care, unfortunately, who is in these bands. They see the logo, and that's what the agents want. They sell the logo and sell the song without looking too closely, actually, as to who's in it. But I also do think there's something to be said, with certain bands and at certain levels, for who is and isn't in the band. You have multiple versions of bands out there, and it bums me out that more people don't know or care about who's actually in the versions of the bands they're seeing.

KATHERINE TURMAN You had that with L.A. Guns, Ratt, Great White . . .

STEPHEN PEARCY With Ratt it kind of hurt the brand a bit because people were confused. But, I mean, I'll say we were never the most functional band on the planet. It's just par for the course.

JACK RUSSELL I had such a hard time getting off drugs. Unfortunately [other members of Great White] just got sober before I did, you know? I wish 'em well. I hope they do well. I just hope I do a little better!

BRAD TOLINSKI Jack Russell's early-2000s version of Great White was involved in that fire at the Station, which was a really horrific incident.

KATHERINE TURMAN Great White, I don't know if '80s metal had more than its share of tragedies than other genres, per se, but that Station fire was one of the worst that I ever heard of. [During a Great White performance at the Station nightclub in Rhode Island on February 20, 2003, the band's tour manager ignited pyrotechnics that set fire to the acoustic foam on the walls and ceiling around the stage and engulfed the venue in flames; an estimated 100 concertgoers were killed, with another 230 injured.] It's just so horrifying that so many people perished there. And I think it probably changed things for a lot of people. The members of Great White who survived it, how can you ever get over the guilt and the horror?

LONN FRIEND I don't think Jack Russell ever really recovered right from that event. I can't speak to his specific physical conditions, but he's hobbled. He's been walking with a cane for a long time. But he's out there touring and I know people that think he's never sounded better.

ALEX GROSSI There's no shortage of gigs and there's no shortage of bands willing to play 'em. Warrant and Dokken and Skid Row have kind of become the new classic rock, whereas when I was growing up, it was Queen and Led Zeppelin and the Who.

LONN FRIEND The first time I heard "Sweet Child o' Mine" on a classic rock station, it just hit me. Classic rock? Guns N' Roses? Yeah, I guess . . .

KATHERINE TURMAN Miley Cyrus has invited Bret Michaels onstage to do "Every Rose Has Its Thorn." It shows that it's not just lip service, that it is a good song and that it can sound great done by a singer of a different gender and in a different musical genre, too.

STEPHEN PEARCY People try to separate and label this music, and the worst thing is this hair metal thing. It's like, "What is that? Please explain." To me it's all just music. Sixties, '70s, '80s, whatever. I think hair is irrelevant . . . It's nice to have it, though.

KATHERINE TURMAN There's still a lot of lovers of this music and a lot of places they can go to hear it. Even though MTV is no longer around, there's YouTube and you can find anything you want from, you know, Bang Tango to Tuff. There's Hair Nation on SiriusXM, there's podcasts. Dee Snider did a radio show called *House of Hair.* On *Nights with Alice Cooper,* which I work on, we'll stick in deep cuts from '80s bands. And there's *Rock of Ages* . . . I mean, you've got these sexed-up, drunked-up hair guys on Broadway and it's a huge hit. That really says something.

JOEY ALLEN It just goes to show you, that whole thing that we were all a part of back in those Sunset Strip days, people like it. Even if, you know, I can't explain it.

MICHAEL SWEET Stryper went over and did the Loud Park Festival in Japan, and I'll never forget it. They had stages at either end of the arena, and one band would play at one end as the band at the other end was setting up. So here we have Limp Bizkit playing, and they have a massive crowd. And we're setting up onstage at the other end, we're on in fifteen, twenty minutes. And I go out there in my pants and my black shirt and I'm setting up my gear. I'm looking at the crowd, they're watching Limp Bizkit. I turn around and I'm plugging in my gear for, like, five minutes. And then I say to our manager, "Hey man, give me my jacket." And he hands me my yellow-and-black jacket and I put it on. And I hear the crowd just go, "Ahhhhh!"

I just kind of assumed it was for Limp Bizkit or whatever, but I turned around and, like, half the crowd was facing me and cheering for me putting on my yellow-and-black coat. It gave me chills.

ALEX GROSSI I think what's important is the brand. And as time passes you're going to see that the brand and the songs are what really live on.

BRAD TOLINSKI Then you have bands like Steel Panther, who are taking everything outrageous about the '80s and just blowing it up into something completely ridiculous and over-the-top.

KATHERINE TURMAN I remember seeing Steel Panther early on and I thought it was kind of a fun shtick. And I have to say I'm super surprised that they're doing well, people like them. I'm not quite sure what that says. I guess it says, "Yes, there's still a hunger for that and you can make fun of something while simultaneously loving it." Which is nice.

TRACII GUNS Steel Panther is vital. They're an outlet and they're relevant to people that remember, and also to people that are really interested in that time frame now. They're able to really push things in a comedic way that is almost reality based.

EDDIE TRUNK I'm not a fan. Nothing personal. The look, the attitude, the misogyny, the goofy lyrics, all the silliness, it just basically re-stokes that whole fire of those bands not being credible bands and these guys really, really sort of taking the piss out of them. I've seen them a couple times and I just don't think it's funny.

LONN FRIEND The debauchery, the decadence, that came from the '60s. It's just that the '80s bands crystallized it. And they crystallized it with hair and volume and questionable behavior and substance abuse and alcohol. I mean, come on! These groups, they glamorized it, they glorified it, and they were shameless about it.

JOEY ALLEN This isn't rocket science. It's not U2. We're not trying to save the world. We're coming from a point of view of, it's Friday night, forget about your day gig, go get a six-pack, let's have some fun . . . and, you know, be responsible at the same time.

STEPHEN PEARCY People are having a great time, they're coming out, and that's what it's all about. My god, we just left, where did we go? A festival in Brazil, Mexico, somewhere like that. And it was like eighty-fucking-thousand people out there. I mean, those events, we love that. The gigs are great.

BRIAN "DAMAGE" FORSYTHE When we first started playing again, everyone, especially our singer, Steve, didn't think it would just keep going. But it seems to get stronger and stronger. That's the crazy part.

SCOTTI HILL People just want to hear those songs. They want to hear "18 and Life," they want to hear "I Remember You," they want to hear "Monkey Business." I mean, I've played "Youth Gone Wild" every fucking show we've ever done since it was written. Even at fifty-six, "Youth Gone Wild." And man, we're not youth. We're just youth *gone*.

JOEY ALLEN Warrant played with Cheap Trick and I asked their bassist, Tom Petersson, who was sixty-nine years old, "You gotta give me some advice. How are you still doing this?" And he looked at me dumbfounded and he said, "What do you mean, man? This is what we do." He looked at me, he goes, "This is what *you* do."

STEPHEN PEARCY It is what it is, and Ratt can't be exterminated anyway, so . . .

DANA STRUM It's the rise and the fall of a music genre that was meant to be extinguished several different times. And funny enough, it still gets played out there to this day.

BRIAN "DAMAGE" FORSYTHE Everybody's sort of waiting for the other shoe to drop, but it hasn't. Hopefully it won't, because I just relocated to Nashville and bought a house. I need to keep working!

ACKNOWLEDGMENTS

The authors would like to sincerely thank all the people who consented to be interviewed for this book for being so generous with their time. We are also deeply indebted to the following individuals who went above and beyond to move this project up the hill: Bill Barbot, Cory Brennan, Steve Brown, Brit Buckley, Amanda Cagan, Tor Caracappa, Josh Cohen, Larry Crane, Lily Cronig, David "Dizzy" Dunton, Pete Evick, "Metal" Maria Ferrero, Gayle Fine, Brian "Damage" Forsythe, Jon Freeman, Röb Gröm, Tracii Guns, Janie Hoffman, DeeDee Keel, Jeff Klein, Andy Langer, Larry Mazer, Marc "the Animal" Resnick, Steven Rosen, Share Ross, Keith Roth, Chris Scapelliti, Madelyn Scarpulla, Mike Squires, Danny Stanton, Nick Stern, Rob Tannenbaum, Corey Taylor, Brad Tolinski, Eddie Trunk, Katherine Turman, Mark Weiss, Jon Wiederhorn, and Mark Yarm.

Apologies are owed to a handful of people who were interviewed at length but who sadly do not appear in the final text because of narrative constraints: Peter Baron, Robert Battaglia, Gary Cee, Anthony Corder, Bob "Nitebob" Czaykowski, Rik Fox, Gary Graff, Chip Hobart, Bruce Kulick, John Lassman, Jack Lue, Jason McMaster, Jizzy Pearl, Bob Rock, Gerry Rothberg, Stuart Simone, Tommy Thayer, and Chip Z'Nuff.

And even greater apologies to anyone who deserved to be included and was thoughtlessly omitted.

Last, four interviewees passed away during the completion of this book. Our gratitude goes out to Frankie Banali, Ron Goudie, Lizzie Grey, and Gina Zamparelli for offering their time and insight. We extend our deepest sympathies to their families and loved ones.

NOTES

Part I: Everybody Wants Some!!

9 *There wasn't any vibe around L.A.:* Steven Rosen interview with Kim Fowley, used by permission of Steven Rosen.

9 *Gazzarri's, we auditioned twice:* Steven Rosen interview with Alex Van Halen, used by permission of Steven Rosen.

9 *They kicked ass:* Steven Rosen interview with Mick Mars, used by permission of Steven Rosen.

10 *There wasn't really very many local bands happening at that time:* Steven Rosen interview with Rodney Bingenheimer, used by permission of Steven Rosen.

11 *Bill Gazzarri called me "Van" for the first two years:* David Lee Roth, *Crazy from the Heat*, Hyperion, 1997, p. 75.

13 *I spoke to this guy Ray who was at the Starwood:* Steven Rosen interview with Rodney Bingenheimer, used by permission of Steven Rosen.

13 *I was invited in 1977 to go see a band called the Boyz:* Steven Rosen interview with Gene Simmons, used by permission of Steven Rosen.

29 *A lot of clubs would say, "Don't do any originals":* Ken Kurson, "Tell Me What You Want: Long Island Legends Zebra Earn Their Rock n Roll Stripes," *The Observer*, January 4, 2017.

33 *I used my Marshall stacks to kind of wall me in:* Steven Rosen interview with Mick Mars, used by permission of Steven Rosen.

45 *London played the Starwood all the time:* Matt Wake, "On the Eve of Mötley Crüe's Final Shows, a Look Back at their Very First Gig," *L.A. Weekly*, December 30, 2015.

46 *I asked the guys [in my band]:* Steven Rosen interview with Mick Mars, used by permission of Steven Rosen.

46 *When I met Mick he had his shoes duct-taped together:* Author interview, 1999.

46 *At the time we first got together I was listening to a lot of different artists:* Author interview, 2014.

47 *We had this little guitar player kid named Robin:* Author interview, 2014.

47 *My first job. Nikki and Tommy were like, "You tell him!":* Author interview, 2014.

47 *And then it was the three of us:* Author interview, 2014.

47 *One day we were rehearsing with O'Dean:* Author interview, 2014.

48 *O'Dean had a Roger Daltrey–sounding voice:* Author interview, 2014.

48 *The first song we ever played together was "Live Wire.":* Author interview, 2014.

48 *We stuck out like a sore thumb:* Author interview, 1999.

49 *You can't use aerosol:* Sylvie Simmons, "Mötley Crüe: Crüesin' and Blüesin'," *Sounds*, February 20, 1982. Retrieved from Rock's Backpages, rocksbackpages.com.

50 *We would take the amp line:* Author interview, 1997.

50 *Those were crazy days:* Author interview, 2010.

51 *I just remember sitting in a fucking cowboy bar:* Author interview, 1997.

59 *We did [Too Fast for Love] at a place called Hit City:* Author interview, 1999.

59 *I think it cost us, what, three grand to make:* Mötley Crüe: Audiobiography, Google Play, 2012.

60 *I'd known him a long time and he was doing a band called Accept:* Steven Rosen interview with Mick Mars, used by permission of Steven Rosen.

60 *When the lights were all white and cut and industrial-looking:* Author interview, 1997.

61 *Bro, we were fucking poor back then:* Author interview, 1999.

64 *I was in a "special" program at my school called Continuation Education:* Author interview, 2007.

64 *Yup. They were "marketing":* Author interview, 2007.

65 *I think it was that same night that I went out to the Whisky:* Author interview, 2007.

65 *Vince and Tommy used to light me on fire in our apartment:* Author interview, 2015.

66 *We would experiment with putting pyro gel on his boots:* Jon Wiederhorn interview with Vince Neil, used by permission of Jon Wiederhorn.

66 *It was a pyro gel, which I only used once:* Author interview, 1999.

67 *I remember back then somebody in my band saying to me:* Author interview, 2007.

74 *Our foundation was in theatrics:* Chris Dick, "Buzz. Kill." *Decibel*, December 2016.

74 *I only did a couple of shows:* Rob Kern, "Blackie Lawless: Ever Met Hendrix?," *Classic Rock*, May 26, 2010.

75 *Sister was put together in 1977:* Jon Wiederhorn and Katherine Turman, *Louder Than Hell: The Definitive Oral History of Metal*, It Books, 2013.

78 *The whole germination came from The Road Warrior:* Chris Dick, "Buzz. Kill."

78 *Not many bands, at the time, were wearing huge nails:* Chris Dick, "Buzz. Kill."

79 *With all the props and everything:* Chris Dick, "Buzz. Kill."

80 *To understand us in the beginning:* Paul Elliott, "Exploding Cod-Pieces, Raw Meat and God: An Audience with W.A.S.P's Blackie Lawless," *Louder Sound*, November 10, 2015.

85 *I saw them first at a Bon Jovi concert:* Stryper, *In the Beginning*, VHS, 1988.

88 *I was living in Ocean City, Maryland:* Talk Toomey podcast, Ep. 30, February 29, 2016.

89 *We did that for about a year before we even played a gig: Talk Toomey* podcast.

89 *Our guitar player at the time, Michael Kelly Smith: Talk Toomey* podcast.

91 *They didn't necessarily want me because I was cool: Behind the Music: Poison*, VH-1, 1999.

91 *The reason I would never join a band:* Sylvie Simmons, "America Gets Poisoned," *Kerrang!*, April 16, 1987. Retrieved from Rock's Backpages, rocksbackpages.com.

92 *We've always worn makeup:* Sylvie Simmons, "America Gets Poisoned."

92 *The motto was "Shake your hiney at the Piney":* Chuck Yarborough, "Bret Michaels and Poison Bring Cheap Trick and a Proud 'Weekend Warrior' Mentality to Blossom," *Cleveland.com*, June 5, 2018.

93 *Somewhere, there's a Polaroid image of me:* Chuck Yarborough, "Bret Michaels and Poison Bring Cheap Trick."

94 *It was New York or Los Angeles: Behind the Music: Poison.*

94 *We sold everything we owned and went to L.A.: Behind the Music: Poison.*

94 *We had a kind of naive belief in ourselves:* Jon Hotten, "Poison—From the Gutter to Glam Rock Superstars," *Classic Rock*, July 27, 2006.

94 *The day we left was my younger sister's birthday, March 2, 1983:* Author interview, 2015.

Part II: Feel the Noize

105 *Four of the most striking looking guys this city has to offer:* "Mötley Crüe: Crüesin' and Blüesin'," *Sounds*, February 20, 1982. Retrieved from Rock's Backpages, rocksbackpages.com.

126 *We had the goods for that record:* Author Interview, 1999.

126 *If* Shout at the Devil *is a darker album:* Author Interview, 1999.

126 *I was doing a lot of drugs, and lots of weird shit was happening:* Author Interview, 1999.

127 *I had to finish the bass on "Red Hot" with a metal pin in my shoulder:* Author interview, 1999.

134 *I was seventeen when I came out to California:* Joe Bosso, "Raunchy Guitars and Reckless Reps," *Guitar World*, March 1989.

135 *The first thing I remember about Axl, this is before I knew him:* Mark Rowland, "If Guns N' Roses Are Outlawed, Only Outlaws Will Have Guns N' Roses," *Musician*, December 1988. Retrieved from Rock's Backpages, rocksbackpages.com.

136 *He came out like three times before he stayed:* Mick Wall, "Izzy Stradlin: Life and Death, Sex and Drugs and Guns N' Roses," *Classic Rock*, November 7, 2016.

138 *When you're coming from towns like Mechanicsburg and Butler, PA:* Author interview, 2015.

138 *Kim and a bunch of other people took us to see Hollywood Rose in Chinatown:* Richard Bienstock, "Decade of Decadence: A Timeline of the Eighties Sunset Strip," *Rolling Stone*, October 23, 2015.

139 *When we pulled into town every band wore leather and studs:* Sylvie Simmons, "America Gets Poisoned."

139 *We stayed at the Tropicana Motel, which was like the rock 'n' roll hangout:* Author interview, 2015.

139 *I saw Poison's first-ever gig in L.A., at the Troubadour:* Author interview, 2015.

140 *Sure, we'd have girls buying our groceries:* Jon Hotten, "Poison—From the Gutter to Glam Rock Superstars."

141 *If you were living in Los Angeles in 1983–84 like we did: Behind the Music: Poison.*

142 *We moved into the back of a dry cleaner's:* Author interview, 2015.

143 *We spent one Christmas in there:* Jon Hotten, "Poison—From the Gutter to Glam Rock Superstars."

143 *You have to survive. You have to eat. You have to have shelter: Behind the Music: Poison.*

143 *We were workaholics with a dream:* Author interview, 2015.

160 *Ozzy is one of the sweetest men I've ever met:* Kory Grow, "The Last Word: Nikki Sixx on Drugs, Groupies and What Dying Taught Him," *Rolling Stone*, March 20, 2019.

160 *I remember Ozzy just had his daughter Aimee:* Steven Rosen interview with Mick Mars, used by permission of Steven Rosen.

178 *Me and Slash, we were walking down Sunset Boulevard:* Video interview with *Rock Scene*, October 29, 2015.

179 *I said, "If we get that singer and that guitar player":* Video interview with *Rock Scene*, October 29, 2015.

180 *There was Izzy and Axl, and then there was Steven and I:* Joe Bosso, "Raunchy Guitars and Reckless Reps."

186 *It was down to Dave and Jeff LaBar: Talk Toomey* podcast.

190 *We dressed and looked like how we thought a rock band should look:* Andrea Seastrand, "Interview with Eric Brittingham from Cinderella: Know What You've Got," *The Aquarian*, August 10, 2011.

192 *He said, "I am going to be a father and we are living like pigs":* Jon Hotten, "Poison—From the Gutter to Glam Rock Superstars."

193 *I had been sort of scrounging around, looking for anything that was happening:* Author interview, 2007.

193 *I really didn't like Poison. I didn't like that whole thing:* Author interview, 2007.

194 *I played the shit out of those songs:* Author interview, 2015.

195 *I got where Slash was coming from:* Author interview, 2015.

195 *He clearly fit the part better than I did:* Author interview, 2007.

199 *After the Poison thing, I joined this band called Black Sheep:* Author interview, 2007.

200 *It just happened, you know?:* Author interview, 2007.

Part III: Knock 'Em Dead, Kid

214 *Who wouldn't want to get signed to a massive record deal?:* Author interview, 2015.

216 *Ric had a different vision:* Author interview, 2015.

217 *And then we finished the entire record by ourselves:* Author interview, 2015.

217 *That was probably the most glam we ever got:* Author interview, 2015.

218 *I one thousand percent will never deny:* Author interview, 2015.

219 *The critics looked at Poison: Behind the Music: Poison.*

219 *That whole androgynous thing was very cool:* Billy Manes, "DeVille Worship," *Orlando Weekly,* September 1, 2000.

236 *Razzle was dead on arrival at the hospital:* Ian Winwood, "The Tragedy of Hanoi Rocks: How a Deadly Car Crash Destroyed One of Metal's Greatest Bands," *The Telegraph,* January 8, 2020.

236 *I wrote a $2.5 million check for vehicular manslaughter:* Michael Odell, "Twilight of the Gods," *Blender,* March 2005.

236 *For us, it was kind of hard to grasp that somebody died:* Paul Elliott, "Competition, Chaos and Car Crashes," *Classic Rock,* January 9, 2020.

249 *With Theatre of Pain we figured out how to take the drum riser and have it lean all the way forward:* Author interview, 2015.

258 *Jani and Steven lived in an apartment just down the street from Jerry and I: Let There Be Talk* podcast, Ep. 363, June 19, 2017.

263 *There were flyer wars, let me say this. It was crazy:* Author interview, 2015.

264 *You know, as sad as it sounds, the concept of marketing has always intrigued me:* Author interview, 2007.

264 *We had a list of fourteen high schools and junior high schools within driving distance:* David Lee Roth, *Crazy From the Heat,* p. 101.

265 *Not a day, not a moment went past that we weren't promoting: Behind the Music: Poison.*

281 *We went out to the Cathouse, and then back to Franklin Plaza:* Author interview, 2007.

284 *My recreation director was named Paul:* David Lee Roth, *Crazy From the Heat,* p. 314.

302 *For a while when I saw that movie I was like, "Oh, god, look at us.":* Richard Bienstock, "Decade of Decadence."

307 *Originally, my character of Kelly Bundy on* Married with Children *was kind of like a tough little rebellious biker kind of chick: Fresh Air,* June 5, 2019.

Part IV: Youth Gone Wild

315 *Well, Kane Roberts . . . Kane had Stallone's body:* Author interview, 2018.

316 *I saw bands like Mötley Crüe and Bon Jovi, and it was the era of the video:* Author interview, 2018.

316 *I heard about Kip Winger from one of my producers:* Author interview, 2018.

326 *All of a sudden, your real life exceeds your dreams: Behind the Music: Poison.*

342 *We were just rebelling against the fact that there were all these bad bands coming out of L.A. who were copping our look:* Author interview, 1999.

346 *Pushing boundaries in terms of what [Van Halen] wore was never an ambition of ours:* Leah Harper, "David Lee Roth: 'My Advice for Aspiring Artists? Breathable Fabrics,'" *The Guardian,* June 25, 2019.

350 *My hair in the "Still of the Night" video was actually a hairdressing accident:* Author interview, 2017.

359 *In working with them as an A&R person, artists learn to hate you*: Artist House Music video interview, 2010.

368 *"Home Sweet Home" for us was our "Dream On" or our "Stairway to Heaven"*: Mötley Crüe: *Audiobiography*, Google Play, 2012.

368 *I believe that that was one of the first hard rock 'n' roll power ballads*: Mötley Crüe: *Audiobiography*, Google Play, 2012.

368 *It came from a guitar figure that I had had since I was seventeen*: Mötley Crüe: *Audiobiography*, Google Play, 2012.

369 *The record company was totally against us putting "Home Sweet Home" on there*: Author interview, 1999.

372 *When we played "Every Rose" for our label and management, they told us it would end our career*: Author interview, 2001.

374 *I mean what the fuck do the lyrics of "Here I Go Again"*: Author interview, 2017.

380 *Beau Hill had produced my band Streets with Steve Walsh of Kansas*: Double Stop podcast, Ep. 92, February 29, 2016.

380 *Beau called me and said, "Look, how would you feel about doing the guitars on this record as a ghost player?"*: Double Stop podcast.

381 *We lucked out in our first single, "Down Boys"*: Let There Be Talk podcast, Ep. 363, June 19, 2017.

382 *Jani could have a hurtful sense of humor sometimes*: Let There Be Talk podcast.

396 *We never had any permits or anything*: Saul Austerlitz, "Moscow Music Peace Festival: How Glam Metal Helped End the Cold War," *Rolling Stone*, September 22, 2017.

398 *All these bikers came and surrounded the hotel*: Author interview, 2015.

399 *It was like in Mad Max, and Ozzy was the guy*: Author interview, 2015.

400 *It was so interesting, this dynamic between all the bands*: Author interview, 2015.

400 *There were a lot of egos because that's what it's all about*: Author interview, 2015.

401 *When Ozzy Osbourne appeared, the fans bum-rushed the stage*: Saul Austerlitz, "Moscow Music Peace Festival."

Part V: The Last Mile

448 *Everybody and their mother was playing all scales*: Author interview, 2014.

449 *Was I kinda overlooked or put in a different category? Yes*: Author interview, 2014.

450 *I hated that whole sort of whammy bar thing*: Author interview, 2019.

472 *At a St. Louis stadium Axl Rose jumped into the audience*: *Sky* Magazine, September 1991.

Part VI: Shut Up, Beavis

483 *I was the sole instigator of calling and getting Alice in Chains*: Mark Yarm interview with Bret Michaels, used by permission of Mark Yarm.

488 *I think on the first two Warrant records we got a lot of love from the fans*: Let There Be Talk podcast.

490 *The* Still Climbing *tour, which was in 1995, was a disaster*: Talk Toomey podcast.

496 *C.C. was getting fucked up and I was drinking:* Jon Hotten, "Poison—From the Gutter to Glam Rock Superstars."

506 *When the album came out, I remember* Rolling Stone *saying:* Paul Elliott, "Competition, Chaos and Car Crashes."

Part VII: Epilogue

519 *All those grunge bands have been gone for a long time:* Jon Wiederhorn interview with Vince Neil, used by permission of Jon Wiederhorn.

520 *The band always prided itself:* Melissa Locker, "Nikki Sixx Says Goodbye for Good: Inside the End of Mötley Crüe," *Time,* February 5, 2014.